THE INTELL
LIFE OF WESTERN
EUROPE IN THE
MIDDLE AGES

Richard C. Dales

UNIVERSITY
PRESS OF
AMERICA

FORWARD

This book has been written for my students, not my colleagues. It originated as a lecture course and it still bears many of the marks of its origin. The annotation too is designed for the needs of students and is in no way intended as a scholarly apparatus.

Both the time limits of the book and the contents are somewhat, though not completely, arbitrary. There is no agreement as to when the Middle Ages began or ended, but in intellectual history the entry of Christian writers into the literary arena of Antiquity is as satisfactory a starting point as can be found. Determining the end is more difficult. I have chosen the middle decades of the fourteenth century for several reasons. Many elements of European intellectual history reach a natural culmination or break-off point at about that time. The Black Death, the Hundred Years War, peasant rebellions, urban uprisings, and other assorted miseries had their reflections in the life of the mind. And to have continued beyond that point would have required greatly increasing the length of the book or being so superficial as to be worthless.

The matter of content is justified with more difficulty. At any point in the book, an almost totally different selection of writers would have been possible. I have used four leading criteria to help me determine what to put in and what to leave out. First of all, what is included must be intrinsically important. Secondly, there must be sufficiently obvious connections among the various parts of the book that it makes sense. I have had to omit several things of which I am very fond because they did not fit. Thirdly, I have tended to emphasize those things which the reader would be less likely to encounter elsewhere and to give rather brief treatment to those aspects of medieval thought which are generally well known. This has resulted in both Hrothswitha and Liudprand of Cremona receiving more space than Thomas of Aquino, and Aldhelm getting about the same attention as Hugh of St. Victor. I have tried to stay as close as possible to the texts when this procedure was at all feasible, and I have frequently given rather full summaries. This takes space and necessitates the omission of other material, but I think that it is the most effective way to present intellectual history. And finally, I can only include those things that I know about. No one can know everything, and I, like all writers, am better informed on some things than on others. The book thus reflects my interests, my knowledge, and my vision of what the intellectual life of the Middle Ages was. Many other views are possible and justifiable, but they are not mine.

I should like to thank my students of the past twenty years for whom this book was written. By trying it out on them bit by bit, I have slowly learned what will work in the classroom and what will not. I should also like to thank several good friends with whom I have discussed various aspects of the book over the years: Thomas W. Africa, who first suggested to me that I write it; John F. Benton, whose intimidating intellect has forced me to sharpen up many of my ideas and statements; and Paul W. Knoll, whose erudition and broad humanity have provided me with both information and insights which I would otherwise have lacked. And finally, sincere thanks are due to Roneale Branning, who typed the final copy, and to Gunar Freibergs, who made the index.

TABLE OF CONTENTS

PART ONE: THE ROMAN EMPIRE

Chapter 1

The Intellectual Climate of the Roman Empire

The intellectual tradition of the western world is derived primarily from the magnificent achievements of Greek and Roman
Antiquity, modified by the Hebrew-Christian world view. The
interaction of these two strains was extremely complex. For one
thing, neither tradition should be considered as though it were
homogeneous; there was vast diversity within each. For another,
the two traditions have much in common, as well as many points of
conflict and basic incompatibility. And finally, much depended
upon the personalities of the men in whose lives these traditions
met. The meetings range from outright clashes in such men as
Tertullian to harmonious blending in such a man as Boethius.
Between these extremes were many gradations, and even in the same
man, the nature of the interaction might vary from time to time,
as with St. Jerome or even St. Augustine.

But traditions, ideas, and value systems do not exist independently, apart from the men who hold them dear. Important as
continuity of tradition is, the determining factor in intellectual
history is the existential situation of thinking men. We are not
concerned simply to document the transmission of ideas, literary
forms, and ethical cliches from Antiquity to modern times, but
rather to see how men continually used the old in new ways to meet
the needs of their own days, and occasionally, sometimes by design
but more often by accident, to create something new.

The true founders of the classical tradition are the Greeks, who,
from the time of Homer to the days of Galen, Ptolemy, and
Plotinus, excelled in virtually every department of intellectual
activity. The Romans, by their own admission, could create only a
reflection or imitation of what the Greeks had done. Still, their
work is by no means despicable. They not only served as mediators
and transmitters of Greek culture, but especially in literature
they created much of considerable merit. Furthermore, it was
mainly through Latin works that the Greek achievement was known to
the men of western Europe in the Middle Ages, through the Latin
poets and orators, encyclopedists, and church Fathers, and to some
extent through the Latin translations or paraphrases of Greek
writings.

During the two centuries before and after the birth of Christ, the
Romans had managed, by using foreign talent, imitating their Greek
models, and giving expression to their native genius, to create a
Latin literature of great merit. Beginning with a crude tongue
suitable for an agricultural and military society, they began
about the middle of the second century B.C. to make a systematic

effort to master their Greek models and imitate them in Latin. New meanings were given to old Latin words, Greek words were Latinized, and even Greek constructions were adapted to the Latin language. Although Latin poetry had originally been accentual, a quantitative poetry was devised, and prose writing, always later to develop, began to take its place as a literary medium.

By the time the political disintegration of the republic was about to enter its most appalling phase, Latin literature came of age and entered its most creative and brilliant stage. This is the period of Caesar, Cicero, Lucretius, and Catullus, a time when the men involved in the great struggles in the state or confronting the basic problems of human existence were themselves the writers rather than the patrons of writers.

The establishment of peace, order, and security by Octavian (Augustus) brought about a marked change in the character of Latin literature. It was technically superior to that of the preceding age and is represented by some of the greatest authors of Western literature, Virgil, Ovid, Horace, Livy, and Sallust.

This plateau of excellence was maintained until the early second century A.D., but from this time on, Latin literature began to atrophy. Despite the attempts of the educational system to maintain uniformity, despite the tremendous prestige of the late republican and Augustan authors and their language, the literature of classical Rome, so artfully contrived and so skillfully employed to speak for a great people at the moment of their triumph, began to lose its integrity and vitality. And although the great classics would continue to inspire men for many centuries to come and to serve as models for many subsequent writers, they already by the third century belonged to the past, to a great age which would never return. Very early -- in many cases by the second century A.D. -- the original works in the tradition (with the exception of the "classics") were epitomized. Summaries of the histories, the scientific works, and so on, were replacing the originals long before the Christians or barbarians exerted any influence on Roman development, and this tendency must be recognized as general throughout the ancient world and as particularly characteristic of the Romans.

The third century was a time of enormous difficulties for the Empire. Economic depression, loss of public spirit, nearly constant civil war, governmental corruption, and the deterioration of the social order all threatened the very existence of ancient culture. But it was during this period of general misery that some very important developments occurred. Apparently despairing of happiness, security, or fulfillment in this world, people on all levels of society sought solace, escape, or assurance in some sort of supernaturalism. There was an increasing tendency to identify the emperors, such failures as human beings, with gods.

The mystery cults of an earlier age, promising personal immortality to their initiates, underwent a great resurgence and tended to become more and more alike. And for the intellectuals, there were several philosophies, or philosophical religions, which could respond to the needs of the time in a more respectable fashion.

Out of this spiritual turmoil came one of the most powerful and influential philosophies of the western tradition, Neoplatonism. As the name implies, it was a development of the ideas of Plato. In 387 B.C., Plato had established a school, the Academy, where to the end of his life he continued his teaching and writing and provided the leisure and means of study for a number of advanced students. This school remained in existence until 529 A.D., preserving the teaching of the master, providing commentaries on it and on the writings of the other major philosophers, serving as a center of study and learning, and going through a significant development in doctrine. From shortly after Plato's death until about 100 A.D., it was primarily concerned with the criticism of rival philosophical systems. Its characteristic attitude during this period was one of tolerant scepticism, and it was in this form that the Platonic tradition influenced the philosophical works of Cicero.

Late in the first century A.D., a more positive and creative philosophical movement was centered at the Academy. Emphasizing the religious and metaphysical aspects of Plato's thought, it attempted to round out into a system certain of the brilliant hints and insights of the master. Using congenial doctrines from other philosophies, especially the Pythagoreans and Stoics and to a lesser extent Aristotle, it considerably improved on Plato's metaphysical thought. Plato had never been especially clear on the relationship between the world of sense and the world of Forms, nor had he been specific about the nature and function of the Idea of Good. The Middle Academy placed the Idea of Good at the apex of the hierarchy of forms, though not yet outside it, and made it the first principle and cause of the rest of the universe. Also known as the Supreme Mind, the One, or God, its essence was to think, and the world of Forms was its thought. A third divine being, the World Soul, served as intermediary between the human soul and the Divine Mind and its thoughts. The vision of God, through a life of philosophical study, was the ultimate goal of human existence.

The fullest development of Plato's thought (Neoplatonism) was the accomplishment not of the scholar of the Academy, but of Plotinus (205-270 A.D.), an Egyptian writing in Greek and teaching in Rome.[1] Plotinus' philosophy is comprised of both a cosmology and an ethical system. The requirements of each of these are not always compatible with the other and occasionally make for inconsistencies and redundancies in Plotinus' thought, but they are closely related and interdependent. Unlike Plato, Plotinus did

-3-

not consider philosophy as a means for preparing a man for a life of action in the world, but rather as a means of escaping from and transcending the world of sense. He therefore emphasized and completed those aspects of Plato's thought which best served his purpose. He built on the entire preceding philosophical tradition, criticizing and correcting the views of many, borrowing some from Aristotle, especially the concepts of potency and act, and matter and form. But the words of Plato were above reproach and needed only to be understood properly.

Let us look first at Plotinus' cosmology. The source, cause, and goal of all being -- though itself above and not involved in being -- is the supreme, perfect, infinitely good, utterly unified hypostasis which Plotinus designated as the One. Because of its perfect goodness it creates continually all of reality, not by any activity on its own part, not even an act of the will, but by a kind of spontaneous "overflowing." This notion of creation without activity (for this would imply change and mutability) or diminution is difficult to grasp and perhaps impossible to explain, and so Plotinus resorts to an analogy: the creative overflowing of the One is like the effusion of light from the sun. (This analogy would have far-reaching ramifications in western thought up to early modern times.)

The second hypostasis, the first result of the overflowing of the One, is the intelligible world, the realm of Ideas, Forms, Eternal Archetypes (Nous). Here all reality exists in its highest form, simultaneously, interdependently, intelligibly. This realm is endowed with a life of its own, and it immediately contemplates the perfection of the One.

The third hypostasis, bridging the gap which Plato left unbridged between the intelligible world and the world of sense, is the Soul or Life (Psyche). It is in the discussion of the nature and functions of the soul that most of the difficulties in Plotinus' thought arise. As a strictly cosmological hypostasis, its function is to give life and being to the world of sense. It soon becomes apparent, however, that this is a multiple being. It is distinguished first as the soul of the entire cosmos and as the individual souls of particular bodies. It does not remain fixed in its position in the hierarchy of being but is capable of descending or falling into the realm of sense and forgetting there its own identity; and of rising not only to the realm of Ideas, but to a vision of the One itself. Neither the reason for nor the possibility of the fall is ever adequately explained. Plotinus sometimes asserts that there are many levels of soul, or that what falls is merely an image of the soul. Thus the entire range of being, contained in its highest state in the Forms, and in an incomplete and imitative way in the sense world, is reproduced in an intermediate way in the various levels of the soul, which thus becomes something quite different from the third hypostasis whose function it is to create and animate the sense world. In fact, since the intelligible world has a life of its own, it could well perform the cosmological function of the soul without an intermediary.

These difficulties are unavoidable, however, because Plotinus' purpose is primarily ethical. The fall of the soul is to him an obvious fact, and the ascent of the soul was a matter of his personal experience. His purpose was to show others how, through the use of reason, they too might ascent to a union with the One.

This ascent is possible because the soul by its very nature, is capable of transcending the limits of time and space which the sense world places upon our bodies. It accomplishes this by pursuing as the objects of its knowledge the abstract and intelligible, beginning with music and mathematics. Through constant rational effort is can ascend to the knowledge of the totality of the intelligible world, the highest form of knowledge; and from there it may go on to a union with the One, the source and the goal of its being, where it no longer knows but simply is. Any soul which is not purified through the study of philosophy must be born again into another body until it finally realizes its true nature, frees itself from the world of sense, and journeys upward to union with the One.

There is much in both Middle Platonism and Plotinus that is much like Christianity.[2] This is not to be wondered at, since these doctrines were influential with the Fathers who laid the basis of Christian dogma. Still, there are important differences which were not always clearly perceived by later Christian enthusiasts and often led them into heresy. In the first place, the three hypostases of the Neoplatonic trinity are not co-equal, but as consequences of emanation are hierarchically subordinated. Thus the Nous is subsequent to and inferior to the One and is in fact created by it. Also, since creation does not result from an act of will or any other activity of the One, the Nous is necessarily what it is and could not be otherwise. The sense world, since it derives its being from the Nous via the Soul, is also necessarily what it is. Although the One is the source of all being, the only thing it creates immediately is the Nous. All else is the result of a decending hierarchy of intermediate causes. The only element of freedom in the system lies in the Soul's ability to escape its imprisonment in sense and ascend to a union with the One.

Nor should the One be confused with the Judeo-Christian God. It is utterly impersonal, without activity, lacking nothing, and thus totally unconcerned about the soul's destiny. It does not, indeed it cannot, interfere in the operations of the sense world and the Soul.

Although Neoplatonism is in many respects a religion of salvation, it obviously could not appeal to a very wide circle. Its uncompromising rationalism makes great demands on its followers. Not by believing, but by thinking, one may be saved. Although Plotinus did not solve all the problems arising from his own doctrine, he alone perhaps among the followers of Plato improved upon and went beyond his master and worked out one of the most comprehensive, logically complete, and intellectually and emotionally satisfactory philosophical systems of the western world. It was through Plotinus' mind that Plato exerted a dominant influence on European thought through the mid-seventeenth century.

In the meantime, however, Neoplatonism had the task of surviving in the environment of the late Empire. Under Plotinus' successors, especially Porphyry and Iamblicus,[3] it took on many of the trappings of a ritualized religion, including the use of prayers and the cult of images, and so was able to appeal to some of those who found the rigorous intellectual discipline prescribed by Plotinus beyond their power.

The general outlook of the ancient world, and of the Romans in particular, has often been misrepresented. Although in a selected few Latin works, one sees the traditional classical view of man as a free, rational, self-reliant being, restrained by the pursuit of moderation in all things and placing a very high value on human capabilities, in most Latin writers one sees quite a different view expressed. The Romans relied heavily, both in life and in their literature, on dreams, visions and omens -- the entrails of slain animals, flights of birds, astronomical and meteorlogical phenomena -- for guidance. The universe they inhabited was full of spooks, evil spirits, and benevolent deities who either used men for their own purposes or who could be bribed to favor a particular candidate for their assistance. The Roman mind as revealed in classical literature was credulous, superstitious, uninquisitive, and careless of chronology, natural causation, and logical consistency. With very few exceptions, the Romans were poor historians, poor philosophers, and poor scientists. But they were often superb poets, orators, letter writers, and satirists.

This intellectual tradition was maintained and passed along through the educational system of the Empire. Designed primarily for the sons of the wealthy and powerful, its purpose was to train "The Orator," a man with at least a superficial knowledge of all departments of learning, a complete mastery of the works of the great authors, such as Cicero and Virgil, and considerable facility in formal public speaking and argument. When he was about twelve years old, the rich young Roman boy, after having received his primary education, went to the grammaticus, under whom he studied Greek and Latin literature, especially poetry (although the study of Greek declined considerably during the fourth and fifth centuries); grammar in its more general sense, as well as syntax; and history, mythology, and arithmetic. After two or three years of these studies, he was sent to a <u>rhetor</u>, where he undertook an intensive study of prose authors, particularly the orators, and was given extensive practice in written and spoken exercises.[4] It was this emphasis on rhetoric, prizing as it did dazzling effects, specious reasoning, and verbal extravagance, and depending heavily on set themes and stock manners of treatment, which dominated the literary output of late Antiquity and extended its influence through the centuries into the Middle Ages and the Renaissance.

The advanced studies of philosophy, science, and law were outside the regular curriculum. Very few studied science, a somewhat larger number studied philosophy. In the Latin half of the Empire, law was the only higher study which attracted any great number of students. Much of this higher education was carried on by teachers connected with the great libraries of the Empire or with the baths, which in Roman society were centers of social and intellectual activity as well as physical recreation.

This education, for all its shortcomings, was a crucial force in maintaining the civilization of Rome. It passed on selected portions of a magnificent literary tradition; it formed a common body of knowledge and values which distinguished Romans from barbarians; and it provided a source of genuine humanity and intellectual inspiration to at least some of those who underwent it. It abounded in didactic works, emphasizing the Roman virtues of character and the blessings the Roman state had conferred upon the world. It contained watered-down and eclectic discussions of Greek philosophical ideas, always with a strongly ethical emphasis. It considered man as a rational, morally responsible being capable of great achievements and much of it investigated the nature of these human potentialities. On the other hand, man was often foolish, venal, or vicious and was so portrayed in works ranging from good-natured spoofing to fierce indignation. It contained stories of the gods, works of history, collections of letters, compendia of general knowledge, and much poetry of a great variety of types.

But however we judge it, the Roman tradition was the only alternative to complete illiteracy: it <u>was</u> culture. When the Christians began attracting recruits from the literate elements of Roman society, and especially after they became the religious majority, the question of the relationship between Christianity and Roman culture became crucial. This question was explored by many acute and sensitive men, and the answers proposed varied a great deal, not only between different men, but even within the thought of the same man. Regardless of what answer was accepted as ideal, however, the inescapable fact of the situation was that the only choice the Christians had was between accepting Roman culture and accepting illiteracy. They had no substitute curriculum, no schools of their own, no learned tradition upon which to draw.

Even those who were most vehement in denouncing the study of the pagan classics shown by their use of language, their choice of words, and their thought processes that they themselves were the products of this education. By and large, the hostility on the part of some Christians to Roman culture tended to become less pronounced as that culture became progressively weaker and the church in turn became stronger. When the chips were down, the Christians were willing to incorporate classical culture, to make it their own, sometimes with the provision that it be purified, but occasionally on its own merits.

There is a danger of confusing the classical tradition with worship of this world and its delights, or with polytheism, and conversely to assume that only Christianity emphasized the superiority of eternal and divine things, and worshipped the one true God. There is of course some truth in this. Many Latin writers did emphasize this world, based their ethics on a mundane standard, sang of man and his accomplishments, and assumed a pantheon of ancient gods. But there were many others, from Cicero to Macrobius, who were monotheists, who placed the spiritual above the worldly, who derived their ethical standards from the divine commands; and they were preceded by five hundred years of similar developments among the Greek writers. It is consequently difficult to draw clear lines between Christian ideas and sentiments among the writers of the late Empire and those which were common to Christianity and much of late paganism.[5]

NOTES

1. On Plotinus, see Kenneth Sylvan Guthrie, Plotinus, Complete Works (Alphine, New York, 1918), Stephen Mackenna, Plotinus (London, 1917-30), and The Cambridge History of Later Greek and Early Medieval Philosophy, and A.H. Armstrong (Cambridge, 1967), 195-268. His Enneads are printed with facing English translation in the Loeb Classical Library edition (New York, 1966).

2. See D. Knowles, The Evolution of Medieval Thought (Vintage Book 246, 1962), 29-31.

3. See The Cambridge History of Later Greek and Early Medieval Philosophy, 298-301, and John M. Dillon, Iamblichus (Leiden, 1973).

4. M.L.W. Laistner, Thought and Letters in Western Europe, A.D. 500-900 (2nd ed., London, 1957; reprint Ithaca, New York, 1957), 34-36.

5. See E.K. Rand, Founders of the Middle Ages (Cambridge, Massachusetts, 1928; reprint Dover Publications T369, 1957), 32-33.

Chapter 2

The Christian Empire

During the third century, the fortunes of Christians in the Empire varied greatly, from vicious persecution under Decius (249-251) to protection and even support under Gallienus (259-268), although they were usually ignored by the government. Among the population at large, however, they were still suspect, and stories of their cannibalism and incest circulated widely. Concentrated largely in the cities of the Greek-speaking part of the Empire, the Christians had nevertheless enjoyed enough success in the Latin world by the year 200 A.D. that they had begun to penetrate the literate classes of the West. By this time, Latin literature had been moribund for about a century, and although the pagan world produced writers of some skill during the second and third centuries, none of these ranks as a major author.

The earliest Christian writers among the Latins would not rank as major authors either, except that unlike their pagan contemporaries, they had some very important things to say, and as things worked out, they were the earliest spokesmen for the winning side. Around the year 200 A.D. two men of vastly different temperament undertook to write in behalf of Christianity.

One of these is Minucius Felix, whose birth and death dates are not known. He was a Roman iuris consultus, well educated, and intimately familiar with classical literature, but particularly with Cicero. He had been born a pagan, and after his conversion retained his love for Rome and its culture. He wrote a work called Octavius,[1] modelled on a Ciceronian dialogue, the purpose of which was to identify Christianity with the Graeco-Roman tradition, showing how the best of the philosophers and poets had taught doctrines similar or identical to Christian doctrines, and how Christianity excelled even the best of pagan thought. Actually, very few specifically Christian doctrines are even mentioned, and the work is more an argument for monotheism than for Christianity. Still, in view of its intended audience -- educated pagans -- this was perhaps the wisest approach. St. Paul, after all, did not talk to the Athenians the same way he talked to the Hebrews.

In striking contrast to the tolerant urbanity and moderation of Minucius Felix is the North African rhetorician Tertullian (160-ca. 240).[2] Like Minucius he had been a pagan and was converted to Christianity about 190-195 A.D. But here the similarity ends. Tertullian was born to be an extremist, and this perversity of character was intensified by his thorough oratorical training, which prized striking effects and startling formulas to clarity of thought or precision of statement. He was a priest (although married) and published a number of works, some directed against heretics, some against paganism, and some at the behavior of professed Christians. He himself joined the Montanists, a heretical sect, in 206 A.D., only to break with them in turn and found his own sect, the Tertullianists, in 213.

Tertullian is usually cited in connection with some of his more outlandish paradoxical dicta, such as "I believe it because it is absurd;" "The son of God died; it is by all means to be believed because it is absurd. And he was buried and rose again; the fact is certain because it is impossible." There are also contained in his writings a number of extreme denunciations of philosophy, dialectic, rhetoric -- in fact of culture in general.

But when one looks behind the blatant sensationalism of Tertullian's language, his meaning is not much different from what has been said many times before and since, though by gentler souls. He is distrustful of the use of philosophy and dialectics in religion and would put his trust in scripture rather than the philosophers and poets; in this position, he has much company. He emphasizes the differences between pagan literary tradition and Christianity and thinks it dangerous to study the pagan authors. But he also recognizes the absolute necessity of these studies, unfortunate though it may be. During some periods, this would have made him a moderate. He was suspicious of rhetoric and fearful of its ability to convince people of the truth of falsehoods, and well he might be. Yet he was a highly skilled rhetorician and not averse from using this art to convince people of the truth of the Christian faith. And although he knew little philosophy and understood less, yet he is himself of some interest in the history of philosophy for his doctrine that the spirtual was material, and that God and soul were material at the same time that they were spiritual.

Tertullian then represents an early and enduring tradition in the church and sets himself apart mainly by the extravagance and forcefulness of his language. But in so doing, he became an important creator of a new Latin vocabulary and diction. It is not quite accurate to call this form of Latin Christian, because there were similar developments among pagan authors and because languages usually undergo such a transformation during periods of vigor and changing times as well as during periods of decadence. Since he was talking about things for which the Latin language had no words, Tertullian coined them, usually from Greek. And since his audience was not made up exclusively of the educated upper classes, he drew freely upon the spoken Latin of his own day. Among the Christian authors of the next two centuries, more would lean toward the classical diction and moderate approach of Minucius Felix than toward the startling diction and uncompromising stand of Tertullian.

A somewhat younger contemporary of Minucius Felix and Tertullian was Commodian,[3] once thought to have been a converted Jew from Gaza in Palestine but now generally considered to have been an African. He wrote two very poor long poems, Carmen apologeticum and Instructiones, intended to defend and elucidate the Christian faith and to vilify its enemies. He made many mistakes in syntax and used a system of versification which, although it seems to be modelled on the Virgilian hexameter, largely ignores quantity and depends rather on stress accent. It is not properly rhythmical poetry either, for the number of syllables in each line is not constant. Commodian seems to have attempted to write Virgilian hexameters without clearly understanding the principles of quantitative verse, and to have substituted stress for quantity in others. F.J.E. Raby has noted that Commodian, "whether consciously or not, wrote the rude verses of the half-educated classes, and his poetry belongs rather to a barbarized classicism than to the new Christian rhythm."

It is not only in form that Commodian's poetry is bad. It is, with the exception of a very few lines, utterly devoid of poetic feeling, as its author was devoid of poetic talent. Crude in sentiment as in execution, it suffers also from Commodian's addiction to adorning his compositions with acrostics, which might reveal the title, the name of the pagan god being excoriated, or the name of the author. It is unfortunate that the earliest Latin Christian poems were written by so inept a writer. It would be a century yet before men capable of writing poetry at least correct, if not inspired, would turn their talent to Christian themes. Yet for all their shortcomings, Commodian's poems were quite popular both in Antiquity and in the Middle Ages.

It was during the fourth century that Latin Christian literature came to maturity and produced its greatest monuments. The two most important writers of the early part of the century were Victorinus and Lactantius, both born pagans during the closing years of the third century, both famous teachers of rhetoric, both steeped in classical culture, both patriotic Romans even after their conversions, and neither a truly first-class mind despite considerably fluency and ability.

Marius Victorinus, an African, was an extremely successful rhetor and migrated to Rome about 340 A.D. when he was between forty and sixty years of age. So popular a teacher was he that the Romans set up his statue in the Forum of Trajan in 353. Two years later, however, he was converted to Christianity, a faith he had bitterly opposed earlier.

He had already published much before his conversion. As one might expect from a rhetor, he had published an Ars grammatica, but unlike most of his profession he was also interested in philosophy and had written commentaries on some of the works of Aristotle and of Cicero. More important perhaps are his translations from the

Greek of the Neoplatonist Porphyry's Isagoge and some of Plotinus' Enneads. The beauty and power of the Neoplatonist system appealed to him mightily and after his conversion significantly influenced his understanding of Christianity. He has been called by one recent scholar "the one great link between Greek philosophy and the Latin world in the fourth century."[4]

As a Christian he continued to make use of his grammatical accomplishments by writing extensive commentaries on Paul's letters, of which only those on Galatians, Ephesians, and Philippians survive. Obliged to give up his teaching in 362 by the edict of Julian the Apostate, he devoted his last years to defending orthodoxy against heresy, especially Arianism. In so doing, however, he came dangerously close to heresy himself. First of a long succession of Christian thinkers to be overwhelmed by Neoplatonist thought, he was never able completely to reconcile Plotinus' One, which is above being, with the Christian God, which is being in the fullest sense, or to avoid the subordination of the Son-Logos to the Father. After making a valiant attempt to do so, he ends by saying that we are not, after all, asked to understand this mystery, but only to believe it. Still, he himself seemed to feel the necessity of understanding it.

Far more important is another African, Lactantius, whose great work, the Divine Institutes, was written at exactly the time that both Christiantiy and Rome triumphed together under the leadership of Constantine, and the work is clearly affected by the historical circumstances under which it was written. As a pagan rhetor, Lactantius had received a teaching position in Nicomedia through the good offices of Dioletian. Becoming a Christian shortly thereafter, he set out to explain Christianity to the educated classes of the Empire and to make it palatable to them.

His Divine Institutes is an attempt to present a systematic, synthetic Christian theology, which sees Christianity as the culmination of the classical tradition. In it, Lactantius attempts to show that paganism is contrary to reason, while Christianity is completely reasonable. He quotes both the philosophers and poets to show that many of them were at least partially in accord with Christian teaching; and he firmly believed that Cicero was in even closer accord with the true faith than he appears to be, but held back from speaking the truth out of fear of persecution. The influence of the classical tradition is evident throughout the work. He not only knows thoroughly and cites such writers as Horace, Ovid, Plautus, Terence, Lucan, Juvenal, Persius, Virgil, Ennius, and Lucilius and the Sybilline books, but his purpose is patriotic as well as religious, and the entire work is an attempt to provide for the Christian Empire what Cicero had done for the pagan.

He was much more at odds with the pagans, however, than was Minucius Felix. Although he is pleased to note accord between the philosophers and the Christians, he is also at pains to excoriate the pagans for their shortcomings. Particularly interesting in this connection, and in contrast to the implications of monasticism, which was beginning to sweep over the Empire at this time, was his attack on the Stoic concept of virtue, which held that the natural human emotions and affections should be suppressed and overcome. Lactantius effectively and originally pointed out that this was both foolish and sinful. The Peripatetics were closer to the truth, he said, in holding that the moderation, not the suppression, of the emotions was the ideal. But even they are wrong. A Christian knows that it is the proper regulation, not the moderation or suppression, of natural human affections, which is the correct course. Sometimes it is proper to fear or to love, to grieve or to rejoice, without moderation. It is proper to fear God, and a man who does so will not improperly fear other things, such as death, pain, or loss of worldly goods. In fact, without the emotions, which are the gift of God, man would not be able to attain virtue, which is his own responsibility.

The _Divine_ _Institutes_ is a masterpiece of apologetic literature. Uncompromisingly Christian, and not slighting inconvenient matters as Minucius Felix had done, it nevertheless shows Christianity as the culmination and fruition of the best in the pagan tradition, fully in accord with reason and philosophy, simple, profound and true. Christianity was superior to paganism because while the pagans had always separated wisdom and religion, Christianity united them. This book was also of value to Christians in that it presented to them a more systematic and comprehensive view of their own faith than had hitherto been available in Latin.

With Marius Victorinus and Lactantius, the Latin patristic age entered its period of greatness. Even with the victory and conversion of Constantine, the church's battle was far from won. In many ways, the early fourth century must have looked like the beginning of a new Golden Age. But there were still heretics within the church, especially Arians, Manicheans, Gnostics, and Donatists; and paganism remained powerful, not only among the rural population, but more important, among the educated Roman ruling class. The ties of Roman greatness with the ancient gods were strong and were broken only with great difficulty. No writer we have yet mentioned was born a Christian. But from the middle of the century, it would be more common, though still far from usual, for an upper class family to be Christian.

It was a fairly simple matter for Christian prose writers to adapt their language to their ends, and there is nothing ludicrous or incongruous in using an elegant, polished, and correct Latin rhetorical prose for apologetic purposes. But it was otherwise with poetry, particularly epic. Poetic diction, the mythological paraphernalia, the extended metaphors and lofty plane of the epic were unsuitable for telling the Christian story, and Christian poets were too completely dominated by their tradition to devise new poetic forms or techniques (with the exception of the Latin hymn). Before the time of Constantine, there had been Christians who were also poets, but with the unfortunate exception of Commodian, whom we have already mentioned, there were, strictly speaking, no poets who attempted to put poetry to Christian uses before Juvencus.

A Christian of Spanish birth, Juvencus published around 330 A.D. a work called Evangeliorum Libri IV, the Gospel story in Virgilian hexameters. Unlike Commodian he was intimately familiar with Virgil and with the subtleties of diction and meter which were a part of the literary tradition. It was this close acquaintance which accounts for both the strength and shortcomings of his work. His task was to provide the Christians with a heroic account of their Lord, and there was no other way to do this than to adapt the dactylic hexameter and epic diction to Christian needs. Juvencus used the Gospel according to Matthew as the basis for his work, and borrowed material at random from the other Gospels. One is struck in the Prologue by the poet's quite un-Christian statement that since Homer and Virgil have achieved great fame even though they write of the false, he should surely gain eternal fame for singing of the truth. One is struck even more forcibly by the incongruity of much of his diction -- God is Summus Tonans (summi per regna Tonantis), the Most High Thunderer; or the High Throned Parent (Iudex, altitroni genitoris gloria, Christus). But given the validity of the enterprise, it is a successful and impressive achievement.

Juvencus is not a poet of genius, but Rome was not, at this time, producing poets of genius among either pagans or Christians. He is, however, a poet of considerable competence. Expert critics claim to be able to find traces of accentual scansion in the poem, but these are certainly not noticeable. As for the Virgilian tone and reminiscences, these are cinching evidence of the solidity of Juvencus' education and the delicacy of his sentiments. As it was, his book was a great success. It became a popular school book and its verses were frequently used by grammarians to illustrate points of syntax or versification. And it started a new type of Christian literature -- the rewriting of Old or New Testament material in classical form. There are anonymous poems on Sodom and Jonah; Cyprianus Gallicus attempted the same thing, with less success, for the Pentateuch, and Sedulius, Dracontius, and Avitus with more success for various parts of the Bible.

Juvencus is of the generation of Marius Victorinus and Lactantius, of Constantine's restoration of the Empire, of the Council of Nicea. The other two major Christian poets of the late Empire were born about the middle of the century and were contemporaries of the great Christian prose writers, Ambrose, Jerome, and Augustine. The lesser of these was Paulinus of Nola, born in 353 at Bordeaux. He was of a wealthy and noble Christian family, married and father of at least one child. He is an excellent example of the unresolved contradictions which plagued a man of good will in the fourth century. In his youth he had studied under the nominally Christian rhetor Ausonius, and from him had imbibed a thorough knowledge of the pagan poets as well as skill in correct versification, and a deep regard for that tradition. Shortly after his baptism in 390, following the example of St. Anthony, he gave up his wealth and position in the world and sought after holiness through a life of poverty and self-denial. After a brief sojourn in Spain, he went in 396 to the shrine of his patron St. Felix in Nola. He remained here until his death in 431, having been made bishop of Nola in 409. Unlike the vast majority of ascetics, he took his wife with him and although they gave up the lusts of the flesh, they continued to live together as brother and sister in Christ.

Paulinus' poems, like his life, are a study in unresolved contradictions. His Christian feeling was deep and sincere, his whole life was motivated by purely Christian values. Yet his poetry is completely classical in form and diction. The depth of his feeling seldom is evident beneath his flatly correct verses. Still, there are some passages in his poems to the glory of St. Felix which are true poetry. One of his elegies, on the death of a young boy, is genuinely moving and is purely Christian in feeling. Among his other writings, several are of interest, though for other than literary reasons. First is a series of four letters in verse explaining to his old teacher, Ausonius, who had opposed the move, his reasons for renouncing the world. He also composed a panegyric on John the Baptist and some paraphrases of the Psalms. He wrote a variety of miscellaneous verse, including some epigrams, some controversial works, and two poems describing the basilica of St. Felix at Nola.

Without a rival as the outstanding poet of the Christian Empire, and the only one who deserves to be ranked with the great poets of the Latin language, is the Spaniard Prudentius (348-ca. 405). While even more skilled in the use of classical meters, and fully as steeped in classical culture as Paulinus, Prudentius uses the techniques and paraphernalia of the pagans with a fitness and originality which raise his work to the level of true poetry. And fully as devout a Christian as Paulinus, Prudentius was better able to place the pagan and Christian traditions in a viable relation to each other. His life too was a successful mingling of Roman and Christian values, as he brought to a career in the civil service the values of a Christian gentleman.

Prudentius' poetic output was considerable and varied, all Christian in its purpose and subject matter, much of it pagan and classical in its form, diction, and devices. Among his major works are two long didactic poems, the Apotheosis and Hamarti-genia. Both are argumentative and polemical in character, but they are more than this. Although each of these works castigates heretics and sometimes suffers from an unregulated use of denun-ciation, still each has a true poetic conception and artistic integrity. The subject of the Apotheosis is the deification of man through Christ, who is fully human and fully God. Christ shares the suffering and temptation of man, and man shares in the apotheosis of Christ. This is truly a grand theme, and it is handled with great skill by Prudentius. It has often been ob-jected of this poem and the Hamartigenia that the argument tends to overcome the poetry, and this is to some extent true. But this is an almost inevitable pitfall of a didactic poet. Even Lucre-tius, whom Prudentius greatly resembles in these works, has been justly criticized for the same failing; and he is a great poet nonetheless.

The Hamartigenia is a similar work, but treating of the origin of sin and the problem of reconciling the existence of evil with an omnipotent and good God. In the course of the poem, he castigates both the Gnostics and the dualist Marcion, and solves his problem in a way which, if not completely satisfactory, is as good as the Christians have yet managed. He insists that God, being com-pletely good, could not be responsible for evil. But because He was good, He endowed man with freedom, and with freedom came the possibility of evil. Its actual existence however was the result of man's free choice, and the fatal result of that choice has been the pollution of the natural world. Prudentius rises to Lucretian intensity in recounting and denouncing the lust, greed, and cruel-ty which have accompanied the progress of mankind. And he rejoices in the sweet gift of the resurrection, which only a good and merciful God could give. The poem closes with a description of the eternal joys of the saved, the tortures of the damned, and of purgatory (not yet so named), where those saved but stained souls are made fit to enter the kingdom of heaven.

Quite different from these long didactic poems, which are written in heroic meter, crammed with erudition, indulging in overblown figures of speech and rhetorical adornments, is the Peristephanon, a collection of fourteen poems of martyrdom. In these poems, Prudentius illustrates his skill in handling a great variety of the more difficult classical meters, and his sense of metrical fitness. It is more than a virtuoso performance. It is poetic composition of a high order, and in a genre (saints' lives) which usually brings out the worst in a writer. Prudentius accomplishes in these poems what so many writers of short works attempt and fail -- the union between the specific event, convincingly por-trayed, and the universal or ideal. Also he exhibits in several of these poems a charmingly simple and direct style, quite in contrast to the florid nature of much of his writing. Modest in his aim, Prudentius has succeeded here better perhaps than in any of his other work in creating poetry of enduring value.

By far the most original of Prudentius' poems, in its conception if not in its execution, is the Psychomachia, an allegorical account of the battle between the virtues and vices for the soul of man. The Introduction recounts the victory of Abraham and his 318 followers over the heathen kings, which signifies the triumph of faith, aided by Christ, over the sins of paganism. In the main body of the poem, however, the action proceeds through a series of indivdual combats: Faith defeats Idolatry, Shame overcomes Lust, Patience conquers Anger. But Pride is a more formidable opponent and is beaten only through the united efforts of Mens Humilis, Spes, Justitia, Honestas, Sobrietas, Jejunia, and Pudor. The outcome, as seemed certain from the outset, is the victory of the forces of righteousness. As poetry, this is far inferior to Prudentius' best work, but it has considerable historical signi- ficance in being the first completely allegorical poem in the West, and in beginning a new poetic genre, the Psychomachia, or battle for the soul, which would enjoy considerable popularity in the centuries to come.

The final two works of Prudentius which we shall discuss can best be dealt with in connection with our account of his well-born contemporary, St. Ambrose. These works are his long poem Contra Symmachum and his collection of hymns entitled Cathemerinon.

Eight years older than Prudentius, but vastly more important as a force both in his own day and in succeeding centuries was the first of the "Four Doctors of the Latin Church," St. Ambrose. He was born about 340 A.D. in the city of Treves in Gaul of a noble family which had been Christian for several generations. His father, a high Roman official (praetorian prefect), died while Ambrose was still a boy, and the family moved to Rome where Ambrose was educated in the best Roman tradition. After com- pleting his education, he entered the legal profession, in which he enjoyed considerable success, eventually becoming governor of Liguria and Aemelia in north Italy about 372. Included in the provinces Ambrose governed was the city of Milan, upon the death of whose bishop in 374 a battle broke out between the Arian and Orthodox factions in the city, each wishing to name the next bishop. Ambrose intervened personally, and while he was attempt- ing to restore order a child's voice (according to his biographer, Paulinus) in the crowd was heard to cry out: "Let Ambrose be bishop;" and both factions took up the child's cry.

Thus Ambrose was thrust, suddenly and against his will, into an ecclesiastical career. He accepted his election with protests and considerable misgivings, but once having made up his mind to be a bishop, he determined to be as good a one as possible. Although Ambrose had had very little instruction in religious matters, and in fact was not even baptized at the time of his election, he had enjoyed all the benefits of a classical education; he had had considerable administrative experience; and he embodied in his person all the best qualities of the Roman aristocratic civil servant.

In addition to restoring peace and order to his faction-ridden diocese, Ambrose determined to perfect himself in sacred knowledge, to which he had hitherto given little thought or attention. Considering how late in life he began these studies, it is amazing how widely and how deeply he read. Among his many duties as bishop were teaching and preaching, and it is his success in these callings upon which his fame chiefly rests. But he was also a fearless defender of the independence of the church, and his verbal chastisement of the emperor Theodosius for his massacre at Thessolonica is well known. In addition to this heroic confrontation, Ambrose was involved in another cause celèbre during his episcopacy. This was the affair of the Altar of Victory.

The statue of the goddess Victory, supposedly captured from the Tarentines in the third century B.C., had for centuries stood in the Senate house in Rome. It was at this altar that incense was burned to open sessions of the Senate, here that senators took their solemn oaths of loyalty to the emperor. The emperor Constantius had ordered the removal, though not the destruction, of this altar. It had been restored by the pagan emperor Julian, at which time it became an emotion-charged symbol to the senators, a majority of whom were still pagan. Consequently, when Gratian in 375 ordered it removed again, a stormy controversy arose, culminating in a formal request to the emperor that the statue be restored. This appeal, by the senator Symmachus, is written with great sincerity, exhibiting a most ingratiating piety and tolerance, and is one of the most attractive pagan productions of the fourth century. Symmachus pleads that without the altar, before which all the senators take their oath, there is no guarantee against perjury, no principle of unity in the Senate, no sanction giving authority to its decrees. After recalling the triumphs which the goddess Victory has given Rome throughout the ages, Symmachus concludes:

> I ask only peace for the gods of our fathers, the native gods of Rome. That which all men worship ought properly to be considered to be a single god. We all look up to the same stars; we have the same sky; and the same firmament encompasses us all. What does it matter by what learned theory each man seeks the truth? There is no one way which will lead us to so great a secret. All this is matter for discussion for men of leisure. We offer your Majesties not a debate, but a plea.

This plea, which was unsuccessful, evoked two replies from the Christians, one immediately from Ambrose, and one about twenty years later from Prudentius. Both replies show the confidence and certainty of the Christians, who had quickly become accustomed to their position of strength, and both assume a doctrine of progress in which Christianity is a culmination of earlier developments. Both are ruthless in their refusal to accept the doctrine of religious tolerance urged by Symmachus. Ambrose' reply was confident and unbending, but not shrill. "How can I believe you," he taunts Symmachus, "who confess you do not know what it is you worship?" But "there is no shame in passing on to better things. Just as the world progressed from elements flying about wildly in the void to the ordered distinction of sky, seas, and earth, and all the things contained in it, and as light and warmth replaced the dark and cold of the first three days, so also has the church grown through injustice, poverty, and persecutions," and Ambrose clearly implies that the world has been improved through the growth of the church.[5]

Near the end of the century, when the immediate battle had been won, but paganism in high places was still a threat to the church, Prudentius wrote a long poem <u>Against Symmachus</u>, which was more sweeping in its scope than Ambrose' work. Prudentius began his poem with an attack on a number of pagan religions and then turned his attack against Symmachus, especially the latter's plea for the toleration of paganism. Written after the heat of battle had cooled, this poem could indulge in a broader view. Symmachus' plea, and the case for paganism in general, is seen in historical perspective; and in Prudentius even more clearly than in Ambrose a doctrine of historical progress is evident. The pagans had been mistaken in attributing Rome's greatness to the ancient gods and in considering the present as a period of decline. Rather, the history of Rome is a record of continuing progress and improvement. The so-called Golden Age was a crude and primitive time which no sensible man would wish to see return. Rome conquered and civilized the world not with the help of the old gods, but by virtue of her armed might, because the only God wished the human race to be unified as a preparation for the coming of Christ. The present is a great improvement over the past, but Rome's mission is far from fulfilled. Augustus brought the Empire, Christ the church, and the work of both has hardly begun. There is no place in this brave new world for the falsehoods and superstitions of earlier and less enlightened ages. Symmachus had pled that both Christian and pagan share a common sky, to which there are many pathways. Truly the sky is common to all, answers Prudentius, to the virtuous and depraved, the harlot and the wife, the priest and gladiator. But this does not minimize the difference between them or mitigate the obvious superiority of the one over the other. There is as much difference between a German and a Roman as between senseless idolators and those who, freed from vain superstition, follow the commandments of God. Certainly the Christians had the better of this encounter, as the confident and vigorous must always overcome the tolerant and the weary.

Ambrose and Prudentius are also the two greatest writers of hymns in the early Latin church, and although this form of liturgical poetry has antecedents among both the Hebrews and Greek Christians, it may be considered a new literary form in the Latin language. Hilary of Poitiers is ordinarily credited with having written the earliest Latin hymns, but of the few remaining ones attributed to him, none is known with a certainty to be his. Most successful in writing hymns for the church service was Ambrose, the lawyer and administrator. His hymns have a simplicity, beauty, and intensity that cannot fail to thrill the most indifferent reader, and they remain to this day some of the finest hymns the church possesses. Although they use quantitative scansion, rather than accentual, their meters are extremely simple, in accordance with the needs of the service.

Prudentius' hymns are of a different sort. Of a genre dating back to Pindar and in Latin to Horace, they are classical in form and diction, though Christian in inspiration. Still, there is much paganism in them, in the interweaving of phrases from the poets into the texture of the hymns and in the parallelisms between Christian and pagan themes. These works were evidently not intended for use in worship. They are too long, too complicated in structure, too erudite, and too lofty in diction. They are rather Christian poems of reflection, whose themes are appropriate to a given hour of the day or year or time of life. Once again Prudentius shows himself a master of many classic meters, and a poet and thinker of considerable merit. There are sections of several of the hymns which have been found suitable for liturgical use in excerpted form. Another interesting aspect of Prudentius' hymns is his extensive use of allegory. Ambrose was one of the first in the West to use allegory as a means of Biblical exegesis, but his hymns are quite straightforward. It was Prudentius rather who introduced this technique on a large scale into the poetry of the church.

Although not a writer of great technical proficiency, except in his hymns, Ambrose was tireless in carrying out the duties of his episcopal office. He published a number of sermons, models of their kind, as well as studies of a variety of Biblical topics, in which he developed the allegorical method of interpreting scripture. Allegorical interpretation of authorities had for long been employed both in profane literature and in the Greek church, where it had enjoyed quite a vogue since the time of Origen (early third century). Even as Ambrose was developing this system for the western church, the mythographer and grammarian Fulgentius was doing the same for Virgil's Aeneid. But it was Ambrose who, in the West, first made extensive and systematic use of this technique in interpreting scripture, although he usually confined himself to searching out the moral sense.

During the Middle Ages, the allegorical interpretation was perfected into the fourfold method, in which each passage of scripture might be read in two or more of four possible ways: the literal meaning, that is, the obvious literary meaning, including the various figures of speech; the moral or tropological sense, indicating how the words of scripture apply to human character; the allegorical or mystical sense, interpreting passages of the Old Testament as prefiguring events of the New; and the anagogical sense, showing how scripture reveals to us something of the life to come. This method rapidly gained popularity and soon was all but universal in the West. To many it seems a perverse attempt to explain away the plain meaning of the text, but it must be remembered that there was a strong tendency to allegorize among both Christians and pagans during the fourth century, and that allegory had been employed by many classical writers from Plato on. There are many reasons for its spread. One must have been the necessity of finding more meaning, or different meaning, in Holy Scripture than was apparently present, in order to make it accord with Christian principles. The pagans had done the same with their myths. But there were also sound literary reasons for its triumph, namely a long tradition coming down from the Pythagoreans through Plato concerning the secrecy of doctrine. What was written was as much a concealment of the truth as an exposition of it; and the puzzle had to be solved by expert interpretation before the divine secrets could be known. With Ambrose the former considerations were no doubt more important, but it was he who set the style.

He used this technique too in his Hexameron, or commentary on the six days of creation, in the form of a series of nine sermons. Intended primarily for the edification of the Christians in his flock, it was also to some extent addressed to nonbelievers, for so great was Ambrose's fame as a preacher that it was not unusual for his audience to include a number of pagans. The first of a long series of Hexamera to be written in the West, it was modelled upon the work of the same name by the Greek father, St. Basil. However, it exhibits several important variations from its model, none more striking that its loving delight in the beauties and minute details of the world of nature, and the lessons these had for God's children if they would but learn. His purpose is essentially moral, and in this work he is both ingenious and profoundly poetic in devising allegories to elucidate the moral significance of the words of scripture. Like Cicero and Augustine, he was capable of writing a highly poetic prose, and the power of his inspiration and beauty of his imagery more than compensate for his limitations as a "literary" artist. This is not meant to imply that Ambrose was not a well-educated man or a competent writer; only that literature was not his profession. His education had included the great writers in both the Greek and Latin traditions, and in his Hexameron he is at pains to show, by implication at least, that Christianity is the fulfillment, not the renunciation of those traditions. By using phrases or paraphrases from the standard Latin authors as integral parts of his own language, by hinting rather than insisting, Ambrose effectively makes his point.

In his De officiis ministrorum, too, Ambrose is at pains to show the affinities between the pagan and Christians, at the same time insisting on the superiority of Christianity. This treatise is closely modelled on Cicero's De officiis (in turn modelled upon a Greek work by Paenitius), whose structure it follows very closely and much of whose doctrine it accepts. The reason for this seems fairly clear. By following such a well-known work on pagan ethics, Ambrose could show the frequent congruence between them and Christian ethics, while at the same time he could conduct a point by point criticism of the older system and show how it had been superceded by that of the Christians. One is therefore surprised to find that the attack on pagan ethics is very mild: the law of retaliation has been superceded, and the summum bonum is no longer virtue itself, but eternal life which is the fruit of virtue. Point by point the scheme of Stoic-Platonic ethics embodied in Cicero's work is gone through, and although a Christian will often apply the old precepts in a new way, the system itself is left intact by Ambrose. Although he holds that the highest and noblest examples of virtuous behavior are to be found in the Old and New Testaments, still the examples of the virtuous pagans are worthy and edifying and should not be despised by a Christian.[6]

The second of the four Doctors of the Latin Church is St. Jerome, born about the same time as Ambrose but in Illyria rather than Gaul. His family was quite wealthy, though of a somewhat lower social stratum than Ambrose'; and it too was Christian. Jerome travelled considerably in pursuit of the best education obtainable at the time, studying at Ambrose' home town of Treves, a major intellectual center, at Aquileia in northeast Italy, and at Rome, where his teacher was the foremost grammarian of the day, the pagan Aelius Donatus. Jerome is a much more complex personality than Ambrose. It is almost as though he had two concurrent personalities vying for supremacy within him. On the one hand he was a humanist, highly cultured, witty, urbane, a lover of book, good food, and polite and refined society. This is the personality with which he seems to have begun life, and although it was sometimes submerged in later years, it remained with him to the end. On the other hand, he was an ascetic hermit, fasting and mortifying his flesh, fearful of the snares of this world, morbidly afraid of sex, fleeing to the desert and dreaming wild dreams of passion, temptation and deliverance. This second personality first became manifest while he was a young student at Aquileia and fell in with a group of reformers who felt that the church had become corrupt and could only be saved through monasticism.

Jerome continued his travels and his studies during his adult life, living for periods in Rome, Syria, Constantinople, and finally Bethlehem, where he founded a monastery. Wherever he went, he surrounded himself with pious virgins, whom he never touched. He constantly enjoined perpetual virginity upon them and told them in obscenely minute detail the stories of his own temptations and deliverance. His closest relationship was with the widowed Paula and her daughter Eustochium, both of whom Jerome loved dearly and to whom he acted as spiritual guide and confessor as well as friend.

While he was still a young man, and during a severe illness, Jerome had a famous dream which both illustrates and further complicated the conflicts of his personality. Most of the writers we have hitherto noted accepted the pagan tradition, albeit purged and transcended, with little or no difficulty. But Jerome, perhaps because he was more keenly and subtely attracted by the beauties of pagan literature, was more sensitive to its incompatibility with Christianity, or at least the monastic-dominated Christian world view of the late fourth century. As he tells the story in a letter to Eustochium, while on the verge of death he was suddenly haled before the judgment seat of God, and being asked to identify himself, answered that he was a Christian. A terrifying reply was returned to him: "You lie! You are not a Christian, but a Ciceronian. For where your treasure is, there also shall your heart be." This was followed by repentance, a severe beating, and a vow from Jerome that he would give up pagan books altogether. Then he awoke, still feeling the pain of the blows he had suffered. He seems, for a time, sincerely to have tried to be more moderate in his cultivation of pagan literature, and surely he plunged with great energy into a study of sacred literature. But he apparently never interpreted his oath literally, and as time went on he took it less and less seriously, finally retorting to a critic that after all the whole thing had only been a dream.

Despite the fact that Jerome was perhaps the best educated man of his day, and could, had he chosen, have written nothing but purely classical Latin, his commitment to Christianity led him to devise a style which, although always lucid and correct, was nevertheless not "pure" by classical standards. He introduced words and locutions from spoken Latin into his writings, and he freely coined new words from Greek and Hebrew as the need arose. He was able to vary his style according to the needs of the moment and is more important even than Tertullian as a creator of a new, expressive, and more natural literary Latin. Without the tendentious bombast of Tertullian before him or Gregory the Great after him, he nevertheless accomplished more in this direction than either of them. He prided himself highly on his scholarship, his taste, and his linguistic knowledge, but he devoted his life to placing these at the service of the Christian religion.

Jerome's literary output was voluminous and varied. He was one of the finest and one of the most active letter writers among the Fathers, and although these letters rank as literature (in fact some of Jerome's best writing is contained in them), some of them are nevertheless genuine letters, intensely personal and immediate, and not as is the case with others, essays disguised as personal letters. They provide us not only with clear insights into Jerome's personality and his relations, both loving and hostile, with many of his contemporaries, but also with innumerable pictures of and comments on the life of his age. His theological writings were numerous and always on the side of orthodoxy, but they are not his best works and are of much less permanent significance than those of his younger contemporary Augustine. Jerome also has some importance as a historian. He translated from the Greek the <u>Chronicle</u> of Eusebius and wrote a continuation of the work, stopping just short of his own day. He intended to wait, he said, until the barbarians were controlled before bringing it up to date. In the related field of biography he composed two quite different kinds of works: an elegantly written <u>Lives</u> <u>of</u> <u>Famous</u> <u>Men</u> for the intelligentsia, to compete with pagan works of a similar nature and to show the world that the church could claim many illustrious authors as well as pious if unlettered souls; and a series of three popular saints' lives (<u>St.</u> <u>Paul</u> <u>the</u> <u>First</u> <u>Hermit</u>, <u>St.</u> <u>Malchus</u>, and <u>St.</u> <u>Hilarion</u>) which, although they hardly rank as great literature, satisfied the popular taste and had the advantage of being edifying as well as entertaining.

Jerome's greatest achievement, for which he was eminently qualified, was the translation of the Bible into Latin. Learned in both Latin and Greek, a scholar and bibliophile, he had also mastered Hebrew. The Latin versions of the Bible then in use were both incomplete and poorly done. Accordingly in 383 at the suggestion of Pope Damasus, Jerome began a revision of the Gospels and Psalms on the basis of the Greek text. This modest design grew into a re-translation of almost the entire Bible, not finished until many years later in Bethlehem. Jerome used the best scholarly resources available to him, including the <u>Hexapla</u> of Origen, but ultimately depended upon the texts in the original languages. Although not devoid of mistakes, Jerome's Latin (or Vulgate) Bible was a great triumph of scholarship. But it was an even greater triumph stylistically. Scorning the rolling Ciceronian period as well as the diffuse style of common speech, Jerome devised what is probably a perfect compromise. His Latin is correct, but contemporary, simple where simplicity is called for, lofty when necessary, incorporating much of the language of the earlier Latin translations but elevating and correcting them. When one recalls Jerome's repugnance at the uncouth style of the gospels in his younger days, his accomplishment appears all the greater. He supplied several of the books of the Bible with individual introductions and commentaries, which provided the reader with the benefit of Jerome's great erudition on matters of history, literature, and language, disucssed some of the problems of translation, and elucidated some of the more difficult passages. They, together with several of Jerome's letters concerning points of translation, provided later ages with a basis for intelligent Biblical criticism and a considerable knowledge of the Greek language.

Contemporary opinion, then as now, tended to be conservative in the matter of tampering with the word of God, and there was much opposition to the novelties of Jerome's translation, thus delaying for a time its universal acceptance. Such acceptance was general, however, by the end of the eighth century, and with minor revisions to bring it abreast of modern scholarship, Jerome's Vulgate remains the standard Latin text of the Bible for the Roman Catholic church.

In Bethlehem, Jerome and Paula had set up a convent and a monastery, which soon attracted great numbers of pious virgins and monks who wished to profit from association with the great scholar-monk. To escape them, Jerome retreated to a private cave which he converted into a study, accompanied, according to tradition, by his pet lion. He did, however, supervise the monastic establishment, and as an integral part of it he set up a school (in which he himself taught grammar) and a scriptorium, devoted to copying manuscripts of both pagan and Christian writings and providing a solid classical education as a preparation for religious studies. This step had momentous significance, for a new educational establishment now existed as an alternative to the state schools and the higher instruction of the libraries and baths. The new education included the old -- or most of it -- but its purpose went beyond the classical ideal. It was education for the religious vocation, but Jerome always remained too good a humanist to think that one could be a very good Christian if he were not also a scholar.

Although as a scholar, Jerome must be ranked with the great, as a man he is not particularly likeable. He was petty, unforgiving, arrogant, conceited, and sharp-tongued, always looking for a fight and usually finding one.[7] Still there is much sweetness in him, and a consuming interest in the salvation of his soul. His services to the church, though, and his title to sainthood, must rest on his intellectual attainments rather than the example of his character.

As has become evident by now, most of the important Latin writing of the late Empire was done by Christians. But there are also some pagan monuments of this period which deserve recognition. We have already had occasion to mention the senator Symmachus' plea for the restoration of the Altar of Victory and for religious tolerance. But Symmachus was pleading for a lost cause. Even the untiring efforts of the apostate emperor Julian had failed to breathe new life into the old tradition. The pagan productions of the period were not creative, but several are nonetheless important. In the teaching of grammar, pagans continued to dominate, and two grammarians of special importance date from this period. We have already mentioned the Ars grammatica of Marius Victorinus who, although he became a Christian late in life, may legitimately be considered among the pagan authors. Of much greater importance than the grammar of Victorinus are the two works of St. Jerome's teacher, Aelius Donatus. It is not completely certain that Donatus was a pagan, though in all probability he was. He wrote an elementary work on grammar, the Ars minor, and a more advanced treatise on literature, the Ars maior. For more than a thousand years these were the most widely used text books in the Latin world.

Of a more scholarly turn of mind was the mythographer Fulgentius.[8] Although nothing whatever is known of his life, and even his dates cannot be established with certainty, it is likely that he was an early fifth-century pagan writer. Four of his works survive, the Mitologiae, Expositio sermonum antiquorum, Expositio Virgilianae continentiae, and De aetatibus mundi et hominis. They are the work of a pedantic antiquarian of mediocre abilities, and indulge in the worst excesses of rhetorical extravagance and perversity in vocabulary and style. Nevertheless they are important, particularly his study of Virgil, because they use allegory quite as whimsically as does Ambrose and to much less purpose, and they systematically employ allegory in the interpretation of the classics. Fulgentius was an extremely popular author during the Carolingian period and profoundly influenced the way men conceived of the function of literature during the whole of the Middle Ages.

Broader in his interests than Fulgentius and possessing a less preposterous style, but also enchanted by the uses of allegory in literary criticism, was Macrobius,[9] a Neoplatonist of the late fourth and early fifth centuries. He wrote two works, both of which were widely used throughout the Middle Ages. One was a commentary on Cicero's Dream of Scipio (a section of book VI of De republica, which circulated separately), which interprets Cicero's work in a Neoplatonic sense. In this commentary, Macrobius used the works of many of the later Neoplatonists rather than those of Plotinus and indulged in numerous digressions to illustrate his own learning on points only remotely connected with his text.

His attitude toward the great authors of Antiquity in this work is extremely interesting as well as profoundly influential on later ages. The great writers, Homer, Virgil, Plato, and Cicero, are infallible authorities on all matters whatsoever, divinely inspired sources of wisdom. It is therefore inconceivable that they might contradict each other, and to avoid apparent contradictions, it was necessary to resort to allegorical interpretation.

But it was in his second work, <u>Saturnalia</u>, that he most effectively employed allegory in his study of classical literature, particularly Virgil. This work, only parts of which are extant, is in the form of a dialogue, and its purpose seems to be to illustrate the author's vast knowledge of a variety of topics, including religion, antiquarian trivia, social customs, and especially language and literature, to which the greater part of the work is devoted. In it he considers Virgil's poetry as embodying profound truths concerning all the secrets of the universe, man, and the gods. Virgil is an authority on religion, philosophy, science, and ethics. One studies him, as all great poets, to gain wisdom, and to do this one must discover the meaning hidden in his allegory. Both of these works were widely quoted during the Middle Ages as authorities on everything from grammar to meteorology, and their influence on the medieval concept of the nature and function of poetry was almost determinative.

As is the case with many authors who did not write controversial religious works, there is no agreement among authorities as to whether Macrobius was a Christian or a pagan. So close were Neoplatonism and Christianity in many of their doctrines that nothing Macrobius says absolutely rules out the possibility of his being a Christian. Still the positive evidence is slight and he is usually numbered among the pagan authors.

Even more important than Macrobius, largely because his book was widely used as a school text, was the African writer of the early fifth century, Martianus Capella.[10] An advocate by profession and a Neoplatonist, he devoted his last years after his retirement from active life to composing a synthetic work on the seven Liberal Arts, the quintessence of late paganism. He uses odd and unusual words, ornate and complicated constructions, fantastic figures of speech -- in short, a tortured and bizarre style. However, he hit upon a device for presenting his instructional matter which, even more than the basic soundness of the book, assured it a place of honor in the schools of western Europe for the next millenium. So influential was Martianus' book, not only on the literature of the Middle Ages, but also on its art, architecture and pageantry, that a fairly full synopsis of its content is in order.

Taking his cue from the popular romances much in vogue at the time, Martianus provided a mythological story, comprising the first two books, to introduce the main part of the work. First there is a hymn to Hymen, conciliator of the sexes and elements and matchmaker among the Gods. Then begins the action. Mercury is still unmarried and decides to take a wife. His first several attempts are unsuccessful, as he is turned down by Sophia, Mantici and Pysche. He then, on the advice of Virtus, asks Apollo for a suggestion. Apollo proposes the learned maiden Philologia, who is well versed in every kind of knowledge. Then the three of them, accompanied by the Muses and delighted by the music of the spheres, make a journey through the celestial spheres to the palace of Jupiter to ask his consent. Jupiter calls an assembly of the gods and it is decided that the match shall take place and that the bride shall be raised to divine rank. Book II opens with Philologia appropriately flattered and willing to be Mercury's bride but afraid at the prospect of so great an honor. Her misgivings are ignored; her mother Phronesis begins getting her ready for the wedding; the four Cardinal Virtues greet her; the three Graces bestow upon her three mystic kisses to give her courage. Athanasia, the daughter of Apotheosis, comes to lead her to heaven, but first, to prove her worthiness of divinity, the bride must vomit up a large number of books. She obliges, and the books are gathered up by the Artes and Disciplinae, with the help of the Muses Urania and Calliope. She now quaffs the goblet of immortality and is carried up to heaven in a litter carried by two young men, Labor and Amor, and two girls, Epimelia and Agrypina. She is met in heaven by Juno, who then escorts her on a journey through the celestial spheres to the Milky Way, where Jupiter's palace is. Assembled at the palace is a vast collection of gods, demigods, heroes, poets, and philosophers, the blessed inhabitants of Olympus. When Philologia has been instructed by Juno about the inhabitants of Olympus, her mother, Phronesis, demands an accounting of the wedding gifts. Apollo thereupon leads forward, as gifts for the bride, seven maid-servants of various aspect. There are the seven Liberal Arts, to each of which one book is allotted in the remainder of this work. Up to this point, Martianus used a mixed form of alternating prose and poetry -- the prosimetrum, derived ultimately from the Roman Menippean satire and later to be used with such striking effect by Boethius. The last seven books, however, are mostly in prose and vary considerably in their value. The books on grammar and rhetoric are the best, that on geometry probably the weakest. Taken as a whole, however, it is quite a competent summary of the Arts, and its allegorical presentation, though offensive to modern taste, nevertheless exerted a strong appeal for both students and writers for a thousand years. His personification of the Arts became standard: Grammar is old and gray-haired, carrying a box with a knife and file to excise errors; Rhetoric is tall and beautiful, wearing a dress adorned by the figures of speech and carrying arms to wound her adversaries. The other personified abstractions also became standard and show up again and again in the works of later writers. They and the journey to heaven through the celestial spheres in elaborately allegorical conveyances formed the basic outline of the world of learned poetry during the Middle Ages.

By a strange chance, one of the best of the Roman historians wrote during the fourth century. This was Ammianus Marcellinus (330-400 A.D.). History had never been the long suit of the Latin authors. Even the best of them, Livy, Sallust, and Tacitus, leave much to be desired. History writing was considered a branch of rhetoric, and as such had to conform to rhetorical requirements whether the events described did so or not. It was also subordinated to considerations of public utility, such as showing the greatness of Rome, instilling patriotism in the reader, providing examples of virtuous conduct to be emulated and of vice punished to be avoided. Still there was a polish and a rhetorical fitness about these historians which deserve for them consideration as fine literature. The last of the really able Roman historians, Marcellinus wrote the history of Rome from the reign of Nerva (96 A.D.) to the battle of Adrianople (378 A.D.) Although only the last portion of the work is still extant, its merits are sufficiently obvious. Although Marcellinus was Tacitus' inferior in point of style, he was at least his equal in other respects. His history is well-written, dispassionate, well informed, and clearly and logically presented. His faults are those of his genre. These are certainly less objectionable than those of the Seven Books against the Pagans of Orosius (of which we shall speak later) or the anonymous Augustan History, an ineptly composed compilation of the fourth century treating the reigns of the emperors between 117 and 284 A.D.

One further man, Calcidius, deserves mention. Though he was not a particularly noteworthy intellect, his work nevertheless had far-reaching influence on later centuries. Calcidius translated into Latin the Timaeus of Plato and wrote a learned commentary on it, thus supplying the West with its only Platonic treatise until the fifteenth century, with the exception of Aristippus' translations of the Phaedo and Meno in the twelfth century.

It can be seen from this short summary (and there are important scholiasts we have not mentioned) that the pagans had already adopted an attitude toward their tradition which the Christians would be forced into during the next century -- they were interested in preserving, organizing, excerpting, and their activities were largely devoted to explaining or reorganizing a literary culture which was no longer living, but a treasured inheritance from the past.

The greatest and last of the Latin Fathers of the late Empire was St. Augustine.[11] In his life he recapitulates the experience of several centuries of religious development; in his experience he plumbed for the first time since St. Paul the very core of Christianity -- man's sinful nature and utter helplessness and God's forgiving mercy in making possible man's salvation through the incarnation and resurrection; in his writings he supplied the church with numerous works of instruction, protected it against heretics from within and pagan attacks from without; and by a combination of all these he exerted a more powerful and lasting influence on western Christianity than any man since apostolic times. The third Doctor of the Latin church, he is, all things considered, probably the greatest. In his thought and life were embodied the best of the Graeco-Roman tradition and an abiding regard for it, but these were completely transformed by the depth and intensity of his Christian feeling and orientation. He brought to completion and perfection what his predecessors from Minucius Felix to Jerome had begun -- the absorption and genuine transformation of the pagan tradition within the new world of Christianity.

Augustine was born in 354 A.D. in the north African city of Tagaste of a Christian mother and pagan father. Although his mother instructed him in Christian doctrine, he remained unconvinced and only arrived at Christianity after trying nearly all the alternatives which the late Empire provided, asking all the basic questions of human existence, and relentlessly criticizing all the available answers. In 383, the very year in which Jerome began his translation of the Bible, his profession of <u>rhetor</u> brought him to Rome, where he heard of the wonderful preaching being done by Ambrose, the bishop of Milan. Prompted mainly by professional curiosity, he journeyed to Milan to hear Ambrose, where he was much impressed by the skill of the bishop but remained unconverted. His way of life up to this point had been that of a gay young libertine, exploiting all the opportunities for sin provided by the corrupt society of the late Empire, even keeping a mistress for fifteen years. Unlike most libertines, however, he was disgusted by his way of life, yet he could not find within himself the strength to reform. He had been tormented by this problem for some time and for awhile had belonged to the sect of Manicheans, who believed in two gods, one good and one evil, constantly battling for supremacy, which in the end would go to the god of light and goodness. He had next adhered to the moderate, humane, scepticism of the Old Academy, as represented by the writings of Cicero. More recently he had been attracted to the religious philosophy of Neoplatonism, a powerful force among the intelligentsia of the time, and although he was deeply impressed by this cult and indeed never turned his back on it, he found it ultimately unsatisfactory since it gave him no assurance that he would be saved and no strength to save himself. To such a person, Ambrose' sermons, lively and pointed though they were, had no deep significance, although Augustine found that Ambrose' allegorical interpretation removed many difficulties for him. His conversion took place as the culmination of a period of anguish and soul-searching. "Suddenly," he writes in his <u>Confessions</u> (VIII, 12), "a voice reached my ears from a nearby house. It was the voice of a boy or girl (I don't know which), and in a kind of singsong the words were constantly repeated: 'Take it and read it. Take it and read it.' At once my face changed, and I began to think carefully of whether the singing of words like these came into any kind of game which children play, and I could not remember that I had ever heard anything like it before. I checked the force of my tears and rose to my feet, being quite certain that I must interpret this as a divine command to me to open the book and

read the first passage which I should come upon. . . .I snatched
up the book, opened it, and read in silence the passage upon which
my eyes first fell: Not in rioting and drunkenness, not in cham-
bering and wantonness, not in strife and envying: but put ye on
the Lord Jesus Christ, and make not provision for the flesh in
concupiscence. I had no wish to read further; there was no need
to. For as soon as I had reached the end of this sentence, it was
as though my heart was filled with a light of confidence, and all
the shadows of my doubt were swept away." The incarnation, he
realized, God's suffering and death for the sins of mankind and
His triumphant resurrection, gave firm assurance of personal
salvation for all those who would accept this free gift of faith.

From this point on, he devoted the totality of his vast energies
to the service of his new faith. In 391 he was elected bishop of
the African city of Hippo and organized his cathedral clergy along
semi-monastic lines. His writings exceed in volume, as in importance, those of any other church Father, numbering 118 titles in
all and filling sixteen closely printed volumes of Migne's
Patrologia Latina. Consequently, despite his enormous importance,
it is impossible to give here more than a brief sketch of some of
his more important teachings.

After his conversion he subordinated everything to his central
purpose in life: the defense and understanding of his faith.
Whatever was irrelevant to his purpose he ignored or discarded.
His approach was nearly always subjective -- that of the individual soul trying to understand itself and to reach God. His
starting point is his own experience, and from that experience he
deduced the necessity of God's existence. If, he says, there is a
higher being than the soul, it is God. Men know absolutely that
they can attain truth through the use of their reason. This truth
which they thus know is not, however, the unique truth of any one
man but is common to all. It is permanent and unchangeable, and
the only possible source of this truth is God. He goes on to call
God Goodness, Beauty, and Truth. He is the only creator and
sustainer of the world, and He is both the source and goal of
knowledge.

But if He is supremely good, and the world is His creation, how
can evil exist? Avoiding both the dualism of the Manicheans and
the virtual denial of evil by the Neoplatonists (although he
accepts from them the denial that it is any positive thing),
Augustine explained that evil arose as the result of the abuse of
free will by man. The world, man, and free will, being creations
of God, were all good, but since they were mere creatures they
were not perfect. The abuse of free choice in Eden led man's soul
to be controlled by his body, thus reversing the proper relationship. This eventually resulted in the soul's forgetting its own
nature and thinking itself to be a body. It is this tragic consequence of a free choice dictated by greed that is responsible for

evil.

The soul, in its fallen state, has not the strength to restore itself to its proper relationship with the body. Augustine spoke from personal experience here. He had led a thoroughly evil life, had hated himself for it, yet could not find the strength to renounce it until God's freely given grace did for him he had been unable to do for himself. Augustine states the necessity of grace for salvation in very strong terms, and this has led many throughout the centuries to interpret his remarks as a denial of free will or a claim that since some men were predestined for salvation and others not, the sacraments of the church were superfluous. But in developing these views, Augustine was attacking the British priest Pelagius, who denied original sin and taught that each man must merit his own salvation by his works. As often happens in works addressed to a single problem, Augustine perhaps over-stated his case in his Contra Pelagium. When we consider his writings as a whole, rather than in isolated segments, it becomes clear that while he considered God's grace to be an indispensable aid to free will, it did not destroy that will. And on the sacraments, Augustine was explicit that they are channels of grace and instruments of salvation and are efficacious whether or not the administering priest is in a state of grace.

Among the most ambitious and influential of Augustine's works is his City of God. Written over a number of years, probably from 413 to 426, it was intended as a reply to those pagans who had blamed Alaric's sack of Rome on the anger of the ancient gods at having been deserted for Christ. This work was neither the first nor the last of its kind, but it is by all odds the most powerfully presented and influential. Its theme is the growth, under God's Providence, of the City of God from slight beginnings to its present flourishing state and its ultimate triumph. The City of God is made up of all those who are united by a common bond of love for God and each other, and it is contrasted to the City of the World, consisting of all temporal states, whose citizens are united by devotion to temporal ends. The two cities are necessarily mixed here on earth, and both exist to fulfill God's purpose. Although the work is, strictly speaking, an apologetic rather than a history, its appeal is to history. Augustine traces the progress of the two cities from the creation to his own time, drawing his information both from the Bible and from the Roman historians, especially Sallust and Livy. He grants the merits and even the necessity of the City of the World, but his main theme emphasizes the emphemeral nature of that city and eternity of God's city. It is a philosophy of history assuming a constant progress and improvement as the City of God grows in strength and numbers. Rome was but one of a fleeting succession of temporal powers. Its aims had been high, but its performance had fallen far short of them. Here the philosophy of history which appeared in rudimentary form in Lactantius and Prudentius, and even

Ambrose, becomes explicit. Augustine is somewhat less sympathetic to Rome and temporal government in general than his predecessors had been, but the underlying theme was the same.

Although the City of God used an argument from history, it was not and did not pretend to be a historical work. To provide a history illustrating the theme he had developed in the City of God, Augustine asked a young Spanish priest, Paulus Orosius, to devote his talents and knowledge. Unfortunately, in this instance Augustine proved not to be a good judge of men. Regardless of what one thinks of the validity of the enterprise, Orosius was second-rate or worse in every respect except his Christian zeal. He fulfilled Augustine's request with a work entitled Seven Books against the Pagans. Taking the least imaginative and most pedestrian way of illustrating Augustine's grand theme, Orosius recites the record of man's atrocities to other men in the ancient world during the days of paganism and contrasts this unfavorably with the heights humanity had reached in his own day under the aegis of the church. True, there was some slight disruption caused by the incursions of several Teutonic tribes, but these were as nothing compared to the universal misery of mankind before the triumph of Christianity. He saw all human history as controlled by God's providence, but even managed to make this theme seem silly by the inept, misinformed, and arbitrary way he either misunderstood or misused his data in relating the ineffable chronological coincidences (very few of which occurred in fact) by which God's providence was made manifest in human history. For his information, Orosius almost certainly confined himself to late Roman epitomes, for although he cites the great historians by name, he shows no evidence of having read their works. But such are the chances of history that this book became the most important authority on ancient history for the Middle Ages, and his scheme of the four monarchies of the ancient world, Babylonian, Macedonian, African, and Roman, corresponding to the four quarters of the world, and God's plan of uniting the human race under Roman rule as a preparation for Christ's coming, formed the framework for all large historical works for many centuries to come.

Although Augustine was, properly speaking, a theologian and not a philosopher, still he was well versed in philosophy, and many of his philosophical positions have had an enormous influence on succeeding ages. As he interpreted the story of creation in Genesis, the six days of creation was merely a metaphor. Creation was really instantaneous. With the creation of the world, time also began, and through time the seeds or "seminal reasons" of all things that would ever be would unfold. And so everything, beginning, middle, and end, was created at the first instant.

Augustine felt that all created beings, angels, and souls as well as physical beings, contained within themselves a principle of mutability or limitation, which he called matter. Matter could be either corporeal or incorporeal, although the incorporeal is superior. The soul was a substance composed of incorporeal matter. It was extended in space yet occupied a body. Augustine defines man as "a soul using a body," but the soul was the essential part. Not only was it immortal by nature, but it knew itself with complete certainty to be a living, thinking being. Therefore, whatever else man might be, he was at least that.

Assuming that inferior beings (bodies) cannot act on superior beings (souls), Augustine developed a doctrine of knowledge which was to have great influence in the Middle Ages. The soul constantly "takes notice of" or "gives attention to" everything that goes on in the body. Sensations arise when the soul takes notice of some physical process in the body and from its own substance produces an appropriate "spiritual image." Knowledge of the image, however, is not derived from the senses, which are unreliable sources of knowledge. Knowledge is possible, first, because the soul contains within itself a reflection of the Divine Ideas, which are the sources of all (created) being and all knowledge; and second, because of divine illumination. This latter is one of the most difficult concepts in Augustine's thought, but apparently he means by it that since full knowledge of a thing involves more than what is contained in the thing or in the knowing mind, something additional must be added to this process of knowing, and this can only be added by God. What is added is a spiritual light, analogous to the function of the sun in aiding the process of sight.

Since Augustine had been a teacher of rhetoric in his youth, he necessarily had a profound and professional knowledge and appreciation of the literature of pagan Rome, as well as some knowledge of Greek literature (the extent of his knowledge of Greek has never been satisfactorily determined). His favorite authors apparently were Cicero, Virgil, Plotinus, and Plato, and his interest in them was not merely literary and intellectual. He was convinced that they had caught glimmerings of the Truth in their writings, and although they were lamentably not Christian, still they could be read with profit by Christians. He also felt, especially in his younger and middle life, that they were a necessary preliminary to Christian studies, and he even began to write a series of text books on the Liberal Arts. Throughout his writings the influence of the classics is obvious, but he completely subordinated them to his purpose. He might borrow the Divine Ideas and much else from Plotinus, the "seminal reasons" from the Stoics, the form and style of several of his dialogues from Cicero, and the theme of Roman Destiny from Virgil, but he always bent them to his needs and was never seduced by them. Near the end of his life, in his Retractationes, he expressed fear that perhaps in his early works he had prized the Liberal Arts too highly, since some holy men were ignorant of them and some who knew them were not holy men. Still, his basic attitude is probably best expressed in his statement that since God is the source of all knowledge, and a philosopher is a lover of knowledge, the true philosopher is a Christian.

At about the time Augustine passed from this world in the city of Hippo in 430, the nearby metropolis of Carthage fell to the Vandals. Spain and much of Gaul had already fallen to other barbarians, and still the pressure mounted. The Empire in the West was on the point of extinction, and a new age with new problems, new needs, and new solutions was in the making.

NOTES

1. The Octavius is translated in the series Fathers of the Christian Church, vol. X (New York, 1950), 313-402.

2. On Tertullian, see Timothy David Barnes, Tertullian: A Historical and Literary Study (Oxford, 1971).

3. On Commodian, see E.K. Rand, Founders of the Middle Ages, 181-83, and especially F.J.E. Raby, A History of Christian-Latin Poetry from the Beginnings to the Close of the Middle Ages (2nd ed., Oxford, 1953), 11-16, who settles the troublesome problem of his dates.

4. "Victorinus' greatest importance lies in the fact that he, more than anyone else, can claim to be the one great link between Greek philosophy and the Latin world in the fourth century," in The Cambridge History of Later Greek and Early Medieval Philosophy, 331-32.

5. Both Symmachus' plea and Ambrose's reply are in Ambrose's Epistle 18, Patrologia Latina, 16:1014-24.

6. See Henry Osborn Taylor, The Emergence of Christian Culture in the West (Harper Torchbook 48, 1958; first published as The Classical Heritage of the Middle Ages, New York, 1901), 74-78.

7. See David S. Wiesen, St. Jerome as a Satirist (Ithaca, New York, 1964).

8. See L.G. Whitebread, Fulgentius the Mythographer (Cambridge, 1971).

9. On Macrobius and the succeeding "handbook" authors, see William H. Stahl, Roman Science (Madison, Wisconsin, 1962). English translation of Commentary on the Dream of Scipio by W.H. Stahl (New York, 1952).

10. English translation: Martianus Capella and the Seven Liberal Arts, tr. W.H. Stahl and Richard Johnson (New York, 1977).

11. Of the voluminous bibliography on Augustine, by far the best is Peter Brown, Augustine of Hippo (Berkeley, 1967). Also useful is Vernon J. Bourke, ed., The Essential Augustine (Mentor-Omega MT601, 1964).

Chapter 3

Debased Roman Culture

The establishment of barbarian kingdoms on Roman soil in the West did not inaugurate a completely new age, but rather the final stage of the decay of Roman culture. The process was gradual and not without temporary reversals of direction. Still the decline of intellectual life between the fifth and eighth centuries was drastic, the more so since it was accompanied by a metamorphosis of society which made it impossible that the old culture could be maintained intact. The amalgamation of the Christian and Greco-Roman traditions had been fairly satisfactorily accomplished before the barbarians arrived and was to be the basis upon which a new culture would later be created, but we are concerned in this chapter with the intellectual responses made by the men of the fifth, sixth, and seventh centuries to the indisputably chaotic conditions of their age.

The note sounded by all the Christian writers of the fourth century, from Lactantius to Augustine and Orosius, had been triumph. They were Romans, and they were Christians, and they lived in a Christian Empire. It is true that there had been considerable disenchantment with the civil power between Lactantius' panegyric of Constantine and Augustine's City of God, but Rome was more than the civil power. Even in the sacking of the City there was a vision of triumph for the Church. But this unbounded confidence wilted under the continuing miseries of the fifth century.

From the time of the barbarian invasions, the separate parts of the western Empire tended to have separate histories, not just because they were ruled by separate groups of barbarians, but because the literary universalism of Rome was broken. This is evident even among those who endeavor to maintain the purity of the intellectual tradition. The cultural integrity of the separate barbarian kingdoms never quite becomes a fact, but it is in the making between the fifth and eighth centuries.

Interest in the particular, the parochial, the personal, was renewed and might well have resulted in the reflourescence of Latin literature had it not been accompanied by the virtual collapse of the educational system and disappearance of the society which had maintained Roman culture. Local peculiarities of language arise and find their way into the written language. Confusions in spellings peculiar to certain areas crop up. And handwriting now begins to take on clearly definable characteristics in certain areas. There is a Visigothic script, a Beneventan script, and Insular script (Irish and Anglo-Saxon) and several well-developed scripts peculiar to particular monasteries or groups of monasteries in Frankish territory -- Bobbio, Luxeuil, St. Gall, Corbie. All are based on the older uncial, half, or quarter classical, of the various barbarian peoples.[1]

The lack of intellectual intercourse between the Latin and Greek worlds, already pronounced during the fourth century, became more severe as time went on. The separation was not, of course, complete. As late as the sixth century, Priscian had taught Latin in Constantinople, though born in Africa, and had a good command of the Greek language; Boethius knew Greek well; and the Spaniards Martin of Braga and John of Biclaro had both spent some time in the East and had some acquaintance with the Greek tongue. But each century the alienation grew sharper. It was not unusual in the fourth century for an educated man to know Greek, although ignorance of it did not brand him as uncultured. In the fifth century a man acquainted with Greek was unusually learned. In the early sixth century there was a brief revival of Greek studies, but by the end of that century a man who knew Greek was a rarity. And by the seventh century a literary knowledge of that language had almost disappeared in the West.

The onslaught of the barbarians did not destroy the Roman educational system, although there was unavoidably much social disruption. Literary production, however, declined both in quantity and quality. The boundless confidence of the Christians was gone, and they took over the attitudes as well as the tasks of their pagan predecessors. Men like Sidonius Apollinaris and Sedulius, who took over the pompous, overly-ornate style of late paganism into their poetry, though nominally Christian, asserted their Romanity and culture against their barbarian masters by continuing the pagan literary tradition. The Christians also became organizers, summarizers, and "transmitters," a function they had been willing to leave to the pagans in the fourth century.

As the fifth century drew to a close, there is evidence that things were settling down. A modus vivendi had been worked out between Germans and Romans in most parts of the West. The Germans, though masters, adopted much of Roman civilization and, even among the infamous Vandals, upper class families sent their sons to Roman schools. A great orator declaiming his speeches or reciting his poems was still a popular form of entertainment and was assured of large appreciative audiences and considerable fame. Two Christian writers, Dracontius in Africa and Avitus in Gaul, composed works of considerable merit in the Christianized classical tradition. The first half of the sixth century sees significant restoration: Priscian wrote the most competent treatise on grammar of the late Empire; Boethius contributed translations of Greek philosophical and mathematical works and of commentaries on them and the great Consolatio; and Cassiodorus envisioned the reform of Christian education.

But the wars of mid-century put an abrupt end to this. Cassiodorus' decision to abandon his plan for a Christian center of higher education at Rome in favor of a monastic studium is portentous. Benedict of Nursia had been preparing the ground. There would be non-monastic writers and scholars well into the seventh century, but the future seemed clearly to lie with the monasteries if anywhere. The decline of education, as of culture as a whole, is marked after 550. During the last century of expiring Antiquity, Christians stepped in to do what pagans had done before. Gregory the Great, Isidore, Fortunatus and Gregory of Tours struggled valiantly against the relentless trend toward illiteracy, ignorance, superstition, violence, and crudity, but they themselves were infected by the shortcomings of their age. They stand high above their contemporaries but far below their Roman predecessors and their Carolingian successors. Good will, industry, and intelligence were not enough. A cultured man must be a member of a cultured society, and what little culture that remained had by the mid-seventh century retreated behind monastic walls.

The writing of history provides us with important insights into the changing tastes, styles, problems, and attitudes of the late imperial period. Jerome had translated Eusebius' Chronicle from the Greek into elegant Latin and had provided a continuation of it up to 378, the year the Visigoths overcame the imperial army at Adrianople. He intended to wait until the barbarians were controlled and things settled down before bringing it up to date. Ammianus Marcellinus had also written an admirable history of the period in the best classical tradition. Sulpicius Severus wrote two quite different works, intended for different audiences, but both composed in the concise and pure style of the best Latin historical literature. One of these was a Chronicle, or Sacred History, published about 403, which is a masterpiece of Latin historical composition. Even more than most Latin historians, he showed great skill, industry, and critical sense as well as an unusual concern for correct chronology. Admirable as this work is, it was almost completely ignored both by his contemporaries and by succeeding ages and today is extant in a single manuscript. He scored a great success, however, with his Life of St. Martin. A model of its type, full of accounts of miracles wrought by the saint, edifying and popular, it became one of the most widely read saints' lives of the Middle Ages. The History of Orosius, for all its faults, marks a sharp break with the preceding historical tradition. It is a Manifesto of a victorious party, little concerned with historical truth, with detailed chronology, or stylistic niceties. It represents the contamination of history with the edifying purposes of saints' lives.

By the middle of the fifth century, however, attitudes had changed considerably. One could not longer simply ignore the barbarians as Jerome had done. And apparently they had not been sent just to punish the Romans. The church, too, had suffered greatly at the hands of these Arians, who seemed to be growing in strength each day. Some people questioned that the Christian God really cared for His people; others even began to repeat the accusations against the Christians made after Alaric's sack of Rome. To answer these doubters and complainers and to justify God's ways to man, a priest from Marseilles named Salvian wrote a book entitled De gubernatione Dei, the first part of which is an argument for God's providential arrangement of human affairs. Then comes the crucial question: Why then is the Empire falling to the barbarian heretics? The reason, says Salvian, is that the Christians have become sunk in vice and corruption. They have become worse than the pagans, and God has sent the barbarians as a just punishment for their sins. Having made his point, Salvian goes on in a vein reminiscent of Tacitus to compare the wickedness and immorality of the Christians with the purity and uprightness of the invaders. Even though they may be Arians, or sometimes pagans, they lead better lives than the Christians. This is a most unusual work in that it, almost alone among contemporary sources, gives a highly favorable picture of the Goths. Most writers, fired with orthodox zeal and doubtlessly supplied with sufficient genuine atrocities, could see them only as hateful persecutors of the true church. Salvian, certainly as devout an orthodox Christian in any, concentrated rather on the shortcomings of his own people than the vices of the invader. The necessities of his argument seem to have led him to err in the other direction, to paint too noble a picture of the Goths and too sordid a one of the Romans. But it is a useful corrective.

Others managed to carry on as though nothing had happened and to continue types of literature which had originated in the fourth century. Even so, in the work of a poet like Sedulius, there is a tendency toward the overly ornate rhetorical artifices of style and language which the Christian poets of the fourth century had, by and large, managed to avoid. Especially since Sedulius was a writer of some ability, this is good evidence of the decadent tastes of his contemporaries. He seems to have worn his religion lightly, choosing a Christian subject (the miracles and passion of Christ) because it was the fashion and employing all the devices of pagan literary technique for the same reason. But he managed nevertheless to write a poem of some merit and great popularity. Entitled Paschale carmen, it was written in hexameters and made up five books. The first book is concerned with the miraculous deliverances related in the Old Testament. The second sings the birth and childhood of Christ. Then come the miracles performed by our Lord, the crucifixion and resurrection and Christ's triumphant ascension. Not content with an epic poem on his subject, Sedulius recast the entire work in prose, expanding it somewhat but otherwise altering little but the form. He seems to have possessed a good measure of talent and cleverness and a compelling urge to write, but there was nothing in particular he had to say. He was, of course, following in the literary tradition established by Juvencus, but his work has none of the motivation of earlier works of a similar nature. There were very few pagans left among the Romans. Orthodox Christianity rather than antique paganism had now become their mark of superiority over the Goths. Late Roman society had simply taken on a veneer of Christianity.

By the end of the fifth century, the note of sincerity and earnestness is sounded once again. Two Latin authors, living on opposite shores of the Mediterranean, composed Christian epics of considerable excellence. Dracontius was an African living in the Vandal kingdom during the reign of the brutal Gunthamund. Dracontius had made some uncircumspect remarks about his king, for which he was imprisoned, and having written an unsuccessful plea for forgiveness (Satisfactio), he devoted his considerable poetic talents to writing an epic on the Creation entitled De laudibus Dei. An example of prison literature, the poem is concerned with finding consolation in the knowledge of God's providence and mercy. Eschewing the literary cliches of his day and blessed with a lively poetic imagination as well as a valid personal reason for writing, Dracontius composed a truly fine poem, abounding in picturesque descriptions and psychological insights. The first book celebrates God's mercy as it is manifested by His creation of the world and in creating and redeeming man despite his sinfulness. It elaborates on the details of creation, showing a genuine love for the particulars of nature, and on the feelings of Adam and Eve during the Temptation and Expulsion. The second and third books are highly subjective and lack the epic unity which was so marked a feature of Book One. The first part of this poem was soon excerpted and circulated independently under the title Hexameron.

The finest of all the Latin Christian epics was written by Avitus, bishop of Vienne, a Gallic contemporary of Dracontius. A master of dramatic action and characterization, though prone to the rhetorical extravagance of style we have already noted in Sedulius, Avitus was a staunch upholder of orthodoxy, and in addition to his great work, The Deeds of Spiritual History, also wrote several treatises against the Eutychean and Arian heresies and a poem in praise of virginity. It is the De spiritalis historiae gestis, however, for which he is best known. It is an epic rendering of the main themes of the Old Testament from the Creation to the Redemption. It is man rather than nature who claims Avitus' interest. From the creation of Eve out of Adam's side, as the Church was born from the side of Christ, to the story of Exodus, in which Moses prefigures Christ, Avitus uses allegory, so that the poem always has two levels of meaning. Unlike Martianus Capella, however, he does not manipulate bloodless abstractions in a contrived plot, but draws vivid and powerful characters in dramatic situations. Eve and the Devil are his best creations: Eve torn between desire for the forbidden fruit and fear of God's prohibition, and her utter anguish after Adam tastes the fruit and shares her sin; the Devil, jealous, proud, miserable, but revelling in his great evil-making power. After the Fall, he gloats over his triumph and the power he holds over man:

> Nor does God, who first formed you,
> Now have more right over you [than I].
> Let Him keep what He has made.
> What I taught you -- the greater part -- remains mine.
> You owe many things to your creator,
> But more to your teacher.[2]

The unity of the entire work depends upon the second level of meaning -- the allegory. On the primary or literal level, the first three books constitute the poem and the last two seem superfluous. Still, it is carefully constructed, executed with great skill, and informed by deep religious feeling.

As the sixth century opened, the cultural revival signalled by the works of Dracontius and Avitus began to gather momentum. It was in Italy, most fortunate of the western territories in her Gothic ruler, Theoderic, that the clearest evidence of this exists. But a grammarian of outstanding importance, of African birth and teaching Latin in Constantinople, also was active at this time. This was Priscian, next to Donatus the most widely read grammarian during the Middle Ages. His major work is a very long and loosely organized Institutiones grammaticae. It is more comprehensive than either of Donatus' grammars and profited from Priscian's first-hand acquaintance with Greek literary theory as well as an abundance of quotations from both Greek and Latin authors and numerous etymologies. It was later divided into Priscian Major (his first sixteen books) and Priscian Minor (the last two books), of which the former was far more widely used. He also wrote a lesser known, but equally important, work on poetics and rhetorical compositions, the Praeexercitamina, which was little more than a Latin translation of Hermogenes' Progymnasmata, a Greek treatise of the second century.

Two Italian contemporaries of Priscian were Boethius and Cassiodorus, both of whom served the Ostrogothic king Theoderic as high Roman officials. As these young men were growing up, the prospects for the return of peace and the revival of culture must have seemed bright. The civil government in Italy had been restored. The Vandals, Visigoths, and Franks were controlled more effectively by Theoderic than they had been by the emperors, a program of rebuilding was under way and a measure of prosperity was returning.

Boethius was born around 480, while Odoacer was still ruling in Italy. Scion of two of Rome's most ancient and renowned noble families, the Anicii and the Severini, he received the very finest education to be had in his day. In the tradition of the best families, he then embarked upon a career of public service and rose rapidly, becoming Consul in 510 and shortly afterwards assum-

-42-

ing the duties of __magister officiorum__, the second highest civilian office in Theoderic's Italy. Boethius was both a devout orthodox Christian and an intense Roman patriot, and it is these qualities which inspired his great intellectual achievement and his untimely demise. As a part of his patriotic duty to the Roman people, he set out to accomplish for his own age what Cicero had done for his: to interpret Greek learning to the Romans. This led him to undertake a grandiose scheme: the translation of the works of the two greatest philosophers, Plato and Aristotle, and of commentaries on their works, the reconciliation of their systems, and the composition of textbooks on the four mathematical disciplines among the __Artes__, to which Boethius first applied the name __quadruvium__ (later corrupted to __quadrivium__), "the four-fold path to wisdom." He only ever completed a small part of this ambitious undertaking, and only a portion of that has survived, but it is nonetheless impressive. Of Aristotle's works, he translated at least the __Categories__ and __De interpretatione__, both elementary logical works. He also wrote two commentaries on the __Isagoge__, or __Introduction to the Categories__, by the Neoplatonist Porphyry. The first of these was in the form of a Ciceronian dialogue and used the Latin translation of Victorinus; but finding this version too full of inaccuracies, Boethius wrote a second commentary based upon his own translation. He may also have translated Aristotle's __Topics__ and __Prior__ and __Posterior Analytics__, but if so they quickly dropped from circulation. In making these translations, Boethius used a clear, simple, and unadorned prose style and took the necessary liberty of devising new Latin technical terms to express the meaning of the Greek and thereby provided at least the basis of a technical vocabulary for Latin philosophy.

Of his textbooks on the subject of the quadrivium, only those on arithmetic and music have survived. His __Arithmetic__, based largely on the Greek work of Nicomachus, was almost the only source of arithmetical knowledge for the early Middle Ages. Although not first-rate by the highest Greek standards, it was vastly superior to the sections on arithmetic in the works of Martianus Capella or Isidore of Seville, and it is far from despicable. His work __On Music__, based on Ptolemy's __Harmonica__, is also of great importance and contains, among other things, an incipient wave theory of sound. Whether any of the works on geometry attributed to Boethius during the Middle Ages are actually by him is still a matter of dispute. One of his best editors definitely assigns one to him. It is an abridged and simplified free rendering of Euclid's __Elements__. His work on astronomy has definitely been lost, as have his translations of several works of Archimedes and Ptolemy and of Aristotle's __Physics__, if indeed he ever made these.

It is important to appreciate the magnitude of Boethius' achievement even in this fraction of his writings. In his coining of new words, he is in no sense to be considered decadent. It was by a similar process that Latin became a literary language in the first place; and he had excellent precedent for devising a philosophical jargon in Cicero, who had taken similar liberties in an earlier age. His own style is pure, simple, unadorned and natural.

His interest in science and philosophy was unusual not only for his own day, but for a Roman at any time. The fact that he devoted his great energies and considerable talents to providing works on these subjects supplied the Middle Ages with better works than existed anywhere else in Latin. Boethius was intelligent and discriminating in the works he selected and in the commentaries he supplied for them. In science and philosophy he is a "transmitter" only by historical accident. Judged by the context of his own times, he was a restorer, and a competent one. Judged by his importance to succeeding ages he was the most important single transmitter of Greek philosophy and science to the early Middle Ages. He is superior to Cicero in the precision of his thought; superior to Pliny or Seneca in his expert knowledge of specific sciences; superior to a host of writers in preferring the original texts to encyclopedic compilations of ill-digested information; and almost unique among late antique writers in being immune from the curse or fascination of rhetoric. His style, though not elegant, was appropriate to his purpose -- dry and precise, popular and familiar, eloquent and moving as the occasion demanded.

Boethius also wrote five extremely important theological treatises. Three of them are in the form of letters and are addressed principally to matters of immediate importance at the time, but they are of great importance for the future of Christian theology. They brought to fruition a trend long evident in Christianity -- the application of philosophical techniques to problems of theology in the conviction that revealed truths of religion cannot be in conflict with truth rationally arrived at. These treatises are mainly concerned with providing rational proofs of orthodox Christianity against the major heresies of the day concerning the Trinity. Using Aristotelian methods and terminology, they did much to put Christian theology on a scientific footing. Boethius provided precise definitions of the terms nature ("the specific difference that gives form to anything") and person ("the individual substance of a rational nature"). He distinguished between substance (that which underlies accidents) and subsistence (that which does not need a subject in which to exist but does not underlie accidents), employed the Aristotelian divisions of philosophy and the concepts matter and form. His procedure is always rigorously rational, sometimes geometrical.

Important as were Boethius' theological treatises, his translations, commentaries, and textbooks, by far his most important and widely read work was the Consolation of Philosophy. Although Boethius had served with honor under the patrician Theoderic, he seems always to have resented the barbarian Arians who had seized power in Italy. During the century and a half that had passed since Ambrose and Symmachus had argued over the Altar of Victory, the Roman nobility had become, almost completely, orthodox Christian. Boethius' father-in-law, another Symmachus, had been accused of treason by Theoderic, and in his defense Boethius had exclaimed that if Symmachus was guilty, then he himself and indeed the whole Senate were equally guilty. Condemned probably by perjured testimony, he was disgraced, imprisoned, and executed in 524 at the age of forty-four years.

While he was in prison he wrote his Consolation of Philosophy.[3] It is composed of alternating sections of verse and prose (prosimetrum) and begins with the author, comforted only by poetry, in deep dejection over the unjust fate that had befallen him. Suddenly there appeared standing above him "a woman of majestic countenance whose flashing eyes seemed wise beyond the ordinary wisdom of men." This was Philosophy, who then began to "cure" Boethius of his malady. After conceding his fate is indeed unjust, she reminds him that the world is governed not by chance but by the rational control of the Creator. Boethius is too overcome with grief and self-pity to understand what Philosophy is telling him, so she proceeds by many arguments gradually to bring him to see his plight in its true perspective. Every objection Boethius brings is answered by Philosophy, and they discuss such topics as what true human happiness consists of, why good men go unrewarded and evil men unpunished, and how God's foreknowledge can be reconciled with man's free choice. As the work ends, Boethius sees that the universe is governed by God for His purpose and that the human will nevertheless remain free because God is not involved in time. We speak of His "foreknowledge" only because we are temporal creatures and do not, as God does, possess the totality of our lives in an instant, but only drawn out through time.

It has sometimes bothered modern readers that a Christian should be so inclined to take comfort from Philosophy rather than from Christ, that he should have spent his time philosophizing rather than praying. But there is no inconsistency. In fact Boethius gives us reason to believe that he did pray. His philosophy is preeminently a Christian philosophy, or rather a solution of a number of philosophical problems in a way consistent with the Christian faith or even suggested by the content of that faith.

Boethius' translations of Aristotle and his commentaries, his use of philosophical techniques in his theological treatises, and his mature distillation and transformation of ancient philosophy in the Consolation, along with various works of St. Augustine, provided almost the sum total of philosophical knowledge possessed by the early Middle Ages, and these works continued to be highly regarded throughout the medieval period. Therefore, although he is not an original philosophical thinker, but rather a competent and discriminating eclectic, some discussion of his philosophical positions is in order. Boethius has often been tagged by scholars

as an Aristotelian or as a Neoplatonist. In fact he was neither--
he was an educated and intelligent antique Christian. His basic
position concerning the relation of faith and reason is the same
as Augustine's -- faith seeking understanding, since true philosophy is the love of God, the highest Wisdom. He established
certain divisions of philosophy which remained standard through
the twelfth century. The primary division was between theoretical
and practical. Theoretical is further divided into physics,
mathematics, and theology, each with its proper procedure. Practical philosophy is divided into ethics, politics, and household
management (economics). Logic, grammar, and rhetoric are useful
tools of philosophy, logic in distinguishing the true from the
false, grammar and rhetoric in facilitating expression. Both his
doctrine of the soul and of cognition are Platonic or Augustinian.
Souls existed with the angels before their fall into the body.
Thus polluted they lost the ability to see Truth directly and
forgot much of what they had previously known. Knowledge is a
process of recollection. The soul, or mind, is active and is the
cause of our perceptions. Boethius attributes to the senses a
slightly larger role than did Augustine -- they stimulate or
activate the knowledge lying latent in the mind, not the data of
our senses, which are the objects of perception. There are four
levels of knowledge of which the mind is capable -- sense, imagination, reason, and intelligence. In our earthly state, however,
reason is the highest power of which it is capable, except in rare
instances.

Although Boethius' proof of God's existence is brief and commonplace, based on the assumption that the existence of incomplete
degrees of perfection implies absolute perfection, he contributed
much to the study of theology, both in his studies of the Trinity
and in his very keen insight into the simplicity of divine eternity, that is, God's eternity does not involve endless extension in
time, but rather the complete and perfect possession of His entire
life in an instant. The categories of time thus do not apply to
God, strictly speaking. It is for this reason that man's freedom
of choice is not obliterated by divine "foreknowledge," since when
we say "foreknowledge" we are improperly speaking of God as though
He, like us, were involved in time. In describing the nature of
being and reality, Boethius resorts to the Aristotelian concepts
of matter and form and makes the fundamental distinction between
essence and existence in all creatures. Only in God is being
itself His very essence.

Boethius is also responsible for providing the early Middle Ages
with a clear statement of their most difficult philosophical
problem, that of universals, as well as a tentative answer. In
his second commentary on Porphyry's Isagoge, he states the problem: Do species and genera exist only as mental abstractions or
are they subsistents? In this work he gives the Aristotelian
solution, that they _exist_ only in things and are _known_ only as

mental abstractions. In the Consolation, however, he follows the Platonic tradition and considers them as subsistent realities which exist ultimately in the mind of God. This provided the Middle Ages with their first philosophical problem of major difficulty, and although the schoolmen talked about many other matters, the problem of universals was still central to European philosophy in the fifteenth century.

Boethius' execution in 524 at least spared him the pain of witnessing the catastrophes which overtook Italy during the remainder of the sixth century; but his contemporary, Cassiodorus, lived on through the holocaust into the early years of the Lombard occupation. Cassiodorus was a man of quite different temperament, although the early careers of the two men have much in common. Cassiodorus came from a wealthy and prominent Italian noble family, and he began his career as a public servant. He was Consul in the year 514, later succeeded Boethius as magister officiorum, and finally in 533 became Praetorian Prefect. His attitude toward the Goths was quite unlike that of Boethius. He did whatever he could to minimize the tensions between the two peoples and went so far as to write a history of the Goths, which has since been lost and is known to us only through an abridgment by the Goth Jordannes. During his career as a public servant he published a collection of state papers and letters on assorted topics entitled Variae, an invaluable source of information about the period.

In about 535, just as Belisarius was launching his attack against Italy, Cassiodorus and Pope Agapetus were planning the foundation of a Christian institution of higher education at Rome, modelled on the pagan schools at Alexandria and Nisibis, in which the Liberal Arts would be taught as a preparation for the advanced curriculum of theological studies. The wars of Belisarius, however, made the establishment of such an institution impossible, and about 540 Cassiodorus abandoned public life altogether and retired to his family estate near Squillace in southern Italy. He made this into a monastery, although a more delightful and sumptuous place then the term might suggest.

As a result of the turmoil in Italy, it was impossible to contemplate the further prosecution of learning in society, so Cassiodorus turned his attention to establishing a center of religious learning in his monastery. He acquired a sizeable library and established a scriptorium for the copying of sacred and profane works. The activity of Cassiodorus and his fellow monks at Vivarium (as the place was known because of its fishponds) was considerable. Cassiodorus' most important writings from this period are his Institutiones divinarum lectionum and Institutiones secularum lectionum, which are outlines of courses of study in religious and secular disciplines and which contain his educational theory. He was convinced of the necessity of studying the Arts before going on to the higher study of theology. His outline, or syllabus, was highly selective and included short sketches of the various subjects as well as select bibliographies. Cassiodorus realized the great power of the written word and so set his monks to work copying manuscripts of both Christian and pagan authors. For those brothers who lacked the ability or inclination to become scholars and copyists, he enjoined labor in the fields and the reading of elementary treatises on agriculture. He set tasks of a more demanding nature for the more gifted brothers, and it was under Cassiodorus' direction that a translation was made of the ecclesiastical histories of the Greek writers Socrates, Sozimen, and Theodoret. These three were combined into one work and given the Latin title Historia tripartita, an invaluable source both now and in the Middle Ages for a knowledge of the early ecumenical councils and related topics. Casssiodorus also was responsible for the translation of Josephus' Antiquities and various works of the Greek fathers, especially Bible commentaries. One of his last works was on orthography, or spelling, quite an essential aid in that period of social and intellectual collapse.

Cassiodorus has often been criticized for his lack of originality, but we should understand that he was what would be called today an "educator," and not a philosopher or man of letters. The purpose of an educator and writer of textbooks and outlines of study is usually to impart to a new generation an existing body of knowledge, certain techniques for dealing with that knowledge, and perhaps certain values, including, we hope, a love of learning. A fresh approach or an arrangement of materials more suitable to the present situation are about all such a man can bring to his work. Cassiodorus is notoriously unoriginal in the content of his writings. He borrows unashamedly from many of the scholars who precede him. His originality lies in his establishment of a system of Christian education in the monastery, including a study of the pagan classics, as part of the monks' service to God and his fellows; and his implementation of this program in his own monastery and the Outlines which he provided for others who might want to follow his example. His system provided virtually the only higher education available in Latin Europe from his own day until the growth of the great cathedral schools of the late eleventh and twelfth centuries.

When Cassiodorus decided, about the middle of the sixth century, to adapt his educational plans to monasticism, the way had already been well prepared for him by Benedict of Nursia, the great reformer of western monasticism. Born about 480 of a noble family, young Benedict did not follow the official career customary with young men of his class. Instead, disgusted by the corrupt morals of society, he sought holiness by following the life of a hermit. The ideal of monasticism had swept through the Empire like a plague during the fourth century, and although it was most popular in the semi-tropical regions of Egypt and the Near East, it extended also into Italy, Gaul, and even Ireland. The perfect type of monastic life was considered to be the solitary and silent, although groups of hermits living in the same area often followed a common rule and a semi-communal existence. The arrangement of monastic communities was often chaotic, given either to morbid excesses of asceticism or lax behavior. Benedict soon gained a reputation for holiness and was sought out by others, so that he eventually presided over thirteen separate communities. About 520 the hostility of neighboring monasteries forced him to move with his followers to Monte Cassino, where he organized his monks into an ideal religious community. Convinced by his own experience that the hermit's life could be successfully and profitably followed only by a few exceptional souls, he determined upon a carefully regulated communal life of labor, prayer, and reading as the proper way to worship and to reach God. For this purpose he composed a Rule, which borrowed much from the earlier "Rule of the Master" and was intended probably as a guide to a general reform of monasticism but also undoubtedly reflecting the organization of Monte Cassino. Its outstanding features were its enjoining manual labor as a worthy way to worship God; its moderation and regulation of all the monk's activities; and its adaptability to a variety of dissimilar conditions.

There is much disagreement over the extent of Benedict's education and whether or not intellectual pursuits were an important part of the monk's life at Monte Cassino. Concerning the former question, it is highly unlikely that a boy of his class was not given a thorough classical education at this time, and Gregory the Great, our major source for Benedict's life,[4] specifically says that he attended the Roman schools. Concerning the second, it is impossible to know what the original situation was a Monte Cassino. But the rule was intentionally flexible, and the monastery soon became a major intellectual center, developing its own script, accumulating a fine library, and serving as a place of instruction and scholarship on a very high level. The union of intellectual pursuits with monasticism is probably due more to Cassiodorus than to Benedict, but without the framework Benedict's Rule provided, Cassiodorus' task would have been much more difficult, if not impossible.

The promise of Avitus and Dracontius was fulfilled by the Consolation of Boethius, but the hope of better things to come was dashed in Italy by the Gothic-Byzantine wars and the Lombard conquest, in Spain by internecine war among the nobles and by attacks from Constantinople in the south and the Franks in the north, and in Gaul by the deterioration of the Merovingian dynasty and the brutal struggle between Fredegund and Brunhild. The European continent during the seventh century would be almost devoid of intellectual attainment. But before the collapse came, other valiant scholars and writers were to make their mark upon the mind of the West.

In sharp contrast to the tolerance and humanity of Cassiodorus is the narrowness and imperiousness of pope Gregory the Great, the fourth Doctor of the Latin Church. He was the kind of person who could boast (probably with some exaggeration) of having lived in Constantinople for six years without learning a word of Greek, and who would arrogantly proclaim his refusal to "restrain the oracle of heaven by the rules of Donatus" in a grammatically impeccable paragraph of balanced periods and prose rhythms. As pope during a critical period in the church's history he performed magnificently and clearly deserved the title of "Great."

Gregory was born in 540, the very year in which Belisarius was laying siege to Rome, of an ancient and wealthy Roman noble family. It is clear from his style of writing that he somehow managed to receive a very good education, at least in grammar and rhetoric, during the days of warfare, plague, and chaos in which he grew up. As was to be expected, he began his career as a public servant and was made Prefect of Rome in 573. Two years later, however, he renounced the world and became a monk, turning his family palace in Rome into a monastery and founding six other monasteries, all observing the Benedictine Rule, from his family's extensive estates in Sicily. Although he protested that he desired only the life of a simple monk, Gregory's administrative talents and dominating personality resulted in his rapid rise through the ranks, first as deacon, then as papal envoy to Constantinople, then as abbot of his own monastery, and culminating in his elevation to the papacy in 590. The problems he faced would have overwhelmed a lesser man, but Gregory attacked them with the vigor, perseverance, and confidence of an ancient Roman. Stepping into the void left by the near collapse of imperial power in Italy he undertook the government of the city, assumed the role of protector of Italy against the Lombards, asserted the primacy of the Roman see over the Christian church, regularized and reformed the liturgy, and fought valiantly to avert the outcropping of ancient rural paganism and superstition or at least to contain these within the framework of the church.

Among Gregory's writings, we should mention first the 854 letters of his pontificate, which are invaluable sources of knowledge of the period. He also wrote a work called Dialogues, a number of homilies on the Gospel and on Ezekiel, and a long and much used commentary on Job, sometimes called the Moralia on Job. In all of these, Gregory employs tales of miracles, visions, dreams, and prophecies together with extremely arbitrary allegorical intepretation. His writings were copied and preserved by the hundreds during the Middle Ages and translated into Greek, Old English, Old High German, and Old French, and they remained immensely popular for seven hundred years.

His Pastoral Rule is much more palatable, since it is a practical handbook and Gregory was a very practical man. It gives advice as to what sort of man a bishop should be, how he should conduct himself, how he should suit his preaching to his auditors, and what particular temptations he should guard against.

His attitude toward the pagan classical tradition is clearly hostile. He considered it a necessary evil, since without it one could not have a correct understanding of scriptures and could not write and speak properly. But the fact that pagan literature was an integral part of that instruction bothered him considerably. Two often quoted remarks of Gregory on this general subject have given rise to some misunderstanding of his position.[5]

The first is his arrogant assertion that he despised the rules of grammar and would not chain the oracle of heaven by the rules of Donatus. This might lead one to think that Gregory was an unskillful, poorly schooled, barbaric author who utterly ignored the techniques of oratorical prose as they were taught in the schools. But this was far from the truth. In the very paragraph in which he denounces pure Latinity, Gregory shows himself to be an accomplished master of this sort of writing, thoroughly trained in the technical aspects of composition, as well as a writer of great emotional power. What he was denouncing was the emptly, lifeless, artificial, "pure" Latinity affected by so many of the educated classes, bound by mazes of precise rules concerning what was and what was not "correct." The language he was denouncing was as dead then as it is now, and he was quite correct in saying that it was not a fit vehicle for divine thoughts. Neither would it be correct to identify his language with that of the "Roman on the street." This would have been equally unsuited to convey the sublime and intense thoughts that impelled Gregory to write. Gregory simply asserted in an extreme and belligerent manner an attitude which many Christian authors during the preceding two centuries had shared. They used words and constructions which were closer to the language of their own time and they ignored taboos which no longer offended any but the most refined stylists. This in itself did not necessarily result in the barbarization of the language. Certainly Augustine's _Confessions_ or Jerome's Vulgate are two of the finest works in the Latin language, but they are far from "classical" if by that much-abused term we mean conforming to the canons of style in effect between Cicero and Quintilian (and there is even quite a difference between these two.) Gregory was a crusty and cantankerous old Roman aristocrat, and he enjoyed saying things in an extreme way.

The second of Gregory's statements, which appears in book after book, is his warning to bishop Desiderius of Vienne that it is unseemly for a bishop to be teaching courses on the pagan Greek poets. We might mention two circumstances which qualify the apparent "plain meaning" of this letter. In the first place, despite the horrors and ravages of the Gothic wars, a considerable amount, if not a high standard, of classical culture survived in

Italy and particularly in Rome; enough so that it still appeared strong enough to Gregory to be a menace. It was generally, though not always, true that Christians tended to oppose or fear pagan culture while it was still strong and flourishing, and to adopt and try to preserve it (and with it their own Christian learning) when it came near to extinction. Gregory had not after all made an absolute condemnation of the Greek poets. He had said, it is true, that "such phrases should not pass the lips of a religious layman;" but what concerned him much more was that a bishop of the Christian church was undertaking a scandalous and inappropriate function -- giving lessons in Greek literature. At a later date this would not have caused any scandal, but in Gregory's milieu there were laymen, even perhaps pagans, whose job it was to give such lessons. Things had evidently decayed much more rapidly in Gaul than in Rome, or it is not likely that Desiderius would have assumed the duties of a school teacher. All this is not to imply that Gregory was liberal in his attitude toward pagan literature-- only that in Rome at this time he could still afford to be hostile.

But if Gregory ignored the rules of the grammarians out of set purpose and worried still about the threat to Christians posed by the pagan poets, his Gallic contemporary Georgius Florentius, better known as Gregory of Tours, had no such problems. Born of a noble Gallo-Roman family of Clermont in Auvergne which had held high position in the church for many generations, he obtained the best education available in his day. The meagerness of this education is striking evidence of the decline of the literary tradition in Gaul. If a better education had been available, Gregory, as the son of a family of senatorial rank, would have received it. By his own testimony, the secular schools of his town no longer existed and he attended the somewhat informal school maintained by his uncle, the bishop, for the education of boys destined for a clerical career.

His writings indicate that he had been given at least some instruction in all seven of the Liberal Arts, but he was master of none of them. He may have used Martianus Capella's Marriage of Mercury and Philology (at least he mentions it with respect) and probably some other later Roman grammars, and from these school texts he derived the sum total of his knowledge of literature except for Virgil, whom he seems to have known at first hand. He did not even know many of the works of the early Latin Fathers of the third and fourth centuries, although he had quite a good knowledge of the Bible (often in a version other than the Vulgate) and of the canons of the church. He was familiar with Rufinus' translation of Eusebius' Ecclesiastical History and Jerome's Chronicle, as well as Orosius' History against the Pagans, which he used as sources for the history of the world through the fourth century. Still, he was an intelligent, high-minded and industrious man and made maximum use of his education, slight though it was.

Gregory was aware of the poor quality of his Latin and apologizes
for using the vulgar tongue. Unlike his papal namesake, he was
not in a position to flaunt the rules of Donatus; he had never
mastered them. This deprecation of one's literary talents was a
widely-used topos in the rhetorical schools, but Gregory seems to
have been quite sincere. Still, he made the effort. The result
is a linguistic disaster. Although Gregory claims in the preface
to the History of the Franks that he was writing in the rude
language of his day so he would be better understood, he in fact
tries to write in literary Latin. But he confuses genders, case
endings, and verb tenses, makes atrocious mistakes in idiom and
syntax, and makes a shambles of the Latin language. He is most at
home in ecclesiastial jargon and in the simple rapid narrative
style, which was probably quite close to the spoken language. For
the most part, however, his language lacks the consistency which
even the dialects of illiterate people display, and his Latin
cannot be considered an example of the spoken language of his
time.[6]

Gregory began his public career in the church and was ordained
deacon in 563. Ten years later he succeded his cousin as bishop
of Tours, a position he held till his death in 594. As head of a
wealthy and powerful family and bishop of the most important see
in Gaul, Gregory played a major role in the political life of his
time. Rather than attaching himself to the circle of one of the
Merovingian kings, he took the position that the church must
maintain its independence of the civil government, admonish kings
who acted immorally, and take an active part in trying to ameli-
orate the spread of ignorance and brutality. There is, however,
no hostility toward the civil power as such in his works, only
toward particular sinful acts of certain kings.

Like Ambrose and Gregory the Great, Gregory of Tours became an
author out of devotion to his episcopal duties, despite a lack of
proper training in that profession. For the edification of his
flock, he composed a number of saints' lives, the most important
being his life of St. Martin of Tours. These are typical of their
genre, intended primarily to instruct and inspire through example,
and emphasizing the miracles worked by the saints over all other
aspects of their lives. Gregory differs from many hagiographers,
however, in the pains he took to verify the reports of miracles
whenever possible. Even in the most uncritical of all biographi-
cal types, his passion for truth is evident. For the use of the
clergy, Gregory composed a practical handbook entitled De cursibus
ecclesiasticis, designed to aid the clergy in performing the night
offices by explaining to them how to tell time at night by noting
the rising and setting of some of the more important constellations. He describes these constellations in plain and simple
language and gives the usual time of their rising and setting,

being more concerned to be intelligible to his readers than to display his own erudition.

His greatest work, however, is his History of the Franks,[7] the most important source of our knowledge of sixth century Gaul and one of the better historical works in our literature. The first two books cover the period from the creation to the death of Clovis, founder of the Frankish state, and are largely based on Eusebius, Jerome, and Orosius. Books three and four are concerned with the Frankish kingdoms from 511 to the beginning of Gregory's episcopate in 573 and are extremely important because they are based on sources now lost. The main portion of the work, however, deals with the Frankish kingdoms during Gregory's tenure of the see of Tours. He was an eyewitness to and participant in much of the action he describes, and he had access to numerous important personages who supplied him with other information.

Gregory lacked many of the desiderata of a literary man and historian, but he possessed others to the highest degree. His language was, judged by any standard, uncouth, graceless, and ungrammatical. But this is largely the consequence of the time and place in which he wrote. More serious, perhaps, are his utter lack of a sense of form and somewhat vague feeling for chronology. By either classical or modern standards, his History is chaotic in arrangement, placing great demands upon the reader to sort out events and place them in their proper relation to each other. It also lacks any principle of unity, and Gregory neglected to ask many of the questions to which we should like to know the answers. But he was a master of the dramatic episode and of character delineation. Many of the stories and personages from the History have become famous: Fredegund, the inordinately wicked witch-queen, enchanting men to carry out her assassination plots and giving them a secret drug to bolster their courage, trying to kill her daughter after an argument by slamming the heavy lid of a jewel chest on her neck, but distraught with grief at the death of her son; Brunhild, the beautiful and single-minded Visigothic princess and queen of Sigebert, devoting her life and the resources of her kingdom to avenging the murders of her sister and husband; Chilperic, "the Nero and Herod of his time," the villain of the History, but highly intelligent and capable, writing poetry and adding four new letters to the alphabet, magnificently contemptuous of his opponents, and almost admirable in his unrelieved evil; Guntram, comic-opera king, kindly and cultured, but given to occasional fits of cruelty and craven fear, and extremely greedy.

More important than his story-telling skills were Gregory's fundamental honesty and earnest desire for truth. He was not without his prejudices and was sometimes too willing to believe the worst of Arians and persecutors of the church, but whenever his information was favorable even to such people he conscientiously reported it. Like nearly everyone of his time, he firmly believed in the frequent occurence of miracles and witnessed several himself. But like Herodotus, whom he resembles in many respects, he had a healthy skepticism and a contempt for those who were taken in by fakes. He applied the same tests of truth to reports of miracles as he did to other information. In some respects, though, he is beguilingly innocent, as when he reports his argument with some Jews and despite the evidence of his own report, assures us that he completely overcame them in argument; or in his judgment on Clovis, where after recording his career of assassination, murder, robbery, cruelty, lust, treachery, and deceit, he concludes that Clovis swept all before him because he had walked in the ways of the Lord (since Clovis was an orthodox Christian).

Gregory was an honest, intelligent, unpretentious and uncompli- cated man with a very lofty conception of the church and of his own episcopal dignity. He was aware of the decadence of his age, and of his own inadequacies. Yet he struggled valiantly against the downward plunge of ancient culture and of Christianity. His death in 594 spared him from witnessing the ultimate triumph of Fredegund and the collapse of the once vigorous and powerful, if brutal, dynasty of the Merovingians, as well as the further degra- dation of the church and the old Gallo-Roman aristocracy.

A contemporary and friend of Gregory was the Italian poet Venan- tius Fortunatus. Born in the town of Treviso between 530 and 535, Fortunatus received his education at Ravenna, where he acquired an intimate knowledge of grammar and rhetoric and studied some law. In 565, just three years before the Lombard invasion, he left his native land, probably to make a pilgrimmage to the shrine of St. Martin at Tours, and spent the remainder of his long and tranquil life among the Franks. Apparently in no great hurry to reach his destination, he proceeded by easy stages, staying for varying lengths of time in the major cities along his route -- Mainz, Cologne, Metz, Verdun, Reims, and Paris -- before arriving at Tours about two years after setting out. Fortunatus seems to have had an ingratiating manner, and he possessed besides a consider- able facility for writing verse for any occasion. These two advantages gained for him the good-will and largess of the power- ful. He arrived in Metz just in time for the wedding of King Sigibert and Brunhild and wrote for them an elaborate epithalamion in the classical tradition which, although it is far from being his best poetry, seems to have made a great reputation for him. When Sigebert's brutal brother Chilperic, out of jealousy and spite, married Brunhild's unfortunate sister, he required a simi- lar wedding song from Fortunatus, and it was obligingly furnished.

Shortly after arriving in Tours, Fortunatus made the acquaintance of St. Radegund in her convent in nearby Poitiers, and in this town he spent the rest of his days (aside from a few years of travel after Radegund's death in 587), finally serving as its bishop from 591 til his death in about 610. Radegund was a Thur-

ingian princess whose family had been murdered by the Frank Chlo-
thar, and who had then been forcibly married to that king. After
his death in 561 she had founded a number of convents in the
vicinity of Poitiers, one of which she entered. Her piety and
good works became well-known, and Fortunatus fell in love with
her, managing to maintain a very delicate, intense, but non-sexual
relationship with her until her death in 587. It was under her
inspiration and patronage that he wrote most of his best poetry --
numerous playful songs celebrating the beauties of the commonplace, poems of great charm and some wit, and a remarkably tender
and ably written elegy on the life and murder of Brunhild's sister, Galswintha, as well as one on the sad lot of Radegund herself. A considerable proportion of his poetry has slight
intrinsic merit. He wrote numerous panegyrics of the great of his
day, epithalamia, the inevitable Life of St. Martin, verse letters, and assorted short poems of almost every description. He
had a respectable command of classical meters, although in this
respect, as in most others, he was inferior to Prudentius. Miss
Helen Waddell has called him "an indifferent poet, but an artist,"[8] and although this perhaps under-rates his finest poetry,
it is by and large just. He had a sharp eye and ear for beauty,
the ability to fashion a charming poem in a short time, and a keen
sensitivity to the tastes of those he was writing for. For all
its classicism, his style is refreshingly natural and free from
the worst extravagances of the rhetorical schools. And in one
form of poetry, the Latin hymn, he deserves to be ranked along
with Ambrose as one of the truly great poets of the Latin church.
Of the hymns attributed to him, three are definitely his, all of
surpassing beauty -- Pange lingua gloriosi, Vexilla regis prodeunt, and Agnoscat omne saeculum. These are technically very
interesting works, since they are written in correct quantitative
meters but are capable to accentual scansion. One can hardly
avoid the stress accents in lines such as these noted by the
sensitive ear of Henry Osborn Taylor:

> Pange, lingua, gloriosi proelium
> certaminis...
> Crux fidelis, inter omnes arbor
> una mobilis...
> Dulce lignum, dulce clavo dulce
> pondus sustinens.[9]

Yet they are metrically impeccable. The same is true of Vexilla
regis prodeunt, which also makes extensive use of assonance and
rhyme. These devices did not originate with Fortunatus, having
been used in varying degrees by both Christian and pagan poets
since the late third century, but his use of them marks a major
step on the way to the purely accentual and rhyming Latin poetry
of the High Middle Ages.

To one familiar with the History of Gregory of Tours, it seems scarcely credible that a poet of Fortunatus' ability could have found extensive patronage and great fame in that age of unbridled passions, endemic warfare and general illiteracy. While it is true that he was a product of the Italian schools and could probably never have developed his poetic talents had he been born in Frankland, it is nevertheless to the credit of the Franks, and particularly to the Thuringian St. Radegund, that they treasured and rewarded his gifts and so kept alive some small measure of literary culture even in a time of general barbarism.

Although the Visigothic kingdom did not produce a poet of the stature of Fortunatus, it apparently maintained a higher general level of culture than existed in Gaul during the sixth century. It was decadent, often crude and barbarized, but it was Roman culture still, and some outstanding scholars such as Martin of Braga and John of Biclaro still had some competence in Greek. Spain had not suffered the extremities which befell Italy during the first half of the sixth century, but its lot was far from happy. Attacked by both Franks and Byzantines, torn by internal strife between nobles and monarch, orthodox and Arian, Latin and Goth, the kingdom nevertheless managed to survive and with the accession of Leovigild in 567 actually to revive. Leovigild, an Arian, was a bitter persecutor of orthodox Christians, and when king Reccared, and with him his kingdom, became orthodox in 589, the zeal of the newly triumphant faction was manifested both in vigorous persecutions of Arians and Jews and in a literary revival whose most famous representative was Isidore of Seville.

Isidore was born around 570 of a noble family and received the normal Roman education in grammar and rhetoric. Because of his father's early death, he was brought up by his older brother, Leander, whom he succeeded as bishop of Seville in 600. He died in 636.

In addition to being a tireless administrator, Isidore was a prolific writer. His literary reputation through the ages has run to extremes. For nearly a thousand years he was held in the highest esteem, copied, rearranged, and cited as an authority by the greatest scholars of Europe. Modern critics, however, have scarcely been able to find words to express their contempt, although there have been some recent attempts to rehabilitate him. He is often dismissed as being a mere compiler and criticized for choosing the most inane, stupid, and fatuous statements of his illustrious predecessors for inclusion in his compilations, and for misunderstanding them at that. There is, of course, as always, some basis for these unfavorable judgments. Isidore's writings are, for the most part, mere compilations, and it is that which makes them valuable. He himself plainly says that he is "collecting flowers from the meadows of the ancients." It is also true that he often did not understand fully the material he was excerpting. But it would be ungenerous in the extreme not to grant the great value of at least some of his works, his indefatigible industry, his wide reading, and his earnest devotion to learning and religion.

Isidore's writings include Questions on the Old Testament, a compilation from earlier Latin Bible commentaries; a lamentation on the woes of this life entitled Synonyma; a defense of the Catholic faith against the Jews, showing an extensive knowledge of the writings of the earlier Fathers and of the canons of the church councils; a Book of Numbers, also a compilation, showing the mystical signficance of certain important numbers (a practice which goes back at least as far as the Pythagoreans); a short compilation of natural science entitled De rerum natura; a continuation of Jerome's Lives of Famous Men; a History of the Visigoths; and a universal chronicle.

By far his most ambitious and influential work, however, is the Etymologies. This is an encyclopedia of universal knowledge culled from a great variety of sources and takes its name from Isidore's custom of introducing each new topic with an etymology and from the contents of the tenth book, which is given over wholly to this sort of thing. It includes treatises on the seven Liberal Arts, medicine, law, geography, astronomy, meteorology, chronology, mineralogy, and numerous other topics, all put together into twenty books without any principle of division or grouping. Isidore, however, is not responsible for this arrangement. It was done by his friend Braulio, and we have no way of knowing whether he would have improved on it.

The range of Isidore's reading was prodigious, and although he relied primarily, though not entirely, on late compilations and handbooks rather than the original works he cites, his accomplishment is nevertheless remarkable. So great was the authority of the Etymologies that even when many original Greek and Latin works had been recovered in the twelfth and thirteenth centuries, it remained a standard reference work. It is certain that he did not understand all that he included, especially concerning the shape of the earth. It is impossible from reading the Etymologies to decide whether he thought it was spherical or flat, and there are other instances of similar vagueness. But with all its undeniable shortcomings, the Etymologies is a noteworthy achievement and was to pass on to the Middle Ages at least a significant fraction of the knowledge of Antiquity.

With Isidore we come to the last significant writer of Antiquity. Those who came after him cannot be considered Roman in any meaningful sense of the term. This outline of the major writers from Avitus and Dracontius to Isidore has not revealed a steady and unrelieved decline. A period which produced Boethius' Consolation of Philosophy, Avitus' Deeds of Spiritual History, Gregory of Tours' History, and Fortunatus' poetry cannot be considered com-

pletely barren of intellectual attainment. Still the end represents a sad decline from the beginning. From a highly cultured,
if somewhat effete, society nurtured on its literary tradition, we
move to a period when even cultivated men seldom know Greek and
when normal communications between intellectuals in different
places is difficult if not quite impossible, and finally to a
period when literary Latin is a tongue beyond the ken of even the
well-educated and when the vigor which had earlier begun the
creation of a new, more contemporary literary Latin is dissipated.
The educational system, the mainstay of Roman culture, has broken
down,[10] books of even the great classics are hard to come by, and
the ruling class is largely illiterate.

During the seventh century men had more elementary interests --
staying alive and getting enought to eat -- than literature,
philosophy and science. What learning survived was primarily in
the monasteries or occasionally in a great cathedral school such
as Seville, York, or Canterbury. Certain influential Christians
had warned against the study of the pagan authors, but the pre-
vailing view recognized the necessity of preserving Roman literature within the new system of Christian education.

NOTES

1. For examples of all known pre-Carolingian manuscripts, see E.
   A. Lowe, Codices Latini Antiquiores, 12 vols. (Oxford, 1934-
   71). For an excellent brief account of the development of
   Latin handwriting, see the same author's essay in Crump and
   Jacob, eds., The Legacy of the Middle Ages (Oxford, 1926),
   197-226.

2. Ed. R. Peiper, MGH: Auc. Ant., VI, 2 (Vienna, 1883).

3. English translation by V.E. Watts (Penguin, 1969).

4. Gregory's biography (Book II of his Dialogues) is available
   in English translation in Fathers of the Christian Church,
   vol. XXXIX (New Yrok, 1959). The Rule is translated by A.C.
   Meisel and M.L. del Mastro, The Rule of St. Benedict (Double-
   day Image Book, 1975). It should be read with The Rule of
   the Master (Kalamazoo, Michigan, 1977).

5. See Pierre Riché, Education and Culture in the Barbarian West
   (Columbia, S.C., 1976), 146-47, 152-57.

6. Max Bennet, Le Latin de Gregoire de Tours (Paris, 1890).

7. The best English translation is by Lewis Thorpe, Gregory of
   Tours, History of the Franks (Penguin, 1974).

8. Helen Waddell, The Wandering Scholars (London, 1927; reprint

of 6th ed., Anchor Book 63, 1961), 29.

9. H. O. Taylor, The Emergence of Christian Culture, 295-96.

10. For the details of this, see Pierre Riché, Education and Culture.

PART TWO: THE CAROLINGIAN AGE

Chapter 4

Antecedent Developments

The late seventh and early eighth centuries are probably the lowest point in continental European culture. The revival of education, literacy and thought lagged behind the restoration by the Carolingian house of order and something approaching political unity, and indeed it is not inconceivable that the western cultural tradition might have been completely lost during this time. It is against this background that the achievement of the Carolingian age can be appreciated as the truly heroic effort it was.

In previous chapters we have insisted upon the continuance, in however debased a form, of the Roman intellectual tradition. The writers we have studied were upper-class Romans by birth, educated in the Roman schools of grammar and rhetoric, and imbibing there the same education, the same attitudes, and the same values. That tradition was broken during the seventh century and had to be reconstituted to meet the needs of a vastly alien society. There were, however, important elements of continuity without which this reconstruction never could have taken place. These were the Irish monastic schools, the English schools at Wearmouth and Jarrow, and the two important cathedral schools at Canterbury and York; a few monasteries on the continent, mostly derived either directly or at one remove from the Irish monks; the remnants of Roman culture in the Carolingians' Visigothic lands; and the perseverance of the antique tradition and perhaps even of lay schools in Italy, from which came Peter of Pisa, Paulinus of Aquileia, and Paul the Deacon.

There is evidence of spontaneous vigor even before Charles purposefully undertook the revival of learning in his realms, but none of this originated in Gaul or Germany. Charles was forced to call on foreigners to be the teachers of his people -- Theodulf of Orleans, a Visigoth, Alcuin of York, an Englishman, Peter of Pisa, an Italian, and numerous needy and talented Irishmen. What intellectual vigor there was in the old Frankish lands must be attributed to the Irish and English missionaries and their foundations.

Charles then did not call a cultural revival into being out of nothing. But on the other hand, without his organizing ability, his willingness to put the material resources of the realm at the disposal of his scholars, his motivating force, and his efforts at revitalizing education on a large scale, it is not likely that our classical intellectual heritage could have survived through the tenth century, much less grown and developed into a new and creative cultural movement, including much of the Roman heritage, but transforming and passing beyond it.

The first people to attempt a reconstruction of intellectual life in a radically un-Roman environment were the Irish teachers of the sixth and seventh centuries.[1] During the sixth and even through the seventh centuries, the Irish were in great demand as teachers. They colonized and converted much of Scotland and England, setting up monastic schools as they went. Their next field of activity was the continent, where Columban established monasteries at Luxeuil, Corbie, Bobbio and elsewhere. Judged by absolute standards, the achievements of these Irishmen were minimal. Their Latin was whimsical, their program of studies and educational aims restricted and practical -- to enable priests to perform the church rituals properly and to understand and expound the scriptures -- although they are also known to have cultivated the study of the classical poets and to write a good deal of verse themselves. Their knowledge of Greek was restricted to meanings of specific words and phrases; few if any knew even the rudiments of Greek syntax. Their knowledge of Hebrew was even slighter. Still they had the virtue of beginning at the beginning, of compiling word lists and eagerly studying whatever grammatical works were available to them. And they instilled in their pupils an awesome reverence for learning. The problems they faced were elementary: to teach Latin, an utterly foreign tongue, to boys and men who were totally ignorant of all things Roman and then to employ this language in the acquisition of the elements of learning and the service of religion. The version of Latin they concocted was fanciful in the extreme, grammatically perverse, full of newly-coined words and misuses of old ones. Their zeal was notorious, and if it often outstripped their performance, still one shudders to contemplate what the future of European letters would have been without them. But it is equally fortunate that the source of Latin learning had not yet completely dried up and that new books and an occasional teacher were acquired from Italy from time to time.

During the seventh century, it was the Anglo-Saxons who performed the most significant service for European learning and education.[2] They profitted from the instruction of Irish masters and from the newly-established connection with Rome as well. In the north, two important monastic schools -- at Wearmouth and Jarrow -- were founded by Benedict Biscop, an energetic and capable abbot who made during his life five or six trips to Rome and each time brought back with him many precious books to stock the library shelves of his monasteries. In the south, at Canterbury, a cathedral school was instituted by two easterners, Theodore of Tarsus and Hadrian the African, who had been sent to England by Pope Vitalian in reponse to a plea from the English church for able bishops following the decimation of the English clergy by the plague of 665. Theodore became archbishop of Canterbury and Hadrian was his scholasticus and abbot of St. Peter and St. Paul's abbey. Both these men had been educated in secular schools, knew Greek well, and perhaps some Hebrew. Theodore had been educated at Athens itself, and Hadrian came from Calabria in southern Italy where Greek was still spoken. And by happy accident they were wonderfully gifted teachers. It is difficult to reconstruct the actual method and content of their teaching, but if teachers may be judged by their pupils, then they were outstanding indeed. Although many studied under the direction of Theodore and Hadrian and from them learned excellent Latin, at least some Greek, and a love for some of those purely literary delights which the classics had to offer, only one of those students is known to us in any detail.

This is Aldhelm, a noble Saxon boy with a thirst for knowledge. He studied first under the great Irish teacher Mailduib at Malmesbury and in middle life continued his education under Theodore and Hadrian at Canterbury. His extant writings show an excellent command of Latin and a reading which is much wider than was then common, including many pagan writers as well as a wide range of Christian authors -- Virgil, Lucan, Juvenal, Juvencus, Prosper of Aquitaine, Sedulius, Augustine, Jerome, Cassian, Gregory the Great, Isidore, Rufinus' translations of various Greek theological works, and numerous saints' lives -- and even some slight knowledge of arithmetic, astronomy, and law. His poetry, too, though not of a high order, shows that he had studied carefully the rules of classical verisification, on which subject he wrote a short treatise. Gifted by a keen intelligence, motivated by religious zeal and a love for learning, and profiting from the teaching first of the Irish tradition and later the superior learning of Theodore and Hadrian, Aldhelm inspired a whole generation of English scholars. When he died in 709, England was ready to assume the intellectual leadership of Europe.

The leading European scholar of his age was the northerner Bede (673-735). At the age of seven he was given by his parents to the monks at Wearmouth, from which he soon transferred to Jarrow. Within a few miles of this monastery he spent his entire life, which he devoted to study, teaching, and writing.

His early works were written for the use of his monastic pupils and are competent though not remarkable. He was clearly a capable young teacher, acquainted with a large number of earlier Latin grammatical works and able to select intelligently and pertinently that which was most useful for his purpose. Among these were a work on metrics (De metrica arte) and one on the figures of speech of the Bible (De schematibus et tropis sacrae scripturae), in both of which he draws his illustrative material almost exclusively from Christian writings, and a work on spelling (De orthographia). He also composed for his students a Life of St. Cuthbert in correct but uninspired verse as well as a prose version of the same saint's life. Two other elementary works were concerned with the sciences: his De natura rerum, which was a selection and rearrangement of material he found principally in Isidore of Seville and Pliny the Elder; and *Liber de temporibus*, dealing with basic problems of chronology and the ecclesiastical calendar.[3]

Although Bede drew his knowledge of the natural world from standard late antique sources such as Ambrose, Augustine, Basil, and Gregory the Great, the *De natura rerum* was derived mainly from Isidore's work of the same name, itself a compilation. It was, however, superior to that work for several reasons. For one thing, Bede had access to Pliny's *Natural History*, or an abridgement of that work, probably the best of the Latin scientific encyclopedias, whereas Isidore had not known it. More important though were Bede's clarity of thought, common sense, and assumption of natural causation. These qualities often permitted him to rise above the level of his sources. Isidore had been confused and inconsistent about the shape of the earth -- he probably considered it to be shaped like a wheel but copied without understanding astronomical information which clearly implied its sphericity. Bede, on the other hand, held it to be a sphere at rest in the center of the universe. The sphere of the stars revolved in a circle about the earth while the various planets followed epicyclical orbits around it. Bede understood enough to be able to give a clear account of the reasons for eclipses and for the phases of the moon. The corporeal world was separated from the spirtual by the waters of the firmament and was made up of the four elements, fire, air, water, and earth, whose combinations constituted the world of corporeal nature. The earth itself was divided into five zones; two frigid, one torrid, and two temperate. Both temperate zones were inhabitable but only the northern was actually inhabited.[4]

The *De temporibus* (written in 703 A.D.) was an attempt to bring order into the chronological chaos of the ecclesiastical calendar, the most pressing problem of which was the establishment of the date of Easter as well as other movable feast days. Since the date of Easter depends on the lunar calendar of the Hebrews, its date fluctuates in terms of the solar calendar of the Romans. A lunation and a solar year are incommensurable, thus making it necessary to adjust the two periodically. The Irish had developed a system of establishing the date of Easter, but it had many faults and was different from the Roman method. Aside from the Irish works, called *computi*, Isidore was the major authority on questions of chronology, and he too left much to be desired. Bede undertook to explain clearly the major divisions of time and to point out the problems caused by their incommensurability. He also introduced his students to problems of historical chronology and general problems of the measurement of time, and explained to them the use of the nineteen year cycle (by which nineteen solar years are considered equal to 235 months) in figuring the dates on which Easter would fall in the future. Although this was an elementary work, it is admirable in the clarity with which it grasps and presents the factors involved in the problem and proposes well thought out solutions.

In 725 Bede published a much fuller and more advanced work on chronology, the De temporum ratione, which is of interest from several points of view. While his sources for De temporibus had been restricted to Irish computi and the pertinent sections of Isidore, in De temporum ratione he also used a large number of antique writers on chronology as well as many chronicles employing different systems of dating, which he endeavored to synchronize according to a single chronological system. He adopted from Dionysius Exiguus, a bilingual writer on legal topics and a friend of Cassiodorus, the method of dating forward and backward from the Incarnation. Then he computed the major dates of world history on this scale and appended to his work an outline history of the world from the Creation to 725 A.D. Included in this work is a very important study of the tides, which combines experience with knowledge gained from literary sources. From Pliny, Bede learned of the correlation between the tides and the motion of the moon. But he also knew that the tides follow the moon at different intervals at different places, the interval remaining fixed for each port; and how the wind can retard or advance the tide. And he explains how the nineteen year cycle can be used to predict the tides for each port.

Important and admirable as Bede's scientific works are, it is his religious and historical works on which his reputation chiefly rests. In his own day his Biblical commentaries were the source of his great fame. He displays in these works great erudition, a degree of originality, keen insight into what in the works of his predecessors was pertinent to his own age, and an uncommon interest in linguistic criticism. He had studied Greek from the time he was a boy and clearly had some knowledge of that language, reading not only Josephus' Antiquities and St. Basil's Hexameron in Greek, but employing also a bilingual version of the Acts of the Apostles (which is still extant) in both his commentaries on that work. The basic Biblical text from which he worked was a copy of the Vulgate brought to England from Rome by Bendict Biscop, from which the still extant Codex Amiatinus[5] was copied; but he also had recourse to older Latin translations and occasionally to Greek versions. He was able to correct the Vulgate at times and often to clarify a passage by comparing it to the wording of the Greek text. His principal method of exegesis, however, was allegorical. Here he depended heavily on earlier writers, especially Augustine and Gregory the Great, although he imposed his own intelligence upon even the material that he borrowed and was far from being a mere compiler. The literal and moral senses of scripture were most often expounded, but Bede sometimes found three or even four senses of a single passage. These commentaries were in great demand while Bede was still alive and for several centuries thereafter. There are still extant numerous letters from the great English missionary, St. Boniface, begging for copies of Bede's commentaries. And so they found their way onto the shelves of missionary establishments throughout central Europe to enlighten and instruct new generations of Christian scholars.

Of somewhat lesser renown in his own day, but considered his greatest work by the modern world, is his Ecclesiastical History of the English People.[6] Bede had long been interested in chronology and hagiography. In addition to the De temporibus and De temporum ratione, and the Life of St. Cuthbert, which we have already mentioned, he had written a history of the first five abbots of Wearmouth-Jarrow (Historia abbatum). Nothing he had done previously, however, promised the magnificent achievement of the Ecclesiastical History, one of the greatest historical works of all time. Strongly influenced by Eusebius' Ecclesiastical History, which Bede knew in the translation of Rufinus, it was also intended as a work of edification in the best sense of that word. For Bede never resorted to the use of fictitious exempla for the sake of a lesson; rather he diligently sought out the truth and let it speak for itself. Except for the first twenty-two chapters of Book I, which he copied from Orosius, Prosper of Aquitaine, and several saints' lives, the Ecclesiastical History is a masterpiece of careful and judicious use of great variety of sources, varying considerably in their value. Bede used local chronicles and traditions, saints' lives, personal interviews and official documents, and secured the cooperation and help of many of his contemporaries who often put themselves to considerable trouble for his sake, checking some information in the records of Canterbury or consulting the papal archives in Rome in his behalf. Bede's History amply justified their pains. Although its reliability necessarily varies with the reliability of his information, Bede's common sense, competent historical method, and persistent intellectual curiosity make his History one of the most trustworthy historical works of our tradition. Following the practice of Eusebius, he always provided a complete list of the succession of bishops from the founding of each see. He also was careful to identify his sources in most cases, thus providing later readers with a standard by which to evaluate the various parts of his work. The style of the Ecclesiastical History, as of most of Bede's prose works, is almost incredibly classical -- not in the strict sense of being confined in its vocabulary and locutions to those used by the Augustans, but in its clarity, appropriateness, and simplicity. Since no one among either his predecessors or immediate successors approached him as a stylist, this quality cannot be credited solely to the teaching he received, but must be attributed ultimately to his own genius in the understanding and use of language. The subject matter of the History is precisely what the title implies -- the history of the English church from the mission of St. Augustine of Canterbury in 597 to the year 731, preceded by a brief sketch of world history from the Creation to Augustine's mission. He adopted in this history the era of the Incarnation as the chronological standard, to which he attempted to make all his dates conform. When he failed, it was the fault of his sources rather than his method. The Ecclesiastical History, which was widely used and copied during the Middle Ages, along with the De temporum ratione, were determinative in establishing the era of the Incarnation as the standard for Latin Europe.

When Bede died in 735, England was culturally the most advanced nation of Europe. Building upon the work of the Irish, invigorated by fresh infusions of the antique tradition from Byzantium and Rome, and motivated by a zeal for Christian orthodoxy, the English had constructed a superb culture. Shortly after Bede's death, his close friend and former pupil, Egbert, became bishop of York. Egbert expanded and regularized the somewhat causal cathedral school of that diocese and installed his cousin Elbert as master of the school. This cathedral school soon replaced the monastic school of Jarrow as the intellectual center of the north (and in fact of England, since the schools at Canterbury seem to have decayed somewhat) and through Elbert's efforts soon possessed an extensive library. It continued the traditions established by Bede. It was at this school that Alcuin was educated, and when Elbert became bishop of York in 767, Alcuin succeeded him as master of the school. It was principally through Alcuin that the vigor, the knowledge, and the educational accomplishments of the Irish and English acquired a dominant place in the Carolingian revival, reinforcing and superseding the work of the continental Irish monasteries.[7]

The other major avenue by which English learning revitalized the continent was the activity of the Anglo-Saxon missionary monks. From about the middle of the seventh century, the English caught from the Irish the desire to wander as missionaries. Their principal field of activity was Frisia and Germany east of the Rhine, beyond the area under Frankish control. Persistent and courageous, they continued despite many hardships and martyrdoms to preach the gospel to the northern pagans. The culmination of this movement was the career of perhaps the greatest of all these English missionaries, Wynfrith, later known as Boniface (ca. 675-754). Although his own writings -- elementary compilations on grammar and rhetoric and some riddles in verse -- are negligible, he is nevertheless of great importance in our intellectual history. After a career as a monastic teacher in his early life, he embarked on a brief missionary journey among the Frisians in 716. Two years later he went to Rome where he was re-christened Bonifatius by Pope Gregory II and given formal authorization to convert the heathens of Germany, being made bishop in 722. He devoted the rest of his life both to preaching among the heathens and to organizing the German church. From 741 on he received valuable support from the Frankish rulers as well as from the Pope. The majority of his comrades and helpers, however, were Englishmen, who often served as teachers as well as preachers, and who brought with them precious books from their native land. Boniface himself was constantly writing home for books, among which the works of Bede figured largely.[8] Of the many monasteries, some doomed to violent extinction, some to be permanent, founded by Boniface and his aides, the most important was that of Fulda, Boniface's favorite and his burial place after his death at the hands of the heathen Frisians in 754. These monasteries, and particularly Fulda, became continental centers of English culture and thence integral parts of Carolingian intellectual life in the ninth century.

There were, of course, a number of monastic intellectual centers on the continent before the arrival of the Anglo-Saxons. The majority of these had been established by the Irish during the sixth and seventh centuries or were offshoots of Irish foundations. The propensity of the Irish to wander is proverbial, but the most important Irish mission was a group of twelve monks, headed by Columbanus, which invaded Burgundy via Brittany in about 590 A.D. They were well received by the Frankish king Guntram, who provided them with land for their first monastery at Annegray. This little settlement grew rapidly, increased both by new arrivals from Ireland and by natives, and two more houses were founded by the end of the century, one at Luxeuil and one at Fontaines. Columbanus was a vigorous and domineering person and became involved in several important disputes, usually over the extreme austerity which he tried to impose on the clergy or over matters of religious observance which differed between the Frankish and Irish churches, such as the tonsure, the method of baptism, and determination of Easter. He was finally forced to leave Burgundy in about 610 and after wandering through the eastern Frankish territories, established another monastery on Lombard territory in northern Italy at Bobbio the year before the death in 615. The previous year, one of his disciples, Gallus, accompanied by several friends, had established a small house in what is now Switzerland, later to become one of Europe's greatest intellectual centers, St. Gall. Another monastery destined for greatness was founded at Corbie by monks from Columbanus' foundation at Luxeuil. There were frequent contacts between these monasteries, and their libraries and scriptoria did much to maintain the existence of the literary tradition, both Christian and pagan, during the seventh and eighth centuries.

Not all the important monasteries were Irish foundations, however. Another great Swiss monastery was that at Reichenau, founded in 724 probably by Visigothic refugees from Spain. The work of Boniface we have already mentioned, and although Fulda was not as yet important, it would be one of the leading intellectual centers of the ninth century.

There were in addition some of the older monastic establishments. Of these, Lerins continued to be active and maintained close contacts with many of the Irish foundations, especially Bobbio. Tours, however, had fallen on hard times since early in the seventh century and would not regain its former eminence until the abbacy of Alcuin (794-804). Monte Cassino had been destroyed by the Lombards in 581, but its monks had escaped, carrying their books with them, and had taken refuge in Rome under the protection of the pope. Here they had maintained their identity until 718 when, again with papal help, they restored their monastery. From that date until its destruction at the hands of the Muslims in 883, Monte Cassino was a dominant intellectual influence in southern Italy.

Meanwhile shattered remnants of the old culture still remained outside the monasteries. Although the seventh century was far from brilliant in Spain, the ecclesiastical culture which had flowered under Martin of Braga and Isidore of Seville persisted until the Muslim conquest and then through its refugees contributed its bit to the Carolingian restoration. The principal intellectual center seems to have been Toledo, three of whose bishops were men of some learning and authors of works of theology, biography, history, and grammar. It is very difficult, from the sources which remain, to form a clear picture of the intellectual life of the kingdom as a whole. It enjoyed a higher measure of political and social stability than the Frankish state, and its church was extremely vigorous. Also the Visigoths were in closer touch with Constantinople than was any part of Latin Europe except Italy. Still their intellectual activity was not impressive. Their libraries were apparently well stocked and sometimes used, but the nation produced no great writers.

In Italy the picture is more complete. In many parts of the peninsula, the combined miseries of the Gothic-Byzantine wars and the Lombard invasion had almost eliminated literacy even among the highest classes. This condition was aggravated by the resulting political fragmentation. Ravenna, Rome, Naples and the extreme south were part of the Byzantine empire. Most of the rest of Italy had fallen to the Lombards, who, however, were disunited themselves, so that warfare and pillage were fairly usual occurrences.

Still some centers of learning remained. In some of the major cities there were literate clergymen who sometimes took pen in hand, and it is possible that even lay schools continued to function. At Pavia and Milan there were at least small circles of educated men who, in their small way, kept alive a knowledge of and interest in letters. Rome too contained a number of educated people, including many Greek-speaking easterners. And at Ravenna an anonymous author composed a genuinely valuable work on cosmography, using an impressive number of sources, many of which have been since lost.

In Gaul itself the situation was uniformly bad. If Charles had had to depend on the resources of his own realm for his restoration of learning, he could have accomplished little. Here and there a barbaric compilation confronts us: a collection of ethical maxims culled from the Fathers by Defensor of Ligugé; two ludicrously inept historical works, one the History of the Franks by the so-called Fredegarius, the other the anonymous Book of the Franks. Of a somewhat higher order, and probably meant as a joke, is the Book of Monsters by the so-called Aethicus Ister. And finally, defying all description or understanding, is the work of Virgilius Maro Grammaticus. This man, probably from Toulouse, wrote two books, Letters and Epitomies, allegedly on grammar, a subject they approach with imagination if not much else, unless it be humor. This Virgil reports a debate by two grammarians lasting for two weeks on the correct form of the vocative of ego, and he drops the names of many famous authors whose works he apparently did not know and others whose names are not known to anyone else. He invents his own parts of speech, increases the number of genders to four, and divides Latin into twelve varieties. He also explains a new way of writing Latin in which the letters of a word or even a whole sentence may be changed around so that only the initiated can understand it. It is difficult to know what to make of works such as these. Were they a joke, or parodies, or did their authors really consider this to be the highest form of literary composition? Few but the Irish were innocent or perverse enough to take them seriously, but even so great a man as the Saxon Aldhelm shows traces of their influence.

These then were the intellectual resources and centers of Europe at the time of Charlemagne's accession in 768. There were areas which were still rich in the remains of ancient culture, but decayed; others that were young and vigorous but foreign to the language and traditions of Rome; and Gaul itself, intellectually inert, arid and inept, except for the foreigners who had come to dwell there. It was Charles himself who harnessed and organized what potentialities existed and gave direction and support to the intellectual revival which bears his name and without which the western tradition could hardly have survived.

NOTES

1. On the Irish, see Ludwig Bieler, _Ireland, Harbinger of the Middle Ages_ (London, New York, 1963).

2. See Wilhelm Levison, _England and the Continent in the Eighth Century_ (Oxford, 1946).

3. The introduction to C. W. Jones, _Bedae De temporibus_ (Cambridge, Massachusetts, 1943) contains an excellent account of the calendric problems of the age.

4. See A. C. Crombie, _Medieval and Early Modern Science_ (two vols., Garden City, New York, 1959), I, 19-22.

5. A photograph of one of its pages is in Lowe, _CLA_, III, 8.

6. English translation: Leo Sherley-Price, _Bede, A History of the English Church and People_ (Penguin L42, 1955).

7. For an excellent account, see Laistner, _Thought and Letters_, 136-188.

8. The letters are translated by Ephraim Emerton, _The Letter of St. Boniface_ (New York, 1940; reprint Norton, New York, 1976).

Chapter 5

The First Generation of Carolingian Scholars

The earlier Carolingians had displayed no particular interest in education or in church discipline. Charles Martel had even shown hostility to the church and had divested it of considerable property, which he used for the support of his cavalry. Late in his life, he had turned down an invitation from pope Gregory III to act as papal champion against the Lombards, with whom he was on good terms. With the accession of Pippin the Short, however, Carolingian policy changed. Pippin and his brother Carloman took the initiative in summoning synods to restore discipline to the Frankish church. They also gave important support to the Anglo-Saxon missionaries working among the east Germans; and when the papal plea for military aid against the Lombards was renewed in 751, Pippin responded and in return received the royal crown of the Franks, first from Boniface in 751 and later from the pope himself in 754. Thus was laid the foundation for the alliance between the Frankish royal house and the Roman see. When Charlemagne became king in 768, the direction of the new Carolingian policy had been clearly indicated, but little or nothing had yet been done to remedy the widespread illiteracy among the clergy, to allay the confusion in liturgical practices or monastic rules, or to arrest the process of contamination of the text of the Bible. Handwriting was another problem. There existed in the eighth century a great variety of book hands, some slovenly, some beautiful but difficult to read, and all restricted to limited areas. It was Charles' task to utilize all the intellectual resources at his disposal for the good government of his realm.

His first step was to discover the best educated men in Europe and then to put them to work on useful tasks. Primary among these tasks was the reconstitution of the educational system. The Roman system had completely broken down. A few scattered monasteries provided a respectable tuition, and the more conscientious bishops conducted, as part of their household, schools for young boys who intended to pursue a clerical career. Under these circumstances, education was bound to be haphazard, and the number of inadequately prepared clergy was much higher than is usually the case.

To correct this, Charles attacked on two levels. In the year 796 in a letter addressed to abbot Baugulf of Fulda and intended for general circulation, Charles attempted to create the means of implementing his earlier injunctions that priests be better educated and that they should teach each of their parishioners the Creed and Lord's Prayer. He commanded that each bishop set up in his diocese a school for all those capable of profiting from education, regardless of their origins. There is no way to determine how widely this order was obeyed, and certainly many dioceses must have remained without schools. But many others established them, the most famous being those of Orleans instituted by the great Visigothic scholar Theodulf. Good teachers were, of course, difficult to come by, and Charles was extremely generous in providing adequate material support for all those he could find.

In addition to this thoroughgoing scheme to broaden elementary educational opportunities, Charles established at Aachen a palace school, or rather reformed a palace school already in existence. Dating back probably to Charles Martel, the school had hitherto been confined to providing training in military virtues and manners for the sons of the nobility. Charlemagne now made it the intellectual center of his realm, to which the pre-eminent scholars of Europe were brought. On the one hand, it provided elementary instruction for young men, noble and common alike. On the other, it served as a sort of Institute for Advanced Study, where the greatest intellects of the day met for learned discussion, sometimes joined by Charles himself. This elite group served as a scholarly task force, providing men to carry out or direct some of Charles' major projects, such as a new edition of the Vulgate, a definitive text of the Benedictine Rule, a collection of suitable homilies for the use of the priests, defining a policy concerning Iconoclasm and other heresies, and purifying and standardizing the liturgy.

Charles' motives in all this were clearly practical. He was interested in letters and education not for their own sake but insofar as they served the common good. But he was a rare man among rulers in his clear perception of the relationship between the two. His practicality was not of the narrow sort, nor was he immune from the delights of intellectual stimulation. His respect for learning was great, and his support of it was intelligent and generous. Though he may never have learned to write even his own name, it would be misleading to call him illiterate. In addition to his native Frankish, he could both speak and understand Latin and could follow a conversation in Greek. He delighted in having books read to him and was able to question and discuss intelligently what he heard.

The guiding principle of his reforms was sound: Back to the sources![1] And this usually meant back to Rome. For the liturgy, for the Bible, for patristic texts, he sent for and received books from Rome. For the Benedictine Rule he sent to Monte Cassino. Only in handwriting did he scorn the ancient example and urge the creation of a new script suitable to the demands of the time. But even in this, his passion for uniformity was manifest. There should be one uniform liturgy, the Roman; one monastic rule, the Benedictine; one definitive Latin version of the Bible, the Vulgate; and one bookhand, intellegible to all and written by all.

The Roman bookhands had been of two types: the rustic capitals, in which the oldest extant Latin books are written; and the uncial which had become universal by the fourth century. These are both majuscule scripts (i.e., their proportions are those of our upper case letters), and although they are large and beautiful, they are neither economical of space nor particularly easy to read. There were two modifications of the uncial script called inexactly "half uncial" and "quarter uncial," in which some of the letter forms are altered and the size of the letters is often reduced. In addition to these bookhands, the Romans had a cursive script which they used for their more commonplace writing. Between the fifth and eighth centuries, all these hands continued to be written, but new combinations and modifications were devised, and the capitals and uncials tended to become display scripts. The new scripts were, for the most part, miniscule, having the same proportions as our lower case letters. They incorporated many cursive elements, including ligatures, and each had a number of highly individual letter forms. The Irish and Anglo-Saxons early developed two new bookhands, a majuscule and a minuscule, derived mainly from the Roman half-uncial. These hands also influenced much of the continental writing, especially in the scriptoria of the Irish foundations. Among these monasteries Bobbio, Luxeuil, and Corbie developed characteristic scripts of their own, as did the Visigoths. By mid-eighth century Monte Cassino had also devised a distinctive script which soon became common to the southern Italian area.[2] The influences which governed these developments were: (1) the scarcity and high cost of parchment, making an economical script necessary; (2) the need for legibility and desire for beauty; (3) the desirability of a uniform bookhand which could be read by all. The approach to the new script, known as the Caroline minuscule, was various, but the crucial line of development seems to have been through half-uncial, a smallish majuscule script, which when crowded changed the proportion of its letters and became a minuscule. There is still extant a manuscript in which this actually occurred, a book written for the abbot Maurdramnus of Corbie.

The new script quickly caught on, although many of the older hands persisted in the outlying regions. Monte Cassino went its own way; the Insular script continued in general use in Ireland and Britain until into the tenth century, and in some areas the Visigothic script lasted even longer. Nor was the Caroline minuscule completely uniform. By mid-ninth century, however, a high degree of uniformity and consistency had been achieved, and the script was the universal book hand of Latin Europe between the tenth and early thirteenth centuries, when it was modified to the point that it virtually became a new hand, the so-called Gothic. The Caroline minuscule was revived by the Italian humanists of the fifteenth century and is the basis for all modern type faces except the seldom used Gothic.

It was the scholars contemporary with Charles who bore the brunt of the intellectual revival and who gave it the impetus which carried it through the dark centuries of civil war and renewed invasion which followed. Although they were more naive, less thoroughly trained in the old learning, and sometimes made silly mistakes, they provided the solid foundation upon which the subsequent intellectual culture of Europe was built.[3]

Foremost among these men was Alcuin,[4] the master of the school and library of York. In 780, while returning to England from Rome where he had gone to receive the pallium for the new archbishop of York, his path crossed that of Charles in Parma. Charles urged him to remain on the continent as head of the Palace School, and after receiving the permission of his king and archbishop, Alcuin accepted. Except for two visits to England, one in 786, the other from 790-793, Alcuin spent the rest of his life in Frankia, renowned, respected and amply rewarded with benefices.

Although Alcuin was involved in some fo the great projects of the time, such as the new edition of the Vulgate, the restoration of the school and scriptorium of Tours, the decision that Charles seek the imperial crown, and the battle against the Adoptionist heresy, yet most of his time was spent as a schoolmaster, teaching the rudiments of "Wisdom" to his pupils and writing textbooks based on the old education, but more pertinent to the needs of his day. Even the best of Alcuin's pupils were simple country boys, to whom the Roman tradition was awesome but nevertheless alien. An effective teacher will tailor his presentation to the needs and capabilities of his students, and a great teacher will produce scholars better than himself. Alcuin did both.

Feeling that none of the available textbooks was entirely suitable, Alcuin wrote his own. He wrote treatises on grammar and orthography which are quite similar in scope and matter to the teaching of remedial English in American high schools, except that they employ a lively dialogue form of presentation, and they exude a love of the subject and place a high value on learning in general. They employ riddles, such as we use in the lower grades, but require a fairly sharp mind to provide the answer. Grammar, in Alcuin's words, "is the science of literature and the guardian of correct speech and writing. It rests on nature, reason, authority, and custom." This is good as far as it goes, but this concept of grammar is far more restricted than the Roman and indeed than that of Alcuin's pupil Rabanus Maurus. Still, anyone who has tried to teach young children will appreciate Alcuin's approach. The Grammar is introduced by a discussion between the pupil and teacher. The pupil begins: "We have heard you say that philosophy is the teacher of all virtues and that she alone of worldly treasures has never left the possessor miserable. Please help me, sir. Flint has fire within which comes out only when struck; so the light of knowledge exists by nature in our minds, but a teacher is needed to knock it out." Then the teacher answers him, "It is easy to show you wisdom's path if only you will pursue it for the sake of God, for the sake of the soul's purity, and to learn the truth, and also for its own sake, but not for human praise and honor." The conversation then turns to philosophical topics, each handled quite simply, and the introduction is concluded by Alcuin exhorting his pupils "that with the help of Divine Grace they will ascend the seven grades of philosophy, by which philosophers have gained honor brighter than that of kings." (He seems to have forgotten his injunction against seeking fame, earlier in the conversation.) The technical portion of the treatise continues the dialogue and is presented as a disputation between two boys, presided over by the teacher. In some respects, the Grammar is ludicrous, because Alcuin consistently misuses and misunderstands his technical terms. It was, however, ideally suited for its purpose. The boys were taught, in an engaging manner, the elements of Latin grammar, culled largely from Donatus and Isidore and occasionally from Priscian. And if they picked up a number of quaintly mistaken notions in the process, they were also put in possession of the means to correct these notions.

Alcuin's treatise on spelling too was practical and adequate. Picking out Latin words commonly misspelled or confused because of similarity in spelling and pronunciation, he warned against and corrected the most common errors.

His work on mathematics (Propositiones ad acuendos pueros) is of the same nature. It had a practical objective -- a working knowledge of the computus. His students were simple and unsophisticated farm boys using a lanaguage with which they had only a tenuous familiarity. Alcuin piqued their interest by using the conversational technique and by posing interesting logical puzzles for the boys to solve. For example: Three boys, each with his sister, reach a river which can only be crossed by a boat which holds two people. No girl can be alone in the company of a boy other than her brother for fear of losing her virginity. How can all six get across the river without any girl losing her virtue? Most of the fifty-three questions, however, were more to the point, and by the time a boy had memorized the treatise he would have possessed an elementary working knowledge of basic mathematics which would enable him to attempt the more advanced treatises.

Among Alcuin's more advanced (and less successful) works were his De dialectica and De rhetorica. The latter of these was composed at Charlemagne's request to enable the king better to handle disputes brought before him to judge. It was an elementary treatise on public speaking, based principally upon Cicero's De inventione and to a lesser extent on Cassiodorus. The other treatise, On Dialectic, has been the object of scorn to modern scholars well versed in the classical tradition. But in some ways its very faults were virtues judged in the context of the early

Carolingian revival. Alcuin derived his information from the compendia of late Antiquity -- Isidore, Cassiodorus, and Boethius mainly -- but he was no philosopher and failed to grasp the basic definitions and categories of ancient philosophy. This is undeniably a fault. But it prevented him from attempting a premature flight to philosophical heights or from pursuing subtle distinctions when what was needed was a guide to the more competent Roman textbooks. It is unfortunate that Alcuin did not have a firmer grasp of his subject, but he at least knew the basic texts: Porphyry's _Isagoge_ and Boethius' (and perhaps Cicero's) logical works.

As M. L. W. Laistner had remarked, "Alcuin's educational treatises are not, judged by any standards, remarkable; indeed, they are mediocre. That he was, nevertheless, a very great teacher is beyond dispute."[5] And his primary responsibility in Charles' school was elementary education. In this task he succeeded brilliantly. His pupils were dispersed as teachers and administrators throughout the realm, all better educated than their master, but none able to inspire, as he did, the love, or the devotion to learning, which is the mark of a truly great teacher.

Alcuin's teaching duties at the Palace School, however, were only a fragment of his services. He was an indefatigable letter writer to the end of his life. He also wrote Biblical commentaries, poems, and theological treatises. And one of the most impressive scholarly achievements of the Carolingian period, the edition of the Vulgate Bible, was largely the work of Alcuin. Confusion concerning the true text of scripture was widespread by Charlemagne's time. The general illiteracy of the preceding century had resulted in numerous corruptions, as well as contaminations by older pre-Vulgate Latin versions. The most trustworthy copies of the Vulgate were the old ones, usually written in uncial characters and therefore very difficult to read. A thoroughgoing work of correction was clearly necessary and Charles ordered that it be undertaken. There were two responses to this command, one by the great Visigothic scholar Theodulf; the other, much more important in its long-range influence, by a group of scholars under the direction of Alcuin, and this edition bears his name -- the Alcuinian Rescension. This Bible, no longer extant, became the exemplar for a number of others, and the process of corruption and contamination, if not halted, was at least appreciably retarded.

In addition to his duties as schoolmaster and Biblical editor, Alcuin was one of the Charles' most trusted advisers and was consulted on a variety of topics. The two major heresies of the time were Adoptionism and Iconoclasm. Of these Alcuin was much more interested in Adoptionism (which asserts that Jesus is the Son of God by adoption, not by nature) and wrote several treatises against that heresy. He was also, however, pressed into service to help determine the Carolingian policy on Iconoclasm, although the extent of his involvement is not yet clear. This policy, stated in the famous Libri Carolini (of which we shall speak further below), was a major factor in Charles' decision to accept the imperial crown, and before making his fateful trip to Rome in 800 A.D., Charles stopped off at Tours to consult Alcuin.

As a reward for his invaluable service to Christianity and to the Carolingian state, and to dissuade him from returning to England, Alcuin was made bishop of the venerable see of Tours in 796. But his labors did not end here. He found the library to be in miserable circumstances and spent much of his time in his declining years in acquiring books for it, many of them from York. He also found his clergy to be deplorably "rustic," and so he became a schoolmaster again. The scriptorium, too, was decayed, and Alcuin exerted himself to introduce and maintain the Caroline minuscule and to attract competent scribes. His great fame attracted many to his retreat, both bright young boys and mature men. These enabled him vastly to improve educational standards at Tours, but they were also a drain on his failing strength. Charlemagne, too, constantly required advice and instruction, and Alcuin was busy writing to his master scores of letters, some of them short educational treatises in themselves. When he died in 804 he had done his job well. The revival of learning was well under way, and others had been prepared to carry on his tasks. Among his students were Einhard, Rabanus Maurus, Amalarius of Metz and Grimald of St. Gall, the leading scholars of the next generation, all of whom attest to the excellence of the instruction they had received from Alcuin. We should more justly judge him by the results he obtained than by his educational treatises, whose cultural context we are hardly in a position to appreciate.

Important though Alcuin was, he was far from being the only scholar employed by Charles for the restitution of learning. Coming from a vastly different cultural background was the grammarian Peter of Pisa, from Lombard Italy. Probably a member of one of those small circles of educated men who sought to keep alive the spark of the antique literary tradition, he was for many years a teacher of grammar at the Palace School and acted as private tutor in grammar to Charles himself. Unlike Alcuin's, his interests were exclusively literary and secular, and his teaching seems to have been of a more advanced nature than Alcuin's. It is well known that there was an intense interest among a small circle in secular Latin literature and that members of the "Academy," including Charles himself, affected classical as well as Biblical names in their discussions. It was probably Peter of Pisa who first kindled this classical enthusiasm which ultimately produced the first-class scholarship of Servatus Lupus and, more immediately, inclined Einhard to model his Life of Charles the Great on Suetonius' Lives of the Caesars and such poets as Angilbert, Ermolaus and Modion to write poems loaded with classical reminiscences. In the early 790s Peter returned to his native land, but his influence continued to be felt even after his departure.

Another Italian whose talents Charles made use of was Paul the Deacon, who, although he spent no more than two years in Frankish territory, was one of the more important scholars and writers of the period. Paul was born of a noble Lombard family, received an excellent education from the grammarian Flavian at Pavia, and very likely served the Lombard court in some official capacity. Charles' conquest of the Lombard kingdom in 774 had a profound effect on his life. Forsaking the world, Paul took monastic vows and eventually entered the great cloister at Monte Cassino.

His writings cover a wide field, including grammar, poetry, hagiography, and theology. Even before his connection with Charlemagne, he was an author of some importance. He had made an abridgment of the encyclopedic De verborum significatu of Pompeius Festus, of great value since most of the original has been lost. He had undertaken an edition of Eutropius' Short History of Rome (Breviarium historiae Romanae), which he expanded by including material from Jerome, Orosius and others, and which he continued up to the reign of Justinian, using an impressive variety of sources. Shortly after becoming a monk, he wrote for his brethren a commentary on the Rule of St. Benedict, which became the basis for several later and fuller commentaries.

Soon after the Frankish conquest of Lombardy, Paul's brother was involved in an unsuccessful revolt against Frankish authority and was made prisoner. In 783 Paul received permission from his abbot to journey to Frankland to intercede with Charlemagne in behalf of his brother. Thus was established his connection with the main intellectual currents of his time. He was well received by Charles and his petition was probably granted. One of the finest poems of the Carolingian age was written by Paul at this time on his brother's misfortune and the sad plight of his wife and children, now reduced to begging their livelihood in the streets. This poem, which preceded its author to Gaul, assured Paul an eager welcome, and Charles, always anxious to increase his store of learned men, prevailed on him to prolong his stay. To this end, Peter of Pisa was charged to write a flattering poem praising Paul's virtues and learning and particularly his knowledge of Hebrew and Greek. Since Charles' daughter was shortly going to Constantinople to marry the emperor, would not Paul teach her and her retinue the Greek language? Paul replied somewhat acidly that if they arrived in Constantinople knowing only the Greek he could teach them, they would be laughed out of town. He had studied a little Greek long ago in school, he said, but had forgotten most of it. And he had never known any Hebrew.

At any rate he agreed to stay (perhaps because his brother had not yet been freed) and soon became a genuinely enthusiastic admirer of Charlemagne, for whom he had earlier had some rather harsh words. While Paul was in the north, he composed, at the request of bishop Angilram, a history of the bishops of Metz. But much more important was the homilary he compiled at the request of Charlemagne himself. The condition of the Frankish church and clergy, despite the efforts of Pippin and Charles, was still far from ideal. There was a shortage of appropriate homiliaries, and the text even of those was often corrupt. Nor did the priests know enough to employ them at the proper offices. To remedy this situation, Paul diligently searched the writings of the church Fathers and selected from them material suitable for sermons throughout the ecclesiastical year. He also took great care to provide a text free from corruptions. The use of this homilary was urged upon the Frankish clergy by the Epistola generalis (between 786 and 800); it was the basis for many later homilaries.

Throughout his life Paul wrote poetry of various kinds. In addition to the poem on his brother's misfortunes which we have already mentioned, he wrote several epitaphs, some mildly satirical poems on the craze among Charles' court scholars of exchanging riddles and letters in verse, although he himself obligingly furnished his share, two poems in praise of St. Benedict, and a beautiful and justly famous description of Lake Como in his homeland.[6] Aside from those on his brother and on Lake Como, his poems are not remarkable, although they are more correct than are Alcuin's. For these two, however, he must be ranked among the major Carolingian poets.

After less than two years, Paul returned to Monte Cassino where he remained until his death. During the last years of his life, he composed the work upon which his fame mainly rests, the Historia Langobardorum.[7] In it he traces the history of his own people from their beginnings to the death of King Liutprand in 744, apparently not caring to record their conquest by the Franks. Unlike the histories of Gregory of Tours and Bede, therefore, it was exclusively concerned with events preceding the memory of the author. Paul used the standard historical works available to an eighth century-writer -- Gregory of Tours, Isidore of Seville, Bede, and numerous Roman authors -- but the great value of the History derives from Paul's carefulness and judiciousness as a historian and from the wealth of sources he had access to. He used two earlier histories of the Lombards (the Origo gentis Langobardorum and the Chronicle of Secundus), and old list of Roman provinces, and oral traditions and legends of the Lombards, all of which are now known only through Paul. The style of the History is straightforward narrative, occasionally interspersed with effectively written dramatic episodes. Its greatest faults are its carelessness about chronology and its haphazard organization. Nevertheless it is a major historical work and quickly attained a great popularity, which it maintained throughout the Middle Ages.

A third Lombard who served Charles was the grammarian, theologian and poet, Paulinus, known to his colleagues of the court circle as Timotheus. After the Frankish conquest of the Lombard kindom, he became a teacher of grammar at the Palace School. Here he formed a very close friendship with Alcuin, who wrote numerous letters in prose and verse expressing his grief when Paulinus left the court in 787 to become Patriarch of Aquileia. In his new post, despite his close involvement in political and missionary affairs, Paulinus continued to write. Although he made some undistinguished theological compilations, his best works were his poems, all accentual rather than quantitative.

He was a poet of considerable originality, skill, and deep feeling. When in 799 Duke Eric of Fruili fell in battle against the Avars, Paulinus composed a beautiful rhythmic dirge lamenting the death of his friend and lay adjutant, ending with the plea: "Eternal God, who from the dust formed in your image our first parents through whom we all perish, but who sent your own beloved son through whom we all miraculously live, redeemed by his crimson blood and holy flesh, grant to your sweet servant Eric, I beg you, the joys of paradise both now and through the unmeasured ages to come." Paulinus may also be the author of an equally fine poem on the Apostles Peter and Paul, and he definitely wrote an excellent poem based on the gospel story of the raising of Lazarus. Although both Alcuin and Walafrid Strabo mention him as a composer of hymns, none of these survives. Paulinus is one of the best of the Carolingian poets. Despite his training in rhetoric, he avoided the typical poetic faults of the rhetorician; and despite his knowledge of grammar he never felt comfortable writing prose or quantitative poetry. His conscious decision to follow the tradition of the accentual poetry of Lombardy afforded him a greater degree of freedom from the heavy weight of the classical tradition and gave free reign to his undoubted originality. His excellent use of this freedom fully justified his choice.

Also ranking among the major figures of Charles' court was the great Visigothic scholar Theodulf. A versatile writer, well acquainted with the Latin classics, a superb poet and writer of hymns, an honest and fearless missus, an energetic adminstrator and educator in his see of Orleans, he was also a leading theologian of the period, and he shares with Alcuin the credit for having edited the text of the Vulgate (although, as we have already mentioned, Alcuin's edition was more widely used). He was perceptive enough to see through the sham learning of the many Irishmen who enlivened the court, and his annoyance at these charlatans involved him in the only personal controversy of his life. Most of his writing which survives is poetry, and nearly all of this is on a very high level. Not only was he adept at the technical aspects of poetry, and steeped in the classical poets, particularly Ovid, whom he could quote or paraphrase easily and naturally, but he had the true poet's ability to perceive beauty and significance in the world around him and communicate it aptly and originally. His poems range from descriptions of nature, through gentle satires and characterizations, to expressions of deep personal emotion, and a few hymns. One of these, the Palm Sunday hymn Gloria, laus et honor tibi rex, Christe, redemptor, was written by him near the end of his life, in the reign of Louis the Pious, when he had been deposed from his bishopric and cast into prison. Ironically, his most famous poem is one of his least impressive. It is a description of the seven Liberal Arts carved on a wooden table top, and its importance for art history has resulted in its popularity.

It now seems fairly certain that Theodulf was the principal author of "the principal source for the intellectual history of the early years of Charlemagne's reign," the famous Libri Carolini.[8] In 787 the Byzantine empress Irene had summoned the seventh ecumenical council of the church to meet at Nicaea, and at this council, which was attended by representatives of pope Hadrian, the heresy of Iconoclasm was officially condemned. The council decreed that the figures of the Holy Cross and the Savior, the Virgin Mary, the angels and the saints might be represented on vessels, garments, and walls, since these figures stimulated the spectator to think of the original; and while the image might not be accorded latreia, the type of worship to be given only to God, they were deserving of proskynesis, an expression of abject humility often involving prostration, which in the east was often accorded to emperors.

A very bad Latin translation of the acts of the council was made in Rome and forwarded to Charlemagne. His scholars then examined these acts and were horrified to find what they considered to be a sanction of idolatry. Both the bad translation and the western ignorance of Byzantine forms and forumlas were responsible for the misunderstanding. Charles' theologians then proceeded in language which was often abusive to answer the acts of the council point by point. This answer, known as the Libri Carolini, held that while images might be permitted in churches for the sake of decoration, no kind of worship or adoration should be accorded them, since this should be reserved to God alone. The Libri deny the authority of the seventh ecumenical council, denounce Irene as a usurper, censure pope Hadrian for sending representatives, and assert the "filioque" version of the Creed. The arguments, although sometimes citing the acts of earlier councils, rely heavily on scriptural quotations and show a distrust of the more fanciful interpretations, preferring rather the obvious literal meaning.

A work of this importance was obviously a joint effort of the leading theologians at Charles' court, but apparently the original draft was prepared by Theodulf and later altered to conform to the sense of the committee. If this is true, it would indicate that Theodulf ranked second only to Alcuin in Charles' esteem. Alcuin

was away in England during the years (790-793) that the _Libri
Carolini_ were composed, although he may have had a hand in their
final revision. Still in all probability Theodulf was their
principal author.

Theodulf was, all things considered, the greatest intellect, the
finest poet, and the best educated member of Charlemagne's court
circle, where he was known as Pindar. Second in renown to Alcuin
perhaps, he was nevertheless highly esteemed by Charles. He was
rewarded for his services with the see of Orleans and served as a
missus in the year 798. Early in the reign of Louis the Pious he
was suspected, probably incorrectly, of complicity in the unsuccessful rebellion of Louis' nephew Bernard, was deposed from his
bishopric and imprisoned in the monastery of St. Aubin. A few
months before his death in 821 he was pardoned and probably restored to his see.

Many other scholars served Charles during his long reign. They
became teachers in the schools, bishops of the cathedrals, and
abbots of the monasteries of his realm. They did invaluable
though unspectacular work in copying and editing classical and
patristic texts, preparing florilegia, writing Biblical commentaries and tracts against heresy, and all of them writing vast amount
of verse, very little of which can accurately be called poetry.
Many of these were Irishmen, some Germans, some Italians, and some
west Franks. By the time Charles died in 814, he had succeeded
both in broadening the educational base of his realm and in pointing the way to major cultural achievements.

NOTES

1. See Heinrich Fichtenau, The Carolingian Empire (Harper Torch-book 1142), 89.

2. See the Introduction to vols. IV, VI, and XII of CLA.

3. For a more detailed survey of the Carolingian period, see Laistner, Thought and Letters.

4. On Alcuin, see E. S. Duckett, Alcuin, Friend of Charlemagne (New York, 1951).

5. Thought and Letters, 201.

6. On these poems, see F. J. E. Raby, A History of Secular Latin Poetry in the Middle Ages (2 vols., 2nd ed., Oxford, 1957).

7. English translation by W. D. Foulke, Paul the Deacon, History of the Lombards (Philadelphia: University of Pennsylvania Press, 1974).

8. There has been much controversy over the authorship of the Libri Carolini. Liutpold Wallach claims Alcuin as the author: "The Unknown Author of the Libri Carolini," Didascaliae (New York, 1961), 471-511; Diplomatic Studies in Latin and Greek Documents from the Carolingian Age (Ithaca, New York, 1977). Ann Feeman has made a very strong case for Theodulf: "Theodulf of Orleans and the Libri Carolini," Speculum 32 (1957), 663-705; "Further Studies in the Libri Carolini," I and II, Speculum 40 (1965), 203-289; III, Speculum 46 (1971), 597-612. The issue has been definitively decided in Theodulf's favor by Paul Meyvaert, "The Authorship of the Libri Carolini," Revue Benedictine 89 (1979), 29-57.

Chapter 6

The Later Carolingian Age

Just as the intellectual revival had lagged about two generations behind the political restoration in western Europe, so it outlasted the political collapse by two generations, reaching its height at the very time that Europe seemed to be falling apart, a helpless prey to new bands of invaders, the Muslims, the Northmen and the Magyars. Even before Charles' death the troubles had begun, and they became more severe as the ninth century progressed. Civil war, the decay of royal power, and general lawlessness added to the miseries inflicted by the invaders. It is against this background that the scholars of the second and third generations of the Carolingian period worked.

The second generation of Carolingian scholars were those whose activity began during Charles' reign but who reached the height of their power and success during the days of Louis the Pious, and who had, for the most part, received their education at the Palace School or at the hands of one of the masters of that school. They include a large proportion of Germanic men, as well as a liberal sprinkling of Irishmen.

Closely connected with the court, well versed in the classical authors, and wielding considerable power during their lifetimes, were two laymen, both Franks, Einhard, and Angilbert. Einhard (ca. 770-840) received his early education at the great monastery at Fulda, whose library was already well-stocked with classical authors. He then studied at the Palace School under Alcuin. He was a favorite of Charlemagne's and became a member of the circle of learned men of the court. At this stage of his life, he was described in a poem of Theodulf "running to and fro like an ant, a great mind in a tiny body." Charles had sufficient confidence in him to send him as a special emmisary to the pope in 806, and to put him in charge of the construction of all royal buildings at Aachen. He was on close terms with the king's family and may have had an affair with one of Charles' daughters. He secured his position in the reign to come by being among the first, in 813, to suggest to Charles that he associate his son Louis with him as co-emperor. His star continued to rise under Louis the Pious, and despite the fact that he was a layman, he was given several abbeys. In 830, he became abbot of Seligenstadt and retired to this cloister for the last ten years of his life.

Three years before he became abbot of Seligenstadt, Einhard managed to have the remains of saints Marcellinus and Peter moved to that abbey and shortly thereafter wrote a detailed account of the occasion and of the miracles performed by the saints in their new home. The only other work which can confidently be ascribed to him is the _Life of Charles the Great_,[1] one of the finest examples of medieval biography and a generally acknowledged classic of European literature. One of the most notable aspects of the work is the classicism of its style. The most important influence on the Life was the Lives of the Caesars by Suetonius, from whom Einhard borrowed the general plan of his biography, his selection of incidents, his vocabulary, and sometimes whole phrases. He used the Life of Augustus as his primary model but drew material as necessary from the biographies of other emperors. Other influences, not so important but clearly evident, are Sulpicius Severus' Life of St. Martin and the works of the Roman historians Caesar, Livy, Tacitus, Florus, and Pompeius Trogus (in Justin's abridgement).

Although literary considerations dictated much of the form of the Life of Charles, it may nevertheless be considered a largely accurate account of the great emperor, somewhat over-zealous to praise him and to compare him to Augustus and suppressing several unflattering episodes of his life, but willing to criticize on occasion. There was a sufficiently large store of descriptions in Suetonius' work that Einhard could pick and choose what was appropriate. The least reliable part of the Life is the early life of Charles, which Einhard was not in a position to know with any degree of accuracy; and the account of the imperial coronation, which has thrown a cloud of obscurity over that epoch-making event to this day. All in all, however, it is one of the most satisfactory biographies of a major figure in our literature.

Einhard probably first imbibed his pure Latin style and his love for the classics at Fulda. While he was a student of Alcuin this bent was probably given slight encouragement, but there was at the Palace School a group of scholars who sedulously cultivated classical letters. Theodulf of Orleans was an excellent classicist and, unlike Alcuin in his later years, was never troubled by their incompatibility with Christianity. However, Theodulf's influence as a teacher is problematical, and this classicism may probably be traced back to the old Lombard grammarian, Peter of Pisa, even though he had undoubtedly left the school before Einhard's arrival.

Einhard's contemporary, Angilbert, a Frank of noble birth, is probably an ideal example of what Charles hopes to accomplish on a large scale. Suited by birth, character and ability to be an administrator and man of affairs, he was educated at the Palace School under Alcuin. He later took his place among the privileged group of court scholars and among this intellectual elite was known as Homer. Like Einhard, he was an ardent student of classical literature. He was also an ardent lover of Charlemagne's daughter Berta, by whom he had two sons, one of whom was Nithard, the outstanding historian of the next generation. Although he was a layman, he was made abbot of St. Riquier and distinguished himself by the excellence of his administration. He also held the

position of Primicerius Palatii to Charles' son Pippin of Italy
and was sent on several important missions to Rome. His two major
surviving poems, one in elegiac verse to his lord Pippin, the
other an eclogue addressed to Charlemagne (David), reveal their
author as a brave but tender man, treasuring his welcome home by
Berta and his two sons, an intimate of the royal family, and a
very skillful poet in his expert handling of several of the more
delicate and subtle of classical verse forms.

Another member of the court circle of this generation was Modoin,
who was highly regarded as a poet in his own day and was known as
Naso (Ovid) at court. Only two of his poems have survived and
from them it is difficult to form a just estimate. One of these
poems is a consolation to Modoin's friend, Theodulf, on his unjust
imprisonment, enumerating all the people, Christian and pagan, he
could think of who had similarly suffered unjustly and suggesting
that despite his innocence, Theodulf confess and throw himself on
"Caesar's" mercy. The verses are quite competently constructed
but the content is commonplace. A more interesting poem is one
which Modoin wrote shortly after the imperial coronation of 800
A.D. It is in the form of an eclogue, or pastoral dialogue, and
skillfully compares the age of Augustus with the age of Charlemagne. He is here clearly playing the part of Virgil, who sang
the praises of the old Empire as Modoin sings the new. The hint
was not lost on Charles. This poem is more impressive than the
later one to Theodulf. It is truly a virtuoso performance, handling expertly the subtleties of versification and sentiment and
showing an intimate acquaintance with the classical poets Virgil
and Calpurnius and particularly with Modoin's namesake Ovid.

A much more typical figure of the Carolingian movement was Rabanus
Maurus (780-856), who became abbot of Fulda in 822. A favorite
pupil of Alcuin at Tours after having received his early instruction at Fulda, Rabanus was the dominating figure of the second
generation of Carolingian scholars. Under his abbacy the school
at Fulda achieved a position of preeminence in Europe, and it was
to Fulda rather than to Aachen or Tours that the brightest young
men journeyed to complete their education. Rabanus embodies the
typical and dominant, if not the highest, characteristics of the
Carolingian movement. Pious without being profound, he devoted
most of his vast energies to ecclesiastical concerns. None of his
numerous writings displays the slightest trace of originality. He
was a compiler, excerpter, rearranger, yet his reputation for
erudition was justifiably enormous. Unlike others of his contemporaries, he showed no interest in classical literature for its
own sake, but solely as an indispensable aid to theological
studies. Still his attitude toward the Liberal Arts was not
narrow or fearful, and he went to some lengths to defend their use
in Christian education in his treatise on the education of the
clergy.

He shared with most of his educated contemporaries a penchant for writing verse, most of it of slight value, although it enjoyed some fame in his lifetime. His verse, like his other writings, was for the most part borrowed from others -- from the Latin classics, the Christian poets, the Irish. His poems reveal a man who is stern, austere and pious, with little of the capacity for warm human relationships that characterized both his master Alcuin and his pupil Walafrid. He wrote both in the classical meters and in the rhythmical poetry which was becoming more popular. One of his more important models for the latter was the Altus prosator of the Irishman Columba, and from the Irish tradition Rabanus also appropriated the extensive use of rhyme and assonance.

A considerable amount of his time between 822 and 842, when he was abbot of Fulda, was taken up in administration and teaching. Still he found time to do much writing and was one of the most prolific Biblical commentators of the ninth century. But he was one of the least original men in an age noted for its lack of originality. His commentaries contain very little of his own, being based mainly on his predecessors -- Ambrose, Jerome, Gregory, Augustine, Isidore and Bede for the most part, although he occasionally borrowed material from other writers, even from heretics and pagans when it served his purpose. Still his reading was extensive, and his commentaries undoubtedly supplied a real need in his day. Many of the works of Jerome or Augustine were too difficult for the average Carolingian theological student, and many of the more suitable commentaries, such as those of Bede, were not readily accessible or did not correspond to the tastes and interest of the ninth century. Unbendingly orthodox, more than a little ponderous, severly suspicious of originality or individuality, Rabanus was nevertheless the most respected Biblical scholar of his day.

He also wrote a widely read work on the education of the clergy (De institutione clericorum), a field in which he clearly excelled. Yet despite his own extensive first-hand experience with the subject, he drew most of his treatise from the works of earlier writiers. The comprehensiveness of its treatment and its organization, however, are Rabanus' own. It is a thorough and authoritative treatise on the ecclesiastical life, ranging from descriptions of the proper vestments, offices, principal feast days, each of the sacraments and divisions of the liturgy, to an outline of the education of the various classes of the clergy, to which is added a short account of each of the Liberal Arts. The most important work in the history of education since Cassiodorus, it is an impressively erudite performance and was widely used throughout the earlier Middle Ages.

In 842 Rabanus resigned the abbacy of Fulda in order to be able to devote himself uninterruptedly to the composition of his great work, De rerum natura (sometimes erroneously called De universo), upon which, along with the De institutione clericorum, rests his title Praeceptor Germaniae, the instructor of Germany. By far his most important source for this work was Isidore's Etymologies. He rearranged the material he found in Isidore, thus providing a much easier book to use. His purpose, however, was not merely to edit the Etymologies, but to provide for Christendom a literal and mystical account of the universe. Even in this latter enterprise, he borrowed his mystical interpretations from previous writers, particularly Jerome and Bede.

In 847 Louis the German prevailed on Rabanus, against his inclinations, to become archbishop of Mainz. Although as abbot of Fulda, Rabanus had sedulously avoided political involvements, such isolation was impossible in his new position. It was during this period that his quarrel with his former pupil Gottschalk came to a head, and throughout this affair, which we shall discuss in connection with Gottschalk, Rabanus appears in a most unfavorable light. His long and fruitful life came to an end in 856 in the midst of bitterness and controversy.

Rabanus' lifetime extended into every generation of the Carolingian period. Many scholars twenty years or more younger than he died before or shortly after he did, and it is to these men that we now turn our attention.

Two of Rabanus' most illustrious pupils were Walafrid Strabo (809-849) and Gottschalk the Saxon (805-869), both oblates from humble families, close friends and schoolmates, both poets of considerable ability, but utterly unlike in temperament and fortune. Walafrid was given by his parents to the monks at Reichenau, and here he was brought up happy and good-natured, studying under four excellent teachers whom he dearly loved, and showing early a great aptitude for learning and for composing verse. When he was about fifteen he had composed a versified account of the life of Mamme, a Cappodocian martyr, and at eighteen had written a long poem recounting the vision which his teacher Wettin had had as he lay dying, a vision of hell and its torments, of purgatory, and of the blessed in paradise. Walafrid loved the beauties of this world, he loved people, he loved literature and knew the classics well, but he was also a sincerely religious young man. So outstanding were his gifts that he was sent to Fulda in 827 to continue his education in theology under the great Rabanus. He continued to excel under Rabanus' care, and he made many friends, of whom one of the closest was the morose and rebellious Saxon boy, Gottschalk, with whom he continued to correspond even after Gottschalk had become seriously involved in controversy.

Apparently without his seeking it, good fortune came to Walafrid when in 829 he was summoned to the imperial court to act as tutor to the young prince Charles, the future emperor Charles the Bald.

His nine years at court seem to have been spent pleasantly. He found an appreciative patron in the empress Judith, whom he addressed as Augusta, and for her he wrote numerous delightful if not distinguished occasional verses. One of these is in the form of a dialogue between the poet and his scintilla, occasioned by the huge equestrian statue of Theoderic which Charlemagne had brought to Aachen from Ravenna. This gives him an opportunity to declaim on a variety of subjects -- the poet's need for solitude, the cruelty of the heretic king Theoderic, and by contrast the virtues of the emperor Louis and his admirable family. In this long poem, Walafrid has recourse to the entire armory of antique rhetoric and shows himself a master of these devices -- the standard topoi, the catalogue, the poet's incapacity for so exhalted a task, the unrestrainted praise of the ruler, comparison with the great figures of classical and Biblical antiquity.

When the young prince's education was completed in 838, Walafrid was rewarded by being made abbot of Reichenau, the monastery where he had spent his youth. Two years later, Louis the Pious died and during the civil war which followed, Walafrid was deprived of his abbacy, but it was restored to him in 842, and he lived the remaining seven years of his life there, writing and teaching.

Of Walafrid's other principal works, perhaps the best is his De cultura hortorum, a delightful poem on the garden at Reichenau. It is generally agreed that this is among the small group of truly fine poems produced during the Carolingian period. Although Walafrid was saturated with the poetry of Virgil and the works of Columella and pseudo-Apuleius, and his poem is full of classical allusions and reminiscences, it is nevertheless an original poetic creation, full of love for the beauties of nature, of spontaneous and sincere delight in his own little garden at Reichenau. In the introduction he describes the preparation of the soil for planting, the sowing and careful tending of the seeds, which he waters by hand in order not to injure the tender sprouts, and how nevertheless the rain destroyed some of the less hardy. Then he describes one by one the twenty-three plants in the garden, including sage, rue, horehound, pumpkin, gladiola, and "ambrosia," which, however, he doubts is the same as the food of the gods. He follows the same formula for each plant, first describing it, then pointing out its medicinal or culinary uses, adorning his description with allusions to religious symbolism, such as the rose (the blood of martyrs on earth) or the lily (the reward of the saints in heaven), or to classical mythology. The poem ends with a dedication to his former teacher, Grimald, whom he pictures reading the poem as he sits in the orchard, while his young pupils engage in sport and pick the ripe fruit for their master.[2]

Walafrid wrote many other poems, though none the equal of the De cultura hortorum. Throughout his life he wrote letters in verse, to his school friends (especially Gottschalk), to the members of the imperial family, to the great men of his day, and to his own pupils. They are of a higher quality than is usual in this sort of composition, and they reveal the gentle, lovable nature of their author and his capacity for warm friendships, as well as a poet of great sensitivity and technical proficiency. He also, with less success, tried his hand at hymn-writing, although his hymn on the martyrs of Agaunum (St. Maurice), De Agaunensibus martyribus, modelled on Prudentius' Peristephanon, stands far above the rest.

Walafrid also wrote in prose, but not much of this remains. Of the commentaries on the early books of the Old Testament, only the introductions to his commentaries on Exodus and Leviticus are still extant. The most important and interesting of his prose works is a treatise on liturgical usage, De exordiis et incrementis quarundam in observationibus ecclesiasticis rerum which, in addition to being an important study of the Latin liturgy, also shows Walafrid's interest in the Greek liturgy and the Greek language. He is one of a small number of Carolingian scholars who possessed at least a knowledge of the rudiments of Greek syntax and the meanings of some words , and phrases, although it could hardly be said that he knew the language well.

Walafrid is probably the most likeable person of the later Carolingian period, and he was its most successful poet in classical meters, employing with great skill a larger variety of difficult meters than any poet since Boethius. He was also widely known and respected as a man of God, and his supposed authorship of the Glossa ordinaria (which he did not write)[3] was the basis for his fame in the succeeding period. In an age of brutality, invasion, civil war, and fierce personal hostilities, Walafrid pursued his peaceful course and, aside from his troubles from 840-842, remained untouched by the violence which surrounded him. He managed to hold the friendship of men who were bitter enemies, and although he continued to write poetic letters of warm friendship to Gottschalk, his epitaph was written by Rabanus Maurus.

Some people are miserable because of bad fortune. A few seem destined for a life of sorrows and will even give fortune a helping hand by creating their own troubles. Gottschalk the Saxon was of this latter select group. Given by his parents to the monks of Fulda, Gottschalk grew up rebellious, miserable and restless. When he reached the age when he was to repeat for himself the vows his parents had earlier taken in his behalf, he refused and tried to be released from his monastic profession. His abbot, Rabanus Maurus, took an inexplicably severe course, used more than ordinary means to induce Gottschalk to repeat the vows, and when the boy sought release, the abbot seems to have taken it as a personal affront. For the rest of his life Rabanus pursued and persecuted Gottschalk with a persistence and intensity equalled only by St. Bernard's later persecution of Abelard. In 829, the synod of

Mainz released Gottschalk from his vows. Rabanus appealed all the way to the emperor to have the decision reversed, but Gottschalk won a partial victory in being transferred from Fulda first to Corbie, then, with or without permission, to Orbais. Not content, Gottschalk made things easier for his enemies by leaving his monastery, writing theological treatises which taught the doctrine of double predestination, receiving ordination from a suffragan rather than from the bishop of the diocese, and wandering about to preach his dangerous doctrines through Pannonia and Italy. In 848, whether through arrogance or compulsion, he appeared at the synod of Mainz to defend his views. His former teacher and now persecutor, Rabanus, was now archbishop of Mainz, and the synod condemned Gottschalk as a heretic, ordering him to be placed in the custody of archbishop Hincmar of Reims. The following year he was inexplicably tried and condemned again, severely beaten, deprived of his orders, and imprisoned at the monastery of Hautvillers. Here he continued to write and teach and to correspond with his friends for about a year, when again unaccountably the conditions of his confinement were made much more severe. He was deprived of his books and writing materials and perhaps condemned to perpetual silence. In this pitiful condition he lived on until about 870. As he lay dying he asked for the sacrament, but it was refused to him unless he subscribe to a confession of faith drawn up by his old jailor Hincmar of Reims. Gottschalk remained true to himself, refused the confession and so died without the final rites of the church.

Gottschalk is one of the earliest examples of a type, utterly foreign to the spirit and attitudes of the Carolingian period, of the original, bold and creative individualist in which the Middle Ages would be so rich. Although he derived his theological ideas from Augustine, he himself said that he had no leader in this affair. And although rhyming rhythmical poetry was hardly a novelty in the ninth century, Gottschalk's poems are as bold and innovative as they are passionate and sincere. Neither his rhymes nor his rhythms are pure, but he used them so effectively and filled them with such intensely felt poetry that one is happy to overlook a certain technical roughness. A man of troubles, deeply religious as are most heretics, he devised one poem of such beauty and originality that it deserves quotation, at least in part. Its stanzaic structure is original, as is the persistent use of the two syllable rhyme. And it stands two tests of great poetry; the beauty and pathos of the sound and rhythm are evident even to one who does not understand Latin; and the content retains its merit even in an uninspired prose translation.

1. ut quid iubes, pusiole,
   quare mandas, filiole,
     carmen dulce me cantare,
     cum sim longe exsul valde
       intra mare?

1. (Why do you bid me, little lad, me an exile far beyond the sea, to sing a sweet song? Oh, why do you bid me to sing?)

o cur iubes canere?

2. magis mihi, miserule,
   flere libet, puerule,
     plus plorare quam cantare
     carmen tale, iubes quale,
       amor care,
     o cur iubes canere?

2. (It is more fitting little
   sinner, for me to weep, dear
   heart, to wail rather a song
   of woe than the sweet song
   you ask. Oh, why do you bid
   me to sing?)

5. scias, captivae plebeculae
   Israeli cognomine
     praeceptum in Babylone
     decantare extra longe
       fines Iudae.
     o cur iubes canere?

5. (You know how the captive boy
   named Israel, in Babylon,
   could not sing since he was
   far from home. Oh, why do
   you bid me to sing?)

10. . . .
     interim cum, pusiole,
     psallam ore, psallam mente,
     psallam die, psallam nocte,
       carmen dulce.
     tibi, rex piissime.

10. (. . . Meanwhile, with my
    little lad, I'll chant with
    my mouth, chant with my mind,
    chant by day and chant by
    night, a sweet song to thee,
    most holy king.)

Another brief example will illustrate the power of his poetry better than any description:

Christe, mearum
lux tenebrarum. . .
respice nunc me,
da, sequar ut te:
iam miserere
iamque medere,
et tibi fac me
iamque placere.

(Christ, light of my darkness,
look on me now, give me strength
to follow You. Pity me and heal
me now. And make me pleasing to
Thyself.)

Although the most vigorous and extensive intellectual work seems to have been carried on in the eastern part of Europe during the ninth century, the west Franks produced the finest classical scholar of the Carolingian epoch. This was Servatus Lupus. Born about 810, he was educated at the monastery of Ferrières, of which Alcuin had once been abbot, and on whose schools the great Englishman seems to have made a lasting impression. This was not a rich abbey. There were not many books in the library, and the teachers, though devoted, were not the best. Still Lupus made optimum use of what educational facilities existed there, and when he had exhausted them he was sent by his abbot to Fulda to continue his studies under Rabanus. He made friends of great scholars throughout Europe and carried on a voluminous correspondence with them, one hundred twenty-seven letters of which are still extant. In 842 he became abbot of Ferrières, which made great progress under his rule despite the chronic civil war and Viking raids which were devastating much of Europe. Lupus was unable to pursue a sheltered scholar's life, but took an active part in the political and military affairs of his king, Charles the Bald.

Although Lupus was a devoted and conscientious churchman and took a decent, if not passionate, interest in theology, on which he wrote at least one excellent work, his real love was classical literature. As a young man, he had written in a letter to Einhard that "wisdom ought to be sought for its own sake." Throughout his life he continued to pursue classical studies, and when he became abbot of Ferrières he devoted vast amounts of time, energy and money to building the classical holdings of his library. Not only did he borrow or copy, sometimes with his own hand, books which his library lacked, but he often procured two or more copies of the same work, so that he could improve the text through comparison and conjectual emendation. As a text critic, he was superior to any of his near contemporaries, and there still exist about fourteen manuscripts which Lupus either wrote himself or annotated, calling attention to omissions or additions, listing alternate readings, and indicating suspect readings which he was not yet able to correct.[4] His classical studies were not without their effect on his own Latin style. Not only as a scholar, but also as a stylist, he was superior to all other Carolingian writers, in fact the first pure prose stylist since Bede. Lupus was also an able teacher, and one of the most important lines of continuity between Carolingian classicism and that of the tenth century runs from Lupus through his pupils.

Since the time of Columbanus, the Irish migration to the continent had continued. From the end of the eighth century, however, it increased significantly as the raids of the Vikings began spreading ruin throughout the Emerald Isle. These Irish scholars, from the beginning, had played a significant part in the Carolingian intellectual movement. There were two unnamed Irishmen who told Charles they had wisdom for sale, the unnamed Hibernicus Exsul, at least two Irishment named Clement, three or perhaps four named Dungal, also Dicuil, the geographer, as well as the unnamed antagonist of Theodulf, and probably many more who, instead of seeking their fortunes at court, sought shelter at one of the numerous Irish monasteries on the continent. None of the above-named Irishmen produced anything of outstanding importance, but in the mid-ninth century, two Irish scholars achieved genuine preeminence.

The lesser of these was a refugee named Sedulius, who appeared one stormy night in the winter of 848 at the door of the palace of the bishop of Liège. He immediately charmed the bishop, as he did most men who knew him, and since he was also a better than average scholar, he became the scholasticus of the bishop's school. Here he taught, studied and wrote for the next ten years, when in 858 he vanished without a trace, possibly a victim of a Viking raid on

Liège. Sedulius was widely read in classical and patristic literature, but his inclination was clearly toward the Latin classics, of which he probably had a more extensive knowledge than any Carolingian scholar except perhaps Lupus. He was not in any way profound. His classical scholarship was largely confined to making collections of extracts from the Roman authors, primarily striking phrases which, taken out of context, might serve to adorn one's own work or provide pertinent comments on a variety of topics. He also knew some Greek, and a still-extant Greek psalter bears the inscription, "I, Sedulius Scotus, wrote it." It is doubtful, however, that his knowledge of this language was more than elementary. He composed two advanced grammatical works, commentaries on the grammars of Eutyches and Priscian, which necessitated at least some knowledge of Greek.

In addition to these literary and linguistic studies, Sedulius composed a Liber de rectoribus Christianis, one of the earliest examples of the Mirrors for Princes of which the Middle Ages would produce so many. Written ostensibly as a guide to the sons of king Lothar, its content is undistinguished and unoriginal, but its style is that of a true virtuoso, combining prose and verse in the manner of Martianus Capella and Boethius.

It was his poetry, however, which won for Sedulius fame in his own day and a high reputation today. He was unusually skillful in handling the more difficult classical meters, and wrote only one accentual poem. Although he seems to have taken his poetic gifts quite seriously, most of his verses were occasional pieces, designed to gain their author employment, wine, and the favor of the great. Like Fortunatus, he could fashion a good poem on short notice, always just right for the situation. He wrote a poem of the most extravagant praise to Hartgar, the bishop of Liège, numerous requests for better food and drink, a poetic dispute between the rose and the lily, a fierce song of praise and thanks for the bishop Franco's defeat of the Vikings, several hymns, and numerous other poems.[5]

Perhaps the outstanding figure of the late Carolingian period was another Irishman, John, usually referred to as Scotus Eriugena. The only Carolingian scholar with a real knowledge of Greek, the first philosopher since Boethius, a theologian of great subtlety, a commentator on Martianus Capella and Boethius, but a rather poor poet, John was an arrogant and overbearing person, quick to take offense, and not afraid to exchange good natured insults with Charles the Bald. He took part in the theological controversies of his day, and died probably about 877.

In about 860, Charles the Bald commissioned John to prepare a new translation of the works of pseudo-Dionysius the Areopagite. These works were allegedly written by St. Paul's first Athenian convert, Dionysius (cf. Acts 17:34), but they were actually composed much later, ca. 500 A.D., by a Syrian Christian. Strongly influenced by the Neoplatonist writers, particularly Proclus (410-485), they first appeared in the West during the reign of Pippin the Short, but remained untranslated. Another copy was obtained in 827 as a gift to Louis the Pious from the Byzantine emperor, and a very bad Latin translation was made about 835 under the direction of Hilduin, abbot of St. Denis (=Dionysius) in Paris, who successfully, if falsely, identified the Areopagite with the founder of his own monastery. What John undertook then was a revision of the earlier translation, and he did quite a competent job. There are many errors in his translation, some caused by misunderstandings of the Greek text, which was written in uncials without word division, others caused by errors in the Greek manuscript itself. John's translations were literal in the extreme, even to translating the article. He did great violence to Latin idiom and construction, sometimes merely replacing Greek words with Latin ones. Still, for the most part, his translation is intelligible. He accompanied these translations with commentaries in which he explained the more difficult passages, justified his own translation, and shows that he had a firmer grasp of their meaning and of the Greek language than one might deduce on the evidence of the translations alone. He also translated several works of the Greek fathers: the De opificio hominis of Gregory of Nyssa, and Maximus Confessor's Ambigua.

John's current reputation rests on his great philosophical work, De divisione naturae,[6] a subtle and difficult work whose meaning is still a matter of some dispute. Part of the reason for its ambiguity is the unusual meanings John gives certain key words, such as nature, God, being, creature, knowledge, etc. His mind was brilliant, bold and original, and he made more extensive and daring use of Neoplatonic concepts than any of the Latin fathers. While he follows Augustine in placing faith before reason and equating true philosophy with Christianity, his approach is wholly rational, and many parts of his system fit with difficulty into Christian teaching. In making his famous statement that "no one enters heaven except through philosophy," he was, it is true, asserting the preeminent truth of Christianity, but he was also making a somewhat extravagant claim for philosophy.

The starting point of his Division of Nature is the utter unity and infinity of God. This is the first division of nature, uncreated and creating, unkowable even to Himself because He transcends every intelligible limit through which alone knowledge is possible. He is above being, above goodness, above knowledge. Creation takes place because of God's desire to know Himself, and it proceeds according to the laws of analysis and division from the most general, through intermediate stages of descending generality, until it finally reaches individuals. First are created in the Son or Logos, the Divine Ideas -- Goodness, Being, Life, Reason, Intelligence, Wisdom, Virtue, Blessedness, Truth, etc. --

the second division of nature, which is created and creates. These ideas are not God, but are the first created things, the archetypes and causes of all the things that exist. Man, in his true nature, is one of these, "an intellectual notion produced eternally in the Divine Mind." In Man is contained the entire universe of nature, and so when Man sinned and was consequently distributed into many temporal individuals, the universe too was scattered through time and space. This condition of spatial and temporal extension, subject to generation and corruption, is the third division of nature, that which is created and does not create. But every individual thing aspires to return to its source. In Man, this return begins with his death. His body will return to its simple being in Man, and thus all things (except the souls of the damned) will reside at last in their origin, the fourth division of nature, which is uncreated and does not create.

Of the end of John's life little is known. According to a legend, he returned to Britain after the death of Charles the Bald and was there murdered by his students.

By the year 880, the political dissolution of the Carolingian state was virtually complete, and the raids of the invaders made any kind of intellectual life extremely difficult. The creative phase of the revival begun by Charlemagne was over and the line of unbroken progress comes to an end. But the Carolingian scholars had done their work well. Europe did not lapse back into barbarism and illiteracy. The gains of the preceding century were maintained and the educational base of Europe was significantly broadened. Europeans met the challenges of the tenth century in an aggressive and creative way. The critical period had been successfully passed.

The Carolingian revival has been variously assessed as a brilliant "renaissance" and as a crude and unoriginal era of near barbarism. Although we have attempted some degree of evaluation in the preceding narrative, it might be worthwhile to assess the nature and value of the period as a whole.

Grammar. Under this head we consider literary studies in general. They were, of course, basic to the entire intellectual revival. Alcuin's textbooks, as we have noted, were quite elementary and contained much misinformation. Not nearly so much is known about the teaching of the other members of the Palace School, and we assume, perhaps on insufficient evidence, that it was of a higher order. At any rate, the level of performance becomes steadily higher until the mid-ninth century. Rabanus, Einhard, and Angilbert are superior to Alcuin in the extent and accuracy of their grammatical knowledge and Walafrid, Lupus of Ferrières, Sedulius Scotus and John Scotus Eriugena are thoroughly skilled grammarians.

The last four men were all, to a greater or lesser degree, students of the Greek language. Some knowledge of that tongue had been kept alive in the West by the Italians and by the Irish. There were many Greek-speaking communities in Italy; contacts with Constantinople on the governmental and commercial levels were frequent; numerous refugees from the East had come to Italy for religious reasons; and there were also frequent embassies between the Frankish court and Constantinople. From the testimony of Paul the Deacon it would seem that the schools, too, continued to teach the language, albeit on an elementary level. But it is very difficult to identify any Italian who possessed a literary knowledge of Greek, although many must have spoken enough to get along in Constantinople. The only definite exception is the papal librarian Athanasius, a contemporary of Erigena who insulted the Irishman's translations but whose own acquaintance with the Greek language seems to have been less than intimate.

The Irish had exhibited an interest in Greek studies from the sixth century, and they persisted in this interest through the Carolingian period. Evidence concerning the success of their efforts in inconclusive. There are several bilingual Psalters, some word lists, and frequent Greek words in the extant writings of Irishmen. There is nothing, however, to prove that they could actually read Greek.

Slightly more is known about the Irish foundations on the continent. In several of these, and particularly at St. Gall, at least the elements of the language were studied, so that a fair number of Carolingian scholars knew the meanings of many Greek words and phrases and may have known a little about Greek syntax. Hilduin was able, after all, to manage some sort of a translation of the works of pseudo-Dionysius with the help of several of the monks at St. Denis, in Paris, the city where Eriugena studied and taught for some time after coming to the continent.

Still the only Carolingian scholar who demonstrably had a genuine reading knowledge of Greek was Eriugena himself. Seen in the cultural context of the mid-ninth century, he is no longer an inexplicable anomaly, nor is it necessary to posit flourishing, if otherwise unknown, centers of Greek studies in Ireland to account for him. The difference between Hilduin and Eriugena is not so great but that it can be explained by assuming merely that John was an unusually gifted language student. The facilities for such a person to learn Greek were clearly in existence on the continent.

It is unfortunate for the reputation of Carolingian poetry that so much of it survives and has found its way into print. Versification was a fad during this time, and many men scribbled poems who in other ages would have held their hands. But in spite of this disability, the poetry of the time comes off rather well. The rules of classical versification and the works of certain classical and Christian poets were extensively and intensively studied. Many Carolingian poets could handle the simpler classical meters, and at least three, Theodulf, Walfrid, and Sedulius, displayed considerable competence in a variety of the more difficult meters. This was also a creative period, and accentual poetry using rhymes and assonance was brought to a high level of excellence in the ninth century. In addition to providing men of technical competence, the Carolingian age can also boast several poets of genuine merit. Theodulf, Paul the Deacon, Paulinus, Angilbert, Walafrid, Sedulius, and Gottschalk, although they do not rank with Virgil, Dante, Milton, or perhaps even Petrarch, are nevertheless excellent poets whose works would stand high in any age.

Although classicism did not dominate the Carolingian period, it was nevertheless a powerful influence. Classicial poetry and prose works provided models of both form and style. The Latin scholiasts were studied, great numbers of classical works were copied, florilegia were complied, and texts were improved. The Carolingian period is of crucial importance in the history of classical scholarship.

Philosophy. The Carolingian was not a reflective or philosophical age. Alcuin's ventures into "dialectic" show a greater than usual ineptitude. However, a general increase in knowledge, improvement of teaching, and growing awareness of abstract probelms -- in short a major improvement in the intellectual climate -- while they did not for two generations produce any works of formal philosophy, at least made men aware of what philosophy was. Again Eriugena stands alone in his accomplishment but comprehensible in his milieu. Because of his knowledge of Greek, he was able to read works containing a much stronger dose of Platonism than was to be found in any of the Latin Fathers. His thought was powerfully influenced by these Greek works, but his own brilliance and individuality made it possible for him to create a genuinely original philosophical synthesis, though of course he was working within an established tradition. He seems, however, to have struck no responsive chord, and the influence of the De divisione naturae between the ninth and thirteenth centuries is still to be traced.

Theology. Theology, in the sense of rigorous thought concerning the problems presented to man by the data of revelation, had all but ceased to exist in the West between the sixth and eighth centuries. Tracts were written against heresies, and Biblical commentaries were composed, but these were for the most part a rehashing of patristic thought. It was during the Carolingian age that new problems arose for the first time since Antiquity, and western theologians were forced to devise new solutions since there were no old ones at hand. The major theological problems of the eighth century were Adoptionism, the dispute over the procession of the Holy Spirit, and iconoclasm, and all three evoked spirited debate. Adoptionism was a rather crude revival of the Nestorian position, originated apparently by Elipandus of Spain, holding that Christ was the Son of God by adoption, not by nature. The dispute over the procession of the Holy Spirit involved the insertion of the words "and from the Son" (filioque) into the Creed. The western church, by and large, favored the insertion, the eastern church opposed it. By far the most difficult problem faced by the eighth century theologians was the use of icons in worship, and the western response, the Libri Carolini, was a noteworthy attempt to grapple with the difficult questions involved in the dispute.

During the ninth century, two disputes of major importance arose: the questions of double predestination and the miracle of transubstantiation. The first of these derived from the writings of Gottschalk, who, apparently while he was at Orbais, became convinced, on the basis of Augustine's writings, that God had decreed irrevocably that some men should be saved and the rest damned. He emphasized man's sinful nature, the absolute necessity of grace for salvation, and man's impotence to save himself. God predestines only the good, but this is of two kinds: justice, by which the damned are punished; and mercy, by which a few are undeservedly saved. Christ died only for the saved, and nothing will help the damned. Despite being persecuted by Rabanus and Hincmar, he preached this doctrine with considerable success throughout Europe until he was silenced by the Synod of Mainz in 848. Nor was he without supporters among the intelligentsia. Prudentius of Troyes, Amolo and Florus of Lyons, Remigius, Ratramnus and Servatus Lupus all wrote treatises according closely with Gottschalk's position. But the consensus was against him, and personal animosity exacerbated the dispute. Even Eriugena entered the battle and wrote a fierce and subtle refutation of Gottschalk's views, holding that since God is absolutely simple, it makes no sense to speak of double predestination, or indeed or predestination, since God is not involved in time.

The belief in transubstantiation had been general in the West for several centuries, but the doctrine had never been explictly formulated and indeed would not be until 1215. Nor was it held by all theologians. Rabanus in particular does not seem to have believed in a physical change in the bread and wine. The question did not issue in a dispute, however, until in the 860s two monks of Corbie, Ratramnus and Radbert, each wrote treatises on the subject (De corpore et sanguine Domini) and came to quite different conclusions. Radbert argued that both in the sacrifice of the mass and in the eucharist, the bread and wine are miraculously changed into the actual physical body and blood of the Lord, although the change is perceived by faith and not by sense. Ratramnus, on the other hand, held that the bread and wine of the eucharist were symbolic of the mortal body of the Lord and that the communicant partook of the spiritual body of Christ through an act of faith. These two books caused a brief flurry of excitement but led to no clearcut definition. Majority opinion continued on the side of Radbert, and the question continued to trouble European theologians until it was finally settled by the Fourth Lateran Council in 1215.

The Carolingian epoch was also rich in theologians of a less daring and original temperament. Alcuin, Theodulf, and Paulinus of the first generation were extremely well-read in the Bible, the fathers, the canons and conciliar decrees, and liturgical works. In the second generation, Rabanus appeared as a veritable paragon of theological knowledge, and by the second quarter of the ninth century, Latin Europe contained scores of thoroughly trained theologians.

Conclusion. One could prolong an investigation of the Carolingian period almost at will. There remain many important men and many departments of knowledge about which we have said little or nothing, either because they have not been sufficiently studied to date or because other men and movements seemed more deserving of mention. The progress made by western European intellectuals in the short space of about a century is most impressive, and a comparison of the end of this period with the beginning strengthens our admiration. The movement received contributions from every part of Europe and intelligent support from the Carolingian rulers. It was conservative and practical in attitude, but produced original thinkers and impractical intellectuals in spite of itself. It not only rescued western Europe from illiteracy and preserved the literary tradition, both classical and Christian, of Antiquity, but it reconstituted that tradition in such a way as to allow it to be a fructifying influence on European intellectual developments rather than a dead weight preventing thought and growth.

NOTES

1. English translation in S. E. Turner, tr., <u>The Life of Charle-magne by Einhard</u> (Ann Arbor Paperback 35, 1960) and <u>Two Lives of Charlemagne</u>, tr. Lewis Thorpe (Penguin L213, 1969).

2. See Raby, <u>Secular Latin Poetry</u>, I, 233-34.

3. On the question of Walafrid's contribution to the Gloss, see Beryl Smalley, <u>The Study of the Bible in the Middle Ages</u> (Oxford, 1952), 56-60.

4. See C. H. Beeson, <u>Servatus Lupus as Scribe and Text Critic</u> (Cambridge, Massachusetts, 1930).

5. For translations of Sedulius' poems, see Helen Waddell, <u>Medieval Latin Lyrics</u> (Penguin L29, 1929; reprint 1962), 130-137, and George F. Whicher, <u>The Goliard Poets</u> (New York, 1949; reprint New Directions Paperback 206, 1965), 7-13.

6. English translation by Myra L. Uhlfelder, with summaries by Jean A. Potter, <u>Periphyseon. On the Division of Nature</u> (Indianapolis: LLA 157, 1976).

PART THREE: THE ROMANESQUE AGE

Chapter 7

The Tenth Century

In the case of the "Tenth Century," as with so many historical
periods, the key events do not always coincide neatly with the
century years. With the death of Charles the Bald in 877 we may
justifiably consider the Carolingian epoch at an end. Few if any
people were still alive who could remember the great emperor, and
he had become a legendary figure, the hero of a golden age far in
the past. The great if somewhat awkward political structure which
he, and three generations of his predecessors, had built up was in
shambles, public authority had fallen into the hands of the local
nobility, the Empire had only a shadow existence. Militarily
western Europe had lost the initiative, and the inroads of Northmen, Muslims, Hungarians, and Slavs met with only sporadic
resistance; many libraries and centers of learning were either
destroyed or badly damaged by these wild invaders.

The tenth century, although building upon the traditions established during the Carolingian period, was different in many
respects, and it is these differences which give it its distinctive character as a historical period.[1] In the first place, the
quality of its classical learning was significantly lower,
although enthusiastic study of the classics and copying of classical manuscripts continued. The attempts to write quantitative
poetry were uniformly unsuccessful except sometimes in Italy, as a
knowledge of quantity became a rare accomplishment. This period
was also much more naive than the Carolingian, and in both philosophy and theology, Europe had almost to start over again.

But if, judged by classical standards, the tenth century represents a temporary decline in the intellectual standards of Europe,
from another point of view it is at least as important as the
preceding age. The centers of education were more diffused and
were self-sustaining, which was fortunate since leadership from
above was no longer forthcoming. Just as militarily the outstanding feature of the period is that Europe pulled itself
together, drove the Muslims out of their alpine strongholds,
contained the Northmen, defeated the Slavs and Hungarians, and set
about creating a new Europe, what strikes one most forcibly about
its intellectual life, despite the undeniable crudity of much of
it, is its creativity, its break with the attitudes and forms of
the past, its boldness and originality, which were often the fruit
of ignorance. The preposterous but fascinating plays of Hrothswitha of Gandersheim, supposedly imitating Terence but written in
prose, the powerful Song of Walthar, drawing its material from
German legend but in form modelled on the classics, the abominable
Ecbasis Captivi, first of the beast fables, and drawing much of

its phraseology verbatim from the classics, the beginnings of important productions in the vernacular literatures and translations from the classics into the vernaculars, the development of the lyric and of rhymed rhythmical poetry, the creation of the Trope and Sequence, the restoration of the study of philosophy, in however elementary a fashion, and the first definite intellectual contacts with the Muslim world, all presaged the magnificent accomplishments of the next three hundred years. It is as a time of beginnings that we should consider and appreciate the tenth century, and when one considers the rampant disorders of the times, it is scarcely short of miraculous that things were as good as they were.

But however much of newness we detect in the tenth century, the theme of continuity with the Carolingian age must not be overlooked. First and most obvious is the fact that many of the schools which existed were in fact Carolingian foundations, and when new ones were established, as many were, both in the older parts of Europe and among the recently conquered Slavic and Hungarian peoples to the east, they were modelled on the Carolingian schools. Also, the curriculum was that established by the Carolingians, supposedly the seven Liberal Arts but in fact usually little more than Latin language and literature, with some work in rhetoric and elementary logic. The mathematical disciplines were taught in some schools, but seldom was instruction in all four of them available in a single school. The textbooks which were employed in the teaching were for the most part those written by the Carolingian masters, especially Alcuin.[2] And finally, in several cases we can trace a succession of teachers and students from the height of the Carolingian period into the tenth century. Two such lines converge in Notker the Stammerer, the leading scholar of St. Gall in the late ninth and early tenth centuries. One of his teachers was Werinbehrt, who had studied at Fulda under Rabanus Maurus. Another was the Irishman Moengal (or Marcellus), who had been a close friend of Sedulius. Another such line runs from Servatus Lupus, the great classicist of Ferrières, through his pupil Eric of Auxerre. One of Eric's pupils was Hucbald of St. Amand, who was called to Reims in the early tenth century to reform the school there. (This was the school which, under Gerbert later in the century, would become the finest in Europe.) Hucbald's most important work is an amusing if undistinguished poem in defense of baldness, in which every word begins with the letter "C."[2] He had a wide acquaintance with classical literature and when he left St. Amand for Reims, he gave its library his copies of the Timaeus and the works of Seneca, Virgil, and Priscian, as well as Alcuin and Rabanus Maurus. Another of Eric's pupils was Remigius of Auxerre, who also taught at Reims, and around 900 went to Paris, the future intellectual capital of Europe, and was the first to open a school there. And finally there is Radbod, later bishop of Utrecht, who had been educated at the Palace School of Charles the Bald, where the traditions of the good old days were sedulously maintained and where the foremost scholars of the late Carolingian period congregated. His own literary contribution is slight but pleasant: a lyric, with some allegorical moralizing, on a swallow that built its next under his eave. F. J. E. Raby calls it "a true German product, worth noting as we try to make out the course of medieval nature poetry."[4] Undoubtedly by diligent search one could multiply these examples many times. But in each case, we can detect in the works of the men living during the last part of the ninth century and the early years of the tenth a new and different attitude toward their tradition and toward the world they were writing about.

In their form the new compositions are decidedly inferior to those of the Carolingians. The most popular type of verse which was cultivated throughout the tenth century was the leonine hexameter, a semi-rhythmical verse form imitating the classical hexameter, but employing rhyme, assonance and alliteration. Usually the rhyme is one one syllable only, the last vowel of the line being the same as that of the caesura (pause in the middle of the line):

> O species cari, cur non ades, alma magistri?
> O quid fecisti? cur nobis nota fuisti?
> O cur rara venis, cur nos tardissime cernis?

It is clumsy and monotonous and encourages padding for the sake of the rhyme, but fairly easy to write, and it became enormously popular. Its principal, but by no means only, use was in the composition of epic or historical poems, which are another marked feature of our period. In some respects, of course, these simply continued a Carolingian genre, but there are some important differences, aside from the form. One now detects a strong feeling of national or local pride and the conviction of the authors that the events of their day are as important and as worthy of being remembered as those of the past. Another feature of the period, perhaps the result of Irish influence, was a predilection for unusual words, intentional obscurity of style, and bizarre stylistic devices. One of the better examples of this sort of writing is the _Bella Parisiacae urbis_ by Abbo of St. Germain-des-Près,[5] written about 897. It is an account of the siege of Paris by the Northmen during the time of Duke Odo, to which Abbo had been an eye-witness. Much of the first two books is lively, informative and entertaining, but Book III contains so many obscure words that the author had to compile a glossary to aid the reader in puzzling out what he had written, and even with the glossary it is very rough going. Not content with an almost unique vocabulary, which included a number of Greek words, he also obscured his meaning, in order to parade his learning, by borrowing high-flown phrases from the classics and by resorting to certain stylistic perversities, asyndeton (omission of conjunctions) and tmesis (inserting a word in the middle of another word).[6] So popular was this third book that it was often copied separately from the intelligible part of the poem.

But by far the finest literary production of the late ninth century, eschewing both the leonine hexameter and the studied
obscurity of contemporary works, is the Waltharii Poesis or Epic
of Walthar.[7] Formerly thought to have been written by Ekkehard I
of St. Gall, it is now considered the work of Gerald of Eichstätt,
otherwise unknown, and was written between 882 and 890.[8] Its
story, drawn from Germanic oral tradition, takes place during the
time of Atilla the Hun and tells the tale of Walthar, Hagen, and
Hildegunde. It is replete with heroism in battle and single
combat, divided loyalties, warrior Christianity, crude rough
humor, love, treachery, and reconciliation. It is Germanic in
tone as in theme but powerfully influenced by the Latin classics.
Its author seems to have been an eye-witness of actual battles,
which he dearly loves to describe, and there are many Germanisms
as well as echoes of the old Germanic alliterative poetry. But he
is also a well-educated man, steeped in the works of the ancient
poets, both pagan and Christian. His principal model was the
Thebaid of Statius, but he also borrows from Virgil, Prudentius
and Boethius, and much of his diction and imagery were derived
from the classics. For example, in the evening Phoebus sinks
toward the western shores, lighting up Ultima Thule with his rays,
and in the morning Lucifer ascends high Olympus and Taprobane sees
the bright orb rising from the waves.[9] There is more of this sort
of thing, but fortunately not enough to become oppressive. There
are quite a few metrical errors, since Gerald attempted to use
classical hexameters, but the poem is of a sufficiently high
quality throughout that these are more than compensated for. The
Epic of Walthar was enormously popular as a school text, not only
because it is interesting and reasonably easy to read, but because
the students undoubtedly already knew the story and thus could
read the Latin more readily.

A poem similar in many respects, but with some important differences, was composed in northern Italy, probably Verona, about a
generation later (916-924). This is the Gesta Berengarii,[10]
written by an Italian professor of classical literature whose name
is not known. It is both better and worse than the Epic of
Walthar, depending upon one's point of view. Its author, being
(apparently) an Italian layman, educated and teaching in a lay
school of classical studies, had a much more competent command of
Latin and of classical versification. He also seems clearly to
consider himself in the unbroken tradition of the masters of old.
They were not foreigners to him, as they were to the northerners,
but rather his own people. He has mastered not only the principal
works of the classical authors and made them his own, but he knows
some Greek (indeed he gives his poem a Greek title), is acquainted
with the scholiasts, and is thoroughly schooled in the techniques
of antique rhetoric. But even he cannot wholly resist the current
fashion of the leonine rhyme and writes such lines as:

>   tu licet exustus vacuas solvaris in auras,
>   pars melior summi scribet amore viri.

However, the author is in the difficult position of writing a panegyric of a living king, Berengar of Italy, who was too often unsuccessful in his battles, and trying to make him out a great hero. To accomplish this task, the poet alters the sequence of events (apparently for aesthetic considerations as often as from prudence), and borrows freely from the works of the classical authors in describing his hero, his excellent qualities, his battles and speeches, his restoration of peace to a troubled Italy, his coronation at Rome, and the villainy of those who stir up rebellion against his just rule. There was, of course, an ample store of appropriate material in the writers of ancient Rome. But in some cases, the poet simply omitted crucial material altogether, such as Berengar's loss of a key battle. The preparations and the battle itself are described; only the outcome is passed over.

Much of the poem has a certain freshness and interest because the author witnessed some of the events (such as the coronation at Rome) that he wrote about. Nor was he without a measure of inventiveness; and certainly he was a skillful rhetorician and composer of panegyric. But the greater part of the poem is borrowed from the authors of a greater time, writing about authentic heroes, and their words applied to Berengar result in hardly more than a caricature. Because of its laudatory purpose and rhetorical structure, this work can be used only with the greatest caution as a historical source, and it hardly merits consideration as great literature. Its main significance is that it provides clear evidence that in the tenth century there were in Italy lay schools taught by men of considerable competence in classical studies; and the author states that there were many more poets besides himself in Italy. The north of Europe, though fresher and more creative, still had need of such people.

In northern Europe, one of the outstanding centers of learning, teaching, copying, literary production, music and art of the late ninth and early tenth centuries was the monastery of St. Gall.[11] It is typical of, but superior to, the average well-managed monastery of the period, and its history, in its main outline, was repeated by the experience of many other religious houses. Founded by Gallus, the companion of Columbanus, when the former was too ill to follow his master from Allemania to Bobbio in about 590, it remained little more than a rustic hermitage inhabited by a handful of monks until 720. In that year, it elected its first abbot, Othmar, who partially substituted the Benedictine rule for the Columban (747), acquired land and put up new buildings for the establishment, and founded a school for oblates. A second, "outer," school for secular clergy and laity was opened near the end of the century as a result of Charlemagne's Admonitio gener-

alis. From this point on, the rise of the abbey was steady and
sometimes swift until 920.

It first came to the attention of the Carolingian rulers when
Pippin the Short's brother, Carloman, stopped there on his way to
Monte Cassino to become a monk and commended the house to his
brother. Charlemagne paid St. Gall the dubious compliment of
selecting it as a prison for his son, Pippin the Hunchback, after
the failure of the latter's rebellion against his father. St.
Gall was still, at this time, a relatively small and unimportant
house, and only in the late Carolingian period did it reach a
position of wealth, influence and intellectual preeminence. The
abbot Gozbert (816-836) added more buildings, founded the monastic
library, patronized art and learning, improved the abbey school
which Othmar had founded, and asked Walafrid Strabo to rewrite in
more elegant fashion the older lives of St. Gall and St. Othmar,
with a view to spreading the abbey's fame.

It was under the abbacy of Grimald that St. Gall first rose to
European prominence and established close ties with the Carolingian dynasty. Grimald, educated under Alcuin in the Palace
School and formerly teacher of Walafrid and court chaplain of
Louis the German, was forced upon the monks by that ruler in 841.
He added greatly to the wealth and influence of the abbey, and
under him St. Gall had its first teacher of European fame. This
was Iso, who became master of the outer school while Werinbehrt
taught the inner school. Grimald also caused the first catalogue
of the monastic library (still extant) to be made. It lists 400
titles, of which Grimald himself had contributed thirty-three.
Grimald and Iso died within a year of each other (871-2). Grimald
was succeeded by two noble, wealthy, and learned men of great
capacity, first Hartmuot and then Salomo, under whom St. Gall
reached the peak of its fame, glory, and influence. Iso and
Werinbehrt were succeeded by the Irishman Marcellus, whose pupils
Notker the Stammerer and Radpert in turn succeeded him. During
this time St. Gall produced great scholars, musicians, calli-
graphers, artists, and physicians.

But the death of the abbot Salomo in 920 was also the end of St.
Gall's preeminence. It had risen to wealth and fame as a result
of Carolingian patronage, and Salomo had been zealous for the
Carolingian cause. Consequently the abbey was not favored by the
Saxon house, which now ruled Germany. Still the vitality of St.
Gall's traditions might have prolonged the "golden age" but for
other calamities. In 925 the monastery was sacked by the Hungarians; in 937 it suffered a terrible fire, set by an oblate in
order to avoid a beating; and in 954 it was raided by the Muslims.
Through all these disasters, however, the monastery continued to
produce teachers, scholars and writers of considerable merit. Its
scholars and teachers were in demand to reform or establish
schools in other places. St. Ulrich introduced the St. Gall

curriculum and teaching methods at Augsburg; bishop Balderich did
the same at Speier; bishop Erkanbald of Strassburg called the St.
Gall monk Victor to teach in his cathedral school; and various
other St. Gall monks held important offices in Salzburg and Liège.
But in the year 1034, St. Gall received a blow from which it never
recovered when Conrad II ordered it to adopt the Cluniac reform.
The monks resisted violently but vainly what they considered "the
fanatical teaching of schismatics." After this date, only one
worthwhile literary work was produced at St. Gall, and that was
Ekkehard IV's continuation of the monastery's history, the Casus
Sancti Galli begun by Radpert. Ekkehard's purpose was to illustrate the low estate of the monastery in his own day by comparing
it with the glorious days of the past, before the coming of the
Cluniacs.

Largely as a result of the account of Ekkehard IV and the lucky
chance that a large part of the monastic library has survived, we
have a much fuller knowledge of the school of St. Gall in its
great days than of any other contemporary school. The picture it
presents is impressive. By the early ninth century, there were
two schools, an inner one for oblates and an outer one for secular
clergy and laity. Each school had its own teacher and sometimes
there would be more than one teacher in each school. The schools
do not seem to have been kept strictly separate. Since many of
the students studied under both teachers, either the boys attended
both schools at different times, or (more likely) the teachers
exchanged schools on occasion. We know for a fact that Ekkehard
II taught in both schools, and it is likely that others did too.

For the study of grammar, the pagan Latin authors along with the
Christian classics were the basis of the curriculum. Among the
latter, Sedulius, Juvencus, Arator, Ambrose, Boethius' Consolation, and especially Prudentius were studied. Among the former,
the major school texts were "Homerus Latinus," Martianus Capella,
Horace, Persius, Juvenal, Statius, Terence, and Lucan, but the
library contained in addition works of Jerome, Augustine, Gregory
the Great, Josephus, Orosius, Einhard, Bede, Alcuin, Donatus,
Priscian, Quintilian, Virgil, Ennius, Cicero, Ovid, and Sallust.
The aim of the teaching of grammar at St. Gall was to teach the
boys to write Latin fluently, both prose and poetry. How successful Notker was in this task is illustrated by the entry of the new
abbot Salomo into St. Gall in 890. Each of the boys addressed him
in Latin, "the smallest as well as they were able, the middle-
sized ones rhythmically, and the others metrically, or even
rhetorically, as though they were speaking from the rostrum."[12]
We also learn from this what the St. Gall teachers considered the
order of difficulty: prose was easiest, metrical poetry next, and
quantitative poetry the most difficult.

At least until Salomo's death, the rudiments of Greek were also
taught. Its study seems to have been introduced there by Marcel-

lus and other Irish brothers in the mid-ninth century. Notker, Salomo and Tuotilo all give evidence in their writings of some knowledge of the language, although only Notker is known to have done any extensive work in Greek, and this he accomplished only "with much sweat." There is in the St. Gall library a Greek grammar of the tenth century written by Dositheius and referred to by Notker I, in which the Latin text is literally translated into Greek, and exercises are added for translating Greek into Latin and vice versa. It was clearly used as a school text. The method of transliterating Greek into Latin at St. Gall shows that its tradition of Greek teaching came from Byzantium, not from the ancient Irish centers, regardless of whether or not its first teachers were Irishmen. After Salomo's death, with the single exception of young Burchard's studying Greek under the Duchess Hedwig, all knowledge of that language seems to have died out at St. Gall.

The study of rhetoric, and indeed the very meaning of that word, underwent a profound change during the tenth century. As we shall see later in this chapter, Gerbert at Reims would turn it into the art of defending one's philosophical positions in oral debate, but at St. Gall and throughout much of the rest of Europe it became the art of composing in prose -- primarily letters and legal documents -- following a strict formula. The technical terms exordium, narratio and conclusio were transferred to the technique of writing letters, and many collections of sample letters and charters for all occasions came into being. Among the best of these is the Collectio Sangallensis,[13] written probably by Notker I for Salomo. It contains forty-seven samples of model letters and charters. In addition to the models, however, the school of St. Gall gave some instruction in this new kind of "rhetoric," putting old classics to new uses. The anonymous Ad Herrenium and Cicero's De inventione, Quintilian's Ars oratoria and two very rare rhetorical treatises attributed to Boethius were their major text books, and the library also contained an impressive collection of legal works, the Leges Barbarorum, collections of canon law, capitularies and edicts.

The study of dialectic was rudimentary in the extreme. Although the library had the standard compendia and introductory works of Boethius, Victorinus, Porphyry, Apuleius, Martianus Capella and Isidore, and Notker Labeo made some advances in the teaching of dialectic late in the century, this art was only cursorily cultivated at St. Gall.

The quadrivium, however, was studied intensively. In arithmetic, instruction was first given in counting and computation, but the extremely clumsy methods described by Alcuin[14] were used. Then came a study of the computi for the purpose of establishing the dates of movable festivals. Finally the higher branches of arithmetic, especially numerology, were studied.

Although geometry was included in the curriculum, it received slight attention, both because it had little practical utility for the monks, and because the available text books -- especially the geometric sections of Martianus Capella and Isidore -- were so poor. Largely because of Martianus Capella's misunderstanding, it was often confused with geography, and to aid in its teaching, abbot Hartmuot had a large and finely-made map constructed. It was not until Gerbert rehabilitated the quadrivium between 974 and 984 and recovered the Geometry attributed to Boethius that this art would be adequately studied.

But the case was far otherwise with music, for music was an important part of monastic life. St. Gall boasted many fine musicians and its library was well stocked with the theoretical treatises of Antiquity, pseudo-Augustine, Cassiodorus, Isidore, and especially Boethius. Both singing and classical music theory were taught at St. Gall, which is also the probable birthplace of the Sequence, one of the more important innovations in the music of the liturgy of the tenth century.

Astronomy, too, was carefully studied. The students first learned the divisions of time and their measurement, the motions of the sun and moon, the reasons for eclipses, the Hebrew, Greek, and Roman calendars, the names of the constellations and the signs of the zodiac, the solstices and equinoxes. Then they went on to the more advanced works, Aratus' Phoenomena in the Latin translation of Germanicus Caesar and Apuleius' work on the spheres of "Pythagoras." Since astronomy had practical value for the monks, its study was not confined to the school. They carried on a certain amount of observation and often recorded eclipses in the monastic chronicle. A still extant early tenth century minature of St. Gall shows a monk measuring the height of a star with a viewing tube supported by a stand and attached to a metal ring which has twelve angle markings. Somewhat later in the century, abbot Burchard caused to be constructed a globe by means of which, writes Notker Labeo, "one can see very well why in the arctic regions there is a day for six months and a night for six months. . . .It has the positions of all the nations, and therefore when it is placed so that the northern pole points straight up then the six northern signs of the zodiac will be visible; the six southern ones are hidden."[15] At about the same time at Reims, Gerbert was constructing even more sophisticated and complicated models.

In addition to the seven Liberal Arts, medicine was of necessity studied by the St. Gall monks. There seems to have been always at least one skilled physician among them, several of whom were widely known for their healing skills. The abbey had its own hospital and surgery, herb garden, dispensary and physician's house. In its library were a pharmacopeia, a book of prescriptions, and the works of the great classical medical writers, Hippocrates and Galen, as well as less well-known medical treatises. It is not clear, however, what place, if any, medicine had in the school curriculum.

In view of the avowedly religious purpose of the monastic vocation, it is surprising to see how little time was spent on Biblical and theological studies. Theology had declined abruptly since Carolingian times, and at St. Gall it consisted simply of reading the Bible with the aid of a few commentators. Apparently the works of Jerome and Augustine which were in the library were too difficult, since Notker I, in a letter to Salomo, recommends only the commentaries of Rabanus and Bede (although a slightly more extensive list is given for the Psalms), and for "Roman delicacies" he urges that Gregory's Pastoral Care be learned by heart but is silent about the same author's Moralia in Job which was also in the library. It is reasonable to assume that Notker himself and other more advanced scholars among the brethren made use of the many patristic theological works contained in the monastic library, but that these were not deemed suitable for school use.

The monastery produced a succession of authors and scholars of European fame from about 860 till the mid-eleventh century. Not all of these were men of genuine importance, but several deserve fuller treatment. As we have mentioned above, the first St. Gall teacher to be widely known was Iso, teacher of the outer school during the abbacy of Grimald. His fame rested on his commentary on the works of Prudentius, but he was also widely reputed to be a skilled physician and a musician of great ability. He was summoned in his declining years by count Rudolph of Burgundy to establish a school at Grandval. In the next generation Ratpert was the best-known writer of St. Gall. He wrote several mediocre elegiac poems in leonine hexameters but is best known for beginning the monastic chronicle, Casus Sancti Galli, and for his German hymn to St. Gall, which exists today only in the Latin version made by Ekkehard IV.

Until the last decade of the ninth century, St. Gall was in a class below such famous German monasteries as Reichenau and Fulda. But in the years between 890 and 920, the life of the monastery was dominated by three talented men of varied skills, whose activities brought St. Gall into the first rank of European intellectual centers and established the traditions which would be maintained for the next 150 years. These men were Salomo, Tuotilo, and Notker the Stammerer.

The youngest of the three, Salomo, although orphaned at an early age and educated under Notker at St. Gall, was of noble birth and heir to considerable property. He entered the service of Louis the German as court chancellor and chaplain after having finished his education. In 890, when he was about thirty years old, he became both bishop of Constance and abbot of St. Gall. He continued his involvement in worldly affairs until his death in 920, but under his rule the monastery flourished in every respect. Despite his continuing duties in behalf of a series of Carolingian rulers, Salomo took an active interest in the school of St. Gall and was himself an author of importance. He either wrote or caused to be written the Vocabularius Salomonis, an encyclopedia of technical terms used in the various fields of learning and arranged in roughly alphabetical order. It was also for Salomo that Notker I wrote the Collectio Sangallensis, which we have already mentioned. The great abbot is also responsible for a Greek-Latin psalter, which is still extant. His literary work consists of two letters in verse,[16] addressed to Dado, bishop of Verdun. The first is a gloomy commentary on the state of the Empire, ruled by a child and torn apart by civil war, while the second laments the death of his brother Waldo, a monk of St. Gall. Though he is also reported to have written German poems, none of these survives.

Of the two older men, Tuotilo and Notker, Tuotilo was the more varied in his accomplishments, Notker the greater scholar. Tuotilo, handsome, personable, intelligent, and talented, was famous at St. Gall in his lifetime chiefly because of his skill in ivory carving, some of which is still extant, and for his expertness in playing musical instruments. But he is of importance in intellectual history mainly because, if not the inventor of the Trope, as formerly thought, he is at least the author of the oldest extant example of that rudimentary form of religious drama.[17] A Trope is an adornment of a portion of a high mass. It consists of inserting words and music in a portion of a high mass elaborating upon the text. It is ordinarily sung by two choruses and has a simple dramatic form. Those Tropes which can with confidence be attributed to Tuotilo are extremely simple in structure and are used to introduce a section of the mass, not inserted as commentary in the midst of it as later Tropes were. Whether he wrote the most famous of all Tropes, the Quem quaeritis, out of which the true liturgical drama developed, is doubtful but possible. At any rate, the simplest form of this Trope exists in a St. Gall manuscript of the tenth century, although a more developed version is contained in an older manuscript of Limoges.

It was in Notker I that St. Gall scholarship reached its acme. Like so many of the St. Gall brothers, Notker came from a wealthy family in the immediate vicinity and had entered the monastery as a boy. He describes himself as "toothless and stammering" and is usually known by the nickname Balbulus, the Stammerer. Despite his physical handicap, he was able, through the saintliness of his character, his sly humor, and ready wit, his love for his fellow man, and the obvious excellence of his mind, to become one of the finest teachers of his century and one of the best beloved of all the St. Gall monks, as well as the outstanding scholar of his age. He spent most of his life as a teacher of the inner school, and one of his works is clearly related to his pedagogical interests. This is the Collectio Sangallensis, already referred to, which contains vast amounts of information on all the subjects of the curriculum, as well as models of epistolary style for every occasion and of a great variety of legal documents. It gives us an invaluable glimpse into the practical intellectual interest of the day and into the manner in which these needs were met.

As St. Gall's most distinguished scholar and teacher, Notker was often called upon to write poetry on behalf of the monastery, particularly in welcoming distinguished visitors. He also wrote much poetry of his own volition -- many verse letters and occasional poems in leonine hexameters and some religious verse in Sapphic strophes. One of his more engaging poetic efforts is the story of the wonderful ram,[18] a superb mock-heroic piece in hexameters. It tells of a very poor peasant, whose only posession was a ram. When the peasant died, his three sons contested for the ownership of the animal and agreed that it should go to the one who could describe the largest ram. A contest in comic exaggeration follows, and Notker slyly ends the poem without saying who the winner was. Despite the charm of this work, it, like most of the rest of Notker's poetry, was hardly above the level of clever doggerel. Only in his religious poetry does he sometimes achieve excellence.

It is in the field of religious poetry, or more properly religious prose set to music, that Notker is of crucial importance. As Tuotilo had pioneered in the development of the Trope, so Notker was one of the earliest, if not the first, to write Sequences. Both these forms seem to have originated in France and to have been popularized and developed in German centers, among which St. Gall was a leader. Like the Trope, the Sequence is an adornment of the mass, but unlike the Trope, which is explanatory in nature and consequently closely tied to the text, the Sequence originated as a prolongation and melodic embellishment of the final "a" of Alleluia, to which words were later added. In a letter to Liutward, bishop of Vercelli,[19] Notker explains how the words came to be added. He says that he had always had trouble remembering the complicated melody of the Sequence and was seeking some aid to his weak memory. Providentially, a monk from Jumièges (in what is now Normandy), wandering after the Vikings' destruction of his monastery, chanced to stop at St. Gall, bringing with him an Antiphonary which contained some crude verses set to the melody of the Sequence. Thinking that the addition of words would aid him, and perhaps others, to remember the melody, Notker set about writing a more satisfactory text than the one the Frenchman had brought with him. He showed these to his teacher, Iso, who liked the idea but suggested that each syllable ought to correspond to one note of the music. Notker corrected his words in accordance with his teacher's suggestion and the result was a virtually new genre of liturgical music. The words of a Sequence can be about virtually anything -- the foundation of a new church, the deeds and virtues of a particular saint, in short whatever the occasion calls for. At first existing melodies were used, although their rhythmical structure was radically altered by making them correspond note for note to the syllables of the text; later new melodies as well as new words were written. Like the Trope, the Sequence is usually sung by two choruses, one of men and one of boys, which sing alternating stanzas. Both the Trope and Sequence were to undergo a magnificent development, becoming ever more complex, until the thirteenth century when the church began to suppress them. But by that time, the conditions under which they had arisen -- the free monastic society of a rural age -- had ceased to exist. These two liturgical embellishments are par excellence the creations of the Romanesque period, and St. Gall was instrumental in the origin and development of each.

Perhaps the best known work of Notker is his prose Life of Charles the Great, in many ways his most typical production, both in its strengths in its weaknesses. Despite his fondness for classical literature, Notker was self-consciously German and loved his people, their language, legends and heroes. He was a great gossip and a superb story-teller, and when in 883 Charles the Fat visited St. Gall, Notker entertained him and all those present with stories about the king's own illustrious ancestor. Charles asked Notker to commit these stories to writing, and the result was the Gesta Caroli Magni. It is notorious for its lack of correspondence to historical fact, but it is highly entertaining. Full of excitingly told exploits and battles, character sketches and engaging episodes, it is an invaluable document in that it records the beginning of the legendary Charlemagne, who was to play perhaps as large a role in European history as the historical figure.

After 920, St. Gall lost its preeminence among European centers of learning and became just one among many similar schools. Ekkehard II (d. 990), a man of some learning, was a successful courtier and politician, who read Virgil with the learned duchess Hedwig of Bavaria and through her gained access to the court of her uncle, Otto the Great, thus establishing for St. Gall a connection with the Saxon dynasty. This never became, however, as close or as advantageous as its previous patronage by the Carolingians had been.

The productions of the second quarter of the century can best be considered together, rather than by schools or localities. Two examples of the typically tedious versification of which the tenth century produced so much are the Gesta Apollonii and the Ecbasis Captivi, both dating from around 950. The Gesta Apollonii,[21] extremely popular during the Middle Ages, is a versified version of the Greek romance of Apollonius of Tyre, made from a Latin prose version by an unknown monk of Tegernsee. It has the appearance of an eclogue, since it is presented as a dialogue between two men, Strabo and Saxo; but in fact it is a simple narrative divided arbitrarily between the two speakers. It is in poor leonine hexameters and depends heavily upon intentional obscurity, including Greek words, for its appeal, and so was furnished with a glossary.

The Ecbasis Captivi,[22] written by a monk of St. Eure whose obscurity of style is not intentional, is even worse, but is nevertheless important as the oldest known example of the beast fable in modern European literature. It, too, is in leonine hexameters, put together in the manner of a cento from the works of Horace, Virgil, Ovid, Marcellus Empiricus, Prudentius, Abbo of St. Germain-des-Près, and Eriugena. It is a moral allegory in which the author, portrayed as a calf escaped from its mother, relates his adventures outside the monastery. Other characters are also portrayed as suitable animals -- lion, leopard, wolf, fox, hedgehog, otter, nightingale, swan -- but there is none of the wit or humor which often makes this type of writing attractive. Its structure is awkward, its jokes jejune, and its style, despite extensive borrowing from excellent authors, is heavy-handed and dull. If one were looking for an example of thoroughly barbarous medieval literature, he could not do better than the Ecbasis Captivi.

But despite the depressing abundance of labored leoninea and generally inept versification in the tenth century, this period produced some truly fine rhythmical poetry and witnessed the birth (or rebirth) of the lyric. Two of the best rhythmical poems are the result of Italian civic pride, one exhorting the city of Modena to be vigilant and brave against the threatening Hungarians, the other praising the city of Rome. About 900, shortly after the walls of Modena were rebuilt and while the Hungarians roamed the land spreading terror, a citizen of Modena composed the poem, O tu qui servas armis ista moenia,[23] a magnificent admonition to the city's defenders to rise to the occasion. The poem thus has an immediacy and validity which add to its interest, and unlike many equally sincere northerners who failed miserably in their efforts in similar situations, its poet was fully competent and was well versed in classical and Christian Latin literature. He reminds the defenders of Hector's vigil at Troy, alludes to several events in Roman history (which he probably knew of from Livy), goes on to appeal to Mary, Christ, and John to protect the city, and ends, as he had begun, with an exhortation to courage and vigilance. Every line but two (which end in "is") ends in "a," and there are occasional internal rhymes. The second poem, O Roma Nobilis,[24] was written for the pilgrims who continued to flock to Rome despite all the dangers of the age. It is in rhythmic dactyls and uses rhyme extensively, both internally and at the middle and end of the line:

O Roma nobilis, orbis et domina

> cunctarum urbium excellentissima
> roseo martyrum sanguine rubea
> albis et virginum liliis candida

But the type of poetry which especially flowered in the tenth century was the lyric. Many new songs were written and old ones, including Gottschalk's _Ut quid iubes, pusiole_, some of Horace's Odes, and several of Aeneas' speeches from the _Aeneid_, were set to new melodies. Several song books of the century have been preserved, but the most important single source for tenth century lyrics is a collection of songs compiled probably by an eleventh century ecclesiastic from the Rhineland, now preserved in the University Library at Cambridge and consequently known as the _Cambridge Songs_.[25] It contains a great variety of lyrics dating from the first to the eleventh centuries, of which several, representing France, Italy, and Germany, are of the tenth century. Several of these are religious but most are secular, some exceedingly so.

Nearly all, however, are clearly influenced in their form by the religious Sequence, and at least three, probably German in origin, could be described as secular Sequences. These are a Sequence on Pythagoras, the story of the Snow Child, and the tale of the friendship of Lantfrid and Cobbo. They are all proses, with very little rhyme but definite hints of rhythmic structure.

Another group, still basically Sequences in their form, are completely rhythmical and use rhyme in varying degrees. These are the story of Heriger (Archbishop of Mainz, 913-927), who chastised a man for falsely claiming to have been to hell and to heaven; a satirical story of an encounter between a priest and a wolf; and the story of Abbot John, who wanted to be perfect like the angels and do completely without food and clothing, but changing his mind after eight days and returning to the monastery was forced by the malicious humor of the monks, who pretended they thought he was an angel, to spend the night outside in the cold.

Much better than these narrative dialogues in verse are the nature poems and love lyrics, which seem all to have been written in Italy or France. One of the more famous of these is the _O admirabile Veneris idolum_, a completely rhythmical (probably dactylic) poem using a two-syllable rhyme throughout. It is a love song of a scholar, fond of classical allusions, to a young boy. Another is a nature poem, _Vestiunt silvae tenera ramorum_, in rhythmic sapphics with sporadic rhymes. Its author simply wanted to name and describe certain birds which delighted him, and the poem is little more than a catalogue. Its structure then is rudimentary, but it is fresh and sincere and full of a genuine love of nature. A more successful nature poem is the _Levis exsurgit zephirus_, "the first 'dramatic lyric' of the Middle Ages."[26] A young girl is pictured as gazing out her window at the world bursting into life

in the springtime -- the light breeze, the warm sun, the budding
flowers, the new leaves on the trees, the young animals, and birds
in their nests -- but she cannot share in its joy because her
heart is heavy.

Clearly the best, as well as the best-known, of the Cambridge
Songs is the Iam dulcis amica, venito. Influenced both by Ovid
and by the Song of Songs, it is an authentic masterpiece, combining elements of nature poetry and love poetry and putting them
into a dramatic setting in dialogue form. A young man urges his
sweetheart to come into a room which he has adorned with flowers
and fragrant herbs and with a table set with all sorts of deli-
cious food and plenty of good wine. There will be sweet songs
sung by a boy and girl to the accompaniment of a guitar and harp.
The young lady is apparently much impressed and answers that, even
more tempting than the delights he has described, is the "dulce
colloquium" which comes afterward. The boy is overjoyed at the
reply and exclaims: "Then come now, my chosen lass, delightful to
me above all others, bright light of my eye, and greater part of
my soul." The girl's response is the loveliest part of the song:
"I have been alone in the forest, and I have loved secret places.
I have often fled the tumult and I have avoided crowds. Now the
snow and ice melt; the leaves and shrubs burst forth; now the
nightingale sings on high, and love burns in my heart.."

> (Ego fui sola in silva
>   et dilexi loca secreta;
>   frequenter effugi tumultum
>   et vitavi populum multum.
>
>   Iam nix glaciesque liquescit,
>   folium et herba virescit;
>   philomela iam cantat in alto:
>   ardet amor cordis in antro.   )

The poem ends with the boy's impatient and impassioned outburst:
"Dearest one, don't dally; we are eager to make love now. . . Do
quickly what you are about to do. In me there is no waiting."

> (Karissima, noli tardare;
>   studeamus nos nunc amare
>   . . .fac cito quod eris factura,
>   in me non est aliqua mora.   )

The Carolingian Palace School had come to an end with the death of
Charles the Bald in 877 and for three quarters of a century European education and intellectual life were completely dependent on
the vitality of local tradition and the enlightenment of individual abbots, bishops, and princes. But about the middle of the
tenth century, the German king, Otto the Great, appreciating the
value to himself and to society of learned men, established an

ambulatory school as part of his household. Although his school never assumed the importance of its Carolingian model, it was nevertheless an important element in the intellectual life of the later tenth century. At its center was the king's brother, Bruno.[27] When this scholar was only four years old, he already showed signs of intellectual precosity and was sent for his education to bishop Balderich of Utrecht. After distinguishing himself in his studies, which included instruction in Greek by certain eastern monks at Otto's court, he was made archbishop of Cologne and established an excellent school and circle of scholars at his cathedral. Wishing to take full advantage of his brother's abilities, Otto summoned him to his court, and for the rest of his life Bruno was the leading scholar of Otto's household, following his brother wherever he went, even on military campaigns, with his books, students, and teachers. In addition to maintaining a school, Otto was constantly on the lookout for able scholars to serve him as teachers, administrators, advisors, or diplomats, and such outstanding men as Gunzo of Novara, Liudprand of Cremona, and Gerbert of Aurillac were among those who enjoyed his patronage. In addition to this conscious fostering of learning, Otto stimulated much writing simply by the example of his rule: his restoration of a modicum of peace and order to Germany and Italy, his defeat of the Slavs and Hungarians, and his assumption of the imperial title in 962. A considerable portion of the intellectual activity of the last half of the tenth century was connected directly or indirectly with the Ottonian dynasty.

Shortly after the middle of the century, at Gandersheim, a convent in northern Saxony, a young Saxon girl of noble birth name Hrothswitha wrote a series of works of so generally a high quality that it has even been claimed that she was a figment of the imagination of the fifteenth century German humanist, Conrad Celtes,[29] who first discovered and published the manuscript of her collected works.[30] This claim, however, rests on no solid ground, and we may confidently assume that Hrothswitha was a real woman of the tenth century. She was born about 935 and as a girl entered the convent at Gandersheim, where she was educated first under the learned Riccardis and later under the abbess Gerberga, a niece of king (later emperor) Otto the Great. Her works show that she had read rather widely in the Latin poets, both profane and Christian, and had absorbed at least the rudiments of dialectic, music, and arithmetic, probably from the works of Boethius and Martianus Capella (see especially her plays Paphnutius and Sapientia). She also had a respectable knowledge of the Bible and of patristic literature.

She realized early that she had a gift for composition, and her realistic appriasal of her own abilities in the preface to her plays is refreshing. She is quite aware that she ranks far below the great authors of the past both in writing and in learning, but God has given her the gift of composition, "and I known," she says, "that it is as wrong to deny a divine gift as to pretend falsely to have received it." And if she is not learned, she is at least "a teachable creature."[31]

She wrote two long historical poems,[32] the <u>Deeds</u> <u>of</u> <u>Otto</u> <u>the</u> <u>Great</u> and a <u>History</u> <u>of</u> <u>the</u> <u>Convent</u> <u>at</u> <u>Gandersheim</u>, both in leonine hexameters. The choice of this verse form was perhaps unfortunate, but in Hrothswitha's hands, if it does not reach the level of great poetry, it at least avoids the worst faults of the same form at the hands of her contemporaries. Her unstudied simplicity, the directness and lucidity of her narrative style, and her lack of pretensions to great erudition, enable the poems to remain fresh, informative and pleasing, even though undistinguished. The first of these, clearly influenced by the works of Virgil, Prudentius and Sedulius, is both a history of the reign of Otto I up to his coronation in 962 and a panegyric of this energetic and capable ruler, the "new David," written by an enthusiastic and adoring country-woman. The second, drawing upon legend as well as historical fact, is a highly favorable history of her own convent and its outstanding inhabitants from its foundation about 850 by Duke Ludolf (at the insistance of his wife) up to the death of the abbess Christiana in 911. She also wrote a number of shorter works of slight importance.

But by far her most striking work is the series of six short plays[33] on which her modern fame rests. In a preface, she explains why she wrote them. "There are many Catholics," she says,

> and we cannot entirely acquit ourselves of the charge, who, attracted by the polished elegance of the style of pagan writers, prefer their works to the Holy Scriptures. There are others, who, although they are deeply attached to the sacred writings and have no liking for most pagan productions, make an exception in favor of the works of Terence and, fascinated by the charm of the manner, risk being corrupted by the wickedness of the matter. Wherefore I, the strong voice (Latin <u>clamor validus</u> = 0. Saxon <u>hrots</u> <u>vit</u>) of Gandersheim, have not hesitated to imitate in my writings a poet whose works are so widely read, my object being to glorify, within the limits of my poor talent, the laudable chastity of Christian virgins in that self-same form of composition which has been used to describe the shameless acts of licentious women. One thing has all the same embarrassed me and often brought a blush to my cheek. It is that I have been compelled through the nature of this work to apply my mind and my pen to depicting the dreadful frenzy of those possessed by unlawful love, and the insidious sweetness of passion -- things which should not even be named among us. Yet if from modesty I had refrained from treating these subjects I should not have

been able to attain my object -- to glorify the innocent to the best of my ability. For the more seductive the blandishments of lovers the more wonderful the divine succor and the greater the merit of those who resist, especially when it is a fragile woman who is victorious and a strong man who is routed with confusion.

Although Hrothswitha tends to equate Christianity with chastity and merit with mortification of the flesh, an examination of her plays will show that she was true to her purpose. While these plays lack a tight dramatic structure, and the motivation of the crucial action is inadequately treated, they abound in effective dramatic episodes, clearly defined characters, and a good deal of humor (much of it intentional), both broad and subtle.

The play which employs farcical humor most extensively is the Dulcitius. In it, a lecherous jailor has had three pious virgins, who have refused to worship the pagan gods, confined in a convenient hall near the kitchen. When he attempts to work his nefarious will on them, God causes him to think that the black, greasy pots and pans are the girls. After making love to the kitchen utensils, Dulcitius appears in public covered with soot and grease and cannot understand why people think his appearance unusual. At the end of the same play, however, Hrothswitha is completely in earnest when the eight-year-old heroine, giving her tormentor no choice but to order her death, says, "To me my death means joy, but to you calamity. For your cruelty you will be damned in Tartarus. But I shall receive the martyr's palm, and, adorned with the crown of virginity, I shall enter the azure palace of the Eternal King, to whom be glory and honor for ever and ever." Most audiences would laugh as much at the one as at the other.

A more subtle humor is displayed at the beginning of the Abraham (one of her finest plays) when the holy hermit Abraham, learning that his niece has become a prostitute, decides to disguise himself as a pleasure-seeker and try to win back her soul for Christ. As he is setting out, his friend Ephrem says, "And suppose that in the world they offer you meat and wine?" Abraham answers, "If they do, I shall not refuse; otherwise I might be recognized." "No one will blame you, brother," says Ephrem. "It will be but praiseworthy discretion on your part to loosen the bridle of strict observance for the sake of bringing back a soul." "I am more eager to try now I know you approve," says Abraham, and off he goes.

The Paphnutius, a version of the Thais story and the best-known of the plays today, has a similar theme, but its treatment is different and in some respects better. The play opens with the hermit Paphnutius giving a long and somewhat tedious lecture on the macrocosm and microcosm and Pythagorean musical and number theory to his disciples (who are as slow to understand as many of the girls in the convent school must have been). But he is sad of countenance, and his disciples elicit from him the information that he is downhearted because there lives in the nearby city a beautiful harlot, Thais, for whose sake men fall to quarreling and fighting, give her all the wealth they have, and unwittingly lose their immortal souls. Paphnutius determines to try to win Thais for Christ and to this purpose disguises himself as a man of the world, seeks her out, and gains admission to her sumptuously adorned bedroom. Asking to be taken to her secret chamber, which no one knows about, he discovers to his surprise that she is a Christian, but is convinced that because of the enormity of her sin, God will never forgive her. Paphnutius convinces her that through repentance and strict penance even she can be forgiven. Burning all her ill-gotten wealth, Thais follows Paphnutius to a convent, where the abbess meets them and offers to be of service.

At this point, it becomes clear that Paphnutius feels a shameful passion for Thais, which he does not admit to himself, nor does Hrothswitha actually say as much. The whole matter is treated with great delicacy and psychological insight. Despite the abbess' advice to the contrary and Thais' fears that her frail body will not be able to endure it, Paphnutius insists that she be confined in a dark cell "no wider than a grave," with no toilet facilities, the only opening being a small window just large enought that "a pound of bread and water" might be put inside. Brusquely overriding all suggestions for leniency and urging that the cell be prepared quickly -- "I am already weary of delay. What if her lovers should pursue her?" -- Paphnutius leaves her and returns to his own cell, advising her: "Let your lips say only this: O God Who made me, pity me."

But for the next three years, Paphnutius thinks of nothing else, day and night, but Thais. Not daring to go to her himself, he inquires among his fellow hermits, one of whom has just had a vision indicating that Thais' penance is complete and a place in Paradise has been prepared for her, to which she would ascend in fifteen days. Relieved of his guilt and joyous at the salvation of his beloved, Paphnutius hurries to her, finds her still repeating "O God Who made me, pity me," and unable to believe that she has been forgiven. Paphnutius leads her out of her cell, and she is put in a bed to await her end. On the appointed day, with Paphnutius praying at her bedside, she dies.

Although Hrothswitha was a nun and an energetic virgin, she was extremely sensitive to the "insidious sweetness of passion." In the Gallicanus, although the hero is converted and consents to give up his beloved fiancee, Constance, a virgin of Christ, he admits that it is a very difficult thing and insists that they should live apart. "What temptation is to be feared more than the lust of the eyes?" he asks Constantine, the girl's father. "None, I know," is the reply. "Then is it right that I should see her too often?" he asks. "As you know, I love her more than my own family, more than my life, more than my soul."

Even her notion of a prostitute's life, though it is hopelessly naive in some respects, is often sympathetic and intelligent. When Abraham in disguise enters the house of ill-fame to rescue his fallen niece, Mary, he is brought almost to the breaking point by grief at the plight of his beloved child. The innkeeper summons her sarcastically: "Luck comes your way, Mary. Not only do young blades of your own age flock to your arms, but even the wise and venerable." "It is all one to me," replies Mary. "It is my business to love those who love me." Then she comes in to Abraham, who says, "Come nearer, Mary, and give me a kiss." As a competent practitioner of her profession, Mary replies, "I will give you more than a kiss. I will take your head in my arms and stroke your neck." "Yes, like that," says Abraham.

Then comes the turning point of the play, done with customary abruptness. "What does this mean" Mary exclaims, probably in an "aside." "What is this lovely fragrance? So clean, so sweet. It reminds me of the time when I was good." Then after an aside in which Abraham exhorts himself to keep up the pretence, she goes on, "Wretch that I am! To what have I fallen! In what pit am I sunk!" The crisis is passed, and the rest of the play has to do with her salvation.

Of the remaining plays, only the Sapientia, a fairly successful dramatic allegory, has much intrinsic merit. In the rest, the virtuous are so virtuous and so well guarded from harm by their faith, the villians are so utterly villainous, and the outcome so predictable, that there is little to engage the attention of the audience. One of these, the Callimachus, has some interest in that it contains a scene similar in many respects to the death scene in Romeo and Juliet, but it is not a well-constructed play and, short as it is, it makes tedious reading. But it is only fair to judge Hrothswitha on her best works, which are quite good, rather than her worst, which are merely silly. In any event, her plays are far in advance of any contemporary drama, either the liturgical drama which was just emerging out of the Tropes to parts of the mass, or the buffoonery of travelling players. It would be several centuries yet before her accomplishment in drama would be equalled, let alone surpassed.

Concerning Hrothswitha's statement that she modelled her plays after Terence, this is true only in a very loose sense. She is innocent of the classical unities and apparently does not even realize that Terence wrote in verse. This would indicate that she was, as she claims, largely self-taught, since a competent teacher of grammar, even in the tenth century, still had access to Quintilian, Donatus and Priscian, and was quite aware that Terence's plays were in verse, regardless of the form the scribe might have employed in copying the manuscript.[34] It is, however, most ungenerous to accuse her, as F. J. E. Raby has done,[35] of a "rather unintelligent study of Terence," since until they are pointed out, the meters of Terence's plays are not obvious, especially to a beginner.

Whether or not these plays were ever acted at Gandersheim, it is impossible to say, although there is nothing improbable in the assumption that they were. It is, however, quite clear that they were meant to be acted. Two of the plays have stage directions in the manuscript, and they are all constructed in such a way that they are playable.[36] And since much of the impact, including the humor, of the plays depends upon the action, we may reasonably assume, although it cannot be proven, that these plays were performed for the nuns, and perhaps for high-ranking visitors, at Gandersheim.

Perhaps the most accomplished writer of the tenth century, and certainly its most entertaining character, was Liudprand,[37] a Lombard of noble birth, excellent education, superb wit, and wide experience of the world, who has provided us with a lively, convincing and entertaining portrait of the Europe of his day, including within his purview all the countries from Muslim Spain to Constantinople. He was born in 920 at the old Lombard capital of Pavia of a wealthy family closely connected with the monarchy.

The Italian throne had been hotly contested since the death of Charles the Bald and was held, not without difficulty, by Hugh of Arles while Liudprand was a young man. In 927 King Hugh sent an embassy to Constantinople to arrange for the marriage of his daughter to the emperor Romanos' grandson and to procure a Greek fleet for an attack on the Muslim stronghold of Fraxinetum in Provence. Liudprand's father was chosen to head this mission, which was successful, but he became ill, entered a monastery, and died shortly after his return, not, however, before relating his experiences at the imperial court to his seven-year-old son. Liudprand then entered the household of King Hugh as a singing page, while his mother remarried, again to a man of wealth, position, and exemplary character. Liudprand, although performing his singing duties and paying careful attention to all that was going on around him, studied diligently and acquired a most impressive mastery of classical Latin literature, the Bible, the Fathers, church history, and canon law.

After Hugh's death in 948, Liudprand became a deacon at Pavia but continued to take an active part in worldly affairs. His parents, aware of his unusual intellectual abilities, were zealous for his advancement and at great cost purchased for him the position of private secretary and chancellor to the new king, Berengar, grandson of the hero of the Gesta Berengarii. His association with Berengar was of supreme importance for all his subsequent career, since he developed a passionate hatred for his new master which resulted both in his fleeing to Saxony and attaching himself to the rising Ottonian dynasty, and in his composing his major work, the _Antapodosis_, which, he tells us, means repayment to the various great men with whom he had been associated, but which was above all an extended libel of Berengar. The occasion for this bitter hatred of his master was a diplomatic mission which Berengar sent to Constantinople. Looking for a way to save money, the parsimonious Italian king prevailed upon Liudprand's stepfather to head (and bear the cost of) the mission because of the wonderful opportunity it would provide for Liudprand to learn Greek. But Berengar had neglected even to provide the customary costly gifts for the emperor, thus forcing Liudprand to do so at his own expense, and he never forgot or forgave this low trick.

From 950 Berengar's harshness and greed alienated increasing numbers of important Italians, who usually journeyed to the Saxon court looking for succor. Some time before 956, Liudprand joined them, learned German and greatly impressed the Saxon king with his learning and ability. At the German court he also met the Spanish bishop Recemund of Elvira, an envoy of the great Muslim ruler Abd-ar-Rahman III, and the two became fast friends. It was Recemund who suggested to Liudprand that he assuage his bitterness by writing a true history of Italy, and for the next four years, between 958 and 962, Liudprand gave whatever time he could spare from his other duties to composing the _Antapodosis_, which traced the history of Italy from the death of Charles the Bald to Berengar's embassy to Constantinople.

He was busy with many other things, however, since Otto had taken him into the royal service and in 960 sent him on a mission to Constantinople, rewarding him for this task with the see of Cremona. Liudprand also accompanied Otto during the Saxon's first intervention in Italy and played a signficant part in the events which led to Otto's coronation as Roman emperor on February 2, 962. Betrayed by Pope John XII and harassed by Berengar, Otto was forced to return to Italy in 964 and quickly dispatched his enemies. Pope John was deposed and a successor elected; and Liudprand had the exquisite pleasure of seeing his enemy Berengar driven into the hills, hunted like an animal, and finally killed in 966. The events of this seond Italian sojourn of Otto's are the subject of Liudprand's second work, the _Liber de rebus gestis Ottonis_.

Henceforth Liudprand played a major role in Otto's Italian policy and in 968 was again sent to Constantinople, this time to arrange for a marriage between the Byzantine princess Theophanou and Otto's son, the future Otto II. This mission was a dismal failure and is reported in full by Liudprand in his final work, the _Relatio de legatione Constantinopolitana_. Upon returning, he took up residence in his see of Cremona. He remained there until late

971, when he was again called upon to go to Constantinople. This time the mission was successful and the marriage between Theophanou and Otto was agreed upon. Liudprand died in January 972, either at Constantinople or Cremona.

Although as a historian Liudprand leaves something to be desired from a modern standpoint, as a writer of vivid narrative, brilliant characterizations and fascinating stories he has few equals. He was a master of the Latin language, which he wrote with naturalness, clarity, power, and elegance. Although his works abound in classical allusions and citations, these are worked in so naturally and appropriately that they enhance rather than mar the overall impression made by his writings. In his prose, there is none of the studied artificiality or imitativeness which we noted in the author of the Gesta Berengarii, none of the intentional obscurity which vitiated so much of early medieval Latin literature. He was a man of culture, of wit, of wide experience, and he was a superb stylist with a keen sense of prose rhythms.

His major work, the Antapodosis, following in the tradition of Varro, Petronius, Martianus Capella, and Boethius, is a prosimetrum, and its poetic sections, fourteen in all, are in an impressive variety of classical meters. Liuprand had great technical competence as a poet, and if his attempts at verse are not apt to stand among the great poetic monuments of the Latin language, they do show the extent to which the classical tradition was still maintained in tenth-century Italy. It is clear that Liudprand assumed in his readers a classical education equal to his own. The authors he knew were, for the most part, the same ones who were studied in the schools north of the Alps: Virgil, Terence, Cicero, Juvenal, Persius, Ovid, Martial, Lucan, and Boethius. He made more extensive use of Horace's Odes than was common at the time, and among the authors we might expect him to cite, Caesar, Livy, and Tacitus are conspicuously absent. But although he does not cite or allude to these historians directly, he was acquainted with both the subject-matter and the stylistic devises of the classical histories. In his own work, he employs direct quotations to a considerable extent and sees to it that his speakers observe the rules of classical rhetoric.

Another aspect of classicism, which seems generally to have eluded medieval writers until the fourteenth century, was a firm grasp of the beauty and function of form. In the carefully wrought structure of each of the books of his Antapodosis, Liudprand stands out not only among the writers of his own time, but indeed of the entire medieval period. This concern for form often plays havoc with the requirements of a consecutive narrative, but history may be either literature or science; it cannot be both. Liudprand clearly conceived it as a branch of literature.

Probably the most striking feature of Liudprand's prose style is his extensive use of Greek, often to no apparent purpose but the adornment of his book. It was, of course, not unusual among classical Latin authors to incorporate Greek words or phrases into their own works, but Liudprand does this to an unprecedented extent. A Greek word or phrase is first written in Greek characters, then spelled phonetically in Roman letters, and finally translated into Latin. In two cases, the tales of "Emperor Romanos and the Lion" and why blind men live so long, the entire story is given first in Greek and then in Latin. One might understand the need for this in the case of technical terms or where there was no appropriate Latin equivalent, but this was seldom the situation. Liudprand apparently felt that the use of Greek would add a certain luster to his own writing and so worked it in wherever possible.

We might ask, in view of this, to what extent Liudprand knew the Greek language. We know by his own testimony that he did not learn it in Italy, but in Constantinople.[38] He also tells us that as late as 968 he had to use an interpreter while dealing with the Greeks, but could often understand what was said before the interpreter provided the translation. Still, Liudprand had a great facility for learning languages and his several visits to Constantinople gave him an opportunity to acquire considerable knowledge of Greek. There does not seem, though, to be any evidence that he studied the language formally, although he may have had a nodding acquaintance with Greek literature.[39] His knowledge of Greek then was that of an intelligent traveller who paid attention to the tongue of a foreign people and made an effort to learn it. This knowledge was often imperfect, as is clear from his use of Greek in the Antapodosis, but it was nevertheless in an immediate and usable knowledge.

Liudprand was perhaps uniquely qualified to write a history of his age. In addition to his intellectual attainments, extensive travel, and personal experience of the great men and events of his day, he had a breadth of view unusual in any age. He wrote of Christian Europe, eastern and western, and its principal neighbors, from the Spanish Muslims to the Bulgarians and Russians. His knowledge of history was sufficient that he could relate his own times intelligently to what had gone before. And he had a set of very strong prejudices which gave consistency and structure to his view.

His primary division of Christendom is between Greek and Latin, and he hates the Greeks and everything about them. They are effeminate, irreligious, filthy, treacherous, and arrogant. He dislikes their customs, their food, their houses, and above all their treatment of foreigners.[40] Compared to them, the westerners are paragons of Christian probity, virtue, orthodoxy, intelligence, and manly vigor.

But all westerners are not of equal value, and some are downright despicable. Of all the westerners, the Romans are worst. Rome is a wicked, fickle, and corrupt city, shot through with lawlessness, cowardice, avarice, luxury, falsehood and vice, saved only by the invigorating and corrective rule of the Germanic peoples. Still, it is mistress of the world and must be respected as such. Liudprand views the Germanic peoples as a unity and speaks of them as "we Lombards, Saxons, Franks, Lotharingians, Bavarians, Swabians, and Burgundians." Among this group, the Burgundians are the lowest, and although Liudprand never insults them in his own person, he seems to delight in reporting other people's derogatory remarks on their gluttony, greed, and filth. The Saxons are the highest, new to civilization and Christianity, but devoted to truth and religion, opponents of heresy, and saviors of Europe from the Hungarians, Slavs, and Muslims.

Liudprand provides us with many vivid and heart-rending pictures of the miseries inflicted upon Europe by these foreign invaders (including the burning of his own city of Pavia), and it is often disconcerting to see with what light hearts ambitious Christian princes, even including the pope, hastened to ally themselves with one or another of these invading hordes if an immediate personal advantage could thereby be gained. It is not necessary to wait till the fifteenth and sixteenth centuries for examples of Christian princes and popes making common cause with the infidel. But despite the constant warfare and the ravages of the fierce heathens, the Italy pictured in Liudprand's works is prosperous, literate, and cultured, and far from lawless. Though there may be dark spots, Lombardy particularly is a land of proud and wealthy cities, well-governed, centers of commerce and intellectual culture. This was the land that Liudprand loved above all. Despite the general excellence of the Saxons and their great king, Otto, they were after all barely won over from barbarism and had great need of the more sophisticated and cultured Italians to advise and educate them. The Italians unfortunately "always preferred to have two kings" and thus were not apt to achieve any considerable political importance except as allies of the Germans, but Liudprand's preference for his homeland and his own people is clear throughout his writings.

Liudprand has never enjoyed a particularly high reputation as a historian, but this at least partly the fault of modern historical taste, which prefers, as source material, the naive, unliterary, factual chronicle from which needed information can be gleaned according to set rules of historical evidence. But Liudprand is not this kind of a historian. He was a man of letters, who had "a soul above documents."[41] His intelligence constantly played upon his material selecting, interpreting, judging, and organizing. He has consequently given us a polished historical work of a very high order, presenting a coherent picture of the Europe of his day and its place in the historical development of our civilization, which no chronicler, and very few modern historians, could equal.

By far the greatest intellect of the tenth century and one of the
key figures in our intellectual tradition was the Aquitainian
Gerbert,[42] born of poor parents between 940 and 945 and dying as
pope Sylvester II in 1003. Counselor of kings and emperors,
ecclesiastical politician and holder of great benefices, he was
happiest teaching the seven Liberal Arts and kept up his intellectual pursuits to the end of his life.

He was educated at the Benedictine monastery of St. Géraud near
Aurillac, where he studied under the monk Raymond, who later
became abbot. It is probable that Gerbert took monastic vows at
Aurillac and may well have spent his life in that cloister in
peaceful obscurity but for the arrival there in 967 of Borrel,
count of Barcelona and duke of the Spanish March. The abbot of
St. Géraud learned from Borrel of the excellence of the schools
and wisdom of the scholars in Spain and asked him to take the
young Gerbert back with him to complete his education. For the
next three years, Gerbert studied under bishop Hatto of Vich, and
whether or not he came into contact with Arabic learning while in
Spain,[43] he became thoroughly proficient in all branches of mathematics, that is, the entire quadrivium.

In 970 or 971 Borrel went to Rome to persuade pope John XIII to
elevate Vich to an archbishopric, and took both Hatto and Gerbert
with him. The pope was much impressed by Gerbert's mathematical
knowledge and brought the young scholar to the attention of the
emperor Otto I, who was at that time in Italy. Thus began the
association of Gerbert with the Saxon dynasty, which would be
maintained until his death and result in his eventual elevation to
the papacy. For the moment, however, Otto was interested only in
obtaining a competent teacher of mathematics for the students who
were part of the imperial court, and which included the next
emperor, Otto II. But Gerbert was restless in his new position
and, pleading that he would rather learn what he did not know than
to teach what he did know, he obtained Otto's permission to leave
and pursue his studies when an opportunity should arise.

Within the year a suitable opportunity did arise in the person of
an archdeacon of Reims, probably named Gerannus, who was reputed
to be a learned philosopher. Gerbert accompanied the archdeacon
back to Reims and gave him lessons in mathematics in return for
lessons in philosophy. But the difficulty of mathematics soon
discouraged Gerannus, who nevertheless continued teaching Gerbert
until the pupil knew more than the teacher. He was now master of
all branches of learning, having studied literature (grammar) at
Aurillac, mathematics at Vich, and philosophy (dialectic) at
Reims. We know that he added a thorough knowledge of medicine to
his attainments, but when he accomplished this is not clear.

The breadth of his knowledge and the quality of his mind attracted the attention of Adalberon, archbishop of Reims, who was to remain on the closest terms with Gerbert until the archbishop's death in 989. Adalberon appointed the young scholar scholasticus (teacher of the cathedral school) of Reims, and here he spent the next ten years building up the library and revolutionizing the curriculum and teaching methods of the cathedral school. His fame as a teacher spread throughout Europe, even as far as Magdeburg, where it aroused the jealousy of another pedagogue of local fame named Otric. Hoping to catch Gerbert in error, Otric sent one of his pupils ostensibly to study under Gerbert, but really to spy on him and report his doctrines to Otric. Basing his case on an inaccurate report from his spy, Otric began to denounce the supposed error of Gerbert. Both principals in this dispute were sufficiently important that the emperor himself (now Otto II) took cognizance of it. Travelling in Italy, with Otric in his entrourage, in 980, Otto encountered Gerbert and Adalberon, who were returning to France from some ecclesiastical business in Rome, and invited them to join his court. The whole party then proceeded down the Po to Ravenna where, at the emperor's command, a public disputation was held in the presence of a large number of learned men, the emperor himself presiding. Gerbert's pupil, Richer, took notes on the debate, which are still extant. These show us both the acuity of Gerbert's mind and the extremely elementary nature of the philosophical discussion of the time. Otric's charge was that Gerbert had subordinated physics to mathematics, as species to genus, and the entire debate was devoted to arranging genera and species, subjects and predicates in their proper order. The majority authority was Boethius, especially his Arithmetic and translation of the Isagoge, and the Timaeus in Calcidius' translation. But though Gerbert's discussion was of an elementary nature, it was thoroughly competent and showed a firm and clear grasp of the material presented in his authorities, even if he was not able to go beyond them.[44]

Having been declared the winner by his former pupil, Otto II, Gerbert returned to Reims loaded down with gifts from the emperor. Two years later, in 983, Otto rewarded him further with the wealthy and famous abbey of Bobbio, but in return for this he required an oath of personal loyalty (which Gerbert gladly gave) and that the new abbot reside in his abbey (a condition which caused Gerbert considerable grief). He continued his studies and book collecting as best he could in his new home, but he soon became embroiled in local squabbles which wasted his time and sapped his energies. When Otto died the following year, Gerbert returned to Reims and resumed his teaching career, but now he also became embroiled in French and imperial politics. He was involved in the election of Hugh Capet to the French throne, and was later caught in the midst of contending parties in Reims, where he was irregularly elected archbishop. This brought him into conflict with the papacy, and when another of his former pupils, the new French king

Robert, supported his rival in this affair, Gerbert retired to imperial Italy, where he was received warmly by Otto III. Through Otto's favor, he became archbishop of Ravenna in 998 and a year later was elected pope as Sylvester II. During the next few years, the pope and his young imperial patron planned the establishment of a perfect peace through a universal monarchy ruled jointly by pope and emperor. But Gerbert died in 1003, shortly after Otto, and their magnificent dreams came to nothing.

Gerbert's interests and accomplishments extended over the entire range of the available learning of his day. He was firmly convinced that education should be a preparation for an active life, and so his own teaching was always practical, but in the highest sense of this word. He was furthermore more acutely aware than most educators or scholars of the interrelatedness of the separate disciplines and therefore of the necessity of teaching them in the proper order. He took great pains to acquire the best books available on each subject, and like Servatus Lupus a century and a half earlier, he was an indefatigable collector and copier of books, although he does not seem to have been interested in textual emendation.

His knowledge of classical Latin literature was extensive and his appreciation of it acute. His favorite author was Cicero, especially the speeches, which he knew intimately and often quoted in his letters. He seemed to feel a special kinship with Cicero, and like the great consul and senator of old, he found in the study of philosophy a solace and a diversion from the tribulations of his political activity.

In his teaching at Reims, he gave lectures on Terence, Virgil, Horace, Lucan, Persius, Juvenal and Statius, and was also familiar with the works of Sallust, Caesar, Suetonius, and Seneca, as well as scholia on many of these authors,[45] and he knew the Timaeus in Calcidius' translation. He constantly made requests for manuscripts of the classical authors from friends in Germany, Belgium, Rome, Bobbio, and other parts of Italy, and from France, and built up a considerable library at Reims. Nowhere is the influence of Cicero more evident than in his letters, in which he "with Ciceronian brevity and admirable lucidity, sets forth the anxieties and difficulties, the hopes and consolations of a life divided between action and study."[46]

To his teaching of literature, Gerbert, in accordance with his practical purpose of exploiting both the wisdom and the style of the ancients as a preparation for an active life, joined the study of dialectic. For this subject he began with Porphyry's Isagoge and Boethius' commentaries. He then proceeded to Aristotle's Categories and De interpretatione in Boethius' translation, along with Cicero's Topics and Boethius' commentary. The course was capped with Boethius' Topics, Categorical Syllogisms, Hypothetical

Syllogisms, Definitions, and Divisions. The method he employed was a verbal commentary, designed to explain difficult sections, resolve apparent difficulties, and sometimes rephrase and rearrange the works in order to get the essential doctrine across to his students. Gerbert is the first teacher known to have commented on Aristotle's logical works. He had managed to gather together, by diligent effort, all the works on logic available in his day, and it is of some interest that a century and a half later, so great a philosopher as Abelard did not know many logical works which were unknown to Gerbert, although, to be sure, he made much more advanced use of them.

The studies of literature and dialectic were not, however, ends in themselves. When his pupils had mastered this fundamental material, they were obliged to put it to use in oral disputations in the classroom, and often a visiting "Sophist" was brought in to test the mettle of the boys, or they were sent to other teachers to defend their views. This was the way in which Gerbert taught rhetoric, thus turning it from a sterile classroom exercise into a living part of the being of each of his students. The classical Latin authors were guides to style and arrangement, the logical works provided the rules of reasoning and of detecting errors, and guided practical experience in the classroom showed the students how to utilize what they had learned.

In the teaching of mathematics,[47] (i.e., the quadrivium), Gerbert insisted upon the importance of teaching arithmetic first, since it is the first part of mathematics. For all the subjects of the quadrivium, he relied heavily on Boethius, as he had in dialectic, but he also wrote several works himself, including three works on arithmetic, the Regula de abaco computi, Libellus de numerorum divisione, and, after he had become pope, a Liber abaci. These are primarily concerned with improved methods of computation and probably do not give a nearly complete picture of Gerbert's mathematical accomplishments.[48]

The next subject of the quadrivium, building upon the foundation laid in the other arts, was music; the third was astronomy; and the fourth was geometry, on which Gerbert also wrote a textbook of his own,[49] drawing both upon the surveying methods of the Romans and the Geometry probably written by Boethius. It was in his teaching of astronomy that Gerbert was most revolutionary and most successful. Most of the standard handbook treatments of astronomy were available in the tenth century, Hyginus, Pliny, Vitruvius, Calcidius, Macrobius, Martianus Capella, Cassiodorus, Isidore, and Bede being the major authorities. In addition to these, Gerbert may have had access to Boethius' lost Astronomy, which he mentions in a letter to archbishop Adalberon, and if so this would be the only trace of the work, except for a possible mention in a tenth century catalogue of the library at Bobbio, since late Antiquity.[50] These authorities, however, present a variety of astronomical hypotheses, some assuming eccentric orbits for the planets, some utilizing epicycles, one (that of Heraclides of Pontus) assuming that only the interior planets, Mercury and Venus, revolved around the sun, while the sun and the other planets revolved around the earth. As we have already noted, there was considerable study of astronomy earlier in the century, especially at Auxerre and St. Gall, and men realized the inconsistencies in their authorities. Gerbert, although fully aware of all this, consciously rejected the more sophisticated explanations and adopted the astronomy of Pliny, which admits eccentric orbits but not epicycles, probably on the pragmatic grounds of simplicity. Then in order to communicate the principles of astronomy to his students, he constructed two models, a celestial globe and a planetarium. Concerning the first, Richer writes:

> He fixed its two poles obliquely to the horizon. Near the upper pole he set the northern constellations, and near the lower one the southern. He determined its position by means of the circle which the Greeks call orizon and the Latins limitans, because it divides the constellations which are seen from those which are not. By this sphere, fixed in this way, he demonstrated the rising and setting of the stars and taught his students to recognize them. And at night he followed their paths and marked the place of their rising and setting on the different regions of his model.[51]

So precisely did Gerbert make this globe that its construction took an entire year, marked by several unsuccessful attempts. Its basis was polished woood, which was then covered with horsehide, on which the various circles and constellations were marked in different colors to aid in their identification. By means of this device, Gerbert was able to demonstrate visually to his students the effect of the obliquity of the ecliptic on changing the rising and setting times of the constellations located on the zodiac.

An even more spectacular visual aid was his planetarium, which indicated the arctic and antarctic circles and the tropics. Inclined to this set of circles he placed the ecliptic, within which the planets, probably represented by metal balls suspended by wires, moved in their proper orbits by an ingenious mechanism.[52] Gerbert was also a patient astronomical observer and constructed at least two fairly complex viewing instruments: a hollow wooden hemisphere, large enough to accommodate a man's head, with the circles of the five zones marked on it and six-inch viewing tubes of equal bore inserted at the intersections of these circles with a longitudinal circle; and a single viewing tube oriented to the heavens by means of two metal rings and outlines of the major constellations made of wire, by means of which wrote Richer, "if one constellation should be pointed out to anyone, even though he were ignorant of the subject he could locate the others without a teacher."[53]

In addition to the customary seven Liberal Arts, we know Gerbert to have been well acquainted with medical literature. In a letter to a sick friend, identified only as "R," Gerbert quotes Cornelius Celsus' De medicina, VIII, 15 verbatim in informing the friend that what he incorrectly calls "postuma" is properly termed "apostema," and was named ΥΠΑΤΙΚΟΝ by the Greeks.[54] While he was abbot of Bobbio, he wrote to an otherwise unknown abbot Gisalbertus, requesting the loan of the Ophthalmicus[55] of the first-century Alexandrian physician, Demosthenes, and later (988) wrote to a monk named Rainardus at Bobbio asking to borrow the same work,[56] apparently the copy he had earlier made himself, so he could have a copy made for the library at Reims. The place of medicine in Gerbert's teaching is not clear, but his pupil Richer was extremely well-read in the medical works of Antiquity and probably owes this knowledge to Gerbert's teaching.

While it is almost impossible to say on the basis of our extant sources whether Gerbert came into direct contact with Muslim learning while he was in Spain,[57] there is clear evidence in one of his letters that he was aware of what was going on in the Muslim world, and that he was not further than one remove from it himself.[58] Writing in 984, he asks his friend Lupitus of Barcelona, otherwise unknown, for a copy of an Arabic astrological work which Lupitus had translated into Latin.[59] The book referred to has never been positively identified, but it is probably the work on astrology often attributed to Gerbert, or the work upon which this was based. Regardless of its precise identification, it is clear from Gerbert's letter that he at least knew of Arabic astrology through a translation made by a friend of his. There is other evidence too that Muslim learning was beginning to penetrate Latin Europe by the late tenth century. At Paris and in the British Museum there are extant manuscripts of the tenth century which very clearly show Arabic influence, and one Paris manuscript (Bibliothèque Nationale 17868, folios 2-12) contains a work attributed to an Alchandrus, which seems to be a translation from the Arabic. So while the great flood of translation into Latin from Arabic was still a century in the future, there was clearly a beginning of Muslim influence before the end of the tenth century.

Except for his letters, the surviving works of Gerbert are disappointing and hardly seem to justify the reputation for learning which he possessed in his own day. His arithmetical works are not extraordinary; his major philosophical work, De rationali et ratione uti, while competent, is elementary in the extreme; his Geometry is merely a compilation from "Boethius" and material he culled from the handbooks; and his theological work is so slight that it has not even been mentioned in this discussion of Gerbert. That he was a figure of truly outstanding importance cannot, however, be denied. In his unceasing search for the best books available on each subject of the curriculum and his ability to make intelligent use of them; in his teaching methods, which combined systematic commentary, visual aids, and practical experience; and above all in his appreciation of the interrelatedness of all the academic disciplines and their vital relationship to the active life, Gerbert represents the very highest type of humanism. And it was from him more directly than from men like Servatus Lupus or from the Italian schools that the humanism of the High Middle Ages was derived.

Probably the most striking aspect of intellectual life in the tenth century is the break with the forms and attitudes of the past and a general willingness to try something new. The Tropes and Sequences are clear examples of this spirit of conscious innovation. So too are Hrothswitha's plays, which, although allegedly modelled on those of Terence, are considered by Hrothswitha herself to be a new and superior type of drama. Also, the leonine rhyme, though not completely without classical antecedents and unhappily a most unpromising verse form, is perfected and widely employed in the tenth century. The lyric, of course, dates back to the sixth century B.C., but its revival in the tenth century and the new forms it took make it virtually a new creation. And most spectacular of all perhaps were Gerbert's new teaching techniques; somwhat less striking but equally important were the subtle changes which occurred in the meaning of many terms and disciplines, especially rhetoric, which we noted in the discussion of St. Gall.

This brings us to a second major aspect of the tenth century, its emphasis on the practical. This was the major reason for the development of the "new rhetoric," both in the Formula Book (Collectio Sangallensis) and in the teaching of Gerbert. It also clearly dominated the study of medicine, astronomy, and law, and to some extent the innovations in music. At the end of the century at St. Gall, Notker Labeo (whom we shall discuss in the next chapter) made extensive use of German, including many translations, in teaching the Liberal Arts and insisted that the Arts were simply a practically necessary preparation for the study of theology.

We might also note the close connection between the religious and secular realms. Just as the monasteries were both religious communities and centers of political and military power, and abbots and bishops were both churchmen and secular political functionaries, so no line was drawn between the secular and religious spheres of life in literature. The monastic schools taught both clerics and laymen, and the religious Sequence soon served as a form for secular compositions, most of which were undoubtedly written by ecclesiastics.

Similarly, there was frequent and often fruitful contact between

the learned and popular traditions. One of the best results of
this was the _Waltharii Poesis_; one of the worst was the _Ecbasis
Captivi_. Somewhere in between were Notker's story of the wonderful ram and _Gesta Caroli Magni_. And a more subtle blending of
popular tradition with both the _Song of Songs_ and the Latin classics was the lyric _Iam dulcis amica_, _venito_.

While the tenth century hardly invented dramatic forms and contrasts, it certainly cultivated them. The Tropes, dialogues sung
by contrasting choruses, developed in time into authentic drama.
The similar form of the Sequence provided a form whereby the
lyric, whether dramatic narrative or dramatic episode, nearly
always involved contrast in its subject matter as in its form.
Even as a soliloquy, the lyric _Levis zephirus exsurgit_ exploits
the contrast between the joy of springtime and the sadness in the
singer's heart.

And finally, by the tenth century there have developed clear
national characteristics and a consciousness of nationality in
European literature. Both Hrothswitha and Liudprand display
considerable national pride in their works, though this was hardly
their dominant characteristic. In the lyrics, we can almost see
the stereotypes of the European nations.

The major division of European peoples was between German and
Latin, and each group considered itself superior to the other.
Liudprand and the author of the _Gesta Berengarii_ were smugly
confident of their superiority to the barbaric peoples of Europe.
But the Germans had their champions, too. They were keenly aware
of the dichotomy of German and Roman. Notker the Stammerer had
defended Bede against the charge that he was a barbarian, had
recommended the works of Rabanus Maurus above all the other
Fathers and had spoken of Gregory the Great as a composer of
"Roman delicacies." The German vernacular, German legend and folk
themes were all employed at St. Gall and other German monasteries.
And even in classical studies, the Germans claimed superiority.
This tension between Latin and Teuton is well illustrated by the
oft-told tale of Gunzo of Novara and the monks of St. Gall. Otto
the Great had summoned Gunzo to establish the Liberal Arts firmly
on German soil. Gunzo made the trip in mid-winter, bringing with
him over 100 manuscripts, including the _Interpretation_ and _Topics_
of Aristotle and Calcidius' translation of the _Timaeus_, and one
night stopped over at St. Gall. The brothers were scrupulously
correct in their reception, but there was clearly an underlying
resentment at this foreigner's being brought in to do something
that the Germans could have done as well. During the course of
the evening's conversation, Gunzo mistakenly used an accusative
where he should have used an ablative. The monks began to murmur,
and the scholasticus, Ekkehard II, called the blunder to Gunzo's
attention. The Italian seems to have said nothing at the time,
and the affair soon became a general scandal. Shortly afterwards,

Gunzo sent a letter to the monks at Reichenau, St. Gall's great rival, in which he admitted his mistake but pointed out with some condescension that since his native tongue was so similar to Latin, it was an easy matter to confuse the two. Then with an impressive display of learning and considerable pedantry he tried to justify his error by piling up many citations of similar usage by the classical authors. He also claimed that he had been very badly treated by the St. Gall monks. The whole affair is silly, but not without significance.

There is no break in European intellectual development as we reach the year 1000. The directions and nature of European intellectual life for the next two hundred years were clearly established, and the eleventh and twelfth centuries would be a time of rapid progress and development of what had begun in the tenth.

NOTES

1. See the extremely important and perceptive group of essays, "Symposium on the Tenth Century," Medievalia et Humanistica 9 (1955), 3-29. The best general account of education and learning in tenth century is A. Hauck, Kirchengeschichte Deutschlands, III, 274-342.

2. For a summary account of the cathedral and monastic schools, their organization, curriculum, and libraries, see Leon Maitre, Les Ecoles episcopales et monastiques en occident avant les universities (768-1180) (Liguge-Paris, 1924).

3. MGH: PLAC, IV, 265.

4. Raby, Sec. Lat. Poetry, I, 250.

5. MGH: PLAC, IV, 77ff.

6. For example: oc-que-cidens, Burgun-adiere-diones. See Raby, Sec. Lat. Poetry, I, 262; and M.L.W. Laistner, "Abbo of St. Germain-des-Pres," Bulletin Du Cange, I (1924), 27ff.

7. Ed. K. Strecker, Berlin, 1924 and 1947. Good English summary in J. M. Clark, The Abbey of St. Gall (Cambridge, 1926), pp. 244-245 and Raby, Sec. Lat. Poetry, I, 263-268.

8. On the authorship and date, see K. Hauck, "Das Walthariusepos des Bruders Gerald von Eichstätt," Germanisch-romanisch Monatsschrift, 4 (1954), 1ff.; and O. Schumann, "Waltharius-probleme," Studi Medievali 18 (1951), 177ff.

9. Clark, Abbey of St. Gall, 246.

10. MGH: PLAC, IV 354ff. See also Sandys, History of Classical Scholarship, I, 504 and Raby, Sec. Lat. Poetry, I, 278-283.

11. See J. M. Clark, The Abbey of St. Gall.

12. Clark, Abbey of St. Gall, 105.

13. MGH, Leges, V.

14. For example, to multiply CCXXXV by IV, first multiply CC by IV, giving DCCC. Then multiply XXX by IV, giving CXX. Then multiply V by IV, giving XX. Add the products of the separate multiplications to get DCCCXL. The actual computation is done on the fingers.

15. Quoted in Clark, Abbey of St. Gall, 123.

16. MGH: PLAC, IV, 297-314.

17. For a more extended and excellent discussion of the Trope and Sequence, see Raby, Christian Latin Poetry, 210-223.

18. MGH: PLAC, IV, 297-314.

19. PL, CXXXI, 1003.

20. MGH: Script., II, 726-763.

21. MGH: PLAC, II, 483. Bibl. in Raby, Sec. Lat. Poetry, I, 277.

22. E. Voigt, ed., "Ecbasis Captivi, das älteste Thierepos des Mittelalters," Quellen und Forschungen zur Sprach und Culturgeschichte der germanischen Völker, VIII (Strasbourgh, 1875). Full summary and bibl. in Raby, Sec. Lat. Poetry, I, 269-277.

23. MGH: PLAC, III, 703.

24. See L. Traube, "O Roma nobilis," Abhandlungen der königlich bayerisch Akademie der Wissenschaften 19 (1891), 299ff.; and B. M. Peebles, "O Roma nobilis," American Benedictine Review, 1 (1950), 67ff.

25. See K. Strecker, ed., Die Cambridger Lieder (Berlin, 1926) and the discussion in Raby, Sec. Lat. Poetry, I, 291-306.

26. Raby, Sec. Lat. Poetry, I, 305.

27. On Bruno, see Pertz, MGH, IV, 252; and L. Maitre, op. cit., 57-58.

28. Sandys, History of Classical Scholarship, I, 505.

29. This is the claim of J. Aschback, Roswitha und Conrad Celtes (Vienna, 1867). It has never been taken seriously.

30. First published by Conrad Celtes in 1501. The best modern edition is by K. Strecker, Hrotsvithae opera omnia (Leipzig, 1930).

31. The foregoing is based upon her prefaces. See C. St. John's translation, pp. xxvi-xxix.

32. For a good discussion of these, see Hauck, Kirchengeschichte Deutschlands, III, 307-308.

33. All six, including the prefaces, are translated by Christopher St. John (Cristobel Marshall), The Plays of Roswitha

(London, 1923). The Paphnutius is reprinted from this work in C. W. Jones, ed., Medieval Literature in Translation (New York, 1950), pp. 211-227. Dulcitius and Paphnutius are printed in John Gassner, ed., Medieval and Tudor Drama (Bantam Classic Q C 286) in the translation of Sister Mary Marguerite Butler, R. S. M.

34. Sandys, History of Classical Scholarship, I, 506, points out that tenth century MSS of Terence's plays are written as though they were in prose.

35. F. J. E. Raby, Christian Lat. Poetry, 208.

36. Sister Mary Marguerite Butler, Hrotsvitha: The Theatricality of her Plays (New York: Philosophical Library, 1960).

37. Liudprand's works are best edited by Joseph Becker (Hanover, 1915). English translation of all the works by F. A. Wright, The Works of Liudprand of Cremona: Antapodosis, Liber de Rebus Gestis Ottonis, Relatio de Legatione Constantinopoli- Lana (London, 1930).

38. Antapodosis, VI, 3.

39. He quotes from the Iliad and from Lucian's Somnium and Plato's dictum that "The responsibility rests with the chooser; the god is free from blame." See Sandys, History of Classical Scholarship, I, 511.

40. Relatio, ch. 37.

41. C. W. Previté-Orton, in Cambridge Medieval History, III, 160, quoted in F. A. Wright, op. cit., 22.

42. On Gerbert's life, I have followed J. Havet, ed., Lettres de Gerbert (983-997) (Paris: Alphonse Picard, 1889), v-xxxix and F. Picavet, Gerbert: Un Pape Philosophe (Paris, 1897), 21-67.

43. On the possibility of Gerbert's having been in contact with Arab learning, see Picavet, op. cit., 30-38.

44. There is an excellent summary and discussion of this debate in H. O. Taylor, Medieval Mind, I, 289-292. See also C. Prantl, Geschichte der Logik im Abendlande (Leipzig, 1927), II, 54-58. For a fuller discussion of the debate and its relationship to Gerbert's De rationali et uti see Picavet, op. cit., 141-158.

45. Sandy's History of Classical Scholarship, I, 509.

46. F. J. E. Raby, Sec. Lat. Poetry, I, 307.

47. See Nicolas Bubnov, Gerberti Opera Mathematica (Berlin, 1899). For a discussion of the mathematical works, see Picavet, op. cit., 75ff.

48. See Picavet, op. cit., 75-76; for a schematic representation of Gerbert's method of computation, se ibid., 183.

49. On Gerbert's Geometry see Picavet, op. cit., 70-84.

50. See J. Havet. ed., Lettres de Gerbert, 6-7 and note.

51. Richer, Historia, III, 48-49.

52. The planetarium is described more fully in Harriet Lattin, op. cit., 16-17. See also the same author's The Peasant Boy Who Became Pope: Story of Gerbert (New YOrk, 1951), 123-130 for a fuller account of his astronomical instruments. Also Picavet, op. cit., 77-80.

53. Richer, Historia, 53.

54. Ep. 169, ed. J. Havet, op. cit., 151.

55. Ep. 9, ed. Havet. op. cit., 7.

56. Ep. 130, ed. Havet, op. cit., 117.

57. See the discussion in Pacavet, op. cit., 30-38.

58. Evidence for tenth century translation from Arabic into Latin is presented by L. Thorndike, History of Magic and Experimental Science, I, 697-718.

59. J. Havet, op. cit., ep. 24, 19.

Chapter 8

Monastic and Cathedral Schools of the
Eleventh and Twelfth Centuries

The developments which had got under way in the tenth century proceeded rapidly in the eleventh and twelfth. Population increased, new land was brought under cultivation, Europe continued her expansion at the expense of her neighbors and even embarked on overseas adventures. Towns continued to increase in size, wealth and power, and new ones were founded where none had been before. The feudal age was taking shape; and despite the sometimes intense but always generalized feelings of nationalism, the slow growth of royal power, and the ambitious and sometimes successful designs of the emperors, the effective units of government during the Romanesque period were for the most part the feudal principalities.

This age can best be characterized as one of rapid, widespread and radical change. Because of this, many tensions were generated, many battles fought both by pen and by sword, and a concept of modernity -- that is, a feeling of the distinctiveness and superiority of the present--- became an integral part of the European world view. Although there was clearly a steady increase in good public order, there was no single authority, not even the papacy, capable of imposing its views on all of society, and the growth and development of Latin Europe at this time were the result of the numerous conflicts between people of different areas, different persuasions, different values and different ways of looking at the world. The idea of reform was perhaps the most important single dominating notion, and it encompassed all aspects of society. New orders of monks attempted to reform the old Benedictine order; a new kind of popes tried to reform the entire church and radically alter the papacy's position in it; a new class of people -- merchants and artisans for the most part -- tried to reform the legal status of the towns and to improve its position in society; new religious ideas, many of them heretical, shook the church to its foundations and resulted in its near transformation during the thirteenth century. Many kings sought to reform their relationship to their realms. This was a time of unusual toleration of dissent and difference, of considerable freedom of thought and expression, of intellectual diversity, creativity and daring.

The most important educational establishments of Europe continued to be the cathedral and monastic schools. As the twelfth century wore on, monastic schools lost their importance, as the vital centers of European civilization shifted from the countryside to the towns, and the cathedral schools gained in importance to the point that their essential character was basically transformed. Still, there were exceptions to this general statement. The monastic schools at Bec and especially at St. Victor of Paris were still of major importance in the twelfth century; the schools of

Salerno and Bologna had only the most tenuous relation to the cathedrals; and "grammar schools," either supported by the church or established and maintained by the guilds or towns, provided a broader educational base and increased the number of Europeans who were literate at least in their own language and were capable of performing basic arithmetic operations.

The number of schools offering higher education was large and growing, though inconstant. The ambition and dedication of individual teachers were the most important factors in establishing a school's reputation. The major European schools were Monte Cassino and Salerno, Bologna, Pavia, Modena, Parma, Reggio, Freising, Bremen, Cologne, Erfurt, Vienna, St. Gall, Montpellier, Lyons, Orleans, Tours, Le Mans, Paris, Chartres, Reims, Laon, Bec, Hereford, Oxford, and Lincoln. This list is fairly arbitrary; several hundred schools are known to have existed, and the ones I have mentioned had their ups and downs. Unfortunately, detailed information about them is usually lacking. In the case of the best documented ones, we might know the names of two or three masters, have a library catalogue or a description of teaching methods, and a vague notion of the curriculum.[1] To say that they all taught the seven Liberal Arts does not tell one much, since these subjects were differently conceived and valued by different masters, and the text books used for them varied greatly in quality and scope. The classics constituted the basis of the curriculum, and the late Roman handbooks and Carolingian textbooks were still widely employed. But we are dealing with a period of rapid change and growth, and the enlargement and improvement of the curriculum was an important aspect of this growth. Then as now, many teachers, finding no books suitable to their purposes, wrote their own. The schools we shall be discussing in detail are those in which significant innovations were made. This makes generalization difficult.

A. St. Gall. We have already spent much time describing the school of St. Gall in the ninth and tenth centuries. One reason we know so much about it is that a monk named Ekkehard, embittered by the destruction of the older easygoing Benedictine monasticism and its humane if parochial culture by the Cluniacs -- foreign fanatics, he labelled them -- has left us a history of the monastery from its foundations to his own day. His theme is the glory of his house in the good old days and its ruin by the Cluniacs in his own time. There is no doubt some truth in this. St. Gall never again achieved its former eminence, and the Cluniacs were much more concerned with singing, praying and architectural adornment than with literary culture. But Ekkehard's history itself is a worthy monument to the culture of St. Gall in the eleventh century.

Much more important though is another monk named Notker,[2] the third of his name, nicknamed Labeo (thick-lipped). Continuing the tradition of innovation which we have already noted at St. Gall, he used German rather than Latin as the language of instruction in the schools and translated many works into German for the use of his students. He was a devout Christian and was fully convinced of the utility both of the Liberal Arts and sacred writings for one following a clerical vocation. He therefore refused to let linguistic pedantry stand between the texts and his students' understanding of them. His earliest translations were predominantly secular and included Boethius' De consolatione and De trinitate, the Disticha Catonis, Virgil's Eclogues, Terence's play Andria, The Marriage of Mercury and Philology of Martianus Capella (a very difficult task), Aristotle's Categories and Interpretation, and an anonymous work on arithmetic. But his real interest was theology. He translated the Psalms and composed a German commentary, based on Augustine, to accompany them. He also translated the first third of the book of Job and Gregory the Great's Moralia in Job, which he completed on his death bed. Of these works, only five are extant today -- the Consolation, the first two books of De nuptiis, the two Aristotelian works, and the Psalms. We know of the others by Notker's mention of them in a letter to bishop Hugo of Sion.

We also learn from this letter that Notker's translations were viewed as dangerous and unworthy innovations by his contemporaries and that Notker was fully conscious of the radical nature of his new methods. Bishop Hugo had apparently deplored Notker's use of the vernacular and his excessive preoccupation with religious texts in his later life, and he urged Notker to confine his teaching to the Liberal Arts. Notker replied that he could do nothing but what the Lord allows, that he could not teach the Liberal Arts for their own sake but only as a necessary foundation for the study of theology. He further explained that in order to make it easier for his students to master the subject-matter of the Arts, he had translated the Latin texts into German and that he explained them to his students in German, using the classical authorities as his guides. "I know you will shrink from them as being unusual," he said, "but little by little they will begin to recommend themselves to you, and you will soon excel in reading them and will recognize how quickly we can understand by means of our mother tongue what can be understood only with difficulty or not at all in a foreign language." It is for his translations that Notker is known as "the father of German prose." The German that he wrote was understandably strongly influenced by the idiom and structure of Latin. Still, his translations were not mechanical or woodenly literal. He used great care in choosing just the right German word, he often paraphrased, and his subject-matter often necessitated the adoption of Latin words. He was also keenly interested in the spelling of his native tongue and insisted upon the use of accents to distinguish short (´) and long (^) vowels.

In addition to the translations for which he is chiefly famous,
Notker composed three quite competent Latin treatises on logic for
use in the schools: De syllogismis, De definitione, and De parti-
bus logicae. He wrote an original work in German, De musica,
which includes a section on the measuring of organ pipes. This is
the earliest known work on music theory in any European vernacular. And he also composed a Computus and a treatise on rhetoric
written in Latin but using many German examples and explaining the
technical terms in German. But important as Notker's works were
for the future, he was working within a dying tradition. The
vitality of rural monasticism had passed its peak. The new age
would draw its strength from the towns and cities.

B. Salerno and Monte Cassino. One of the most remarkable areas
of Europe in the eleventh and twelfth centuries was southern
Italy. Never conquered by the Franks, largely neglected by Byzantium, harrassed but never ruled by the Muslims, these lands south
of Rome had grown wealthy and populous, ruled by a number of
virtually independent local powers, whose frequent wars upset
public order somewhat but did not arrest the development of a high
literary culture. It seems to have been the Italian custom to
educate a significant percentage of her young men, quite often in
secular grammar schools. The two dominant intellectual centers
were the monastery of Monte Cassino and the city of Salerno, famed
for its teaching of medicine.

We have already noted the misfortunes which had befallen Monte
Cassino in an earlier age. After the recovery of the Carolingian
period, the great monastery was again destroyed, this time by the
Muslims, in 883. For nearly three generations the monks preserved
their identity in exile in Campania, and in 949 returned to
rebuild their monastery. From the beginning of the eleventh
century, a series of able and powerful abbots accelerated the
process of recovery and initiated a golden age of Benedictine
culture in southern Lombard Italy. Hundreds of books were copied,
of both pagan and Christian classics, the buildings were adorned
by columns from Rome and mosiacs from Byzantium, the school
regained its former preeminence, and the monastery provided men to
lead the papal battle against the emperors. In addition to diplomats, popes and pamphleteers, the house also produced poets who,
while not ranking among the best of the Middle Ages, still give
evidence of the tenacity of the classical tradition in southern
Italy through all its difficulties and its careful blending with
Christiantiy, to produce a characteristically southern Christian
humanism quite different from that which was simultaneously emerging in northern Europe. The best of these poets, Alfanus of
Salerno,[3] felt himself to be a Roman and took great pride in that
city's illustrious history. He was also an unabashed lover of
secular literature, of which he had a deep and broad knowledge.
With one possible exception, all his poems are quantitative and
are written with impeccable accuracy in even the most difficult

meters.

But Alfanus' life was more closely tied to the city of Salerno, where he began his career as a physician, and after a sojourn as a monk at Monte Cassino, he ended it as abbot and archbishop of that city. Salerno had been famous at least since the year 985 for her physicians, who had acquired a European-wide fame for their practical medicine. During the eleventh and twelfth centuries it was the most renowned school in Europe, a center for the composition of original medical treatises, for the translation of works from Greek and Arabic, and for the development of a large collection of questions and answers concerning a vast array of physical problems -- the so-called Salernitan Questions. Its greatest period extended from the mid-eleventh century, the time of Gariopontus, Petroncellus and Alfanus, to the early thirteenth, with the death of its two most illustrious medical writers, Maurus and Urso. Alfanus, as a young man, had been a physician at Salerno, and from this period of his life date a number of medical writings and a translation from the Greek of the very important and influential The Nature of Man by the sixth-century bishop of Emesa, Nemesius. A young monk from Monte Cassino named Desiderius, having fallen ill, journeyed to Salerno for treatment, met the young physician Alfanus, and the two men became fast friends. Alfanus then became a monk at Monte Cassino for a short time, but he was called back to Salerno first as abbot of the Benedictine house there and then as archbishop. Desiderius later became abbot of Monte Cassino and eventually pope as Victor III. Alfanus made another important friendship while he was at Salerno. In about 1077 a refugee named Constantine[4] from Muslim north Africa arrived in Salerno. Alfanus was greatly impressed by his intelligence and learning. He taught him Latin, converted him to Christianity, and was instrumental in Constantine's taking monastic vows at Monte Cassino, where he wrote diligently until his death in 1087, two years after Alfanus'. Constantine's works are all translations (or sometimes Latin paraphrases) of Arabic medical works which in turn were based on Greek. His major work, the Pantegni, provided Latin Europe with a far more rationalized, orderly, complete and theoretical medical treatise than it had previously possessed, although this work does not seem to have been much used at Salerno until about the middle of the twelfth century. At this time, medical teaching at Salerno underwent a change from the essentially practical approach of its earlier history to a more theoretical and systematic emphasis. Philosophy became a part of the curriculum, the range of problems discussed far exceeded simple medical matters, and works of primary importance for the study of nature generally were written. This trend culminated in Urso of Calabria, whose works made use of Aristotle's natural philosophy, continued the strong practical and experimental trends of earlier Salernitan works, but also exhibit a highly developed theoretical sophistication.

In the early days, teaching seems to have been carried on exclusively by the question and answer method, and this was maintained throughout the medieval period. But by the second half of the twelfth century, commentaries on the standard texts were being written at Salerno, and by the end of the century large-scale original treatises were being composed. Despite the fact that we possess many of the texts used in medical teaching at Salerno, we have very little direct information on how they were employed.

Although Salerno declined in relative importance during the thirteenth century, the works of its masters exercised a significant influence on all subsequent study of medicine in Latin Europe.

C. <u>Bologna</u>. Contemporary with the flourishing of intellectual culture in southern Italy was the rapid growth of the north Italian towns. Technically subject to the western emperor, they managed for the most part to maintain a <u>de facto</u> independence while growing wealthy on trade and manufacturing. They developed an intense civic life and organs of government which necessitated a large number of literate citizens, trained in the <u>ars dictaminis</u> and law. Like the south Itailians, they too maintained close contacts with the eastern Empire, and in the twelfth century north Italian scholars played an important part in the translating of works from Greek into Latin.

The town which seized the intellectual leadership of northern Italy during the twelfth century was Bologna,[5] a place whose earlier importance seems to have been slight. There are several legends purporting to explain the sudden appearance in Bologna in the late eleventh century of a number of excellent teachers of Roman law, but the surviving evidence does not permit us to identify the cause of this phenomenon with any confidence. That it occurred can, however, be asserted with certainty. There is evidence of an Arts school at Bologna by the mid-eleventh century, not widely famed but of respectable quality. Several well educated bishops had received their education there, and two different bishops gave substantial endowments to the school to facilitate the studies of their canons and seminarians. It was not for teaching the Liberal Arts, however, that Bologna became famous. It was rather because of the coincidence of a rising interest in Roman law in both the Italian cities and Europe as a whole and the appearance in Bologna in the late eleventh and early twelfth centuries of a series of able law professors that Bologna developed quite rapidly into the leading law school of Europe. About the earliest teachers we know little but their names and dates -- Alberto, Pepo, and Iginolfo (1050-1079), Pietro di Monte Armato, Rusticus and Lamberto di Fagnano (1090s). We do not know their status (the terms master and doctor were loosely used at this period), whether they were professors at a regularly established school or simply private teachers. Still, the simultaneous activity of so many teachers of Roman law in one small town suggests a most unusual concentration of specialized teaching, far more than can be documented for any other European school of this period. Several of these men were praised by contemporaries as being completely skilled in all the Arts, which would indicate (as we should guess in any case) that they had been trained as grammarians and had subsequently used their grammatical training in the teaching of a specialized subject, namely Roman law.

But by far the most famous of the Bolognese law teachers, having the same legendary position in the rise of the Bolognese studium that his contemporary Peter Abelard has in the rise of the schools of Paris, is Irnerius. He was probably educated at Bologna and Ravenna, the old imperial capital of Italy, and his new methods, his fame, and his activities brought to Bologna a preeminent fame in legal studies.

According to a persistent and widely quoted story taken from the works of a thirteenth-century Bolognese law teacher, writer, and city booster, Odofredus, Roman law had disappeared from the West as a result of the barbarian invasions and was revived by Irnerius in the early twelfth century when he found a copy of Justinian's Corpus Juris Civilis in Ravenna, brought it home to Bologna, and there singlehandedly revived the knowledge of Roman law in the West. However, it can be shown that the study of the Roman law survived in Italy throughout the Middle Ages, first at Rome, then Ravenna, Pavia (the old Lombard capital), and finally at Bologna, where it flourished and slowly permeated the legal theory and practice of all the rest of Europe.

Irnerius seems to have been the first to have lectured on the entire corpus of Roman law in a systematic fashion, explaining it as he went along by a series of glosses. This procedure of glossing the text occasioned the use of the term "glossators" for him and his followers, the most famous of whom are Azo, Accursius, and Azone. Their fame and that of their method attracted large numbers of students both from Italy and from other parts of Europe, men who, for the most part, had already studied the Arts and were considerably older than was common at a medieval school. It was through these men that the reputation of Bologna and the methods and attitudes of her teachers influenced legal studies throughout Europe. John of Salisbury tells of a friend of his who, after studying law in France, went to Bologna to hear the lectures of Irnerius. Here, he said, he "unlearned what he used to teach, and on his return untaught it."

Bologna's fame was not restricted to the civil law. In the middle of the twelfth century, a Bolognese monk named Gratian composed his Concordia discordantium canonum, or Decretum as it was popularly called. This work dealt with the law of the church in a comprehensive and systematic way and became the authoritative text (later augmented) of canon law. Thus in both branches of the law, civil and ecclessiastical, Bologna became the leading school in the twelfth century. It was on this basis that the university of the thirteenth century was established.

In spite of the fame of twelfth-century Bologna, no surviving text enables us to state with certainly what the teaching was actually like at this time. The best we can do is extrapolate from the words of Odofredus in the thirteenth century describing his own lectures:

> Concerning the method of teaching, the following order was kept by ancient and modern doctors, and especially my own master, which method I shall observe. First I shall give you summaries of each title before I proceed to the text. Second, I shall give you as clear and explicit a statement as I can of the purpose of each law. Third, I shall read the text with a view to correcting it. Fourth, I shall resolve apparent contradictions, adding any general principles of law to be extracted from the passage and any distinctions or subtle and useful problems arising out of the law with their solutions. . . .And if any law shall seem deserving, by reason of its celebrity or difficulty, of a repetition, I shall reserve it for an evening repetition, for I shall dispute at least twice a year, once before Christmas and once before Easter, if you like.
>
> I shall always begin the Old Digest on or about October 6 and finish it entirely, by God's help, with everything ordinary and extraordinary, about the middle of August. Formerly the doctors did not lecture on the extraordinary portions; but with me, all students can have profit, even the ignorant and newcomers, for they will hear the whole book, nor will anything be omitted, as was once common practice here. For the ignorant can profit from the statement of the case and the exposition of the text; the more advanced can become more adept in the subleties of questions and opposing opinions. And I shall read all the glosses, which was not the practice before my time.[6]

This is probably a more complete and formal approach and one less dependent on grammatical exegesis than was the case in the twelfth century, but it provides us with a first-hand account of how law was actually taught at Bologna.

D. France. The schools of France dominated intellectual life north of the Alps. Although we know of the existence of some respectably good schools both in England and in Germany, almost no specific information concerning them has survived, and students from these areas who were serious about pursuing advanced studies customarily went to France for their higher education (although a few of the more adventurous went to southern Italy or Spain). There seems to have been an intellectual continuum reaching from Tours on the Loire river to Laon in Picardy within which students and teachers moved rather freely. Hardly any scholar is associated with only one of these schools; most studied or taught at from two to four of them. In the eleventh century they seem still to have been utterly dependent on the fame of individual teachers. They possessed no institutional structure, set curriculum, examination or degrees.

By the second half of the eleventh century, the curriculum was heavily laden with the classics, although the standard compendia and textbooks of earlier times were still much in evidence. Medicine and law continued to be studied and, although no French school would be so important in medicine as Salerno or in law as Bologna, Montpellier was widely known for its medical teaching, and Ivo, a bishop of Chartres, is one of the major figures in the history of law. The tendency seems to have been, as we have mentioned, for the monastic schools to decline in importance and for students and teachers to congregate in the towns. As the twelfth century wore on, there was increasing specialization and fragmentation of learning. As a result of this, the literary classics necessarily played a less important part in the overall curriculum, as enthusiasts concentrated their attention and abilities on dialectic, law, medicine, the ars dictaminis, or natural science. By mid-century these people had become so important that there were numerous complaints about the decline of learning from the "good old days" of sound classical scholarship and gentlemanly philosophy, when all departments of knowledge were just so many appendages to literature. John of Salisbury, of whom we shall speak later, was the best known and most eloquent of the spokesmen for the old way, but many shared his concern. During the last quarter of the twelfth century, European thought was given radically new direction by the acquisition of huge amounts of Greek and Arabic learning in Latin translation. But the assimilation of that material was accomplished for the most part during the thirteenth century.

We can perhaps best gauge the nature of the eleventh century French cathedral schools by extrapolating from the works of some of their most illustrious teacher and products. The lives of the young men who studied at them were apparently little different from their secular counterparts. They seem to have engaged in a healthy amount of sexual experimentation, to have been in close touch with the life of the city of which they were a part, to have been ambitious for worldly gain and high office in the church. But they were set apart from the rest of society by the fact of their clerical vocation and by their learning. For the most part, they were sincere if not fanatical Christians (the fanatics tended to gravitate to one or another of the reforming monastic orders).

Their attitude toward the world and its values was one of tolerance, often even acceptance, unless the rights and privileges of
the church were threatened.

A galaxy of four poets, scholars, and administrators attests to
the high quality of classical studies in these cathedral schools,
as well as the close relationships among them. These are Godfrey
of Reims, Marbod of Rennes, Baudry of Bourgueil and Hildebert of
Lavardin, whose lifetimes stretched from 1035 to after 1125.[7]
These men were all steeped in classical poetry and were themselves
poets of considerable merit. Although they took their ecclesiastical duties seriously, they are evidence of what may almost be
called a cult of Antiquity and of a narrow (that is, classical)
humanism. They exchanged literary letters of friendship in the
antique tradition, they were masters of panegyric, of pastoral
poetry, of satire and of love poetry. All were enchanted by the
idealized vision of Roman Antiquity derived from Latin literature,
and all were famous, powerful, influential and highly respected in
their lifetimes.

The oldest of these four poets was Marbod of Rennes. He was born
at Angers about 1035 and was educated at the cathedral school of
that city. In 1069 he became chancellor of Angers and then head
of the cathedral school. In 1096 he became bishop of Rennes and
found the life of an administrator not to his liking. In his old
age he became a Benedictine monk and lived until 1123.

The range of his poetic activities is typical of the scholar-poets
of his milieu. To aid his students he wrote a brief essay on
versification called De ornamentu verborum. Following a long-
established tradition he composed poetic versions of the books of
Ruth and Jonah. He pursued the cult of friendship in a series of
poetic letters. His output also includes erotic verses, which he
had composed as a young man, and a series of essays called the
Liber decem capitulorum on standard "serious" topics -- De tempore
et aevo, De meretrice, De Matrona, De senectute, De fato et genesi, De voluptate, De bono mortis and De resurrectione corporum --
in his old age. In De tempore et aevo he gives us what may be a
revealing glimpse of life in an eleventh-century cathedral school,
detailing the sexual excesses of youth, when the fervid heat of
the genital organs pulsing through the hearts of lascivious boys
and dirty girls breaks the bonds of shame, and nothing can stop
them from rushing to copulation. And he even complains that in
old age, when the pleasure of coitus has been removed, nevertheless the unsated pleasure continues to itch, and a man seeks in
his desires that which he cannot do in act. In De fato et genesi
he opposes astrology because it is stupid, not because it is
un-Christian.

But his most famous poem, the work which made his reputation in
his lifetime and during the following two centuries, was his Liber

lapidum, describing sixty different stones and gems along with their natural and magical virtues. The substance of this book was derived largely from Solinus and Isidore, but the book was an immediate and lasting success. It exhibits the same concern for secrecy of doctrine that we have noted many times before and shall encounter many times in the future; while these wonderful secrets of nature are of great value and utility to the good and the wise, they could be very dangerous if they should fall into the hands of the ignorant and unworthy. The _Liber lapidum_ was early translated into Old French, and somewhat later into English, Italian, and Danish. Although a naturalistic world view was appearing among small groups of men from Salerno to Chartres and Hereford, the magical lore inherited from Antiquity still had a strong hold on the minds of educated Europeans throughout the twelfth century.

Baudry of Bourgueil was born at Meun-sur-Loire in 1046, received his education at the cathedral school at Angers, retired to a monastery for some years, in 1089 was elected bishop of Bourgueil, and became archbishop of Dol in 1107. Raby correctly characterizes him as a "man of letters, pure, and simple, whom the schools were to produce in increasing numbers." He was above all a student of literature and a poet. Like most Latins for the next 200 years, his favorite poet was Ovid, and love of one sort another was his favorite topic. He exchanged letters of friendship with the other great poets of his day. He wrote a poem to an educated nun named Emma, celebrating the delights of the rural life, and several poems to another nun, Constance, concerned largely with their "blameless love." He composed an exchange of letters between "Ovid" and "Florus" full of tender sentiments and great learning. But his pièce de resistance, the work for which he is chiefly famous, was a poem which he wrote for Adela, daughter of Duke William of Normandy, describing her (imaginary) bedroom. He tells the countess that his poem can "spead her name o'er lands and seas, whatever clime the sun's bright circle warms." The bedroom he describes, in its decorations, furnishings and arrangement, is a symbolic presentation of the whole of human learning. He saw the room in a vision, with its intricately laid mosaic floor a map of the world, the ceiling with the constellations and signs of the zodiac, the walls hung with rich tapestries, the bed laden with learned symbolism, the statue of Lady Philosophy.

Somewhat less famous than these two men but still deserving of mention is Godfrey of Reims. Little is known about his early life, but it is known that he was educated at the cathedral school at Reims, whose reputation and library had been so greatly enhanced by Gerbert a century earlier, and that he spent his later years as scholasticus and chancellor there. Like his contemporaries, he wrote letters of friendship and erotic verse, influenced by Ovid, and was also a master of flattering rhetoric. Like Baudry, he wrote a poem to that much praised lady countess Adela, outdoing even Baudry in the extent of his flattery. The poem is saturated with classical mythology and reminiscences and ends with a bit of the "reverse causality" which appears frequently in twelfth-century poetry: Fate decreed that duke William should conquer England so that this most excellent lady might be a princess. When Godfrey died, his dear friend and admirer, Baudry of Bourgueil, wrote five poetic epitaphs for him, claiming, in the attractive flattery of this genre, that Godfrey was greater than Cicero and second only to Aristotle.

But the greatest and most important of this group was Hildebert of Lavardin. He was educated in the cathedral school at Le Mans, where he later taught. In 1096 he became bishop, and in 1125 he was made archbishop of Tours. Like many men of letters, he did not relish the pressures and tribulations of an administrator's life, but he nevertheless performed his duties. But it is as a poet and scholar rather than as a statesman of the church, that he is known to posterity, "the first man of letters of his age."

The cult of friendship found a worthy devotee in Hildebert, as many of his letters attest, and in one case this led to a moving panegyric of Berengar of Tours, a theologian who had denied transubstantiation and had been attacked as a heretic by so important a man as Lanfranc. Hildebert came to the rescue of his friend's reputation with an elegy praising Berengar's kindness, his personal virtures and his charity to the poor.

Hildebert was also a moralist, and for this purpose he used the epigram (modelled on Martial) and the satire. His poem on Lucretia was long considered a product of classical Antiquity. He also wrote letters of flattery, loaded with classical apparatus, to many of the great of his day, including the fair countess Adela. He exchanged some letters with women, with whom he seems to have got along quite well, but he also wrote a savagely anti-feminist satire, Quam nociva sunt sacris hominibus femina, avaritia, ambitio. A hint of the reason for his change of heart is the elegy On the Faithless Mistress (De perfida amica) -- if Hildebert was indeed the author. Its author tells of his mistress who left him for another who was richer and goes on to denounce women and wealth. The style certainly suggests Hildebert as the author, and if we assume it refers to an actual love affair, it would explain why a man who had had such easy and natural relationships with women changed into a woman-hater. But the theme is so old and so persistent in literature that such an assumption might not be warranted even if we accept Hildebert as the author.

Hildebert's three greatest poems were written as the result of his personal troubles. Feeling overwhelmed by the troubles attendant to his bishopric, he journeyed to Rome in an effort to get the pope to relieve him of his post. His request was denied, but he was overcome by the spectacle of ancient Rome, with its marble buildings, its arches, its statues of the gods. He wrote two poems about his experience. In the first, he addresses Rome, so grand, so full of glory, so beautiful and awe-inspiring. In the second poem Rome answers, replying that she is today even more glorious under St. Peter than she had been under Caesar.

And finally there is the poem he wrote on his exile (De exilio suo). He had been forced to flee overseas by the Count of Maine, against whom he had unsuccessfully tried to defend the rights of his church. This gives him an opportunity to reflect on the whims of Fortune, who had earlier given him so much, and on the assorted miseries of man, and finally to affirm his faith in the Providence of God, before Whom even Fortune is powerless. But even his providence is not so much that of Augustine as of Cicero and Boethius.

It would not be stretching even the most restricted meaning of the term to call these men humanists. They were professional teachers of the litterae humaniores, deeply steeped in the literature of classical Antiquity and accepting of its values. The cult of friendship lived again in their elegant epistles. They numbered themselves among the "sacred poets," and they used their poetic talents to express a wide variety of human thoughts, values, aspirations and reflections. They were masters of moralizing epigrams and satires, of poetic essays, of courtly flattery, of penetrating and delicate wit. They had an eye for bucolic beauty, for human frailty as well as human excellence, for the grandeur of historical development, and for the value of poetry in conveying esoteric learning. Although masters of their ancient models, they were not mere imitators but genuinely creative poets applying the forms and techniques of older poets to their own time. They were part of a growing urban society and culture centered in the rising towns of France and making possible the development of an urbane and literate class of scholars and ecclesiastical administrators, among whom these poems circulated.

One can hardly avoid asking the question of whether the more worldly poems had any basis in the personal experiences of these authors. Did Hildebert really have a mistress who left him for a richer rival? Did all these men engage in youthful love affairs? Did they describe womanly beauty from personal knowledge or from imagination? Questions like these cannot be given a definite answer. Although it is more than likely that as young students they did have amorous adventures, many of these poems have the look of the school exercise: they were simply ways of demonstrating poetic aptitude on a theme which has universal appeal. These students were not monks, after all. Although the four men we have discussed all took higher orders later on, many cathedral school students did not, at least not until the possibility of ecclesiastical preferment induced them to do so. And, although art is usually based on experience, it is usually a transformation of that experience by the genius of the artist. So while we should not look upon these cathedral school students as sober little celibates, we should nevertheless be cautious in using their poems as literal documents of their lives.

Even as the classical revival was reaching its peak, other scholars in other places were developing specialized interests and tended to look upon literature merely as a necessary preparation for more advanced studies. Since we shall devote separate chapters to many of these, we shall give only a general sketch here.

One of the most general and striking developments of the eleventh century was the renewed enthusiasm for dialectic. This cannot be attributed to the acquisition of any new texts, for the recovery of the "New Logic" of Aristotle still lay in the future. These men had the same texts which had been available ever since late Antiquity, but they were approaching them with greater care and understanding and with much greater enthusiasm. Berengar of Tour was using dialectic in an effort to understand the sacrament of the eucharist; Anselm of Canterbury, while he was still at Bec, was implored by his students to give them a proof for God's existence based strictly on reason and independent of revelation; William of Champeaux and Roscelin began their fateful investigation of the nature of universals; Peter Abelard and Thierry of Chartres, attempting to comprehend the mystery of the Trinity by the rules of logic, found themselves accused as heretics at local church councils; Adelard of Bath, an Englishman who had studied at Tours and taught at Laon, denied the possibility of magic, and finding his Latin contemporaries too bound by authority and tradition, sought out the wisdom of the Muslims in Spain. Theology was the special interest of the school of Laon under Anselm, medicine of Montpellier, dialectic of Paris, literature and philosophy of Chartres, natural science of Hereford in England.

Among the schools whose masters were most catholic in their interests, most sensitive and receptive to new ideas, and most famous for their writings was Chartres. Its first teacher of European-wide reputation was Fulbert, a pupil of Gerbert's at Reims who later became bishop of Chartres and under whom the school flourished. Many of the major figures of the mid-eleventh century had been his students, and even his former classmate at Reims, Richer, came to Chartres to complete his education in medicine. Although the school undoubtedly continued to function after Fulbert's death, it seems to have had only local importance until the beginning of the twelfth century, when once again a teacher of uncommon ability raised it to the forefront of European education and inaugurated a period of brilliance which lasted for half a century. This was Bernard of Chartres, primarily a teacher of grammar, whose reputation lasted for two generations after his death. The English man of letters, John of Salisbury, has left us a detailed account of Bernard's teaching, which he undoubtedly got from one of the master's pupils:

Bernard of Chartres, the most abundant fountain of literature in Gaul in modern times, followed this manner of
teaching. He pointed out, in reading the texts of the
authors, what was simple and followed the rule, and in
the course of doing this he also pointed out aspects of
grammar, rhetorical "colors," the quibblings of sophists,
and in what respect the text under discussion was related
to other disciplines, without however trying to teach
everything at one time but measuring his teaching in any
one session to the capacity of his students. And, since
the beauty of a composition lies either in its elegant
and suitable union of verbs and adjectives with nouns, or
in the use of metaphor and other figures of speech, he
took every opportunity to inculcate these in the minds of
his students. And since memory is strengthened and
mental abilities sharpened by practice, he urged his
students to imitate what they had heard, some by warn-
ings, others by beatings or other punishments. Each
student was required each day to recite something from
the lesson of the previous day, some more, some less, and
thus with them each day was the disciple of the preceding
one. The evening "review session," which was called the
declination, was so chock full of grammar that if anyone,
unless he were slow-witted, should attend for a full
year, he would have at hand the rules of speaking and
writing, as well as the words and phrases in common use.
But since it is not proper that any school or day should
be without religion, such matter was included in the
lesson as would build faith and character and inspire
those present to the good. . . .He explained the poets
and orators to those who had been assigned prose exercises or imitations of the poets and told them which
traits should be imitated, pointing out the way the words
were linked and the elegant clausulas of passages. And
if, for the sake of adorning his own work, someone had
sewn on a patch of cloth filched from another, Bernard
would quietly reprove him but usually not punish him.
After he had reproved the student, if the borrowing had
been clumsily done, he would, with modest indulgence,
tell the boy to write so that he who imitated his predecessors would be imitated by his successors. He also
taught among the first essentials and impressed on their
minds what the virtue of economy was; which matters are
to be praised by the fitness of things, which of words;
where brief and frugal expression is appropriate, where
fullness, where bombast, where the proper expression for
any occasion. He warned his students to go through their
histories and poems carefully and not as though they were
being spurred to flight. And from each of them he demanded as a daily debt something committed to memory.
Nevertheless, he said that the superfluous ought to be

shunned and that those things written by the most famous authors sufficed; for to pursue what everyone, even the most contemptible of men, has said is either excessively humble or vain, and it deters and destroys those mental capacities which should be free for better things.[8]

There seems to be nothing in this which we have not already noted at St. Gall and Reims. It was not so much Bernard's method as his execution which made him a teacher of great effectiveness and repute. The curriculum and textbooks at Chartres also, although they were extensive, contain nothing new or surprising; the Latin classics, the handbooks of late Antiquity, the textbooks of the Carolingian age, and some of the works of Gerbert, plus some basic texts in medicine and law, still constituted the basic reading matter in a twelfth-century school. But this was a restless and inquisitive time, and the best teachers pushed relentlessly on. The library at Chartres had some rare and valuable books in medicine and mathematics for the advanced scholar, and its chancellors and teachers for half a century were quick to acquire and assimilate whatever new materials became available through translations from Greek or Arabic. The attitude of the school was perhaps best expressed by Bernard, who said: "We are like dwarfs that sit on the shoulders of giants; hence we can see more and further than they, not because of the keeness of our vision, but because we have been raised up and are being carried by these men of great dimensions."

The intellectual character and reputation of Chartres was the work particularly of three men, Gilbert of la Porrée, Thierry of Chartres and William of Conches. These men had wandered like most scholars, and they had connections also with the schools of Paris, Laon, Poitiers and Tours, as either students or teachers or through close personal contacts. Among them they crystallized what was best in the modern currents of thought without losing touch with the older grammatical tradition. Their writings tell us much about their teaching, since most of them are lecture notes or, in one case, a syllabus of texts for the entire Arts curriculum.

Gilbert of la Porrée had been a pupil of Bernard at Chartres as a young man and had then gone to Laon to study theology under Anselm. He probably also taught for a time at Laon, and it was there that he wrote his Glosses on the Psalter, his first work to attract wide attention. In 1124 he became a canon at Chartres, and in 1126 he was made chancellor. In all probability, he continued to teach and write. In 1141 he was teaching at Mt. Ste. Geneviève near Paris. The following year he was named bishop of his native city, Poitiers, where he died in 1154. In addition to his Glosses on the Psalter, his most important work was a commentary on Boethius' De trinitate. Written in the same milieu and until recently attributed to Gilbert was a philosophical treatise

<u>De</u> <u>sex</u> <u>principiis</u>. The latter work was adopted into the curriculum of most European universities in the thirteenth century along with the newly translated works of Aristotle. It was an essay on the last six of Aristotle's <u>Categories</u> (action, passion, place, when, where, and <u>habitus</u> or permanent possession).[9] The <u>Categories</u> had been available in Boethius' translation since the sixth century, but this author was no longer content simply to learn the work. Like many of his contemporaries, he was squeezing every possible bit of knowledge out of the old sources, using them as occasions for original thought, and grasping eagerly at any new bits of knowledge that might become available.

The other two men, Thierry of Chartres and William of Conches, have much in common, both in the scope of their writings and in their ideas. Thierry is generally thought to have been Bernard's brother, although this is far from certain. At any rate, he was <u>scholasticus</u> at Chartres when Bernard was chancellor. In 1126 he went to Paris and there he established his reputation as one of the foremost teachers of his day. He compiled a superb teaching syllabus, the <u>Heptateuchon</u>, in which he combined the most important texts representing the traditional and the new learning in each of the seven Arts. He bequeathed his own copy of his book, along with forty-eight others, to the cathedral library at Chartres, where they remained until they were destroyed during World War II. In 1141 he became chancellor of Chartres, a position he held for the next ten years. He spent the last few years of his life as a Cistercian monk.

There is no certain proof that Thierry taught at Chartres, although it seems unlikely that a teacher of his reputation, author of the famous <u>Heptateuchon</u>, would not have continued to do some teaching. In any case, he must certainly have exerted a considerable influence on the intellectual climate there. Thierry was especially interested in mathematics and medicine, both of which subjects were well represented in the Chartres library. The oldest manuscript of James of Venice's translation of Aristotle's <u>Physics</u> (made <u>ca</u>. 1120) was in the Chartres library, as was Adelard of Bath's translation of Al-Khwarismi's astronomical tables. His extant writings are the lecture notes he compiled for his teaching, whether at Paris or Chartres is not clear. We have his glosses on Boethius' <u>De</u> <u>trinitate</u>, Martianus Capella's <u>De</u> <u>nuptiis</u>, Cicero's <u>De</u> <u>inventione</u>, and most important of all, his <u>Hexameron</u> or <u>De</u> <u>sex</u> <u>dierum</u> <u>operibus</u>. This last work was one of the most important examples of the tendency so pronounced among the avant garde of Europe in his day to attempt the explanation of the formation of the world purely in terms of natural causes. Thierry of course accepted the fact that God created matter, which he understands as the four elements. But from that first moment on, everything evolved according to physical laws through the agency of the vital heat (<u>calor</u> <u>vitalis</u>). First came inanimate nature; then, from it through the intensification of the vital heat, came the vegetable kingdom, then the animals, proceeding from lower to higher, and finally man. There was no separate creation of man. Although he was considered to have been created in the image and likeness of God, the agencies of his creation were the four elements and the vital heat. Thierry's notion of the soul had more in common with the thought of the physicus, or student of material nature, than with that of the theologian; that is, he considered it a product of the vital heat rather than as a separable substance capable of an independent existence.

William of Conches was another pupil of Bernard of Chartres who later (1141) became chancellor. We do not know the details of his early academic life, but he was clearly teaching at Chartres between 1138 and 1141. He wrote his major work while he was still quite a young man, that is, the famous Philosophia or Dragmaticon,[10] as the later redaction is called. William is typical of the intellectuals of the first half of the twelfth century in his utter mastery of the traditional material, his reinterpretation of much of this material, and his eagerness for whatever new works might become available in Latin from either Greek or Arabic. Although the classical poets and the handbook authors Calcidius, Macrobius and Martianus Capella, are used extensively by him, he also knows Constantine the African's Pantegni and the Isagoge in artem parvam Galeni of Johannitus, both from the Arabic, as well as Theophilus Protospatharius' De urinis and Alfanus' translation of De natura hominis, both from Greek. He was also familiar with many of the Salernitan medical questions or with the still obscure sources of those questions. Clearly he was much indebted to the authors of Salerno. But he also gave them something in return. In puzzling over the exact meaning of the word "element," and especially Constantine the African's definition of it as the simplest and minimal part of what exists, he devised the concept of the "elementatum." Reasoning that the so-called elements, earth, water, air, and fire, were actually compound, each having two of the basic qualities (i.e., hot, cold, moist, and dry), he asserted that the true elements can only be known by reason; they are the primal intelligible qualities which exist only in combination but whose existence can be inferred. The "elements" which we experience are therefore really "elemented things," (elementata), or things made from the elements. This concept of the elementata quickly made its way to Salerno and by the end of the twelfth century was generally known as a Salernitan doctrine.

But more important than the separate concepts and details of William's work was its basic concept: to present a systematic and unified account of the world of nature on the basis of a limited number of scientific principles. William shared with Thierry a thoroughly naturalistic attitude, and like Thierry he radically transformed his sources in the course of his work. The Philosophia is not simply a well devised patchwork of authorities, but an original and highly creative work, bending its sources to give

-162-

a coherence and novelty to its world view. It was one of the most
popular books composed in the twelfth century, 140 manuscripts of
it still being extant, and it strongy influenced the educated
European's view of nature for 200 years.

The works of both William and Thierry exhibit a kind of naturalism
which is commonly called "Chartrian." However, it extended far
beyond the walls of the little city of Chartres. Bernard Silvestris in his De universitate mundi and Alan of Lille in his
Anticlaudianus and De planctu naturae, two of the most widely read
and influential learned poets of the twelfth century, shared this
view of the world and had the same tendency to reinterpret their
sources rather radically. This was, in fact, a common feature of
twelfth-century thought. These Chartrian authors were therefore
not unique.[11] They were, however, at the forefront of European
thought, and just as much as the masters of Salerno, Bologna, and
Paris, they were helping to set the patterns of European thought
for the rest of the Middle Ages.

Still, it was the schools of the city of Paris which would, before
the twelfth century was over, constitute the first full-fledged
university in northern Europe. Like those of Bologna, the Parisian schools seem to have been of slight importance before the
late eleventh century. The cathedral undoubtedly maintained a
school for the training of future cathedral clergy, the numerous
monasteries in and near the city had schools of some sort, and the
canons of the church of Mt. Ste. Geneviève on the left bank of the
Seine and outside the twelfth-century city walls maintained a
school of some repute. An occasional master of some fame taught
in one or more of these schools, but Paris from the eighth to the
eleventh centuries ranked as one of the minor intellectual centers
of Europe. Then quite suddenly, paralleling the rise of the
French monarchy and the growth of the city of Paris itself, it
pushed with dramatic rapidity to the forefront among European
studia, drawing students from Brittany, the Low Countries,
England, Germany, and Italy, as well as the whole area of northern
France. It remained true that most of the Parisian teachers of
this period also spent portions of their careers teaching elsewhere, but a large number of quite famous men spent at least some
time teaching at Paris. Here they seemed to find an adequate
supply of eager students willing to pay for competent instruction.

The abbey of St. Victor, founded early in the twelfth century by
the philosopher William of Champeaux in what was then the countryside, found itself caught up in the growth of the royal city. Its
abbot, Hugh, was one of the main writers of the first part of the
century, and in addition to teaching the brothers, Hugh also
provided instruction for advanced scholars from outside the cloister who had been attracted by his great reputation.[12] St. Victor
was the last monastic school to play a major role in the development of European education and thought, and to do this it had to

-163-

abandon the exclusivist policy of earlier monastic schools and join in the life of society as a whole and of the city of which it was rapidly becoming a part.

Within the city itself, the chancellor of the cathedral of Notre Dame enjoyed a monopoly on education, and any master wishing to teach in the city had first to secure a license from the chancellor. The resulting educational system, however, was far from being simply a large cathedral school. The masters were not necessarily members of the cathedral chapter (although many were), and the students often had vocations other than clerical in mind. The teachers had to find their own facilities, often renting appropriate rooms or teaching in their own homes. The school of master Adam on the Petit Pont was conducted in the teacher's living quarters.

By about the middle of the century, the number of masters and students in Paris necessitated some sort of informal organization, in which the masters took the lead, and some regulations concerning length of study and curriculum were agreed on. From this point on, the schools of Paris can better be considered as the incipient University Paris, which, with Bologna, was the earliest city in Europe to have such a concentration of academicians.

NOTES

1. See Leon Maitre, Les Ecoles episcopaux et monastiques de l'Occident depuis Charlemagne jusqu'à Philippe-Auguste (768-1180), 2nd ed., (Paris, 1924).

2. On Notker, see Clark, The Abbey of St. Gall, 248-54.

3. For Alanus' poetry, see Raby, Sec. Latin Lit., I, 377-83.

4. There is no satisfactory work on Constantine in English. The two best accounts of his activity are Heinrich Schipperges, Die Assimilation der arabischen Medizin durch das lateinische Mittelalter (Wiesbaden, 1964), 17-49, and Boubaker ben Yahia, "Constantin l'Africain et l'école de Salerne," Les Cahiers de Tunisie 9 (1955), 49-59.

5. On Bologna, Rashdall, Universities of the Middle Ages, ed. Powicke and Emden (3 vols., Oxford, 1936), I, 87-141. Very useful for the twelfth century is Patricia Ann King, The Origins of the University of Bologna, unpublished M.A. thesis, University of Southern California, 1970.

6. Odofredus' account is printed in C. H. Haskins, The Rise of the Universities (New York, 1923; reprint Cornell University Press, Ithaca, New York, 1965), 42-44. I have altered his translation somewhat.

7. On the following four poets, see Raby, _Sec. Latin Lit._, I, 312-48.

8. _Metalogicon_, I, 24, ed. Webb, 57-58.

9. On this work, see Edward Grant, "The Concept of _Ubi_ in Medieval and Renaissance Discussions of Place," _Manuscripta_ 20 (1976), 71-80: 72-73. It is edited by Lorenzo Minio-Paluello, _Aristoteles Latinus_, I, 6-7 (Bruges-Paris, 1966).

10. The _Philosophia_ is printed under the name of Honorius of Autun in _PL_ 172:39-102. The _Dragmaticon_ has been printed as _Dialogus de substantiis physicis ante annos ducentos confectus a Vuilhelmo Philosopho_, ed. G. Gratarolus (Strassburg, 1567; reprint 1967).

11. See R. W. Southern, _Medieval Humanism_, 61-85 and the rejoinders by Peter Dronke, "New Approaches to the School of Chartres," _Anuario de estudios medievales_ 6 (1969), 117-140 and N. Häring, "Chartres and Paris Revisited," in _Essays in Honor of Anton Charles Pegis_ (Toronto, 1974), 268-329.

12. The best work on the Victorine school is Penny McElroy Wheeler, _The Twelfth-Century School of St. Victor_, unpublished Ph.D. dissertation, University of Southern California, 1970.

Chapter 9

The Romantic Love Literature of the Twelfth Century

Modern European civilization is set off sharply from all others, past and present, by several distinctive features, among which is its notion of romantic love, the subject of the present chapter. Undoubtedly, the feelings that members of the opposite sex have had for each other have changed little, if at all, since men and women have existed, but the rationalizations of these feelings and the value systems of which they are part have taken many forms. Modern romantic love is the child, however perverse, of medieval love literature. The elements of romantic love very likely began as literary conceits, but as time passed, they have influenced the language, social customs, and sexual expectations of our culture. The very notion of being "in love" and of this being a sufficient justification for sexual activity; of love's being an ennobling passion, on the one hand, or an illness, on the other; the blasphemous use of such words as angel, divine, or paradise in an erotic connection; the man's affectation of performing services for his beloved -- all these and more are modern survivals, often taken quite seriously, of what began as a literary game. But we have lost the medieval awareness that love's world is a fiction, that love turns reason and morality on their heads, and that although love is wonderfully alluring, it can only lead to grief if not kept in its place.

Love seldom looms large in the heroic literature of a people, but it often becomes an obsession during times of civility and sophistication. The Middle Ages drew upon the love literature of both the Roman (especially Ovid) and the Biblical traditions (especially the Song of Songs), and these two sources nurtured a profuse flowering of amorous and erotic writing from the tenth century onward. Much -- even uniqueness -- has been claimed for this literature, and much has been blamed on it. C. S. Lewis has said of it: "French poets, in the eleventh century, discovered or invented, or were the first to express, that romantic species of passion which English poets were still writing about in the nineteenth. They effected a change which has left no corner of our ethics, our imagination, or our daily life untouched, and they erected impassible barriers between us and the classical past or the Oriental present. Compared with this revolution, the Renaissance is a mere ripple on the surface of literature."[1] Another Englishman, Peter Dronke, of somewhat more prosaic mind and sounder scholarship, has pointed out the characteristics of "courtly" romantic love in the literature of many peoples and has asserted that romantic passion is universal in human experience and not after all the invention of eleventh-century Frenchmen.[2] Regardless of one's stand on this matter, the texts themselves are a joy to read. They display a wide variety of attitudes toward love, sex, and marriage, from vulgar lust to refined romanticism.

Although romanesque love literature owed much to Ovid and the tradition of the Latin love lyric, it was in the poetry of the southern French vernacular (commonly called Provençal or Occitan) that the new sentiment was first developed and expressed. It was the poetry of the small courts of southern France at a time when the nobility was beginning to consider itself superior to the general run of mankind not only in power, but also in its more refined perceptions and its more demanding moral code. In short, nobility was coming to be looked on not simply as a status, but as a quality. Some of the poets were of the high nobility, some of the lesser nobility, some were base-born, and a few were women.

Of the history of the genre before duke William IX of Aquitaine (1071-1127) we know nothing, but in a group of poems attributed to this noble troubador we find the establishment of a tradition which would last for nearly two centuries. Provençal poetry was governed by strict conventions in matters of content and treatment of content but allowed for some freedom of stanzaic structure, rhyme scheme and meter. They were songs intended for performance, and only thus can they be understood. The composer himself was not necessarily the performer, although he spoke in his own person, striking different poses and addressing specific people or groups in the audience, indeed, he sometimes even addressed the person singing the song. The person or group addressed was indicated by a senhal, or clue of some kind -- a nickname or veiled reference to some feature of personality, deeds, or appearance. The make-up of the audience and the poet's interaction with it became increasingly complex during the twelfth century. These songs were about many different things, including religion, ethics, and warfare, but a large proportion had to do with love. One finds in them a variety of attitudes toward love, sex, and women, so such terms as "courtly love" used without qualification are apt to be misleading. In the early poems of duke William, women are considered only as objects of lust, and sexual relations have only a physical component. These are the "songs of the

cunt," a genre in which William excelled:
My companions, I have had so much miserable fare,
I can not keep from singing and from feeling vexed.
Still I do not want my little doings known in great detail.

And I shall tell you my thoughts:
these things do not please me: a cunt under guard, a fishpond without fish, and the boasting of worthless men when there is never to be any action.

Lord God, King and Ruler of the universe,
why did he who first set a guard on cunt not perish?
For no servant or protector ever served his lady worse.

But I shall tell you about cunt, what its law is,

as one who has done badly in this matter and suffered worse: as
other things diminish when you take from them, cunt increases.

And those who will not believe my advice,
let them go and behold in a private preserve near the woods:
for every tree that gets cut down, two or three grow up in its
place.

And as the wood is cut, the thicker it grows,
and the lord does not lose any property or dues.
A man is wrong to cry damaged goods when there is no loss.
It is wrong to cry loss when there's no damaged goods.

This attitude remained a constant feature of Provençal poetry,
though not usually the one favored by the poet, who would play
against it, regret it, or condemn it -- but it was always there.

In his own later poems, William expresses the new "courtly" sentiment, and in his poems most elements of the tradition are found in
at least a rudimentary form:

I begin, rejoicing already, to love
a joy that I want most to settle down in;
and since I want to come back to joy,
I must go, if I can, the best way:
for I am made better by one who is, beyond dispute,
the best man ever saw or heard.

I, as you know, am not one to boast,
I do not know how to praise myself,
but if ever any joy has put forth a flower,
it should, before all other joys, bring forth fruit
and shine in perfection above them,
as when a dark day fills with light.

No man has ever had the cunning to imagine
what it is like, he will not find it in will or desire,
in thought or meditation.
Such joy cannot find its like:
a man who tries to praise it justly
would not come to the end of his praise in a year.

Every joy must abase itself,
and every might obey
in the presence of Midons, for the sweetness of her welcome,
for her beautiful and gentle look;
and a man who wins to the joy of her love

will live a hundred years.

The joy of her can make the sick man well again,
her wrath can make a well man die,
a wise man turn to childishness,
a beautiful man behold his beauty change;
the courtliest man can become a churl,
and any churl a courtly man.

Since man cannot discover, nor eye
behold, nor tongue praise anyone more noble,
I want to keep her for myself
to revive the heart within me,
and renew my flesh,
that it may never grow old.

If Midons choses to give me her love,
I am ready to receive it and be grateful,
to keep it secret and pay it compliments;
to speak and act only to please her,
to cherish the goodness in her,
to make her praise resound.

I don't dare send her anything with a messenger,
I'm that afraid she might flare up in anger;
and I myself, I'm so afraid to fail,
do not show her a single image of my love.
But she must pick out what is best in me,
because she knows: in her alone I shall be restored.

Of course, not all the stock elements of courtly love are to be
found in any one poem; indeed, many of them are mutually inconsistent. But we might characterize the elements of the courtly
tradition generally as follows: The poet asks the lady to believe
that he (and often he alone) is sincere and not a lecherous hypocrite like the others. He describes himself as her vassal, and
the lady herself is often addressed as Lord. Love then becomes
analogous to feudal service. The identity of the lady must be
kept secret to protect her against gossips, scandal-mangers, and
perhaps a jealous husband, although her physical attributes are
admiringly described. She is always blonde and white-skinned,
with wondrously white teeth and red lips, sweet breath, a long,
graceful neck, smooth throat, high, firm, small, white breasts, a
small waist, and shiny legs. Sometimes the poet has enjoyed the
lady's favors and celebrates them in song, but more often he is a
suitor, with varying degrees of hope for success. In any case,
the lover must be a man of outstanding excellence and spotless

reputation to deserve love, and a lady is wrong not to favor such a suitor, although she must never be too easy to get. There are also poems of unattainable or unrequited love, and the theme of the absent lover is one of the most persistent in tradition. The effects of love can be either devastating or incredibly salutary. On the one hand, it results in trembling, unspeakable suffering, sometimes even madness, loss of appetite and sleep. But on the other hand, it can cure a man of illness, make him brave, wise, and courteous, and, quite often, impervious to cold. The ladies are often cruel and sometimes faithless, and capable of terrifying outbursts of haughty anger, but they are essential to the courtly life.

It was also frequently perceived that love was contrary to reason and to all the requirements of society and religion. This perception provided the context of a special kind of dramatic lyric, the alba or dawn song.[3] The dramatic situation is always the same: a loyal watchman warns his master that the night is ending and he must leave the lady with whom he has been spending the night before her husband catches them. The personae include the watchman (always), the lady (usually), and the man (sometimes). The watchman represents the calls and values of the work-a-day world, of society. The woman, who always replies to him to keep quiet and go away, represents Love's world, with its own inverted moral order, its timelessness, its hostility and superiority to the world governed by nature and reason. She is always married to an "unworthy" husband (old, ugly, impotent, cruel); her lover is always "worthy;" and so her adulterous love is justified. The lover has attachments to both worlds; at first he denies the coming of dawn and joins his mistress in berating the watchman. But he is, after all, a part of the "lower world," and so he must at last reluctantly acknowledge the day, put on his clothes, and lamenting leave her. In an Occitan alba by Giraut de Bornelh (ca. 1200), the action is all conveyed by the watchman's song alone, with the lover replying in the last two stanzas:

"Glorious king, true light and brightness,
  Powerful God, Lord, if it please you,
  be a faithful help to my comrade,
  for I have not seen him since night came,
    and in a moment it will be dawn.

"Handsome comrade, whether you are sleeping or awake,
  do not sleep longer, wake yourself gently,
  for in the east I see the star rising
  that brings the day, for I have certainly recognized it,
    and in a moment it will be dawn.

"Handsome comrade, I call you by my singing,
  do not sleep longer, for I hear the bird singing
  that goes seeking the day in the foliage,

and I am afraid that the jealous one may attack you,
  and in a moment it will be dawn.

"Handsome comrade, come out to the window,
and look at the stars of the sky;
you will learn whether I am a faithful messenger to you;
if you do not do this, yours will be the harm,
  and in a moment it will be dawn.

"Handsome comrade, since I left you,
I have not slept nor risen from my knees;
on the contrary, I have prayed God, the song of Saint Mary,
that He might give you back to me for loyal companionship,
  and in a moment it will be dawn.

"Handsome comrade, out there at the entrance-steps
you begged me that I not sleep,
that, on the contrary, I stay awake the whole night until the
  day;
now neither my song nor my friendship pleases you,
  and in a moment it will be dawn."

"Handsome sweet comrade, I am in such a precious resting-place
that I would not want there ever to be dawn nor day,
for the most noble lady that ever was born of mother
I hold and embrace; for which reason I do not care at all
  about the foolish jealous one or the dawn."

  (Translated by Jonathan Saville, The Medieval Erotic Alba New
  York: Columbia University Press, 1972. Reprinted by permission of Columbia University Press.)

Another, by Cadenet, divides the poem between watchman and lady,
the most common form of the alba:

"If ever I was beautiful or renowned,
now I am changed from high to low,
for I am given to a boor
all for his great wealth;
  and I would die
if I did not have a true lover
to whom I could tell my sorrow,
  and a complaisant watchman
who could warn me of the dawn."

"I am such a fine-hearted watchman
that I do not want a faithful and justly established love affair
to be undone, for which reason I am attentive
  lest the day should come,
in order that a lover who is lying with his lady
may freely take his leave,

        kissing and embracing,
        because I cry out when I see the dawn.

"If I were on watch in some castle
and false love ruled there,
I would be false myself if I did not hide
the day as much as I could;
        for I would want
to break up false love-making;
but among faithful people
        I watch faithfully,
and cry out when I see the dawn.

"I like the long dark night
in the wintertime, when it is longest,
and not for the cold will I cease the least bit
to be a faithful watchman
        always,
so that a true lover
may be safe when he is taking enjoyment
        of a worthy lady;
        and I cry out when I see the dawn."

"Not for any jibe or threat
that my wicked husband may offer me
will I refrain from lying
with my lover till daylight,
        for it would be
ignorant boorishness
to rudely separate
        one's worthy lover
from oneself, until the dawn."

"I never saw a lover rejoicing
because he like the dawn.

"For that reason it does not suit me,
nor do I like it, when I see the dawn."

        (Translated by Jonathan Saville, The Medieval Erotic Alba,
        New York: Columbia University Press, 1972. Reprinted by
        permission of Columbia University Press.)

The alba was not confined to the southern French area, but occurred in most of the European dialects. The Germans were particularly adept at it, and probably the finest alba of all is Wolfram
von Eschenbach's Sine Klawen:

"His talons have struck through the clouds,
he climbs upward with great power,
I see him becoming gray, dawn-like, as if he will dawn,

the day, who intends to turn the worthy man away from
    companionship,
the man whom I let in with such worry.
I will bring him away from here, if I can.
His very many virtues have called upon me to do that."

"Watchman, what you are singing takes much joy from me
and increases my lamentation.
You always bring news that unhappily does not suit me at all,
always in the morning towards day-break.
You must be completely silent with me about these things:
I order you by your faithfulness.
I will reward you for it as I dare,
if my companion remains here."

"He really must get away from here immediately and without delay;
now give him leave to depart, sweet woman.
Let him make love to you at some later time, secretly,
so that he may keep his honor and his life.
He entrusted himself to my faithful promise
that I would also bring him out again.
Now it is day; it was night then,
when, as you pressed him to your breast, your kiss won him from
    me."

"Whatever pleases you, watchman, sing! But leave him here
who brought love and received love.
By your clamor he and I have always been frightened,
when no morning-star at all was rising
upon him who came here seeking love,
nor was daylight gleaming anywhere.
You have often taken him
from my white arms, but not out of my heart."

"Because of the glances that the day was sending through the
    window-panes,
and when the watchman sang his warning,
she was forced to become alarmed on account of him who was
    there beside her.
She pressed her little breast against his breast.
The knight did not lose the battle-zeal
from which the watchman's song wanted to turn him aside.
Their parting, coming near and yet nearer,
with kissing, and other things, gave them the reward of love."[3]

    (Translated by Jonathan Saville, <u>The Medieval Erotic Alba</u>,
    New York: Columbia University Press, 1972. Reprinted by
    permission of Columbia Univeristy Press.)

With the Old French romance, we are in quite a different and more
complex world. The courts are larger and wealthier, and in them

converge a multiplicity of literary currents. First was the vigorous Latin learning of the north French cathedral schools, which we have noted in the preceding chapter. Second was the earlier Old French vernacular literature, especially the Chanson de Geste, which had been flourishing for about a century. Third were many Celtic tales, especially those concerning King Arthur and the knights of the Round Table, which had probably been carried from Britain to Brittany and thence into France (these tales had had some, but very slight, influence on Occitan poetry). And finally there were the Provençal lyrics themselves, which seem to have spread through northern France as a result of the marriage in 1137 of the French king Louis VII and Eleanor of Aquitaine, grandaughter of the first troubador, duke William IX. The confluence of these traditions gave rise to a new genre of vernacular literature, the Old French romance.

By far the most successful author of romances was Chrétien de Troyes, who flourished from 1148 to about 1190 and who found an eager patron in the countess Marie of Champagne, a daughter of Eleanor of Aquitaine, as well as in Count Philip of Flanders. Chrétien had received a sound cathedral school education and was well versed in the Latin classics. The fact that he translated three works of Ovid -- Ars amandi, Remedium amoris, and parts of the Metamorphoses, now lost -- is evidence of the growing sophistication and literary interests of the courtly class, which constituted his audience. He was also, of course, familiar with the Celtic tales, the Chansons de Geste, and the older romances, and he adapted this older material to matters of contemporary interest. Chrétien himself was much interested in exploring the meaning of different ethical values in his works, and he pioneered in the use of allegory to achieve this end.

His first romance, Eric and Enid,[4] is a sensitive investigation of alienation and reconciliation, as Eric seeks to discover both true chivalry and true love. Pursuing a wicked dwarf, he stops at a knight's castle, falls in love with the knight's daughter Enid at first sight, and is given the girl in marriage by her hospitable father. But Eric then spends all his time making love to his wife and neglects his knightly duties. People gossip, and his reputation (a thing of great importance to a knight) suffers grievously. He overhears Enid lamenting his loss of reputation and is furious. Taking her with him, and forbidding her to speak to him, he sets out to wreak havoc on as many adversaries as he can find in order to prove that he is in truth a proper valorous knight, and he tests Enid's love for him by being completely beastly to her. Her loyalty never wavers. She warns him of impending danger in spite of being forbidden to speak, and when Eric is badly wounded she nurses him back to health, thus bringing about a reconciliation between man and wife. But Eric is not yet reconciled with himself. He fights a duel with another knight, who is completely given to sensual pleasures (i.e., his "other self") and kills him.

He then receives news of his father's death, and, having proved his true valor, he is crowned king of Nantes to succeed his father.

Eric and Enid explored married love and a man's responsibility both to society and to Amor. But the love considered by most Provençal poets, and by much of the northern French love literature, was adulterous. Chrétien tells us that his patroness, Marie of Champagne, provided him with the subject for the romance that was to become Lancelot, or The Knight of the Cart,[5] the first French romance to use the theme of adulterous courtly love. Chrétien's attitude toward the new sentiment is not clear. It has appeared to many critics that he satirized that which he was supposed to praise. Lancelot contains all the conventions of "courtly" love carried to an extreme and it looks much like a parody, whether intentional or not. In this romance, the wicked king of Gorre has won Arthur's queen Guenevere as a prize in single combat with Arthur's champion Sir Kay. Gawain and Lancelot set out to rescue her, but everything goes wrong. The two knights become separated, and to make matters worse, Lancelot, who is "sick with love" for Guenevere, loses his horse, and in any case has no idea of where to look for his queen. At this point a surly dwarf comes by driving a cart and offers to make good the lack of both information and transportation -- if Lancelot will get into the cart, the dwarf will take him to where he can obtain news of Guenevere's whereabouts. Since riding in such a lowly conveyance was beneath his station and would surely bring ridicule and loss of reputation upon him, Lancelot hesitated just for an instant, but his love for Guenevere overcame all other considerations and he climbed aboard the cart. Sure enough, he was jeered at and suffered every humiliation for riding in the cart, but he eventually reached the land of Gorre and crossed over the sword bridge which provided the only access to that land, suffering many wounds on the way. The king of Gorre permitted Lancelot to fight a duel for Guenevere, which Lancelot won, thus freeing her from her captivity. Now, one thinks, he shall surely enjoy her favors. But Guenevere is unexpectedly petulant and cruel to him. She has heard (we are not told by what means) of Lancelot's moment of hesitation before getting in the cart, thus indicating that his love for her was not so pure and overpowering as it should have been. However, the king intercedes with Guenevere for Lancelot, and she allows him into her bed. Guenevere goes back to Arthur, though Lancelot remains prisoner of the king of Gorre. But when Arthur holds a great tourney, Lancelot requests and receives permission to take part in it. When Guenevere recognizes him, just to test his love for her, she orders him to fight badly. He obeys and for two days is beaten and jeered at. On the third day she relented and bade him to do his best. He did and was victorious. Chrétien never carried the story beyond this point, although it was provided with a conclusion by Godfrey of Laigny.

Contemporary with the romances of Chrétien de Troyes was one of the most puzzling works of medieval love literature, De arte honeste amandi.[6] Its author was Andrew the Chaplain (Andreas Capellanus), who is often identified as the chaplain of Marie of Champagne, but it now appears that he was the chaplain of Philip Augustus. The book is difficult to understand because it clearly does not mean what it says, but Andreas was not a skilled enough craftsman that we may approach the work on the assumption that he had a clear idea of what he was about, and that if we apply sufficient critical intelligence the work will yield up Andreas' secret purpose. It has been labeled everything from a manual of seduction to a bitter renunciation of courtly love.

De arte honeste amandi (often anachronistically translated as The Art of Courtly Love) is addressed to Andreas' nephew, Walter, who has asked for advice on love. Andreas replies in three books, the first two dealing with the acquisition and maintenance of love, and the third denouncing love (and women) as the source of all wickedness and misery in the world and hurling a barrage of antifeminist cliches at the reader. Even in the first two books, he is not quite serious about the excellence of love, but whether he is attempting humor or has something higher in mind is not clear. For example, in the eight dialogues in Book I, supposedly models of the art of seduction, the man fails in his attempt every time; the women are much cleverer, keep using the would-be lover's own words to confute him, and quote the Rules of Love to show why the suitor should be denied his request. Andreas also makes a ridiculous distinction between ordinary love, which naturally leads to coition, and "pure love," in which the lovers do everything, including nude petting, except the "final solace" of love. Upon hearing this, the woman exclaims (and the reader agrees with her): "You are saying things that no one every heard or knew of, things which one can scarcely believe." And later (Book II, ch. 6) Andreas lets it slip that he really doesn't believe in the possibility either, when he counsels that even though two lovers had agreed to practice only pure love, if one of them wanted more, the other must oblige. "For all lovers are bound, when practicing love's solaces, to be mutually obedient to the other's desires." His treatment of married love, too, seems ironical in a heavyhanded way. His arguments in brief are that since between married people there is no suffering, danger, fear, or jealousy, there can be no true love. The woman's rebuttal to this, that "love seems to be nothing but a great desire to enjoy carnal pleasure with someone, and nothing prevents this feeling's existing between husband and wife," goes uncontradicted. And finally, Andreas' explanation of why it is excusable for clerks, despite their profession, to be lovers, is hardly to be taken seriously: "Since hardly anyone ever lives without carnal sin, and since the life of the clergy is, because of the continual idleness and abundance of food, naturally more liable to the temptations of the body than that of other men, if any clerk should want to enter into the lists of love, let him speak and apply himself to Love's service."

These are only the more obvious instances. They provide us with a standpoint from which to judge the work as a whole. Once we adopt this standpoint, nearly every line of De arte seems to be intended ironically. Unfortunately however it is only almost every line, and the ambiguity remains. All we can be certain of is that the work is not, as most authors assert, a manual of seduction.

Let us now turn to the text and summarize the contents of De arte honeste amandi. Book I explains what love is and how it may be attained. It contains all the commonplaces of the "courtly love" tradition, written in Latin and put forth in the manner of an academic treatise. The organization and development are poor, there is much repetition, and not a few inconsistencies. (This may have been intentional and had satiric intent.) One learns that "Love is a certain inborn suffering derived from the sight of and excessive meditation upon the beauty of the opposite sex, which causes each one to wish above all things the embraces of the other and by common desire to carry out all of Love's precepts in the other's embrace." It "causes a rough and uncouth man to be distinguished for his handsomeness, endows a man of even the humblest birth with nobility of character," and in general is the source of all the moral and social graces (although a man might be so depraved that he is beyond even Love's help). The personal quality which is most deserving of love is excellence of character, but since this is also supposed to be the result of love, we have an inconsistency which is cleverly exploited later by several of the reluctant ladies in Andreas' model dialogues. The bulk of Book I is made up of the dialogues, in which is embedded most of the love lore of the twelfth century. Women are supposed to take lovers, but they have the right to choose among several suitors. They are supposed to show discrimination and be hard to get (these precepts too are used to advantage by the ladies). Both lecherous promiscuity and aloofness are blameworthy, and Andreas tells a fearsome story of Love's afterlife, showing the beatitude of wise women, the pains of the promiscuous, and the torments of the cruel women who refused all lovers. Andreas tells two stories of the acquisition of Love's commandments and gives two sets of laws. Quite a bit of space, in several different places, is devoted to the impossibility of married love. Jealousy, secrecy, danger, and suffering are essential to true love. One may not love two people at the same time, and infidelity, impotence, or defect of character are grounds for terminating a love affair. (A man is permitted frivolous indiscretions, but a woman must remain absolutely true.)

Book III is devoted to the rejection of love. Andreas tells Walter that he has written the first two books because they had been requested, but he hopes that Walter will "read this little book not as one seeking to take up the life of a lover, but that, invigorated by the theory and trained to excite the minds of women to love, you may, by refraining from so doing, win an eternal recompence and thereby deserve a greater reward from God. For God is more pleased with a man who is able to sin and does not, than with a man who has no opportunity to sin." Then follows a diatribe against Love, accusing it of setting friend against friend, making men squander their patrimony, acting in a foolish way -- in short, of being the source of all the evils in the world, even so far as causing men to lose their immortal souls. This is followed by an extended libel of women.

Book III has the same inconsistencies and apparent ironies as the first two books, thus complicating our understanding of the work as a whole. Despite C. S. Lewis' beautifully and convincingly written interpretation of De arte -- i.e., that following the Ovidian tradition, Andreas wrote a Remedy for the love he espoused in the first two books, and that Books I and II are concerned with the secular moral order and Book III with the divine[7] -- when one looks at the text, it is difficult to believe that Andreas was any more serious in Book III than he was in Books I and II. There is actually not much in Book III that had not already appeared in different contexts earlier in the work.

Near the end of the last book, Andreas tells Walter that the book may "seem to present two different points of view." Indeed it does, but they are the points of view that were part and parcel of the "courtly love" tradition. Love and reason were always perceived to be enemies. They ruled two different worlds, exhibiting two different and opposed value systems. The realm of Love was always known to be fragile, fleeting, dangerous, but so beautiful. It is ultimately incompatible with the ordinary world, and lovers must inhabit both. True love never last long, but it is worth the pain, humiliaton and danger. Still, one must have a defence when it is over -- hence the palinode. Andreas seems to have had his tongue in his cheek throughout all three books. It has interfered with the clarity of what he was trying to say.

The most nearly perfect bit of courtly love literature is an unfinished allegorical romance, The Romance of the Rose,[8] written in the early thirteenth century by William of Lorris. It takes the courtly tradition seriously and treats it with great delicacy and sensitivity, incorporating all the elements of the tradition from the lyrics of the Provençal poets and northern French writers, presented in the form of a carefully wrought dream allegory. It is a consciously idealized story of a young nobleman who has fallen in love and may be told discursively as follows: A young man, twenty years old, has reached the point in his career between education and responsibility when he has nothing to do, and so he savors the pleasures of courtly life, flirting and playing the field, when he unexpectedly falls in love. He presses his suit gently at first, so as not to offend the young lady. The girl was pleasant to him and perhaps even did a little flirting herself, although she was not serious. The young man, misunderstanding, became overly bold; the girl became angry and sent him away. The disconsolate lover realized that pursuing his quest was foolish and would bring him even further pain but decided to do so anyway. A friend gave him some advice, which he followed, on how to get back into her good graces. He was greatly aided by the girl's native generosity and pity for his wretched condition and by the fact that she was beginning to feel a sexual passion for him. After the reconciliation she granted him a kiss, and the affair proceeded apace. But then the girl heard untrue rumors alleging her lover to be of evil character and to be guilty of improper past actions; and in a fit of rage, compounded by jealousy and shame, she dismissed him again. The story breaks off unfinished with the heartbroken lover bemoaning his undeserved fate and hoping again to be able to put things right.

However, William chose not to use straight discursive narration but instead to tell the story as an allegory. As the story is actually told, the young man dreams that he has awakened on a beautiful day in May, dressed himself in his finest clothes, and gone strolling along the banks of a broad, slow-flowing river. He comes upon a beautiful garden enclosed by a high wall on which are painted images of those who are excluded forever from it. Each figure is carefully described. We are not surprised to find Hate, Felony, Villainy, Covetousness, Avarice, Envy, Pope Holy the hypocrite, or even Sorrow, excluded, though it may seem a little hard to discover Old Age and Poverty also among the banished. The Dreamer is admitted to the garden by Idleness, a lovely young woman who informs him that the garden is owned by Sir Mirth. He is bidden by Courtesy to join in the dance with the other inhabitants of the garden, Gladness, Beauty, Wealth, Largesse, Franchise, and Youth. Also among the dancers were the God of Love and his squire Sweet Looks, who held the god's two bows, one beautiful, the other ugly and gnarled, and his ten arrows: Beauty, Simplicity, Independence, Companionship, and Fair Seeming for the beautiful bow: and Pride, Villainy, Shame, Despair, and Faithlessness for the ugly one.

The Dreamer strolled through the Garden of Delights enjoying its great beauty, when he paused to gaze into two crystals at the bottom of a fountain. In the crystals he saw reflected a rosebush surrounded by a hedge and was siezed by a great desire to possess one rosebud in particular, more beautiful than all the rest. The God of Love, who had been stalking the Dreamer, now shot him with the five arrows from the beautiful bow, and the Dreamer (whom we may now call the Lover) became the vassal of the god, giving his heart as a pledge of his fidelity. The God of Love then instructed his new vassal in Love's commandments and warned him that he had undertaken a hard service; and to help him bear the pains he must endure, the god gave him Hope, Sweet Thought, and Sweet

Speech.

The Lover then encountered Fair Welcome, who agreed to let him
smell the flower's sweet perfume, but his approach toward the rose
alarmed Danger (with his cohorts Evil Tongue, Shame, and Fear),
who sprang from his hiding place and drove off Fair Welcome.
Reason then advised the lover to abjure the God of Love, but he
refused, saying he would "rather die than that I should deserve
Love's charge of treason." The Lover confided his woes to a
friend, who advised him to flatter Danger into allowing Fair
Welcome to return. This ploy was successful and was aided by the
intercession of Franchise and Pity, and even Venus, whose help
tipped the scales in favor of the Lover. Fair Welcome returned an
let the Lover kiss the rose.

But now Shame, Evil Tongue, Fear, and Jealousy reproved Danger for
being too lax. Danger returned, arrested Fair Welcome, and imprisoned him and the rose in an impregnable castle. The Lover was in
despair and pondered how to free Fair Welcome from his prison.

The story breaks off at this point. It was provided with endings
by several authors, the best known of whom is Jean de Meun, of
whose continuation we shall speak in a later chapter.

This summary fails to transmit some of the more admirable qualities of the poem. One of these is the skill with which the
allegory is handled. Each figure is given an apt characterization, and the author avoids confusion between his allegorical
figures and literal characters (e.g., the Lover himself and
Friend) and thus successfully allows the story to be coherent on
both the literal and allegorical levels. The allegorical significance of each of the figures is usually obvious enough, and if
it is not the author either explains outright or allows the meaning to emerge from the context. The only serious problem of
interpretation is the crystals at the bottom of Narcissus' fountain.

The other quality of the poem to which we must call attention is
the richness of the description, which nevertheless is never
prolonged to the point that it slows the story down. This is a
tightly constructed and richly ornamented poem of very high quality.

The Romance of the Rose, with its continuation by Jean de Meun,
was without any close competitor the most popular and influential
work of the later Middle Ages, far outdistancing the works of
Dante, Chaucer, Petrarch, and Boccaccio, which are much better
known today. It was especially through this poem that the concept
of romantic love influenced the erotic literature, the manners,
the courtship rituals, and the very notion of what love is, from
its own day to the present.

NOTES

1. <u>Allegory of Love</u>, 4.

2. <u>Medieval Latin and the Rise of the European Love Lyric</u> (Oxford, 1965), I, xvi-xvii, 2-3.

3. See Johathan Saville, <u>The Medieval Erotic Alba</u> (New York, Columbia University Press, 1972).

4. English translation by W. Wistar Comfort in <u>Arthurian Romances by Chrétien de Troyes</u> (London: New   York,   1955).

5. English translation by Comfort, <u>Arthurian Romances</u>.

6. A good English translation is John Jay Parry, <u>The Art of Courtly Love, by Andreas Capellanus</u> (New York, 1959).

7. <u>Allegory of Love</u>, 41-43.

8. English translation by Harry W. Robbins, <u>The Romance of the Rose, by Guillaume de Lorris and Jean de Meun</u> (New York: Dutton Paperback 90, 1962).

Chapter 10

The Medieval Renaissance

Beginning about the middle of the eleventh century, Europe experienced a multi-faceted outburst of intellectual activity -- literary, scientific, philosophical, devotional, legal, tehnological, artistic, and historical -- which reached its acme during the twelfth. Some historians label this entire movement the "Twelfth-century Renaissance."[1] But the ambiguity of the term "renaissance" and the fact that it was originally used to denote the recovery of classical Antiquity by the Italians between the fourteenth and sixteenth centuries, makes it an inappropriate catch-all label tor the maturing of medieval European culture. The term is by now so firmly established that one can hardly avoid using it, but we shall confine it in this chapter to that twelfth-century Latin literature which is particularly indebted to the classics of Antiquity, using them as models, as sources of inspiration, or as guides.

One noteworthy aspect of the medieval renaissance was the tendency of men to preserve, embellish, and publish collections of their personal letters. Although, as we have seen in previous chapters, this was hardly new, it became a very popular practice in the eleventh and twelfth centuries, and many famous men -- Fulbert and Ivo of Chartres, St. Anselm, Hildebert of Lavardin, St. Bernard, Peter the Venerable of Cluny, John of Salisbury, and Peter of Blois, to name only the best known -- collected and published their letters for the instruction and enjoyment of their contemporaries and posterity. These collections were literary works, conforming to the rules of the rhetorical tradition.[2] They were nearly always revised for publication, and they consisted only of the letters written by one person, never the replies.

Standing out among these collections, both because of the intensity and depth of the personal revelations they supply, and because they differ in some respects from the norm, are those exchanged by the great philosopher and theologian, Peter Abelard, and the woman who was successively his mistress, wife, and "sister in Christ," Heloise.[3] The first letter, by Abelard and known by the title Historia calamitatum or Story of my Misfortunes, was addressed not to Heloise, but to an unnamed friend in need of consolation, and it just happened to fall into Heloise's hands. The remainder of the collection is an exchange of letters between the two former lovers, providing a narrative of their relationship and a discussion of its most intimate aspects, and finally a Rule specifically designed for the needs of women for Heloise's convent, the Paraclete.[4]

The collection carries the story from forty-year-old Peter Abelard's first seduction of his landlord's seventeen-year-old niece, through the ecstasies of their love affair, Heloise's pregnancy and her uncle's discovery of his betrayal, their marriage, Abelard's castration, and the entry of both lovers into religious orders. It tells of Heloise and her nuns being expelled from their convent and Abelard's establishing them in his former oratory, the Paraclete. It explores Heloise's total devotion to Abelard and the hypocricy of her religious life. It shows us Heloise imploring Abelard for erotic sustenance -- "words, of which you have a store" -- and, the real crux of their tragedy, the total inability of either to understand the state of mind of the other. Abelard considers his castration a just punishment for his sin and the means by which he has been led to a more holy life. But Heloise neither accepts not regrets anything. Abelard is the center of her life and the sole focus of her desire, and now he seems to have abandoned her in her hour of desperate need (in fact, she had waited for ten years). If he will not write her words of love, will he not at least give her something else to occupy her mind?

Abelard began the affair out of simple lust. He says so baldly in the Historia calamitatum, and when Heloise later accuses him of it, he freely admits it. But he must surely have got more than he bargained for in Heloise. He became completely obsessed by her and seemed not to be able to get enough of her. He neglected his work, and made no effort to conceal their affair, which he even advertised in song. He seemed careless of consequences, totally consumed by his sexual passion. But then there were consequences. Heloise was pregnant; uncle Fulbert knew of the affair and wanted revenge.

Abelard's behavior at this point was neither despicable nor admirable. He offered to marry Heloise but insisted that the marriage be kept secret in order that his reputation not be damaged. This led Abelard to send Heloise to live with the nuns at Argenteuil for safety. But his passion did not abate, and he could not stay away from her. He later reminds her in a letter of how, during one of his visits, they made love in a corner of the convent's refectory, so eager were they for each other that they could not wait to find a more suitable place. The marriage did not mollify Fulbert, and his hirelings castrated Abelard. Abelard says plainly in the Historia calamitatum that he felt more shame and revulsion at his new condition than he did physical pain, and that he entered the monastic life because he needed a haven during a time of trauma. But he remained fiercely possessive of Heloise and confesses that he forced her to become a nun so that no one but him should ever have her.

But in time, Abelard's conversion became sincere. He re-evaluated his castration and came to see it both as a just punishment for his sin and as the means of leading him to salvation. He fully accepted the rightness of what had happened to him and thanked a merciful God for rescuing him (and Heloise, as well) from sin. He must also have supposed that Heloise shared his views, and knowing that she had already become prioress at Argenteuil, he assumed that she was making the best of things. In any case, Heloise's first letter must have come as a rude shock, and Abelard seems to have been at a loss as to how to reply. After her second letter, he realized that she was indeed serious, but he neither could, nor thought he should, do as she asked. He tried to explain to her God's justice and mercy towards them, and should that fail to convince her, he simply ordered her to stop. She agreed, but only on condition that Abelard would give her something else to occupy her mind, and she specifically asked for a history of the order of nuns and for a modification of the Benedictine Rule which would be more suitable for women.

Abelard shows a good deal of sweetness and genuine solicitude from this point on for both Heloise and her nuns. He granted her request for a history of nuns and a Rule, he visited them frequently, he wrote letters of exhortation and advice to them, he composed 133 hymns for their use, and thirty-four sermons. In addition, he composed one of his major scholarly works, the Hexameron, in response to Heloise's specific request.

Abelard then did not behave badly in the relationship. It was after all he who had been castrated and thus prevented from fulfilling Heloise's request even if he had wanted to. And the view of their affair and its consequences at which he finally arrived conformed to the most highly valued ethic of his day, that of monastic Christianity. He must have felt morally secure in it. In his view, his life had been a progress from the depths of sin and carnality, through a just and merciful punishment, towards a life of increasing holiness.

But in Heloise there was not progress. She had at the beginning embraced a position from which she never wavered. She loved Abelard because he was the best of men. She subjected herself to him wholly. She gloried in his triumphs, suffered in his defeats. She freely submitted her will to his, without giving up her right to argue her point of view. Heloise never regretted their love affair, only its end. She never felt guilt for what she had done, only that she had been the cause of Abelard's ruin, and she was never capable of repentance. "I can find no penitence with which to appease God, whom I always accuse of the greatest cruelty in regard to this outrage. By rebelling against his ordinance, I offend him more by my indignation than I offend him more by my indignation than I placate him by penitence. How can it be called repentance for sins, however great the mortification of the flesh, if the mind still retains the will to sin and is aflame with its old desires?" As for accepting Abelard as her lover, she remarked defiantly: "Every woman, married or maiden, desired you when you were absent and burned when you were present. Queens and great ladies envied me my joys and my couch. . . .Your manhood was adorned by every grace of mind and body; among the women who envied me then, could there be one now who does not feel compelled by my misfortune to sympathize with my loss of such joys?"

She opposed their marriage for two reasons. First, she clearly saw that it would not achieve its purpose of placating her uncle. And second, and more important, their relationship was not of that kind. It consisted of love freely given, not constrained by the bond of marriage. "The name of wife may seem holier or more binding, but sweeter for me will always be the word mistress, or, if you will permit me, that of concubine or whore. I believed that the more I humbled myself for your sake, the more gratitude I should win from you, and also the less I should damage the brightness of your reputation." And marriage was no fit state for a philosopher. "What harmony can there be between pupils and nursemaids, desks and cradles, books and distaffs, pens and spindles? Who can concentrate on thoughts of Scripture and philosophy and be able to endure babies crying, nurses soothing them with lullabies, and all the noisy coming and going of men and women about the house? Will he put up with the constant muddle and squalor which small children bring into the home?"

If Heloise should be the cause of Abelard's diminished reputation, she would be ruining not only him but herself. She loved him for himself alone, not for anything he could give her, and she said she would rather be his whore than the wife of Augustus. In fact, Abelard had replaced God as the center of Heloise's life. She saw this clearly, but it did not alter the fact. "At every stage of my life up to now, as God knows, I have feared to offend you rather than God, and tried to please you more than Him. It was your command, not love of God, which made me take the veil."

She could neither forget nor regret their lovemaking.

In my case, the pleasures of lovers which we shared have been too sweet -- they can never displease me and can scarsely be banished from my thoughts. Wherever I turn, they are always there before my eyes, bringing with them awakened longings and fantasies which will not even let me sleep. Even during the celebration of the mass, when our prayers should be purer, lewd visions of those pleasures take such a hold upon my unhappy soul that my thoughts are on their wantonness instead of on prayers. I should be groaning over the sins I have committed, but I can only sigh for what I have lost. Everything we did and also the times and places are stamped on my heart along with your image, so that I live through it all again with you. Even in sleep I know no respite. Sometimes my thoughts are betrayed in a movement of my body, or they break out in an unguarded word.

-186-

Heloise's second letter ended with a desparate plea for help. It elicited a seiously concerned response from Abelard, stating his case as comprehensively, clearly, and firmly as he could, ending in a prayer, and closing: "Farewell in Christ, bride of Christ; in Christ fare well and in Christ live." The opening of Heloise's next letter shows us both her lack of any change of heart and her willingness still to obey any of Abelard's commands. The salutation is a masterpiece of subtle and concise expression. In Latin it is _Domino_ specialiter, _sua_ singulariter. It is untranslatable, but it implies resistance to the closing of Abelard's previous letter and a reassertion that she is Abelard's alone.

But she obeycd. "I would not want to give you cause for finding me disobedient in anything, so I have set the bridle of your injunction on the words which issue from my unbounded grief. . . .I will therefore hold my hand from writing words which I cannot restrain my tongue from speaking; would that a grieving heart would be as ready to obey as a writer's hand."

She remained obedient and devoted to him for the rest of his life, and after his death her solicitude did not slacken. She badgered Peter the Venerable, Abbot of Cluny and Abelard's host at the time of his death, both for Abelard's body and for a formal document of absolution. She received both and lived exemplarily for another twenty years, still obedient to her only master.

Late in the summer of 1142, there was written in Paris a brilliant Latin poem in rhymed accentual verse. It was a very clever adaptation of the _Marriage of Mercury and Philology_[5] to the contemporary Parisian academic scene, and its ostensible theme was the wedding of Wisdom and Eloquence. In addition to the gods and goddesses, a considerable number of the Parisian teachers of the time were present as wedding guests, but when the bride asked where her "courtier" was (the Latin word for courtier, Palatinus, was a code word for Abelard), she was told that he had been silenced by a mob of obscurantist monks. This was undoubtedly a reference to Abelard's condemnation at Sens in 1140 (largely the result of Bernard of Clairvaux's persecution) and his subsequent withdrawal from the Parisian schools. The wedding guests, the champions of the union of wisdom and eloquence, are a disgruntled elite, highly educated in the classics-based, old-fashioned curriculum of the earlier part of the century. The poem is entitled the _Metamorphosis Goliae episcopi_, or _Metamorphosis_ by bishop Goliath. In one of the manuscripts containing the poem there are also an _Apocalypse_ and a _Confession_ ascribed to Goliath (the Latin from is _Golias_). By the third quarter of the twelfth century there existed a large body of poetry purportedly written by members of an _Ordo vagorum_, or Order of Wayfarers, whose founder was Goliath (hence they are also known as _Goliardi_).

This make-believe Order had resulted from the confluence of several earlier developments. The use of the term "Tribe of Goliath" to indicate a band of disreputable rowdies goes back to Sedulius Scotus in the ninth century and had since been used several times in this general sense. The development of rhymed accentual Latin poetry had been rapid since the days of Gottschalk, and by the twelfth century it was a polished literary form. And there had always been students who wandered and often, no doubt, got into trouble with the authorities, but by the mid-twelfth century there were large numbers of such people, and they were undergoing a crisis of expectations and status. Whereas previously a sound classical education was considered the proper training for an administrator, and those who possessed one could reasonably expect to reach positions of wealth and importance, it was becoming more and more common by mid-century to favor people with a narrower, more technical education (usually legal) for church preferment. And so there appeared a body of poetry expressing the values of this bitter and very expressive group.

Their poetry exhibits a consistent fatalistic hedonism, a joy in nature, sex, and wine, but a feeling of alienation from a society for which they were too good, a bitter satiric wit, and a good deal of self pity. If we took these poets at their word, we should imagine them as penniless, unemployed (or unsatisfactorily employed) wanderers, completely given over to drinking, gambling, and lechery. There may well have been some who conformed to this image, but it is largely a fiction. We know something about a few of these poets -- what they did for a living, and sometimes even their names -- and it does not square with the literary personae they present in their poems. Hugh Primas (Hugh the Primate), for example, was a successful and much admired professor of rhetoric at Paris. The "Archpoet" was a member of the court of the arch-bishop of Cologne, and while there may be at times a tiny kernel of truth behind some of his poems, his major talent seems to have been comic exaggeration. Walter Map was a beneficed clek and had been employed by Henry II of England. And Walter of Chatillon held a number of lucrative offices at Reims, like Walter Map was once employed in the English chancery, and ended his life as canon at Amiens. These positions, of course, were of the second rank and surely meant keen disappointment for ambitious, able, and highly educated men. But they kept men from starving and should have made possible even some degree of ease and comfort.

The poems of the Goliardi are impossible to transalte (although very effective English poems which are roughly equivalent to them have been written).[6] They are full of mocking echoes, often with puns or other word play, of the Bible, the Creed, the Liturgy, or well known hymns. They are also show-pieces of men who possess classical educations. Pagan mythology abounds, to the point that much of the poems cannot be understood by a modern reader without the help of many footnotes, and echoes of the classics are as frequent (or more so) as those of religious works, but without the mockery. Take, for example, this description of sunrise:

> Axe Phebus aureo
> celsiora lustrat
> et nitore roseo
> radios illustrat.
> Venustata Cybele
> facie florente
> florem nato Semele
> dat Phebo favente
> aurarumve suavium
> gratia iuvante
> sonat nemus avium
> voce modulante.
> Philomena querule
> Terea retractat
> dum canendo merule
> carmina coaptat.

To a reader ignorant of the identification of Phoebus, Cybele, Semele, Tereus, and Philomela, it would have little meaning.

The popular notion of the Goliards is derived largely from their own self-portaiture. Hugh Primas was a poet of great ability, and most of his poems purport to be autobiographical, although this was surely only a device. His "Dives eram et dilectus" did much to establish the stereotype of the Goliard as an educated but ill-used beggar. In it, Primas was supposedly addressing his former colleagues (socii -- whether these are Parisian professors or a cathedral chapter is not clear). He says that he was once rich and highly thought of, but now, bent over by age, he is cast out even by outcasts. He had taken unworthy employment in an almshouse, and a brutal chaplain tricked him out of his money and then threw him out into the wind and rain. He then wandered and led a shameful life and is now begging them for food and drink. "Where should I, nurtured on the Pierian spring and taught by Homer, beg my food except from the clergy? I will not go to the laity. I eat and drink very little, and if I should die of hunger, I will put the blame on you." He then asks if they would like to hear more of the particulars of the quarrel which brought such troubles upon him, and they say yes. In a separate poem Primas tells them a tragi-comic story of his interfering to protect a crippled old man. He ends the poem with a call for judgment against the wicked chaplain.

Another important poem in establishing the Goliardic stereotype is the "Estuans intrinsecus" of the Archpoet, also known as the Confession of Goliath. It is a mock confession, which praises the very vices the poet is confessing. Its opening stanzas set the tone:

Estuans intrinsecus	(Inwardly seething with violent anger, I
ira vehementi	speak in the bitterness of my mind. I
in amaritudine	am made from the matter of the light
loquor mee menti.	element; I am like a leaf with which the
Factus de materia	winds play.)
levis elementi,	
folio sum similis	
de quo ludunt venti. . . .	

Via lata gradior	(I tread the easy path, as youths are
more iuventutis,	wont to do; I tangle myself in vices,
implico me viciis	forgetful of virtue. I am more eager
immemor virtutis,	for pleasure than safety. Since I am
voluptatis avidus	dead in the soul, I take good care of my
magis quam salutis,	skin.)
mortuus in anima	
curam gero cutis.	

Then he goes through each one of the pleasant vices, love of young
women, drinking, and gambling, on each of which he dwells loving-
ly. In the midst of this section comes the most famous stanza of
the poem; it gets to the very heart of the Goliard _persona_ and
ends with a typical irreligious parody, substituting "potatori"
(drunkard) for "peccatori" (sinner):

Meum est propositum	(I propose to die in a tavern. Let wine
in taberna mori:	be placed near the mouth of the dying
vinum sit appositum	man, so that the choirs of angels, when
morientis ori,	they come, may say: 'God, be merciful
ut dicant cum venerint	to this drunk.')
angelorum chori:	
'Deus sit propitius	
huic potatori.'	

At the end the poet claims, somewhat unconvincingly, that he is a
changed man and asks his patron, the archbishop of Cologne, to
have mercy on him and give him a penance.

But there is much variety within the corpus of Goliardic poetry.
One encounters a range of voices and attitudes in the poetry of
Walter of Chatillon. He wrote an epic on Alexander the Great in
classical hexameters, but he is best known for his Goliardic
verses. Among the latter is a conventional love poem on the
much-used theme that love keeps the poet warm in the coldest
weather. Another is more original in the turn it gives to the
"Spring is here, let's make love" theme, although it has more of
the feel of a set-piece than of autobiography. In the poem,
Walter's mistress gave birth to a little girl, whom he optimistic-
ally sees in the last stanza as being a future support and comfort
to him in his old age. But Walter's old age was to be more hor-
rible than he could have dreamed when he wrote this little poem.

Although he was eventually made canon at Amiens and so had some measure of worldly success, he contracted leprosy, of which he eventually died. He wrote two poems which call attention to his illness, but neither is a poem of self pity. They are both savage denunciations of the worldiness and corruption of the Church. In the second of these, he uses his own affliction to accentuate the seriousness of the Church's malady. The first stanza states his theme clearly:

Versa est in luctum	(The harp so often plucked by Walter's
cythara Waltheri,	hand
non quia se ductum	Now sounds an elegy,
extra gregem cleri	Not that he mourns his self-exile or,
vel eiectum doleat,	banned
aut abiecti lugeat	From clerics' company,
vilitatem morbi,	Bewails his leprosy:
sed quia considerat,	But that he sees the dreadful face
quod finis accelerat	Of doom for all of mortal race
improvisus orbi.	Rushing upon this unsuspecting world
	apace.)

The feeling that the world was going to hell was not confined to Walter, but, as is common in times of rapid change, was common to all ranks of society. An anonymous poem on the decline of education bemoans the eroding of academic standards, the shortening of the course of study, and the desire of students and teachers alike to turn their learning into ready cash. Dozens of other poems decry the omnipotence and abuse of wealth and the corruption of the church from the pope to the parish priest, many of them quite clever and all tinged with genuine venom.

Probably the largest number of Goliardic poems have to do with love of one sort or another. Many of them follow an old formula: It's springtime, the juices are flowing, and I'd like to get a pretty young girl. They treat many of the same themes that we noted in the Occitan lyrics -- the lost love, the absent lover, "you keep me ablaze when it's cold outside," love is pain and suffering, Venus conquers all, women should not be too easy to seduce, the secrecy of love affairs, the superiority of "true love" to animal lust, the opposition of love to reason and/or religion -- and often in quite similar fashion. But the Goliards never used a courtly setting, they wrote in Latin, and their poems were much more heavily laden with classical apparatus. They also dispensed with the conventions of "courtly love," even when they were treating similar themes. Compare, for instance, the "Lingua mendax et dolosa" with the similar episode in the Romance of the Rose:

Lingua mendax et dolosa,
lingua procax, venenosa,
lingua digna detruncari,
et in igne concremari,

que me dicit deceptorem
et non fidum amatorem;
quam amabam dimisisse,
et ad alteram transisse. . .

Volo fedus observare,
et ad hec dicemus quare:
inter choros puellarum
nihil vidi tam preclarum. . .

Ergo dum nox erit dies,
et dum labor erit quies. . .

cara mihi semper eris;
nisi fallar, non falleris.

(That lying poisonous tongue that
said I was not true to my mistress
should be yanked out and burned in
the fire. I call to witness the
nine Muses, Jupiter, and Danae.
God knows, the gods know, that I
wouldn't do a thing like that. I
swear by Apollo, Mars, and Cupid,
whose arrows have so often been
shot at me, that I wish to keep our
pact. And let me tell you why:
You are the most beautiful girl I
have ever seen. Among other women
you stand out like a pearl set in
gold; your shoulders, your breast
and waist are so beautifully
shaped. Your forehead, throat,
lips, and chin provide nourishment
for a lover. And so, until night
is the same as day, and work the
same as rest, and there are forests
without trees, and water is fire,
and the sea is without sails, you
will always be dear to me. I won't
deceive you if you don't deceive
me.)

Before leaving the Wandering Scholars, we should call attention to
one more anonymous love poem, which in some ways strikingly anti-
cipates the Romance of the Rose, and in other ways is vastly
different. In this poem, which begins "Si linguis angelicis," the
girl is symbolized by a rose which is guarded by an old crone
(vetula). The girl's love has exalted the poet above all Christians. The demand of secrecy prevents his disclosing her name.
The sight of her occasioned the greatest elation in him, and he
hastened to her and knelt. His love is described as wounds inflicted on him by the rose. He suffered grievously, could not
eat, drink, or sleep, and told the rose that only she could cure
him. Deprived of her, he phantasized about her. The girl replied
that she too had suffered wounds, and asked the poet to speak out
and say what it is that he wants. Is it gold or precious gems?
she asked coyly. In answer, the poet siezed her, kissed her, made
love to her, and was in a state of unequalled bliss. And he was
not bitter about having to work so hard for it. Good things do
not come easily.

The story is very nearly the same as that of the Romance of the
Rose (except that we cannot be sure of how William of Lorris would
have ended his story). There are also the metaphor of the rose,
the duenna, the false start of the courtship and consequent suffering. But there is none of the weight of the allegory. Both

the poet and the girl speak. And, while many of the conceits of the "courtly love" tradition are found in this poem, they do not get in the way of the rapid narrative of directly experienced sexual attraction. Nor was there any need to imbue love with any mystical virtues. It was enough by itself to make the poet "luckier than any man in Christendom."

The concept of poetry as the highest vehicle for the communication of wisdom was an inheritance from Antiquity. Both Greek and Latin commentators had interpreted their own epics in this way, and the Middle Ages continued the practice. Not only were the great poems seen to be repositories of almost divine wisdom, but the garb of poetry prevented the knowledge of the highest things from falling into the hands of the unworthy, and it provided delight as well as enlightenment to those who were suited by nature and education to receive them. Homer and Virgil were the poets par excellence, but many others were also considered great authorities -- Prudentius, Martianus Capella, and Boethius especially, the last two of whom had employed the Menippean satire, or prosimetrum, as the vehicle for their expression. But it had been enough between the sixth and twelfth centuries to study, try to understand, and delight in these ancient gems, and no one had tried to outdo the ancients in the genre of didactic epic.

But late in the 1140s, there appeared a work entitled De universitate mundi; sive Megacosmus et Microcosmus,[7] a poem which still elicits contradictory critical judgments and explanations. Its author, Bernard, was nicknamed Silvestris because he used the word silva for unformed matter, which was usually called hyle or chaos by other writers. Very little is known about Bernard, aside from the fact that he was bishop of Tours, that he had some connections with Thierry of Chartres, to whom he dedicated his poem, and that he was also probably the author of a widely used and very influential commentary on Virgil's Aeneid. But he was a man of wide reading and a poet of enormous imaginative and expressive powers.

The subject of his poem is a great puzzle, and I do not pretend to have solved it: the creation of the universe (the macrocosm) and of man (the microcosm), from the standpoint of a Neoplatonic poet. The twelfth century was a time of great interest in the creation story, and scores of commentaries were written on the first two chapters of Genesis. But Bernard does not use the biblical account as a framework. In fact, he seems totally to ignore the existence of the Bible, Christianity, and the church, and to draw his material wholly from pagan mythology (the exceptions are a passing mention of the Virgin and of the current pope, Eugenius III). And not only the surface details, but even the basic ideas, seem essentially pagan. Do we have then a truly pagan poet masquerading as a Christian bishop? And what of the numerous people who read this poet with pleasure and approval?

The answers to these questions are not obvious, but I offer several suggestions. First, I think that we must assume that Bernard was a believing, practicing, perhaps even devout, Christian. We must then try to understand how such a man could have written such a poem -- one that strikes us as being pagan, although it did not strike his contemporaries in the same way. We must bear in mind the very great prestige of the epic poetry of Antiquity (both Christian and pagan), and of the power of the conventions of the epic tradition. It had overcome both Juvencus and Prudentius, who had lived at a time when the opposition between Christian and pagan was felt much more keenly, and who nevertheless succumbed to the poetic diction and mythological paraphernalia of pagan epic. This awe of the machinery, diction, and personae of the epic was canonized in the writing of late Antiquity -- Servius, Macrobius, Martianus Capella, and Fulgentius -- and represented an ancient and highly regarded way to write poetry. If one were aiming for the sublime, this was the tradition he followed. The incompatibility between this sort of thing and Christianity, which seems so apparent to us, did not present itself to the twelfth-century intellectuals at all. Although some groups (especially Cistercians) railed against the use of pagan works, as they had been doing since Tertullian, the majority view considered truth to be a unity and felt confident (naively perhaps) that there could be no conflict between pagan truth and Christian truth, since in both cases its source was the only God. And poetry is not a literal or discursive type of exposition. It is imaginative; it uses myth, tropes, and allegory, and so its "plain meaning" is not its real meaning.

Now let us look at the poem itself, written in alternating sections of prose and verse. The first book, Megacosmus, concerns the creation of the universe, the second, Microcosmus, the creation of Man. It beings with a wonderful conceit, which makes perfect sense from the standpoint fo the Platonic creation story, the Timaeus. Plato had posited three eternal principles: the World of Forms; the Giver of Forms, or Artificer; and matter, which he said was "between something and nothing." Matter's basic property was to take on form and intelligibility, both of which it wholly lacked, although it was the seat of unbridled brute energy. Bernard has silva, or matter, desiring that it might be brought into full existence. Matter's desire is voiced by Nature, who complains to Noys (i.e., the Neoplatonic nous, the first emanation from the highest divinity). Noys agrees to remedy the situation, but the inherent intractability of silva prevents it either from being perfectly formed or from receiving the Eternal Ideas directly. Noys therefore works through two emanations from herself: first Endelechia (i.e., the Aristotelian entelechy), which impresses "species" (i.e., second order forms derived from the Eternal Forms) upon all things, separates the four elements, and brings into being the heavens, stars, and lower world; and second, the World Soul, which imposes harmonious order, life, and intelligence upon the cosmos as a whole and enables it to maintain itself everlastingly.

This is followed by a verse section describing the universe thus created, from the "superessential God," through Noys, the orders of the angels, the fixed stars, planets, and finally the earth. The book closes with the assertion that the universe is everlasting, since its causes are eternal. And, although everlasting time is different from eternity, it comes from eternity and returns to it again; and so, while the two are different, they are in a way the same.

At the beginning of Book II, Nature is pleased with what she has accomplished. It now remains to crown her creation with the microcosm, Man. But she is not competent to do this without help. She consults Noys, who tells her that she must have the assistance of Urania (the spirit of heaven), who lives on the aplanon (i.e., the sphere of the fixed stars), and of Physis, who inhabits the Eden-like garden of Granusion on earth. "Physis," of course, is simply the Greek word for nature, but in accordance with the usage of his day, Bernard considers her as a separate, lower, and more specific deity than Nature. "Physica," in the twelfth century, was coming to mean the physical sciences, including medicine and biology.

Nature first sets out to find Urania, who greets her warmly, approves her plan, and fortells Man's future character and greatness. His soul, she says, must before birth be taught the influences of heaven, to which it shall return after death. Then together they go to the throne of Tugaton (i.e., to agathon, Plato's Idea of the Good), the highest God, and they pray to his "triune majesty." Urania then accompanies Nature to earth in search of Physis. This gives Bernard an opportunity to describe each of the spheres and their inhabitants, down to the fairies of the upper air and the water and wood sprites of the earth. The two goddesses find Physis in the beautiful garden of Granusion with her two daughters, Theory and Practice. Like Nature, Physis finds the face of Urania too bright to gaze on directly and so looks at her reflection in a well.

Noys now rejoins them and tells them what kind of a creature Man shall be: He shall be both heavenly and earthly; he shall care for the earth and pray to the gods. His two natures shall be aptly matched in him. He shall be able to discover the hidden causes in nature. He shall rule the earth, all of whose creatures shall be subject to him. Noys then gives to Urania the Mirror of Providence, to Nature the Table of Fate, and to Physis the Book of Memory, and the three set out to make Man, each contributing the best of which she is capable. Since he is to be a small world, he corresponds in every detail to the large world. His make-up is described from beginning to end, the last part to be made being his genitals, which receive a startingly naturalistic evaluation: "Their employment will be pleasant and useful, if it respects the qualifications of when, what kind, and how much. They prevent the death of the cosmos and the return of chaos. Unconquered, they fight against death with genial weapons; they repair nature and perpetuate the race."

Bernard's sources are manifold; most are the well known ancient authors of the schools, but the source of his identification of the human genitals as the weapons with which the spirit of universal sexuality battles the forces of death and dissolution comes from the Hermetic work, Asclepius, sometimes wrongly attributed to Apuleius. But De universo is much more than a pastiche of ancient authors. It is a highly original poem, using for background the literary works Bernard could expect his audience to know intimately. If we have trouble understanding him today, it is because we do not read the same books.

During the second half of the century, Bernard's influence made itself felt in the work of the Fleming, Alan of Lille (Alanus de Insulis). Alan was one of the most learned and versatile men of his generation (ca. 1116-1202). He was a famous theologian, the author of a polemic Against the Heretics, and a student of physical science, but he was preeminently a powerful, imaginative, and original poet, a virtuoso with words. Ironically, it is this very virtuosity which has brought down on him the scorn of many modern critics, who prefer leaner, less elaborate literature. But whether one enjoys Alan's style or not (and six generations of readers considered it to be the absolute acme of fine writing), he was a complete master of it. He has all the rhetorical devices at his fingertips, but, like a true master, he can go beyond them and manipulate them at will. Although he took a firm stand in the preface to his Anticlaudianus against the moderns and with the ancients, he was also a conscious innovator, arrogantly proud of the superb work he had created in a new genre, the "philosophical-theological epic."[8] He dismissed with scorn and contempt those future readers who either would not or could not understand what he had written. He was aiming for the heights, and so much the worse for those who were unable to follow him there.

Alan's great work was the Anticlaudianus (1182-3),[9] a lengthy and complex poetic allegory, whose subject was the construction of the perfect man. The explanation of the title alone is complicated. In the late fourth century, the Latin poet Claudian had written a poem In Rufinum, a libel of Theodosius' hated minister Rufinus. In it, Alecto, worst of the Furies, filled with rage because her realm was diminished by a world which was happy, peaceful, and prosperous, summoned all the Vices and evil demons to an underworld conference to determine how to upset this state of affairs. They agreed to entrust the thoroughly wicked man Rufinus with the disruption and destruction of the earth. Alan's poem is the counterpart of this, the construction of the perfectly good man.

After the prose prologue, which we summarized above, the poem gets underway with Nature working at her forge, dissatisfied with her most ambitious creation, Man. She would like him to be a finer being than she is capable of making by herself, so she summons her sisters -- Concord, Abundance, Favor, Youth, Laughter, Modesty, Reason, Prudence, Piety, Faith, Liberality, Nobility, and others -- to help her. They answer her call and arrive at her sempivernal garden. Nature's palace is described, especially the paintings which adorn its walls. These are of exemplary figures, each embodying some human quality in a preeminent degree. Nature explains her problem to her sisters and says that her defects must be repaired by some perfect model, whose mind shall be heavenly though his body walk the earth, a mirror to them of what their faith, power, and excellence ought to be. Prudence then elaborates on Man's double nature, compounded of spirit and body. Nature and her sisters, she says, can make the body, but only God can make the soul. Reason concurs and adds that Man should unite in his being all the gifts they can bestow and be their champion against the Vices. Prudence and Wisdom are prevailed upon to ask God for a suitable soul.

They now set about building Wisdom's chariot. The seven Liberal Arts each form a part of it. Reason, the driver, harnesses the five horses (Sight, Hearing, Smell, Taste, and Touch), and the chariot, bearing Prudence, Wisdom (called both Sophia and Phronesis), and Reason, begins its ascent. At the limit of the material world, they encounter Theology and tell her the purpose of their journey. Since Reason and the chariot are able to go no further, Theology agrees to accompany Wisdom alone, and they continue their ascent into heaven. Wisdom is overawed by its magnificence and falters. Theology and Faith support her and shield her eyes from the heavenly brilliance by giving her a mirror to look in. In it she sees the hidden, eternal causes of all things.

They reach the palace of God Himself and humbly present their request. God agrees and summons Noys to provide a perfect model for the human soul. Noys collects the virtues of the greatest figures of human history. On this model God makes the soul, which Noys then anoints against the Vices. They all return to the chariot and speed back to Nature's garden.

Nature now fashions an appropriately beautiful body for this soul. Concord unites them, and the perfect man has been made. Each of those present now gives him her greatest gifts. Alecto hears what has happened and summons all the Vices and ills of mankind, who agree to make war on Man and his Virtues. A Psychomachia follows, from which the new man and the Virtues emerge triumphant. But the battle is never completely won. We must constantly exercise our virtues, especially through the study of philosophy and theology, in order to maintain the excellence of the new world.

This has been a very short and simplified summary of a very long and complex poem, and it has necessarily suppressed much that is most characteristic of Alan, especially the richness of detail, the piling up of images, the word play, the puns, and the extensive use of the catalogue and the technique of _amplificatio_. This is, it must be remembered, not simply a story told for amusement (although the giving of pleasure was one of its purposes), but a vehicle of sublime instruction. It is packed with information, but it is also very tightly constructed. It is not a collection of all the things Alan knew (C. S. Lewis to the contrary),[10] but a careful and coherent selection of material forged into a work of high art.

The quintessential representative of the older classical education, and generally considered to be the finest prose stylist of the Middle Ages, was John of Salisbury.[11] John was born of poor parents at Old Sarum, England between 1115 and 1120. He received his elementary instruction from the village priest and in 1136 went to France to complete his education. During the next twelve years he studied under some of the most illustrious teachers of his day, including Peter Abelard, William of Conches, Thierry of Chartres, Gilbert of la Porrée, Peter Helias, Robert of Melun, Adam of the Petit Pont, Richard Bishop, Robert Pullen, and Simon of Poissy. He worked for several years at the papal court and in 1154 became secretary to Theobald, archbishop of Canterbury. In this capacity he travelled frequently on diplomatic missions to Italy and France, and in Theobald's declining years John seems to have been largely responsible for running the business of the archdiocese. After Theobald died in 1161 John continued in the same post for the new archbishop, formerly Henry II's chancellor, Thomas Becket, with whom he had ingratiated himself several years before by the dedication of his two major works, the _Policraticus_[12] and the _Metalogicon_.[13] John remained loyal to Becket through all the latter's troubles with his monarch, suffered exile with him, witnessed his murder in 1170, and spent the last four years of his life (1176-80) as bishop of Chartres, a position he obtained through the good offices of the French king, Louis VII.

John's most important works were the _Policraticus_, a discussion of political theory and of a courtier's life, which among much else argues that it is just to kill a tyrannical king, and the _Metalogicon_, a defence of the trivium, which is both a defense of grammatical and logical studies against an unnamed innovator whom John designates as "Cornuficius," and a program of liberal studies, giving much information on the curriculum and the teachers of northern France during the 1130s and 40s. Much of John's adult life was spent in the service of the archbishops of Canterbury, and his paramount allegiance was to this see. He wrote biographies of two of its archbishops, St. Anselm and his own friend,

Thomas Becket, both of whom had suffered at the hands of strong-willed kings. He also wrote the _Historia pontificalis_, a history of the papacy from 1148 to 1152, and two poems, both entitled _Entheticus_, on philosophy. John was one of the most prolific and accomplished letter writers of the twelfth century, and his busy and troubled political life gave him much to write about. Over three hundred of his letters survive and constitute an invaluable source for the history of the period and the personality of their author.

Humanism, as we have mentioned earlier, is an ambiguous word, but E. K. Rand has given us a superb description of what a humanist is, based not on any _a priori_ definition but induced from our intuitive perceptions. "A humanist," he says,

> is one who has a love of things human, one whose regard
> is centered on the world about him and the best that man
> has done; one who cares more for art and letters, par-
> ticularly the art and letters of Greece and Rome, than
> for the dry light of reason or the mystic's flight into
> the unknown; one who distrusts allegory; one who adores
> critical editions, with variants and variorum notes; one
> who has a passion for manuscripts, which he would like
> to discover, borrow, beg or steal; one who has an elo-
> quent tongue, which he frequently exercises; one who has
> a sharp tongue, which on occasion can let free a flood
> of billingsgate or sting an opponent with an epigram.[14]

John is one of the people Rand had in mind when he wrote the description, so it is not surprising that it fits him well. John's interests, even his ecclesiastical ones, were very much centered on this world -- its politics, loyalties, philosophy, literature, and teaching -- and his praise of literature in the prologue to his _Policraticus_ shows that among its principal values are to preserve the memory of great human actions as well as to provide personal guidance, consolation, and delight to those who read. The literature he had in mind was preeminently that of Greece and Rome, but great as was his respect for the ancients, he also felt that his contemporaries (or some of them) were equally important, and so he quotes their writings alongside those of Augustine, Martial, Lucan, and Virgil. His distrust of allegory was that of a literary scholar who knew and approved of the use of the figures of speech, even extended metaphors, when done with sufficient reason by competent writers, but who was suspicious of the play of uncontrolled imagination in the interpretation of a text. His love of books and learning is evident in everything he wrote. He was eloquent if nothing else, and nothing nurtured his eloquence so much as hatred. His description of his enemy Cornuficius is an excellent example:

> I would call him openly by name and reveal to public

view the bloatedness of his belly and his mind, the
lewdness of his mouth, the rapacity of his hands, the
callousness of his behavior, the filthiness of his
habits (which disgust all those near him), the obscenity
of his lust, the deformity of his body, the evilness of
his life, the foulness of his reputation, if reverence
for the Christian name did not restrain me. . . .It is
proper to impugn a man's opinion without derogating his
character. Nothing is more shameful than to attack the
name of an author because his opinion is displeasing.
. . .Insofar as it is permitted to a Christian, I des-
pise both the person and his opinion. So let him snore
away till noon, drink himself into a stupor in his daily
carousing, and lie around wallowing in those mudholes
which would shame Epicurus' pig. But I shall confine
myself to attacking his opinions.[15]

The Latin of this passage is a masterpiece of balanced periods,
antitheses, prose rhythms, and echoes of classical and Christian
authors, as well as a very effective, if unfair, bit of denuncia-
tion.

In addition to being a student of literature and philosophy, John
was also an administrator of some importance, and like Gerbert he
felt a special kinship with the Roman scholar-politician, Cicero.
Both his letters and his Policraticus show him using the classics
as guides, as sources of consolation, and as a means of amplifying
and understanding his own problems (as well as providing hundreds
of gratuitous decorative exempla). His view of philosophy as of
literature was utilitarian. Like a good humanist, he distrusted
philosophers who were too subtle. John was convinced that God had
imbued creation with a natural law, which the judicious use of
human reason could discover. Once a man had discovered this law,
he could then use it as a moral guide to his political and personal actions. He knew that he was no philosopher (or at least
that he did not possess the competence of a professional philosopher), and he wrote in the prologue to his Metalogicon: "Even
though I cannot do what they (i. e., professors of philosophy) do,
indeed it is my intention to love, honor, and respect them."

But he had a mightly love of learning and a very great respect for
it, and it was to vindicate the study of the Liberal Arts, especially the trivium, that John composed his Metalogicon. He
explains the Greek title (which he invented) as meta, i.e., on
behalf of, and logicon, i.e., logic, and he explains that logos,
the root of logicon, means both the science of verbal expression
and reason, and so logic can be taken to mean all the arts and
sciences having to do with words, as well as logic in its more
restricted sense. A man identified by John only as Cornuficius
(and who may be simply a literary invention who stands for all the
things John is against), and a fair sized group who followed him,

had taught that he had discovered a shortcut to learning, which would teach his students all they needed to know about eloquence and philosophy without any work on their part. He had claimed that the formal study of grammar and rhetoric was a waste of time, because eloquence is an innate gift and one either has it or he does not. "Grammar was made over; logic was remodeled; rhetoric was despised. Discarding the rules of their predecessors, they brought forth new methods for the whole quadrivium from the sanctuaries of philosophy." They cared not for truth or usefulness, but only for making money.

John, like a true grammarian, countered that man's dignity is superior to that of all other creatures because he possess the powers of speech and reasoning. And if he surpasses all other creatures because he possesses these powers, one man exceeds another in value in the degree to which he possesses them. The power of speech is primary, because without it reason would remain barren; the concepts of reason could not be clarified through discussion nor communicated to others. Neither grammar nor logic is natural, although both imitate nature. They are not innate and can only be acquired through much hard work and the reading of the proper authors. The Metalogicon both argues against the Cornuficians' claims by sarcasm, logic, authority, exempla, and common sense, and puts forth an educational program which is best suited to make a man both eloquent and rational. John criticizes his old logician friends at Mt. St. Geneviève for treating logic as an autonomous discipline instead of a tool to be used by the other Arts, but he shows himself au courant of the latest and best books (namely Aristotle's "New Logic") available at the time.

The number of authors he cites -- Latin and Greek, secular and religious -- is prodigious, but many of them he did not know first hand. He quotes some authors who are mentioned in other author's works, he clearly made extensive use of florilegia, and his Greek authors are cited only through mention in Latin authors or in translation, so his reading appears, on the basis of his citations, to have been much wider than it actually was. But even making allowances for all this, John had read much classical literature and had committed much to memory; a florilegium is of limited usefulness to a man who is not quite well acquainted with his subject. And he continued to read, even as he was writing the Policraticus and Metalogicon, as his use of pertinent works in the latter which he did not yet know in the former makes clear.

John was a man of considerable ability and accomplishment, who was aware of both his strengths and his shortcomings. He was a man of the world and was intimately involved in some of the major political events of his day, but he was also a man of the schools, with a very high regard for knowledge. It was his conviction that the latter should inform and improve the former. His closing prayer from the Metalogicon makes a fitting conclusion to our examination of him: "May Christ enlighten me with his knowledge and make me a zealous investigator, lover, and observer of the truth."

The attitude of twelfth-century scholars toward the literature and philosophy of Antiquity was notably different from that of the better known Italian renaissance. Between the twelfth and fifteenth centuries there intervened a vigorous "scientific," anti-literary culture, against which the Italian humanists reacted by rediscovering the literary ideal of the ancients. But in the twelfth century there was as yet no feeling of a break from Antiquity. Although there were differing opinions as to whether the present was better or worse than the past (and Bernard of Chartres had it both ways by picturing moderns as dwarfs on the shoulders of giants and thus seeing farther), the ancient tradition was still thought to live in the schools and writings of the time. Even the pagan-Christian dichotomy, which seems so obvious to us, was not part of the twelfth-century perception, and the great Christian authors were lumped together with the pagans as ancients.[16] This often resulted in what looks to us like extreme naivete in the almost universal tendency of twelfth-century writers to read contemporary values and institutions into classical works, while borrowing copiously from them. The twelfth century was steeped in the classics but not enslaved to them. Its use of classical authors is sometimes tedious, mechanical, and artificial, but it is often much more.

Abelard and Heloise, in their letters, can scarcely get through a paragraph without a classical allusion -- in fact, usually a set of them carefully chosen to illustrate a given point and sometimes demonstrably added later during revision. This was the way one wrote letters. But they knew their ancient authors well and quoted them aptly. And the influence of the classics sometimes went beyond this, especially if we accept as literally true Heloise's blurting out Cornelia's speech from Lucan's De bello civili, VIII, 94-98 through her tears as she spurns the pleas of her friends and obediently precedes Abelard into the cloister: "O maxime coniunx, o thalamis indigne meis, hoc iuris habebat in tantum fortuna caput? Cur impia nupsi, si miserum factura fui? Nunc accipe poenas, sed quas sponte luam." (One assumes that she spoke this, if at all, in Latin.) And she seems consciously to have modelled some aspects of her relationship with Abelard on Ciero's De amicitia. Plato (Calcidius), Ovid, Jerome, Augustine, and Boethius also supplied more than verbal ornaments to the correspondence.

The Goliards were at the same time radical innovators and determined classicists. They brought rhymed accentual Latin poetry to its fullest development; they used a form of Latin which in both word order and diction were often very close to the vernacular; and they explored new themes and new genres. But they did all this with a learned wit, throwing phrases from the Poets around

with ease and abandon, and employing the mythological machinery of
the ancients (principally Ovid). Their hedonism is often labeled
pagan, but in fact it was sui generis. It may sometimes reflect
an ancient poem or viewpoint, but it was preeminently medieval,
and it introduced a welcome element of freshness and immediacy
into what had become largely a bookish tradition, even in poems
about love and dissipation.

Both Bernard Silvestris and Alan of Lille drew their inspiration
from the classics but transformed their models by their own powerful imaginations. The outline and many of the details of their
universe are from Martianus Capella, fleshed out with details from
the Timaeus, Virgil, Macrobius, Boethius, Claudian, Ovid, Cicero,
Prudentius, Fulgentius, pseudo-Apuleius, pseudo-Dionysius, and
probably Nemesius of Emesa and Gregory of Nyssa, but the subject
matter and manner of treatment are original. The "flotsam of the
ancient world" (in Henry Osborn Taylor's somewhat unkind phrase),
was used to build a brave, exciting, and confident new world.

Even in John of Salisbury, we find neither a consciousness of a
break with the ancient literary tradition, nor what by modern
standards would be called a true appreciation of it. He plundered
it for maxims, for apt phrases, and for values taken out of context, and he certainly had mastered its language, but there is no
mistaking John for a man of the first century (or of the fifteenth). He was preeminently a gifted man of his own time.

The tension between "humanists" and specialists which we noted
behind much of the Goliardic poetry, in the Philosophia of William
of Conches, in the Metamorphosis Golie, the preface to Alan of
Lille's Anticlaudianus, and especially in John of Salisbury's
denunciations of the Cornuficians, was resolved by the victory of
the specialists. The change was gradual but nearly complete. By
the 1220s the Liberal Arts were considered even by their champions
to be preparatory subjects, the knowledge of which would enable
one to go on to really important things. About 1230, Henri
d'Andeli wrote an allegorical poem called The Battle of the Seven
Arts. The literary tradition, personified as Grammar and represented by Orleans, the last bastion of the old education, battled
against the new scientifically conceived curriculum, represented
by Paris and personified as Logic. Grammar was soundly defeated.
Henri was only registering (and deploring) what had actually taken
place during the preceding half-century.

NOTES

1. Of the numerous books with this title, or something very like
    it, one of the earliest remains one of the best: Charles
    Homer Haskins, The Renaissance of the Twelfth Century (Cam-
    bridge, Massachusetts, 1927; reprint Meridian Books, New
    York, 1957).

2. This undeniable point is made by R. W. Southern, Medieval Humanism and Other Essays (New York, 1970), 86-7.

3. The Latin text has been most recently edited by J. T. Muckle in Mediaeval Studies, XII (1950), 163-213; XV (1953), 47-94; XVII (1955), 240-281; XVIII (1956), 241-292. The only reliable English translation is by Betty Radice, The Letters of Abelard and Heloise (Penguin Classics L297, 1074). An interesting interpretive essay is E. Gilson, Heloise and Abelard (Ann Arbor, 1960). See also the beautifully written "The Heart of Heloise" in H. O. Taylor, The Medieval Mind, II, 3-27.

4. I have assumed, for the purposes of this chapter, that the correspondence is genuine, but the reader should realize that there are some very strong reasons for considering it a forgery. See John F. Benton," Fraud, Fiction and Borrowing in the Correspondence of Abelard and Heloise," Pierre Abélard - Pierre le Vénérable, Colloques internationaux du Centre national de la recherche scientifique 546 (Paris, 1975), 471-511.

5. See John F. Benton, "Philology's Search for Abelard in the Metamorphosis Goliae," Speculum 50 (1975), 199-217. I have followed his interpretation of the poem.

6. See John Addington Symonds, Wine, Women, and Song (Oxford, 1884), Helen Waddell, The Wandering Scholars (Oxford, 1927) and Medieval Latin Lyrics (Oxford, 1929; reprint Penguin Classics L29, 1952), and George F. Wicher, The Goliard Poets (New York, 1949).

7. Latin text edited by C. S. Barach and J. Wrobel, Bernardi Silvestris De mundi universitate libri duo, Megacosmus et Microcosmus (Innsbruck, 1876; reprint Frankfurt, 1964).

8. It is so designated by Curtius, European Literature and the Latin Middle Ages, 120.

9. Latin text edited by R. Bossuat, Alain de Lille, Anticlaudianus, Texte critique avec une Introduction et des Tables (Paris, 1955); English translation by James J. Sheridan (Toronto, 1973).

10. The Allegory of Love, 99-100.

11. A most useful recent work is Hans Liebeschütz, Medieval Humanism in the Life and Writings of John of Salisbury (London: The Warburg Institute, 1950).

12. Edited by C. C. J. Webb, Policraticus, sive de nugis curial-

ium et vestigiis philosophorum, (2 vols. Oxford, 1909).

13. Edited by C. C. J. Webb, Ioannis Saresburiensis Metalogicon (Oxford, 1929). A fairly reliable English translation is Daniel D. McGarry (Berkeley, 1955).

14. E. K. Rand, Founders of the Middle Ages, 102-3.

15. Metalogicon, I, 2, ed. Webb, 8-9.

16. See Curtius, European Literature, 48-54.

PART FOUR: THE AGE OF THE UNIVERSITIES

Chapter 11

The Universities

It might be well, before beginning our discussion of the universities, to devote a paragraph to clarifying a few terms. In the first place, the word _universitas_ was not used until quite late in the Middle Ages exclusively to designate what we mean by a university. The standard term for a place which provided organized advanced teaching on a continuing basis was _studium_. During the last part of the thirteenth century, a distinction was often made between two kinds of _studia_. The more famous and longer established ones were known as _studia_ _generalia_ and the others were designated as _studia_ _particularia_, _studia_ _specialia_, or simply as _studia_. Of course they all aspired to the status of _studia_ generalia, as these days all colleges want to be known as universities. The distinction was at first customary, a matter of informed opinion concerning a school's excellence, but from the mid-thirteenth century on some were designated as _generalia_ by official decree of pope, emperor, or king, and from this point on the term does not have much meaning except concerning the privileges enjoyed by those designated by them. Supposedly the degree of a _studium_ _generale_ conferred the _ius_ _ubique_ _docendi_ (the right to teach anywhere) upon its holders, but this right was always imperfectly recognized. No matter what else the organization of a medieval university might have, it always had a guild of masters, a privileged corporation which controlled its own membership, and these guilds were frequently hostile to outside attempts to infringe on their rights. When foreign masters were allowed to teach, they were nearly always subjected to new examinations by the local masters, regardless of where they may first have received their degrees. Ideally a true university should have a full faculty of Arts which granted degrees and at least one, and preferably more, of the higher faculties, namely canon law, civil law, medicine, and theology, although for most of the thirteenth century Paris had a monopoly on theological degrees on the continent. Both the truncated Arts course of Salerno and the fact that it had only one higher faculty, that of medicine, made it an anomaly among medieval universities. We should also realize that the corporation which achieved legal recognition in the Middle Ages was often not what we would conceive of as the university, that is, the teachers and students considered as a single legal unit. There were often several corporations based on commonality of interest. For example, at Bologna there were two (originally four) "universities" of students and one of masters, often hostile to each other. There was a tendency though toward considering the entire collection of masters and students as the university, especially after _de_ _novo_ foundations by public authorities became popular.

The emergence of universities in the late twelfth and early thirteenth centuries brought about several major changes in European culture. As Europe's first attempt at mass education, it vastly increased the number of educated people. It institutionalized learning and gave political, social, and legal power to privileged corporations of intellectuals, students, and teachers. The universities provided an adequate supply of trained and humanized minds to staff the hierarchy of the church, the chanceries of secular rulers, the bureaucracies of the towns, and the ranks of the professions. Their methods made possible detailed analysis of a large body of recently acquired learning and the systematic investigation of specialized topics. Their institutionalized disputations assured that any view proferred by a professor would have to undergo tough hostile criticism.

Enormous progress was made in a short time, but at considerable cost. Specialization hampers intercommunication between disciplines. A rigorous specialized vocabularly (jargon) tends to cut off the humanistically educated "universal man" from access to what is happening at the forefront of knowledge. This is a problem which is not solved yet and probably will not be until humanity produces individuals who can be both specialists and humanists simultaneously. And perhaps not even then, since much of the difficulty derives from differing frames of reference and guiding values rather than from lack of intellectual competence. It is difficult to say whether a man who thinks abstractly, deliberately simplifies, and insists on rigor and precision in thought and expression is better or worse than one for whom the complexities of thought hold the greatest hope for attaining truth, style is as important as substance, and elegant erudition is the hallmark of a truly cultured man. In any case it was the first type who made the universities and to whom is due the praise or blame for the intellectual culture of the last phase of the Middle Ages.

The earliest universities were not founded; they emerged slowly out of the changing needs of society and the changing academic situation.[1] It is not even possible to say when they became universities. The details of their evolution vary from place to place, and documents are usually lacking for just the sort of thing we are curious about, but generally speaking we may say that between 1150 and 1200 the earliest universities, Salerno, Bologna, Paris, and Oxford, assumed roughly the shape they have when documents of the thirteenth century began shedding some light on them. We may say that when a studium has a core of required texts, has established a course of a set number of years marked by definite stages, has acquired control over the granting of degrees (that is, of admitting new members to the guild of masters), has assumed some sort of internal organization and self-government, and, most important, has achieved legal recognition of the masters and/or students as a corporation by a public authority, it has become a university.

I have included Salerno,[2] even though its history is quite different from the other universities, because it was one of the earliest major centers of higher education and because its medical curriculum largely determined that of the rest of Europe. We discussed the school briefly in chapter 8, emphasizing the beginning of its period of rapid development in the eleventh century. It was at this time that a medical literature written by Salernitan masters first appears. These early works were essentially compilations from ancient sources on topics the masters needed for their teaching. Of this character were Gariopontus' Fevers and Passionarius, Petroncellus' Practica, and the Antidotarium of Nicolaus. They were purely practical in attitude, caring little for medical theory, and were culled from the traditional medical treatises which had been available since the sixth century. Salerno had not yet established a characteristic type of medical instruction.

Two men we have discussed earlier were instrumental in bringing about a significant improvement in Salernitan medicine, one directly and one indirectly. These were Alfanus and Constantine the African,[3] both near contemporaries of the authors mentioned above. Alfanus is the author of two medical works, The Four Humors and Pulses. Since they apparently soon became part of the standard curriculum and were revised and brought up to date many times, we do not have these treatises in the form in which Alfanus wrote them, but rather in the form they had achieved by the thirteenth century. Alfanus also translated into Latin Nemesius of Emesa's The Nature of Man, which contained much Greek medical material as well as many philosophical doctrines. This work was influential on Salernitan writers for over a century.[4]

The second man, Constantine the African, made available in Latin a number of crucially important Arabic and Jewish medical texts: the Pantegni of Ali ibn Abbas, the Viaticum of Al Ja'afar, and many works by Isaac Israeli, including De dietis universalibus, De dietis particularibus, De febris, and De urinis, as well as some Greek material which had not previously been available in Latin, especially Hippocrates' Prognostics, Aphorisms, and Acute Diseases, with Galen's commentaries, some minor works of Galen, Theophilus' Urines, and Philaretus' Pulses. The rational organization and philosophical sophistication exhibited by these works would effectively raise the level of Salernitan teaching signficantly. Their influence, however, was not immediate. Constantine had made his translations at Monte Cassino, and it was not till the mid-twelfth century that they had been fully received at Salerno.

By the beginning of the twelfth century, Salernitan treatises, undoubtedly written for teaching purposes, increased both in number and in quality, showing a growing interest in theoretical matters without losing the close connection with experience which

had been characteristic of Salerno in the past. One of the outstanding teachers of this period was Matthaeus Platearius, who was
apparently the first to dissect animals in the course of his
anatomy lectures, and who composed the first commentary by a
Salernitan physician; it was on an earlier Salernitan work, the
Antidotarium of Nicolaus. Many more commentaries followed this
one, both on Salernitan works and increasingly on the great texts
which Constantine had translated.

The Salernitan school reached the peak of its development, reputation, and influence during the last quarter of the twelfth century. This period was dominated by two men, Maurus and Urso.
Both were well versed not only in medical literature, but also in
the Arts, and both were famous as skilled practicing physicians,
as teachers, and as authors. Maurus wrote a series of superb
commentaries on the major medical texts, the most important of
which are those on Hippocrates' Aphorisms and Prognostics,[5] and he
is very likely the person who established the standard medical
curriculum as it would remain throughout Europe for the rest of
the Middle Ages and the early Modern period -- The Aphorisms and
Prognostics of Hippocrates, Johannitus' Isagoge, Theophilus'
Urines, Philaretus' Pulses, and Galen's Tegni, to which was added
Avicenna's Canon medicinae during the thirteenth century.

Urso carried the development one step farther. He wrote original
treatises, both on practical medicine and on more theoretical and
philosophical topics. One of his works, entitled Aphorisms,
modelled on the Hippocratic work of the same name, he supplied
with a lengthy commentary. He also wrote works entitled The
Effects of the Qualities, The Effects of Medicines, and, most
impressive of all, The Mixture of the Elements,[6] which is not
strictly speaking a medical treatise at all, but a brilliant and
innovative work on natural philosophy. Urso is also of importance
as being among the first authors we know of who explicitly quote
or cite the Aristotelian works on natural philosophy, and from
Greek-Latin rather than Arab-Latin translations.

With Urso and Maurus the school reached its height. Although the
flow of original works of Salernitan masters slowed considerably
during the thirteenth century, the school maintained its level of
excellence and influence for about a hundred years. Still,
throughout the entire period we have been describing, there is no
evidence to indicate that there was any formal association of
teachers and students at Salerno. Apparently teaching was private, each teacher accepting certain pupils, who paid him directly. Nor do we know if there was a specified length of time for
medical study.

The earliest official document which throws any light on the
institutional development of the Salerno medical school is the
Constitutions of Melfi, issued by the emperor Frederick II in

1231. From this we learn that a candidate for a license to practice medicine must first pass a public examination by the masters
of Salerno and then present a certificate signed by the masters
and a representative of the king, attesting to his medical knowledge and political loyalty, to the king, who alone had the right
to grant the license. This represented an extension of the rights
of the masters, who during the preceding century had had no voice
in the granting of licenses. The same article of the Constitutions (47) forbids anyone to teach medicine or surgery in the
kingdom anywhere but at Salerno, or to assume the title of master
unless he had passed an examination by the masters of Salerno.
Ten years later another decree of Frederick had to do with the
study of medicine in the kingdom (and so with Salerno), requiring
three years of study of logic as a prerequisite to the study of
medicine, and another five years in the study of medicine, including surgery. A candidate for the license had to present a certificate to the effect that he had satisfied these requirements. He
was also required to have one year of practical training under an
experienced physician.

It is not clear whether this represented a confirmation of existing custom or was designed to correct abuses; it was probably the
former. There is no doubt though that a decree of 1277 by Charles
I of Anjou had the correction of abuses as its objective. It
states that unqualified students had been receiving medical
degrees at Salerno and ordered that in the future no one was to
receive a degree in either Arts or medicine at Salerno without a
special royal permit. This is the first definite information we
have that a full curriculum of the Arts (i.e., leading to a
degree) was available at Salerno. This decree also implies, for
the first time, the existence at Salerno of a corporation of
students on the Bolognese model. Charles also granted tax exemptions to all Salernitan students (1269), and in 1280 this
exemption was extended to the masters. In 1280 Salerno received
from Charles a document of great importance, explicitly recogniz-
ing the school as a studium generale and setting out the
requirements for the degree. In order to receive the degree of
Bachelor of Medicine, one must have studied medicine for forty
months if he had previously taken a degree in Arts, otherwise for
fifty-six months. He must have held disputations and given two
"cursory" lecture courses (this term will be explained later in
the chaper). He must have taken at least one course each on
Theophilus' Urines, Philaretus' Pulses, Isaac Israeli's Universal
and Particular Diets, Fevers, and Urines, and at least two other
courses on approved books. (This is the same curriculum which had
been established by Maurus a century earlier and was by now standard at most European universities.) The candidate then had to
pass an examination by all the Salernitan masters, then at the
court by the royal physicians, and promise to teach at Salerno for
sixteen months.

The studium at Salerno had by now become a full-fledged university, offering degrees in Arts (although these had only local importance) and medicine, with a recognized corporation of masters and another of students, a core of required courses, a set period of time and other specific requirements for a degree. It continued in existence with varying fortunes until it was abolished in 1812 by Napoleon's puppet, Joachim Murat. It was the most important force in European medical education from the twelfth to the seventeenth centuries.

The university of Bologna shared with Salerno the fact that it first achieved fame in one of the advanced subjects, and the Arts faculty was consequently always in an inferior position. But at Bologna the Arts school had existed first and the school of law, originally taught as a branch of grammar or rhetoric, emerged out of it. It was only during the course of the twelfth century that a clear distinction was made between students of law and students of Arts at Bologna. We do not know much more about Bologna during this period than we do about Salerno, but it is clear that the leadership in achieving legal status and securing privileges and protection for scholars was exerted not by the masters, but by the students. The great historian of medieval universities, Hastings Rashdall, has noted that law students far outnumbered Arts students, and that they tended to be older, usually already held Arts degrees, and came from more important, often noble, families. Furthermore many of them already held responsible positions in church or secular government before they came to Bologna to study Roman or canon law. Additionally, most of them were foreigners (i.e., non-Bolognese) and therefore enjoyed no civil rights in Bologna.[7] Unlike those in Paris and most northern universities, the Bolognese students seem never to have been under clerical control and were therefore without clerical protection. In 1158 the emperor Frederick I had issued a grant of privileges and protection to the scholars at Bologna, which later became the fundamental document upon which their claims to liberties were based. This document, the Authentica "Habita," did not imply the recognition of a corporation of masters and students, but simply granted to anyone teaching or studying law at Bologna imperial protection while he was travelling to and from that city as well as protection against exploitation and humiliation by the townsmen, and a choice of being tried by his own master or the bishop in both criminal and civil matters (later, jurisdiction passed to the rectors of the student university).

How much actual protection this afforded the studium is difficult to say. In any case, friction between the town and the scholars continued and even worsened. During most of the twelfth century masters and students seemed united against the town, but this situation changed during the last quarter of the century. Most teachers were Bolognese citizens and therefore protected by the law of the city and subject to its jurisdiction. When the town began insisting on loyalty from the masters, the latter complied. Without the leadership of their masters, the students took things into their own hands. After a period of coalescence about which we know very little, two powerful associations of students emerged, the Cismontane, composed of Italians, and the Ultramontane, composed of northerners. Their enemies were both the masters and the town, and they reduced both to subservience within a very short time. Their major weapon against the masters was the boycott, and against the town the threat of migration (which was actually carried out on several occasions). They thus used their economic power to extort obedience and cooperation. By about 1242 they had forced the city to grant them the protection of its laws without imposing upon them the responsibilities of citizenship, and probably earlier than this they had reduced the masters to nontenured hirlings who contracted to teach them, subject to very stringent conditions, for one year at a time. Both masters and students who were Bolognese citizens were excluded from these "universities."

Both the Cismontane and Ultramontane universities elected governing officials and made statutes regulating university life. Each was directed by a student rector (who had to be at least twenty-five years old), elected for a two year term and assisted by a small group of councilors, who handled all the financial, legal, and disciplinary matters for the students and who virtually monopolized legal jurisdiction over the students, at the expense of the masters and the bishop.

Although masters were excluded from membership in the student universities, they were required to obey their legislation. Each year a committee of students would decide which teachers would be hired for the coming year. Both student fees (collected and disbursed by the rectors) and the quality, time-table, and content of the teaching were specified, and the master was then required to deposit a sum of money against which fines were levied if he should violate any of the conditions of his employment. He was fined if he started his lecture late or failed to finish by the end of the hour, if he failed to explain any part of the text clearly or if he omitted something, if he left the city without student permission, or if he failed to attract an enrollment of at least five students. Four students, whose identity was kept secret, were deputed each year to act as spies and report all magisterial infractions to the student authorities.

One area upon which the students never infringed was the strictly academic -- the curriculum, examinations, and granting of degrees. The masters of Bologna had their own guild, limited as its powers were, and it had absolute control over who was admitted to it (i.e., who was granted a degree). The license to teach was conferred, upon the recommendation of the masters, by the archdeacon of Bologna, who was named chancellor of the studium. Unlike the situation in Paris, there seems to have been a minimum of friction between him and the academic community, perhaps because his powers were so limited.

Late in the thirteenth century the city government of Bologna began a counterattack against the enormous power of the student universities by establishing paid professorships, thus lessening the students' power over their teachers. By the middle of the fourteenth century this process was complete, and the students were reduced to a position of subservience. This was facilitated by the growing importance of the combined faculty of Arts and medicine which had been established about the middle of the thirteenth century, and the consequent diminution of the relative importance of the law school. In 1364 Bologna was given the right by the papacy to confer degrees in theology, which had hitherto been taught by resident mendicants but had not led to a degree.

The university of Bologna was the prototype for subsequent universities of Italy and other parts of southern Europe. This resulted partly from the fact that several universities were founded by student migrations from Bologna (Vincenza in 1204, Arezzo in 1215, Padua in 1222, Pisa in 1243, and Siena in 1246) and they naturally reproduced the Bolognese organization, and partly because the prestige of the university was so great that it became a model to be emulated, even by universities which were founded by decree.

The university of Paris also came to self-consciousness and eventually to corporate existence as the result of recurrent conflicts, but the circumstances were quite different from Bologna. The number of students and masters was very large, by the early thirteenth century between 2,500 and 5,000, and both students and masters came from all parts of Europe. Also, ecclesiastical control was exercised much more rigorously at Paris than elsewhere. The cathedral school at Notre Dame had been an important teaching center since the early twelfth century, and the bishop of Paris, through his chancellor, insisted that all the masters and students at Paris of whatever status were under his control. The studium enjoyed considerable benefits as a result of this, since its members were considered ipso facto clerics, even though many were not in orders, and they were perfectly willing to profit from this clerical status, which was officially confirmed by a bull of pope Celestine III in 1194. But the chancellor insisted on his untrammelled right to grant or withhold teaching licenses, imprison students and masters for even trifling offenses, and deprive individuals of their scholarly rank.

It was especially in the masters' fight against episcopal control that the Parisian university was born. The masters had established themselves as a customary guild at least by 1170 and perhaps earlier. They had probably established requirements for length of time of study and a basic curriculum, they had taken the lead in establishing student boarding houses and protecting their young charges from insults and exploitation at the hands of the townsmen, and had coalesced into five "faculties," those of Arts, civil law, canon law, medicine, and theology. It was the Arts and theology faculties which enjoyed the greatest repute, but the others were also of distinguished quality. During the last quarter of the twelfth century, the fight against both the chancellor and the town became more intense. The townsmen were brought to heel with the aid of the monarchy in a rather sordid episode, which resulted in the grant of the first written privilege to the university. In 1200 several students (including the bishop-elect of Liège) had been killed by the provost of Paris and his men in the aftermath of a tavern brawl. The infuriated masters appealed to the king for redress and were granted exemption from the municipal police power. The provost was imprisoned for life and his successors, as well as the burghers of Paris, were required to swear to protect the privileges of the university. This was not the end of town and gown violence, but it proved to be the turning point in favor of the scholars.

The fight against the bishop and chancellor was more protracted and was won only with the help of the papacy. The papal alliance proved to be a most important short-term advantage, but it brought the university under papal control, which might be (and in the case of the mendicants, was) used against the masters' interests. In 1215 the papal legate Robert Curçon granted the university some important rights. The chancellor was required to grant the license to teach, without any fee or oath of obedience, to any candidate from the higher faculties who was recommended by six masters. The chancellor did not acquiesce willingly, and tension continued. In 1231, after a bitter fight with the city, as a result of which lectures had been suspended for two years, pope Gregory IX in the bull _Parens scientiarum_ granted the university its most important document of privilege. The chancellor was forbidden to maintain a prison or to arrest students for trifling offences, and then never without bail; and he was required to grant the license within three months to all candidates proposed by the masters. The chancellor retained his position, which he had held since the eleventh century, as head of the _studium_ and as the authority which legally conferred the license. Tension between chancellor and university concerning his precise relationship to it continued throughout the century. But from 1231 on, his powers were strictly subordinated to those of the masters, whose obsolute control over inception reduced the chancellor's licensing power to a _pro forma_ exercise. _Parens scientiarum_ also specifically granted to the university the right to suspend lectures, thus confirming its possession of a most potent weapon in fights against either town or chancellor.

By the first quarter of the thirteenth century, the university had acquired its fully developed structure; we do not know how much earlier it may have been so organized. By far the most numerous faculty was that of Arts (about two-thirds of the total), and its masters had played a leading role in the battles of the preceding half-century. The higher faculties seem to have been organized only to the extent of determining curriculum and degree requirements and conducting examinations, and not for protracted legal battles. They consisted of canon law (civil law had been suppressed by Honorius III in 1219, since it was threatening to extinguish theology), medicine, and theology, of which the last had the greatest prestige, though the smallest numbers. There were only seven chairs of theology at the beginning of the thirteenth century, and never more than fifteen. Of these the medicants at one time held twelve; it is no wonder that the secular masters were alarmed.

The Arts faculty was divided into four nations, the French, Norman, Picard, and English-German, which were the most important organizational units of the university. Each had its own proctor, elected for a very short term, who acted on behalf of the nation. Each nation maintained its own schools and every year assigned them to the available regent masters. Most of the actual governing of the university was done in the congregations of the separate nations, but quite often the entire university (i.e., the masters) would meet. The university as a whole was represented by the rector of the Arts faculty, by whose authority law suits were prosecuted, money was sometimes borrowed, and taxes on the masters were levied and collected; and who was responsible for disciplining all members of the university. In the congregation of the entire university, each nation of the Arts faculty had one vote and each higher faculty had one vote, so that if the nations were in agreement the Arts faculty could always outvote the rest of the university. But this was frequently not the case. There was much ill feeling and competitiveness among the nations, who sometimes fought pitched battles in the streets of Paris. Among the higher faculties, theology often found itself at odds with the rest of the university. It was much more amenable to the authority of the chancellor than the other faculties and was often suspicious of the dangerous doctrines being taught on the faculty of Arts.

Still, by medieval standards, Paris was an unusually coherent university. Dominance clearly lay with the Arts faculty, and its rector gained in power as time went on as a unifying force. Paris was the most renowned of the European universities, truly the Parens scientiarum. It was genuinely international, drawing both students and teachers from every corner of Europe. It provided the model for most subsequent university foundations in northern Europe, and to some extent even in the south.

The fourth of the earliest customary studia generalia was Oxford, and its development shows how difficult it is to generalize about the history of universities. There had been masters of international reputation teaching sporadically at Oxford since the beginning of the twelfth century,[8] but it was certainly not one of the leading intellectual centers of England. Oxford was a small town of no particular importance, its location was convenient but hardly strategic, and it was not even the site of a bishopric. It was included in the gerrymandered diocese of Lincoln a considerable distance away. As late as the third quarter of the twelfth century it had by no means begun to outstrip other English centers of learning. Lincoln, Hereford, Exeter, London, York, and Northampton were all more famous for studies in grammar, the physical sciences, law, and theology, but none of these quite achieved the status of studium generale and gradually faded into insignificance, while Oxford from about 1170 on rapidly developed into a major studium. Its origins have been intensively studied, but no convincing explanation for this has yet been given. By 1190 it had a large number of students and teachers of Arts, law, and theology, who in that year assembled to listen for three days to Gerald of Wales recite his Topographia hibernica.

We lack specific information on its structure until the thirteenth century. Apparently the number of scholars and the complexity of academic life had made necessary the appointment of a magister scholarum even before 1200. We know nothing about this office and its powers, but its holder was probably a local ecclesiastic, most likely the archdeacon, who was appointed by the bishop to oversee the schools. Oxford was shut down by papal decree between 1209 and 1214 as a result of king John's troubles with pope Innocent III, but when it resumed its activities in 1215 it was given a statute by the papal legate conferring clerical status on its scholars and permitting a chancellor to be appointed.[9] The first several chancellors were officially episcopal appointees but were always Oxford masters with strong feelings of loyalty to the university. The masters soon acquired the right to nominate one of their number for the position, and the bishop would then appoint him. Hence the bitter strife which had characterized the relationship between chancellor and university at Paris was avoided.

Oxford's growth in numbers and quality was rapid. While the Paris theologians and artists were fighting over allowing Aristotle's libri naturales to be taught, and the bishop was forbidding them, Oxford took the lead in the acquisition of the New Aristotle, untoubled by ecclesiastical interference. From its inception, Oxford had been an important center of scientific studies; and although for most of the thirteenth century Paris had a monopoly on granting theological degrees on the continent, Oxford had a theological faculty from the outset, as did Cambridge, founded in 1222 by a migration from Oxford. The nations (one northern, one southern) were never important at Oxford and eventually disappeared. When the mendicants began invading the universities, they were cordially received at Oxford and became an important fructifying element of the studium. And it was at Oxford that the collegiate movement thrived most vigorously and eventually transformed the structure of the medieval university.

Unlike Bologna and Paris, Oxford did not attract students from everywhere; its importance was largely restricted to the British Isles. But the works of many of its masters were copied and used all through Europe, and an insular attitude was avoided by the fact that many English masters studied, taught, and worked abroad.

The earliest universities were composed of students and teachers. There were no campuses, buildings (these were hired as needed), libraries, boards of trustees or endowments (although these all appeared later). The most useful kind of information one can have of medieval universities is therefore about their curriculum and teaching. We are faced here with the same sort of difficulty that we encountered with their institutional development, namely a dearth of reliable evidence for the thirteenth and fourteenth centuries. The sketch which follows is therefore a composite one, based on such scattered evidence as is available, dating from the mid-thirteenth to the early fifteenth centuries.[10] It also comes from all over Europe rather than from a single university, and we are therefore forced to make the reasonable assumption (borne out in fact by what we do know) that there was a high degree of uniformity among the various European universities. There were minor differences from place to place, but what follows is a reasonably accurate general picture of the career of a medieval student from bejanus (literally "yellow bill" -- a fledgeling bird, or freshman) to regent master.

The pre-university education received by a young man varied according to family circumstances and the locality in which he lived. Some were educated by private tutors, others by grammar schools maintained by the towns, the guilds, the church, or a private master, and some were trained by a literate parish priest. This preliminary education consisted primarily of grammar and practical arithmetic, although it would obviously vary considerably. But the young man must, above all, be able to speak and understand Latin before going to a university, since this was the language of instruction. Most commonly he was fourteen or fifteen years old when he matriculated. It was necessary for him to place himself under a particular master and not just enroll in the university. This master would then be his principal, but not sole, teacher, and would have the responsibility of a parent toward the young men studying under him.

Once enrolled, the student began a course of study lasting, on the average, seven or eight years and culminating in his admission to the guild of masters and giving lectures and holding disputations for a minimum of two years. Many of the courses he took -- probably slightly more than half -- were required by custom or statute (these are called <u>ad formam</u>), the rest being what we would call electives. Every morning he would attend the "ordinary" lecture of his own master, which would be followed by an informal disputation dominated by the master. These "ordinary" lectures (contrary to the usual connotation of the word today) were the most formal and difficult ones to be given. The master would read portions of the text, amplifying points that interested him, explaining difficulties, giving various opinions of other writers on the subject, and defining authoritatively the doctrine of the author being studied. After each lecture the student had to "repeat," that is, recite to one of the master's bachelors the content of the day's lecture, and once a week he was expected to "repeat" to the master himself.

Since the master seldom read the entire text, and in any case frequently interrupted it with his explanations, another kind of lecture was given, usually in the afternoons by a bachelor. These lectures were known as "cursory" or "extra-ordinary" and consisted of a complete reading and simple summary of the text upon which the master was lecturing. The morning hours were reserved to the masters on the assumption that the students were more alert then, and no bachelor was permitted to lecture during this time, although he was free to choose any other time that was not preempted for disputations.

During the first two years, the student heard books primarily on grammar and logic, then moved to the physical and moral sciences and finally to metaphysics, although, since masters were free to offer any courses they chose, it was often impossible to take courses in the ideal sequence. During his last two years as an undergraduate (or sometimes the last year only), the student was also required to attend and participate in the public disputations held once a week by the masters. His principal function would be as <u>opponens</u>, raising objections to the arguments of the masters, but he was required at least once to act as <u>respondens</u> and reply to the objections raised by others. He could avoid this last requirement by attending lectures for an additional year.

During this fifth year, the student was ready to become a bachelor, or apprentice master. Shortly before Easter each year, a special committee of masters investigated the qualifications of each fifth-year student, and if they found that he had fulfilled all the requirements and was of good character and appearance, they would so swear and present him for the ceremony of determination. Determination, that is, giving an authoritative answer to a question, was a right usually reserved to masters but conceded to bachelors just on this occasion as a sort of practice lecture under the supervision of a master. There would be an official <u>respondens</u> (usually another bachelor who often had to be bribed to perform this difficult function) and as many objectors as chose to participate. The subjects of the determination were always grammar or logic (the more elementary disciplines), and the affair was supposed to be solemn and dignified, although frequently the high spirits of the other bachelors got out of hand. The ceremony would end late in the afternoon, and the new bachelor would then immediately deliver his first cursory lecture to the undergraduates. A student could avoid the baccalaureate determination by attending lectures for an additional year.

As a bachelor, the student had three main responsibilities: to give cursory lectures; to continue attending his master's lectures (but now only two or three times a week instead of daily) as well as taking other specified courses; and to attend and take part in both public disputations and the private ones of his own master, both as opponens and respondens. After two years as a bachelor (not including the year in which he was promoted), the student was ready for consideration for admission into the masters' guild. All the masters (or in some places a designated group of them) examined the candidate as to sapientia and mores (learning and character) and verified that all requirements for the degree had been fulfilled. (It frequently happened that one or more of the requirements would be waived or substituted. In fact, the only source for the existence of a requirement is frequently a grant of exception to it.) Those candidates who received an affirmative vote were then recommended for the licentia docendi, or license to teach (which was granted by the masters at some universities, the bishop's chancellor or even the king at others) and for "inception," that is, admission to the masters' guild.

Inception consisted of two ceremonies, Vespers and Investiture. The Vespers service was presided over by a master (usually the inceptor's) and began with a disputation of a previously announced question, with the candidate playing the role of opponens and the newest master that of respondens. This was a ceremony, not a genuine disputation, and so the disputation was over rather quickly. Then the presiding master gave a short talk, which included praise of the candidate (or candidates; quite often more than one person incepted at the same time) and some witty remarks about his personality or career. This was followed by the candidate's taking an oath of allegiance to the university.

At a new master's investiture, all the regent masters had to be present. After the celebration of mass, the presiding master invested the candidate with the ring, the open book and the biretta, or cap, the insignia of the master's office. This was followed by the new master's immediately exercising the functions of his office: he delivered a brief lecture and then took part in two mock disputations in which he "determined" a question. The ceremony ended with the new master's taking an oath to safeguard the privileges of the university and to teach as a regent master on the Arts faculty for two years. He was then required to entertain his new colleagues at a banquet.

Accurate numerical data for the Middle Ages are very hard to come by, and we do not know what percentage of those who matriculated under some master at a university persevered through the seven or eight year Arts course to become masters, nor do we know what percentage of the masters chose to make teaching a career, or after two years went on to a higher faculty, or petitioned to be released from their two-year teaching requirement so they could begin their professional training sooner. Obviously many who started did not finish. Otherwise there would have been far too many masters, and this was never the case. It seems that not many were content to remain as masters on the Arts faculty, although every master had the right to continue teaching as long as he chose. Probably the greatest portion of the masters taught for two years and then went on to the study of civil or canon law, medicine, or theology, in that order of popularity.

Being a regent master was a demanding job. There were frequent convocations of the masters to regulate university life, eradicate abuses, protect themselves against incursions on their rights, consider petitions for exceptions to the requirements, and examine the qualifications of candidates for the bachelor's or master's degrees. But this was peripheral to the master's main function of teaching and disputing. Most masters gave two sets of ordinary lectures concurrently, and some would also teach cursorily if they felt it necessary for their students' sake or if they were working on something that particularly interested them. The choice of books upon which he lectured was the master's, but the course offerings would to some extent be regulated by demand. The required courses would, of course, have the highest, or at least the most certain, enrollments. But a master could lecture on any other book he chose unless he was forbidden to do so by his peers or, as very rarely happened, by the church. He was also required to hold disputations regularly. The frequency of these disputations varied considerably from place to place, but they were considered an essential part of the teaching process and occupied much of the master's time and energy.

The curriculum of the universities underwent constant change, sometimes slow, sometimes rapid. We possess a slightly idealized version of the Parisian curriculum of about 1200 in the Sacerdos ad altare of the famous English scholar Alexander Neckam.[11] Neckam was conservative in his tastes and probably included more literature than was actually read, but the list does give us some notion of what was being taught at Paris at the beginning of the thirteenth century. After a preliminary list of authors who should be read, probably much of it wishful thinking, the list is arranged according to subject: the seven Liberal Arts and the advanced subjects of canon and civil law, medicine, and theology, corresponding to what we know of the Parisian faculties at that time. Alexander recommends that after a boy has learned his alphabet and the rudiments of grammar, he should read Donatus,

Cato, the _Ecloga Theoduli_, and Virgil's _Eclogues_. He should then proceed to the satirists and historians, the _Thebaid_, the "divine _Aeneid_," and Lucan's _De bello civili_, as well as Juvenal and the works of Ovid (particularly the _Remedium amoris_). He also suggests Virgil's _Georgics_, Sallust's histories, and Cicero's _De oratore_, _Tusculan Disputations_, _De amicitia_, _De senectute_, _De fato_, and _De officiis_ (but he warns that many disapprove of the same author's _De natura deorum_), Martial, Petronius, Symmachus, Solinus, Sidonius Appollinaris, Suetonius, Quintus Curtius, Trogus Pompeius, Livy, and Seneca's _Ad Lucilum_, _Natural Questions_, _De beneficiis_, and tragedies. This list of recommended authors surely exceeds what any Parisian student (and maybe even Alexander himself) actually read. Perhaps Alexander means that ideally a boy should have read these authors before coming to the university.

For grammar, Donatus' _Barbarismus_ and Priscian Major are recommended; for dialectic Boethius' _Topics_ and _Categorical Syllogisms_, Porphyry's _Isagoge_, Aristotle's _Categories_, _Interpretation_, _Sophistical Arguments_, _Prior_ and _Posterior Analytics_, Cicero's _Topics_, and Apuleius' _Interpretation_. He then goes on to recommend Aristotle's _Metaphysics_, _Generation and Corruption_, and _De anima_, which were just beginning to be known in the schools, but he curiously includes them under dialectic, which may mean that he had not read them. For rhetoric there are Cicero's _De inventione_ and _De oratore_, pseudo-Cicero's _Ad Herrenium_, and Quintilian's _De institutione oratoris_.

The quadrivium gets short shrift: Boethius' _Arithmetic_ and Euclid's _Elements_ (probably Books VII-X) for arithmetic; Euclid's _Elements_ for geometry; Ptolemy's _Canons_ (no mention is made of the _Almagest_) and Alfraganus' _Introduction_ for astronomy; and Boethius' _De musica_ for music.

The medical curriculum is much like that recently established at Salerno by Maurus: Johannitius' _Isagoge_, Hippocrates' _Aphorisms_ and _Prognostics_, "Galen's" _Tegni_ and _Pantegni_, Isaac Israeli's _Universal_ and _Particular Diets_ and _Urines_, and _Viaticum_, Theophilus' _Urines_ and _Pulses_, Dioscorides and Macer on the nature of herbs, and the works of Alexander of Thralles. For canon law there are Gratian, Burchard, Ivo of Chartres, and the decretals of Alexander III; for civil law the _Digest_ of Justinian, for theology the Bible (not yet Lombard's _Sentences_).[12] If there are inaccuracies in this list, they result from the inclusion of books which were not used rather than from the exclusion of books which were.

But things were changing rapidly. Already some particularly bold teachers were lecturing on Aristotle's natural philosophy (part of which Alexander had mentioned), and by 1210 the university was in an uproar, which resulted in the condemnation of these books by the archbishop of Sens. This condemnation was repeated by the papal legate in 1215. It was presumably still in force in 1231 when Gregory IX appointed a commission to purge Aristotle of errors so that his books might be safely lectured on. The earliest documents we have concerning the Paris Arts curriculum is from 1255, and by this time all of Aristotle's libri naturales are required ad formam. From this point on we have a much clearer idea of what books were actually used in classrom teaching.

Although the ideal program for the Arts course was alleged to be the seven Liberal Arts and the three philosophies (natural, moral, and metaphysics), the curriculum was in fact not arranged by subjects but by books. Each of the Arts subjects was represented by one or more books, but it sometimes takes a sharp eye to see the old structure which allegedly underlay the actual curriculum of the Arts faculties. We shall nevertheless follow the traditional canon for the sake of convenience.

For grammar both Donatus and Priscian (especially the latter) continued to be used, but early in the thirteenth century a new and more rigorous type of grammar came into vogue, called "speculative grammar." Two of the earliest and most widely used were the Doctrinale of Alexander of Villedieu (1202) and the Grecismus of Eberhard of Bethune (1214),[13] and even Priscian was commented upon from the new viewpoint. These grammars were more precise and logical than the old and more consonant with current accepted Latin usage. Their intensely scientific attitude toward language places them closer to modern linguistics then to literature. They assumed that "grammar had a basis outside language itself. . ., that there was one universal grammar dependent on the structure of reality, and that the rules of grammar were quite independent of the language in which they were expressed."[14] It was the task of grammar to discover these rules.

For rhetoric, Boethius' Topics (Book IV), Aristotle's Rhetoric, and Cicero's De inventione were usually among the required texts, although especially in the southern universities the rapidly developing ars dictaminis was invading the university curriculum.

Of the seven Arts, logic was by far the most important. At Oxford it occupied about half of the curriculum[15] and everywhere was a signficant fraction of the undergraduate education. It consisted of the so-called Old Logic, i.e., Porphyry's Isagoge, Aristotle's Categories and Interpretation, and the De sex principiis customarily attributed to Gilbert of la Porrée; and the New Logic, consisting of Aristotle's Topics, Prior and Posterior Analytics and Sophistical Arguments.

Arithmetic was covered in a very short time, and no new texts were used -- usually only Boethius' Arithmetic, a short practical arithmetic by Sacrobosco called Algorismus, and Books VII-X of Euclid's Elements. We frankly know little or nothing about the texts used for music until very late in the MIddle Ages.

Geometry, however, was the most popular of the mathematical disciplines and even influenced the way Latins conceived of algebra. The basic text, of course, was Euclid's Elements, usually in the translation of Adelard of Bath, and many original works were composed by various masters and probably lectured on as electives. Optics was included under geometry, and as we shall see in chapter 13 was intensively studied in the thirteenth century. The basic texts were Ptolemy's Optics and Euclid's Optics and Catoptrics (Mirrors). Also on this subject many original works were composed and lectured on.

Nearly as important as goemetry, and more interesting because more controversial, was astronomy. The most important text was the very difficult Almagest of Ptolemy, and most schools also taught their students to use the computus, of which there were various versions. Also touching on astronomy, and implying quite a different cosmos, were Aristotle's De caelo and Metaphysics. Many Arabic works of a very high order were also available, one of the best and most difficult being the De motibus caelorum of the Spanish Muslim Al-Bitruji (Alpetragius),[16] which was translated into Latin by Michael Scot in 1217. Its mathematical models were physically inconsistent with Ptolemy's (as were Aristotle's), and it was generally felt during the Middle Ages that astronomy could not grasp the true structure of the heavens but could only "save the appearances."

A very large portion of an undergraduate's career was spent studying the physical sciences, or natural philosophy. They, along with logic, dominated the curriculum at most universities. They consisted almost exclusively of Aristotelian (or pseudo-Aristotelian) works, namely: Physics, The Heaven and the World, Generation and Corruption, Meteorology, The Causes of the Properties of the Elements (not really by Aristotle), The Soul, Animals (actually three Aristotelian works, History, Generation, and Parts of Animals, translated as a single work with some omissions by Michael Scot about 1220), and the so-called Parva naturalia, a group of brief psychological and physiological works.

Moral philosophy too was dominated by Aristotle, whose Nicomachean Ethics, Economics, and Politics constituted the entire curriculum. Aside from the Ethics, this category does not seem to have been given much importance. Metaphysics, the most difficult part of the Arts course and usually heard in the undergraduate's fourth or fifth year, was represented by Aristotle's work of that name.

This looks like a very demanding curriculum even for a five year course, especially considering the care with which each text was expounded. And many of the books are extremely difficult. Are we to assume then that medieval students were much brighter and worked much harder than modern ones? We must keep in mind two mitigating factors. First, many of the books we have listed were taught in a very short time; every course did not have to last an entire term, and a few were as short as a week. This left time for hearing the more important and difficult books more than once, so that the student would acquire a genuine mastery of them. Second is the fact that in many cases the ideal text, even if required by university statutes, was quite often not the book which was actually used, and many universities explicitly permitted summary treatments of the major texts. Some of these works were abridgements of the major text, such as the short version of Boethius' Arithmetic made by Thomas Bradwardine late in the thirteenth century, and an abridgement of Adelard's translation of Euclid's Elements. Others were summaries of the subject, similar to the modern "textbook," such as Kilwardby's De ortu scientiarum,[17] Pecham's Perspectiva (Optics)[18] and on the very difficult subject of astronomy two extremely popular works: The Sphere by John of Holywood (Sacrobosco),[19] largely Ptolemaic but with some material from Arabic astronomers; and a work called Theorica planetarum[20] attributed to Gerard of Cremona, Gerard of Sabionetta, Robert Grosseteste, Simon of Bredon, and Walter Britt,[21] which exists in numerous versions all with a considerable core of common material. These last two works, which were simplified, non-technical astronomical books without tables, were used much more frequently than the actual text of Ptolemy to teach astronomy. During the late fourteenth and fifteenth centuries, a new work, the Theorica planetarum of Campanus of Novara,[22] gained considerably in popularity.

This brings medieval university education into somewhat better focus. Few students could in fact master Ptolemy's Almagest or Euclid's and Ptolemy's works on optics and mirrors. The Aristotelian libri naturales were required to be mastered, but many of the other books which had become available in Latin translations from Greek, Arabic, and Hebrew were not themselves read in university lectures, although they were available to mature scholars, and echoes of their doctrines were to be found in the commentaries of various professors on the required books.

The Arts course covered an enormous range, and so abbreviations of many of its subjects were more common than on the advanced faculties of law, medicine, and theology. The medical curriculum had been largely determined by the Salernitan canon of the late twelfth century, from where it spread very quickly to Montpellier and Paris and thence to all of Europe. Law too became standardized. A gloss on the civil law was brought to completion by Accursius by the mid-thirteenth century[23] and was almost universally employed from that time on. Canon law was based on Gratian's Decretum (with the addition of subsequent decretals of various popes), and it had also received a standard gloss by the middle of the thirteenth century. Theology was based on the text of the Bible with the _Glossa ordinaria_ (see below chapter 12) and from the second quarter of the thirteenth century the _Sentences_ of Peter Lombard, but it drew upon an enormous range of literature and developed both the _Commentary on the Sentences_ and the theological _quaestiones_, which focussed attention on the innumerable disputed points of theology. The method used in these _quaestiones_ was a stylized, highly scientific procedure which often disguised the deep religious feeling of their authors.

Undoubtedly the most powerful spiritual force of the thirteenth century was exerted by the mendicant orders of friars, the most important of which were the Dominicans and Franciscans. They affected every level of European society from the illiterate poor of the towns to the masters of the university theological faculties. Both orders had been founded early in the thirteenth century largely to combat the spread of heresy. They originally owned no property, held no benefices, and lived by begging (hence the name mendicants, or beggars) or by manual labor. St. Dominic had from the first valued education, especially in theology, as a powerful tool in his missionary task, and every Dominican province maintained a school taught by a brother who was a master.[24] The curriculum was much like that of the universities, but probably with more emphasis on theology and less on the Arts, although some of the most important elucidations of Aristotelian texts were done by the Dominicans Albert the Great and Thomas of Aquino. If there were no university in the town, the convent school of the Dominicans was self-contained, but if there was, they usually participated in university life.

The original Franciscan attitude toward learning was quite different. St. Francis felt that a pure and simple heart full of love was all that was needed and was hostile to formal education, but even before he died some Franciscans were beginning to attend theological lectures at Oxford and Paris.[25] At Paris this was facilitated by the entry into the order of one of the luminaries of the theological faculty, Alexander of Hales. The reaction of the Parisian masters was not friendly and resulted in a major battle, with the secular masters in 1262 expelling the friars from the university. Only papal intervention finally brought about a compromise, which allowed the friars to hold four of the fifteen chairs in theology, thus ending the legal battle but not the ill feeling.

At Oxford things were handled in a more civilized fashion. The early relationship between the mendicants and the university had been cordial, since the Oxford chancellor Robert Grosseteste prized them highly and even served as the first lecturer to the Oxford Franciscan school, although the order provided its own lecturers thenceforth. The legal problem at both universities was that the statutes of the universities forbade anyone to study theology without first taking a degree in Arts and required an oath of loyalty to the university, whereas the Rules of both mendicant orders forbade them to study Arts. At Oxford the problem was solved by granting exemptions on an individual basis to friars who wished to study theology without an Arts degree. There is some evidence that the friars, or at least the Dominicans, reciprocated by teaching much of the Arts curriculum in a shortened form in their own school.[26] Although there were some later squabbles between secular masters and friars at Oxford, there was never the animosity which poisoned the academic atmosphere at Paris for much of the late thirteenth century.

A development which eventually altered the basic structure of many universities was the growth of colleges. These were most important at the English universities of Oxford and Cambridge and to a slightly lesser extent at Paris, but they significantly influenced the structure of many late foundations, especially in Scotland and Germany, and they played some part in all the European universities.

The earliest colleges we know of were appropriately enough at Paris, but they were strictly limited in their function. They were founded and endowed by pious patrons as boarding houses for impecunious undergraduates, or sometimes for clerics in general. But the foundation of an endowed boarding house exclusively for theological students at Paris by the royal chaplain Robert de Sorbon in 1258 marked a turning point in the evolution of this institution. Its fellows were all holders of masters degrees in Arts; it possessed its own building and endowment and soon acquired a fine library;[27] and its fellows were given the right by the founder to co-opt their membership. By 1300 about nineteen colleges, some of them ephemeral, had been founded at Paris, and in the fourteenth century there were at least an additional thirty-seven. These were of various types, some exclusively for graduate students, some for undergraduate or even grammar students, and some with mixed memberships. But it was customary at Paris to place the ultimate authority over the colleges in the hands of some external body, often the university authorities, and as a result the growth of colleges at Paris did not have so dramatic a decentralizing influence on the university as it did at Oxford and Cambridge.

The English colleges, on the other hand, were usually completely autonomous corporate bodies, with endowments and the rights of cooptation and self-government. They were also almost exclusively for graduate students. As they grew in importance, began to finance tutors and lecturers, and eventually admitted nonmember undergraduates to their lectures, they virtually destroyed the older structure of the universities. This development, however, had not made much headway by the end of the fourteenth century, the terminus of our investigation. Even by the end of the thirteenth century, however, the early Oxford foundations of Merton,

University College, and Balliol, by bringing together masters with common interests, had already begun to exert some influence on the university's intellectual life.

The spread of universities was rapid after the first quarter of the thirteenth century. By the end of that century there were about twenty, some the result of a natural evolution of previously existing schools and some the result of foundation documents by emperors, kings, or popes. Two centuries later there were about seventy, most of which had been founded by municipalities or other public authorities. During the later phase of university growth, they became more involved in local secular or ecclesiastical politics, and indeed many were founded for just that purpose. They consequently became less international, and even the great university of Paris witnessed a dramatic diminution of foreign scholars and became largely a French university under the protection, and increasingly under the control, of the French king.

Germany came late to the university system and "scholastic" culture. During the thirteenth century there were no universities on German soil, and those who wished to pursue the new type of higher education had to study abroad, usually in France or Italy. Despite the intellectual brilliance of the court of Frederick II, German learning constituted an intellectual backwater in the thirteenth and fourteenth centuries, derivative and inferior. The earliest university foundation in the Empire was not even in Germany, but at Prague in Bohemia in 1348, and the second was at Vienna in 1356. There were only two more by the end of the century. The great age of German university foundations was the fifteenth century. The curriculum, teaching methods, and university organization were borrowed from the older universities of France and Italy and were old-fashioned in their homelands by the time they were established as novelties in Germany.

The universities came into being in response to pressing social needs, and this social function was always their most obvious characteristics. An increasingly urbanized society ruled by increasingly bureaucratic governmental units put a premium on legal education; the educated and wealthy citizens of the towns required scientific medical attention; and a society which was still deeply Christian and assailed from all sides by reforming and heretical groups required thoroughly trained theologians. The elements of local pride, a desire to have the support of sympathetic intellectuals, and the financial benefits to be derived from resident bodies of students and teachers also entered into the near-craze to found universities during the fourteenth century. An unforeseen result of the proliferation of university education was the narrowing of the gap between the educated elite and the intelligent laity. We have already mentioned the fact that many of those who matriculated did not graduate. But they had learned Latin and they had had a taste of the intellectual stimulation of university life. There is no way to estimate the relative numbers of such people, but they must have been considerable. They constituted a new "market" for literary productions in western Europe -- simplified, summary, encyclopedic, or vernacular versions of university learning. We shall discuss these productions at greater length in a subsequent chapter.

NOTES

1. There are many excellent studies of medieval universities. I list only a few titles: Hastings Rashdall, The Universities of Europe in the Middle Ages, ed. Powicke and Emden (3 vols., Oxford, 1936); Stephen d'Irsay, Histoire des universités francaises et etrangères des origines à nos jours (2 vols., Paris, 1933-35); and A. B. Cobban, The Medieval Universities, their Development and Organisation (London, 1975). Many of the documents published in Denifle and Chatelain, Chartularium universitatis Parisiensis (4 vols., Paris, 1889-97) are translated in Lynn Thorndike, University Life and Records in the Middle Ages (New York, 1944). A good brief popular treatment is C. H. Haskins, The Rise of the Universities (New York, 1923; reprint Ithaca, New York, 1965); see also Gordon Leff, Paris and Oxford Universities in the Thirteenth and Fourteenth Centuries (New York, 1968).

2. The coverage of Salerno in most general works on the universities is inadequate. The best two works are Paul O. Kristeller, "The School of Salerno: its Development and its Contribution to Learning," Bulletin of the History of Medicine 17 (1945), 138-194, reprinted in Kristeller, Studies in Renaissance Thought and Letters (Rome, 1956), 495-551; and Brian Lawn, The Salernitan Questions (Oxford, 1963).

3. See above, chapter 8, n. 4.

4. See Lawn, Salernitan Questions.

5. Edited, with an English translation and superb introduction by Morris H. Saffron, Maurus of Salerno, Twelfth-Century "Optimus Physicus," with his Commentary on the Prognostics of Hippocrates (Philadelphia, 1972).

6. Recently edited by Wolfgang Stürner, Urso von Salerno: De commixtionibus elementorum libellus (Stuttgart, 1976).

7. Rashdall, Universities, I, 149-51.

8. See Cobban, Medieval Universities, 100-101.

9. On the vexed question of the origins of the Oxford Chancellorship, see D. A. Callus, Robert Grosseteste, Scholar and

Bishop (Oxford, 1955), 6-10.

10. I have drawn heavily for what follows on the excellent article by James A. Weisheipl, "The Curriculum for the Faculty of Arts at Oxford in the Early Fourteenth Century," Medieval Studies 16 (1964), 143-185.

11. Neckam's authorship and the true nature of the Sacerdos ad altare have been established by C. H. Haskins, Studies in the History of Medieval Science (Cambridge, Massachusetts, 1924; reprint New York: Ungar, 1960), 357-71.

12. Ibid., 372-76.

13. See G. L. Bursill-Hall, Speculative Grammars of the Middle Ages (The Hague, 1971).

14. Ibid., 35.

15. Weisheipl, "Curriculum of the Faculty of Arts," 169.

16. Latin text and English summary by F. J. Carmody, Al-Bitruji, De motibus celorum (Berkeley, 1952). See also the excellent edition and translation by Bernard R. Goldstein, Al-Bitruji On the Principles of Astronomy (2 vols., New Haven and London, 1971).

17. Edited by Albert G. Judy, Robert Kilwarby, O. P., De ortu scientiarum (London, 1976).

18. Edited and translated by David C. Lindberg, John Pecham and the Science of Optics (Madison, Wisconsin, 1970).

19. Edited by Lynn Thorndike, The Sphere of Sacrobosco and its Commentators (Chicago, 1949).

20. Edited by F. J. Carmody (Berkeley, 1942).

21. See Richard C. Dales, "Grosseteste, Aristotle, and Astronomy. A Manuscript in the Hoose Library," Coranto 2 (1965), 7-11.

22. Edition and translation by F. S. Benjamin and G. J. Toomer, Campanus of Novara and Medieval Planetary Theory (Madison, Wisconsin, 1971).

23. See the most useful note by Hermann Kantorowicz in Beryl Smalley, Study of the Bible in the Middle Ages, 52-55.

24. See William A. Hinnebusch, The Early English Friars Preachers (Rome, 1951), 332-419; and R. F. Bennett, The Early Dominicans (Cambridge, 1937).

25. See A. G. Little, "The Franciscan School at Oxford in the Thirteenth Century," _Archivum Franciscanum Historicum_ 19 (1926), 803-874 and John Moorman, _A History of the Franciscan Order from its Origins to the Year 1517_ (Oxford, 1968), 123-139.

26. See R. C. Dales, "R. de Staningtona: An Unknown Writer of the Thirteenth Century," _Journal of the History of Philosophy_ 4 (1966), 199-208.

27. See Richard H. Rouse, "The Early Library of the Sorbonne," _Scriptorium_ 21 (1967), 42-71, 227-51.

Chapter 12

The Philosophy of the High Middle Ages

The Latin Europeans were heir to a long and complex tradition of philosophy. The knew the outlines of pre-Socratic thought through the handbooks, and especially through the admirable summary in Augustine's City of God. They knew too of the definition of the philosopher as a "lover of wisdom" attributed to Pythagoras and repeated by many writers, including Pliny, Augustine, and Isidore of Seville. Although they had only a smattering of Aristotle's works before the late twelfth century, they were aware of his view of philosophy as a rigorous logical inquiry.

But in fact philosophy as a system of inquiry had long since ceased to be a reality. To the Romans it had been largely a system of rationalized morality, and in any case a body of doctrine to be learned rather than a method of inquiry for the discovery of truth. Although the earliest Neoplatonists, especially Plotinus, had been vigorous original thinkers, their thought too was expressed as a series of truths from on high. So although the name "philosophy" and several definitions of it were known to the early Middle Ages, its practice virtually died out until the late Carolingian age. Although the Carolingians were primarily concerned with correct rituals and purified texts, such thinkers as Eriugena, Gottschalk, Ratramnus, and Radbertus impress us with the power of their thought. But the writings of these men had no immediate issue, and it was another two hundred years before the philosophy of the Middle Ages began to take shape.

It was in philosophy as it was in literature, law, science, and medicine, that late in the eleventh century a significant change occurred in the European outlook, and from that time on till the end of the fourteenth century, development was rapid.[1] This change is exemplified in the story St. Anselm tells us of his students at the monastic school of Bec requesting that he provide them with a proof of God's existence based solely on reason, with no recourse to the Bible or other data of revelation. Anselm's first attempt at such a proof, given in his Proslogion, was a reworking of Boethius' argument that our perception of degrees of perfection in the world necessarily implies the existence of an absolutely perfect being as a standard by which lesser perfections are ordered. But he considered this proof to be too complicated and not to carry absolute conviction. After much more hard thought, he devised one of the most famous of all proofs of God, the so-called ontological proof, which he presented in his Monologion. Taking it for granted that all men have a concept of God as "that than which nothing greater can be conceived," whether or not they grant His existence, he then argues that since it is greater to exist in reality than only in the mind, if God existed only as a concept in the mind, it would be possible to conceive of a being still greater, namely one which also existed in reality. Therefore, our very concept of God necessarily entails His existence.

That his students should want this kind of a proof is in itself remarkable. Even more so is the fact that Anselm spent so much of his life trying to oblige them. Anselm and his students were not unique. They were representative of a large body of opinion which was seeking for more and different meaning than was available within the old curriculum with the old techniques. They professed a faith in human reason and its consonance with revelation which would run throughout the rest of the Middle Ages and would constitute one of the major legacies of the Middle Ages to the European intellectual tradition. It was with this new bold use of reason that philosophy was reborn in the West as a system of inquiry. Its range was cosmic, all the way from the elemental bodies of the physical world to the nature of God Himself. As was the case with the revival of scientific inquiry in Latin Europe (see below, chapter 13), this new philosophy came into being before any significant translations of ancient Greek or Arabic philosophy had been made. It was an indigenous phenomenon, and although it provided the motivation for much of the translating activity, it took place prior to it. Latins then eagerly read and interpreted exotic philosophies in their own way, but the integrity of the Latin Christian tradition bent even the stubbornest and most coherent ancient systems to its own values. There were times when the outcome of the struggle was in doubt, but during the twelfth century Plato and his interpreters, pseudo-Dionysius, "Hermes Tresmegistos," and Avicenna, and during the thirteenth Aristotle, Averroes, Proclus, and a host of others eventually succumbed.

It was the use of dialectic in the study of theology that produced much of the excitement (and much of the controversy) of the eleventh and twelfth centuries. As early as the 1040s, Berengar of Tours had asserted the competence of reason to explain the eucharist. Man possesses reason, he said, because he is made in God's image, and he should use this divine gift. Reason teaches us that the accidents (concomitant attributes such as color, weight, texture, taste, etc.) of the bread of the sacrament cannot exist without their proper substance. Consequently there is no change of the substance of the bread after its consecration. Rather, another form, that of the body of Christ, is added to it. This teaching engendered a major controversy over the eucharist not settled until the Fourth Lateran Council of 1215. Berengar's position was condemned by several councils, but his attitude and methods presaged those of the new age.

The single problem which occupied the attention of philosophers during the first decades of the twelfth century was that of the ontological status of universals, and reputations were made and lost on a man's success in defining the relationship between individually existing things and the classes to which these individuals belonged (universals). The problem had been formulated by Boethius in his commentary on Porphyry's Introduction to Aristotle's Categories, as follows: "The question concerning genera and species is whether they have a substantial existence, or whether they are bare intellectual concepts only; or whether, if they have a substantial existence, they are corporeal or incorporeal, and whether they are separable from the sensible properties of individual things, or are only in these properties and subsisting about them." Boethius declined to give an answer in this place on the grounds that the question was extremely profound and in need of further investigation, but the Europeans of the early twelfth century were eager to conduct this further investigation.

The earliest known participant in this controversy was the Frenchman, John Roscelin, a teacher of the late eleventh century. He seems to have taught that a universal was nothing more than the sound of the word (flatus vocis) we use to indicate a class of individual objects. Hence the sound used in speaking the word "man" is a universal. It has no independent existence of its own; it is not higher in the cosmic hierarchy than the individual; it is not a part of a causal chain in bringing individuals about. It is just a name (nomen), and so Roscelin and those who followed in his tradition are called nominalists.

Roscelin's position was vigorously attacked by William of Champeaux. As is the case with Roscelin, William's pertinent works have not survived, and we know his doctrines only through others' reports. But William apparently taught that a universal exists completely and essentially in each individual of which it is predicated, and to have modified this slightly under criticism to say that the whole universal exists indifferently in each individual of which it is predicated. The universal exists prior to the individual and is something real. Hence William's followers are called realists.

Roscelin and William of Champeaux represent the two extreme positions. Many other eager minds joined the argument, and virtually every possible answer to the question as it had been posed by Boethius was offered. Personalities as well as doctrines were involved, and the academic arena often took on the aspect of a battlefield. Berengar had attacked the intelligence of those who believed in transubstantiation. He was in turn attacked by Lanfranc of Bec, who also, somewhat more gently, castigated his former pupil Anselm for the lack of scriptural quotations in his theological works. Roscelin attacked the orthodoxy of Anselm's essentially Platonic philosophical position, and Anselm retaliated in kind and more successfully. Both Abelard and William of Champeaux joined the attack on Roscelin and seem to have effectively destroyed his reputation (and Roscelin later wrote a vicious letter mocking Abelard for his castration). Abelard then turned on William, publicly humiliated him, and forced him out of teaching to a refuge in the countryside which later became the abbey of St. Victor. Abelard himself had no dearth of enemies. His doctrine on. the Trinity was condemned by the council of Soisson in 1121, where he was forced to consign his own book to the flames, and again, following a vindictive persecution by St. Bernard and William of St. Thierry, at Sens in 1140.

Abelard had probably the sharpest mind of the first half of the twelfth century, as well as a naturally combative nature which made it possible for him to thrive in the academic jungle (it just looks like a grove from a distance). He complained that his contemporaries gave too much attention to the problem of universals, "as though it were the whole of philosophy." He solved the problem to his satisfaction, carefully criticizing the answers proposed by others and offering meticulously worked out answers to Boethius' questions. Universals, he said, exist only in the human understanding, but they signify real things, namely the particulars of which they are predicated. As to their corporeity, he said that inasmuch as they are names, they are corporeal, but in their function of signifying a group of individuals they are incorporeal. They exist in sensible things, not apart from them, except when they designate forms of bodies or other non-sensible things.

But Abelard's view of philosophy was much broader than the problem of universals. Philosophy was the highest calling, informing life, elucidating faith, seeking truth. He wrote an important work on ethics, Scito teipsum, which developed his famous doctrine that the morality of the intention determined the morality of the act. But most of his work was devoted to theology. His Sic et non, listing difficult points of doctrine and marshalling opinions for and against, is characteristic of his inquisitive, bold, and undogmatic approach. His three books on Christian Theology, each of which he revised several times and which got him into trouble with the ecclesiastical authorities, come to definite conclusions, but only after exhaustive grammatical investigation of his texts and rigorous logical argumentation.

Abelard's view of philosophy was shared by many men of his day. His older contemporary, Adelard of Bath, has given us an admirable apologia for the philosopher's life, scorning wealth and status and devoted solely to seeking truth, in his De eodem et diverso. In some ways more traditional than Abelard in his nontechnical philosophising, in other ways he is more advanced, as in the extreme claims he made for human reason in his Natural Questions and his active quest for exotic knowledge which led him to travel to southern Italy and the Middle East, and probably to Spain, and to learn Arabic, in order to possess the treasures of more advanced peoples. William of Conches, Thierry of Chartres, Gilbert

-236-

of la Porrée, Bernard Silvestris, and a host of others were of a like mind. Plato's _Timaeus_ and the works of Boethius (both the _Consolation_ and the logical works) were among their most important sources. They had mastered only the "Old Logic" but they put it to impressive new uses and were in the process of acquiring the "New Logic" (Aristotle's _Topics_, _Prior_ and _Posterior_ _Analytics_, and _Sophistical_ _Arguments_). They shared the conviction that reason is omnicompetent in human learning, and they took their technical logic seriously. But they still insisted on the union of wisdom and eloquence and were all highly conscious stylists. William of Conches spoke for them in his quotation of Cicero in the Preface to his _Philosophia_: "Since, as Cicero says in the prologue to his _Rhetoric_, 'eloquence without wisdom is harmful; but wisdom without eloquence, although insufficient, is something, it nevertheless shows itself in the highest degree with eloquence,' those men err who, setting aside that which is profitable and does no harm, adhere to that which is harmful and of no use."[2]

But not everyone in the early twelfth century was so enamored of reason as the men we have been discussing. Many of the ablest and most sensitive young men of the time were being attracted to the Cistercian reform movement, which confronted the archaic ritualism of Cluny with a demand for a more interior, emotional and personal Christian experience. This movement was dominated by Bernard of Clairvaux, who, with his lackey, William of St. Thierry, carried on a vigorous campaign against what they considered to be the presumptuous misuse of reason in trying to comprehend the unfathonable divine mysteries.

A somewhat more moderate position was taken by the great monastic writer, Hugh of St. Victor, who, all things considered, probably exerted a deeper and longer lasting influence on European thought than any of his more colorful contemporaries. Although Hugh was critical of undirected or misdirected secular knowledge, he considered nothing to be useless if properly employed. Within the context of the monastic vocation he gave the arts and sciences an important place and did not shrink from using them, including dialectic, in his studies of theology. He himself was extremely learned and, although a monk, very much in touch with the life of his day. He devised a new classification of the sciences in his _Didascalion_, more applicable to his own day than the old and well known one of Boethius.[3] First came the theoretical sciences, whose aim was to discover truth. These are theology, mathematics, and physics and their subdivisions. Next are the practical sciences, whose aim is moral action, and which are divided into individual, group, and political ethics. Hugh's third division, the mechanical arts, is new and shows the vast change which had occurred in the European value system since the days of Boethius, who had only contempt for the mechanical arts. Hugh includes in this category weaving, armament making, agriculture, hunting, medicine, and theater. His final division of human learning is logic, which in Hugh's broad view includes grammar, rhetoric, and logic proper, a definition which would later be adopted by John of Salisbury.

Rationality in a broader sense also influenced the organization of materials in several disciplines during the twelfth century. Between the late eleventh and early thirteenth centuries, a standard gloss (or body of explanatory material) had been provided for the Roman law. Gratian did much the same thing for canon law, and the Salernitan masters were standardizing both the texts and commentaries on them for the medical curriculum. To do the same for theology was both more difficult and more necessary. An attempt at organization had been made by Abelard in his Sic et non, but this work was concerned with doctrine only, and it was a strictly preliminary sort of undertaking.

Essential to theological studies were the mastery of the text of the Bible itself and some sort of basic agreement in understanding what it said. This had for centuries been accomplished through the use of glosses, usually culled from the writings of the Fathers but occasionally composed by a teacher himself. There is evidence of collections of glosses going back to the seventh century, but they were usually confined to certain parts or books of the Bible, and in any case none of them ever gained general currency. In the mid-eleventh century a movement began to provide an adequate gloss for the whole Bible. This movement seems to have originated either with Fulbert of Chartres or Berengar of Tours, and to have spread to Bec, Reims, and Paris by 1100.[4] From 1100 to 1130 the crucial work was done on this project by the brothers Anselm and Ralph of Laon and their students. Anselm had hoped to provide clear and accurate glosses for the entire Bible, but his episcopal duties interfered with his work and he died (1117) without having completed his project. At the time of Anselm's death, his gloss (or apparatus) was still just one of a number of competing partial glosses on the holy text. But one of his pupils, Gilbert of la Porrée, carried it further, and the famous Peter Lombard both brought it to completion and used it in his own masterwork, the Sentences, thus achieving for it a pre-eminent status as the gloss (or Glossa ordinaria, as it would later be called), the generally accepted and used body of explanatory comments on the scriptural text.

Peter Lombard also contributed a major service to theological studies by rationalizing them under four main headings and treating each one comprehensively in his Book of Sentences (1152). We do not know of any previous similar works which it superseded or displaced; it seems to have been the first book in the field, and its acceptance was rapid. By the end of the twelfth century it was the commonly used textbook for the teaching of theology, and from the early thirteenth century to the end of the Middle Ages, every doctor of theology in a European university wrote a commentary on it. It provided the framework for theological teaching and discussion for 300 years.

The middle of the twelfth century constitutes a watershed. Most of the great thinkers of the early part of the century died during the 1140s or early 1150s. The second half of the century was dominated by the acquisition of large amounts of exotic material, translated into Latin from Greek, Arabic, and Hebrew,[5] and the attempt to assimilate this very rich and diverse body of doctrine. The lines of development which had become evident in the first part of the century were temporarily obscured, but some clarity of focus was restored during the last quarter of the century, as a new canon of authors slowly replaced the old, new problems occupied the best minds of the day, and new teaching methods were devised to deal with the new and vastly larger curriculum.

While its is clearly impossible in a short space and a general work to elucidate thoroughly the doctrines of all the newly translated thinkers, some presentation of the main teachings of the most influential is necessary. The most important of the new authors was Aristotle. His basic difference from both Arabic and Christian thought was that his cosmos was not created. God was its first principle and eternal cause, and it, like Him, had always existed and would exist forever. In analyzing being, he accepted the individually existing substance as the ultimate reality and considered it to be composed of two things, matter and form, which were correlative aspects of actual existents and could not exist separately from each other. But the world was not static; it was in constant, though not haphazard, flux. Aristotle accounted for change as a passage from potency to actuality, and all changes were described within this framework -- the mixture of the elements, the growth of living organisms, local motion, and alteration of accidents. (An accident is a concomitant attribute, such as color, size, texture, etc., which is not essential to the definition of the substance in which it inheres.) In his analysis of motion, Aristotle distinguished between the moved thing and the mover of that thing, and taught that they were separate entities -- "everything which is moved is moved by something else" (Physics, 7.1). He thus argued that the spheres of the heavens, being corporeal even though composed of the highest kind of matter, the fifth element, could not be the causes of their own motion but were rather moved by separate intellectual substances, the first of Whom was God. Thus God in Aristotle's thought is included in nature and is connected to the rest of the world through a hierarchy of intelligent and corporeal beings. The only composition he admits in substances is that of matter and form.

In living things the soul is the form (also called act or perfection) of the body. There are three degrees of living beings, vegetable, animal (sensitive), and rational, with corresponding levels of souls. Only man possesses a rational soul, and even it requires bodily organs to be what it is. Consequently the human soul, being a form, cannot exist apart from the animate body whose form it is. But in one fleeting thought, expressed near the end of Book III of his De anima, Aristotle considered the possibility that the very highest part of the intellect might not require a bodily organ and so might be capable of an independent existence. This obiter dictum was seized upon and elaborated into the doctrine of the separable active and passive intellects by both Arabic and Latin philosophers.

When Aristotle was recovered by the Muslims, they were already in possession of much Neoplatonic literature, and they tended to view Aristotle from a Platonic standpoint. For Muslims as for Christians, God was a creator and not just a first cause. But most of them tended to view creation as emanation and to attribute to God directly only the creation of the first intelligence, which then created the second, and so on down to the last intelligence, which both moved the sphere of the moon and was the active intellect for all men; that is, it was the active cause of human knowledge. To Avicenna the highest part of the individual human soul was the passive intellect, which was put in possession of knowledge by being "activated" by the agent intellect. To Averroes the passive intellect too was separate from individual human beings and was distinguished from the active intellect as that which acquires knowledge is distinguished from that which causes knowledge. This latter view completely denies personal immortality and grants man only a sensitive soul, which perishes with his body.

Avicenna's analysis of being went beyond Aristotle's in attributing to substances a composition of essence and existence (Avicenna did not originate this doctrine, but he was the Latins' major source for it), that is, except for God, the essence of a thing does not require that the thing actually exist -- existence is a separate state. This distinction, stated somewhat imprecisely by Avicenna, would be the cornerstone of Thomas of Aquino's metaphysics. Avicenna's doctrine of form was also seriously contaminated by Neoplatonic concepts. Aristotle had meant by it the form, actuality, or perfection of an individual substance, as opposed to the matter of that substance. But Avicenna assumed a hierarchy of forms, beginning with the most general and going on to the most specific, and he maintained a distinction between substantial forms (the form by which a thing is what it is) and accidental form (the form of the accidents possessed by a substance), so that there was a plurality of forms in everything that existed and a hierarchical arrangement of forms. This doctrine seriously distorted what Aristotle had meant by "form" and introduced untold confusion into Latin philosophical speculation during the thirteenth century.

But more basic even than the specific doctrines of these works was the implication they contained that the universe is necessarily as it is because it is a consequence of the divine nature. By thus connecting God to His creation through a sequence of necessary causes, they denied both His freedom and His omnipotence. There was consequently some legitimate cause for concern on the part of the thirteenth-century opponents of the new learning, who are too often dismissed simply as unintelligent obscurantists.

The successful assimilation of this huge amount of new material occurred as a result of university teaching. The earliest works attempting to accomplish this were literary compositions, which followed the manner of Avicenna in being free paraphrases of Aristotelian works (or a section of one), which both elucidated and altered Aristotle's teaching.[6] This type of work remained in vogue until about 1240, although there are some later examples (especially the works of Albert the Great). But systematic commentaries were also being written as early as the first decade of the thirteenth century; for example, Alfred Sareshel's commentaries on the Meterology, Generation and Corruption, and The Heaven and the World, and Grosseteste's on the Posterior Analytics. The most important early teachers of whom we have any reliable knowledge are John Blund and Robert Grosseteste.

John Blund, who was born in England about 1180-1185, became a master of Arts at Paris and then continued his teaching on the Arts faculty at Oxford. Shortly after 1200 he composed a work On the Soul[7] which shows the influence of traditional Christian sources, the Arabs (especially Avicenna), the Jew Avicebron, and Aristotle himself, although his major source was Avicenna's On the Soul, after which Blund modelled his own treatise. However, Blund was extremely independent and did not follow anyone blindly. In his treatise, most of the crucial questions of the later part of the century are posed and discussed, although his method was quite elementary. He defines the soul as "the perfection of an organized body having in it the capacity for life," and insists that its study is solely the province of the Artist, not the theologian. He argued that there was only one soul in man, i.e., the rational, which included within it the vegetative and sensitive, although he did not, as is sometimes claimed, opt for the unity of substantial form in man; the question had not been raised yet. And, resisting the teaching of his main guide, Avicenna, Blund denied that the heavens are moved either by their own souls or by intelligences, saying that they move according to nature. Blund's De anima seems to have influenced many subsequent thinkers through a large part of the thirteenth century.

One of the most powerful minds of the thirteenth century was Robert Grosseteste.[8] He was born about 1168, taught on the Oxford Arts faculty from ca. 1190 to 1209, then probably took a degree in theology at Paris, and returned to Oxford in 1215. He taught theology there until 1235, when he became bishop of Lincoln. Most of his active academic life consequently coincided with the period of eclecticism, when men were struggling to understand and deal with the newly acquired works. His thought continued to grow and develop throughout his life, as he acquired new books and thought more deeply about his reading. Consequently he did not develop a philosophical system or synthesis, but he exhibits some constant attitudes and adopts some fundamental positions which would be a major influence on European philosophy through the fifteenth century. According to him, the Bible contains all knowledge, both natural and supernatural. But it is difficult to understand, and so expertise in grammar, languages (especially Greek and Hebrew), and physical science (including mathematics) is necessary. Like Augustine and Abelard, he was willing to hazard tentative solutions to difficult questions, but always with the warning that his words should not be taken authoritatively.

In epistemology he held that absolutely certain knowledge was only possible through divine illumination, but this occurs very rarely. So we must usually depend on reasoning from sense data (the senses, he said, never deceive us, although our judgments about them may be false). What we are able to conceive is limited by what our mind aspires to, or in Grosseteste's phraseology, the mind's gaze cannot rise higher than the mind's desires. This is why Christians have succeeded where even the greatest of the pagan philosophers failed. Since they could not perceive the simplicity of eternity or the infinity of God, they were led into many errors, the most serious of which was the eternity of the world.

On the subject of human dignity, Grosseteste summed up and perfected a tradition stretching from Gregory of Nyssa and Gregory the Great through Scotus Eriugena and William of St. Thierry, and in the process provided a solution for one of the knottiest problems concerning the soul, namely, if it is an immortal spiritual substance and the body is a mortal corporeal substance, how can man, who is composed of both these things, constitute a true unity? The rational soul, he said, shares with angels the possession of rationality, and its vegetative and sensitive aspects share with the animal and vegetable kingdoms their functions. Man's body is composed of the four elements and thus shares their qualities with the rest of the material universe. And since the rational soul is naturally suited to be the perfection of the organic body, it is joined to it in a personal unity; the entire created universe, corporeal and spiritual, is thus summed up in man. And the totality of creatures could be united to the Creator, not by any natural bond, but only by God's assuming humanity in the unity of person. This, even more than the redemption of man from sin, is the reason for the Incarnation. "But when God assumes human nature in the unity of person, He is inserted into this circle like a gem in a ring of gold. . . .[This act] unites the entire universe of things, because man shares sensation with animals and vegetation with plants, and he has a natural community with all other bodies through his assumption in personal unity; thus all things have a fuller coupling with the Creator in the assumed man. In this coupling was made not only one universe of creatures, but one universe of all things."[9] Grosseteste considers man to be the highest of God's creatures, higher even than the angels, and he has managed to explain man's supreme worth in a way that preserves the soul as a separate substance but also achieves a sophisticated explanation of human unity.

Grosseteste had a great respect for the pagan writers of Antiquity, as well as the recently translated Arabic and Hebrew works. He had read nearly all of them and had made several translations of his own from Greek. But he was also one of the earliest Latin authors to give a reasoned warning about the errors these books contained. His solution though was not to ban or burn the books—he used them extensively. It was rather to face the questions they raised and refute their positions by argument. The one exception to this statement was books on astrology, which he said were false and written at the dictation of the devil. Astrology was bad science and, since it denied human free will and derogated from the majesty of God, it was also heretical and its books should be burned.[10]

Grosseteste was intensely aware of the (naturally) impassable gulf between a perfect, infinite, and omnipotent God and His mutable and finite creation. In spite of his considerable knowledge of Arabic authors, he denied the existence of the intelligences as movers of the heavens. He knew too much about astronomy to give any facile explanation, and said simply that we do not know much about the actual movements of the heavenly bodies and even less about what causes them to move as they do. They do so because God made them in such a way that they would, but the details of this he considered unknown and perhaps unknowable.[11]

Grosseteste's works were extremely influential in both mendicant orders (Albert the Great, a Dominican, and Bonaventure and Roger Bacon, both Franciscans, used them extensively, and Grosseteste willed his library to the Oxford Franciscans), and it was also considerable among the secular masters. Manuscript copies of his writings are to be found in the libraries of Spain, Italy, France, Germany, and Bohemia, as well as England.[12] He dealt more successfully than any of his contemporaries, such as Alexander of Hales or William of Auxerre, with the problem of maintaining the integrity of the Latin Christian tradition in the face of new exotic thought, while at the same time learning much from the new works.

Thus, Aristotelian studies took firm root early and without controversy at Oxford,[13] and they continued to flourish there. Largely because of Grosseteste's influence, it was mainly logic and mathematical physics that attracted many of the brightest Oxford masters and gave the university's teaching its characteristic excellence during the Middle Ages.

At Paris during the same period there was violent opposition to Aristotle, which hindered the development of philosophy for some time. Aristotle's _libri_ _naturales_ were first introduced at Paris about the same time they were at Oxford, that is, around 1190-1200. But the situation at Paris was far different from that at Oxford. For one thing, the Paris theological faculty was very strong and at that time was extremely conservative in outlook and distrustful of the use of any pagan authors. For another, two of the leading proponents of Aristotelian studies at Paris came to some rather bizarre conclusions concerning Aristotle's teaching, which were both heretical from the standpoint of Christianity and false to the doctrine of Aristotle. Of one of these men, Amalric of Bène, we know almost nothing except that he was regent master first of Arts and then of theology at Paris. About the other we have somewhat better information. David of Dinant[14] was probably a regent master in Arts at Paris and had been one of the most enthusiastic exponents of the _libri_ _naturales_ early in the thirteenth century. David's doctrine is one of the few instances of genuine pantheism in Christian thought. He first divides all being (his ultimate category) into three "indivisibles," matter, mind, and God, and then argues that they are in fact identical with one another.

David died around 1208, but his followers and those of Amalric seem still to have constituted an enthusiastic minority on the Arts faculty. The theologians were outraged and pressed the archbishop of Sens to take action. The archbishop, Peter of Corbeil, was himself a former regent master on the Parisian theological faculty and so inclined to be favorable to its wishes. He summoned the Council of Paris in 1210, and it condemned as heretical the teachings of Amalric, David, and a third person known only as Mauricius the Spaniard, and ordered their books to be burned. It then went on to prohibit Aristotle's works on natural science from being lectured or commented on, either publicly or privately, under penalty of excommunication. It did not of course forbid individual masters to read these books, so long as they did not use them as texts in the classroom.

The next five years were marked by great tension and hostility between the Arts and theological faculties, which was settled only by the intervention of the papacy, probably at the request of the theologians.[15] Pope Innocent III had been a theological student at Paris, and his legate in this affair, Robert Curçon, had been a regent master of theology at Paris. It was not likely then that the matter would be decided in favor of the Artists, and it was not. Curçon gave the university its first statutes and renewed the earlier ban on Aristotle's _libri_ _naturales_.

While we have no explicit information on the Paris Arts curriculum for the next fifteen years, the works of those master which have been studied, both Artists and theologians, show an increasing use of and familiarity with Aristotle's banned books, but it was far inferior to the Oxford teaching of the same period. We are probably justified in assuming that the prohibition was not strictly obeyed, because in 1228 Pope Gregory IX sent a sharply worded letter to the new generation of theologians at Paris (he too had once studied there) protesting the "profane novelties" which were being introduced into the theological teaching. Shortly thereafter, one of the more serious fracases between students and townsmen took place, and the university, failing to obtain redress for what it considered legitimate grievances, suspended lectures. Its masters and students dispersed to other university towns, such as Oxford, Orleans, and the newly-founded university of Toulouse, which brazenly advertised that the books of Aristotle forbidden at Paris could be freely studied there. Only the Dominicans continued to teach, thus increasing the hostility that was already felt towards them.

Pope Gregory now actively intervened. His _Parens scientiarum_, a comprehensive set of statutes for the university, ended the suspension of lectures. The pope also modified the ban on Aristotle by appointing a commision, headed by a former regent master in theology, William of Auxerre, charged with examining Aristotle's works and removing from them any doctrine which might contain even a suspicion of error, so that they might be safely taught.

The timing could not have been worse. William died within a year, and we are not aware that the commission over even began its job. But more important, in that same year, 1231, there arrived in Paris a translation from Arabic of the commentaries of Averroes on Aristotle's _libri naturales_, accompanied by new translations of the texts themselves.[16] These had been made by Michael Scot and sent to his friend Stephen of Provins at Paris, as well as to several Italian schools. Aristotle's works are notoriously difficult and in need of commentary. Averroes' commentaries were superb explanations of Aristotle's meaning, with very few contaminating doctrines from other sources. Within a decade he was commonly known in the schools as The Commentator, as Aristotle was known as The Philosopher, a title which had earlier been accorded to Plato. With the acquisition of Averroes' commentaries, Aristotle's works made steady inroads into the Paris Arts curriculum. By 1240 all the _libri naturales_ were being lectured on, and by 1255 (and probably long before) they had become required books for the Arts degree.

The writings of the Parisian masters during the first half of the thirteenth century help us to fill out somewhat the picture presented by official documents. These are nearly all the works of masters of theology, which have been better preserved and more thoroughly studied than those of the Artists. Peter of Poitiers, who died in 1205, had mentioned Aristotle's Metaphysics in his commentary on the Sentences, and John Blund, whom we have already mentioned, also taught at Paris during this early period. Alexander Neckam's list of "great books"[17] gives us a glimpse of the Paris Arts curriculum about the turn of the century, and David of Dinant's works, insofar as they have been recovered, provide some notion of what the teaching was like. During the 1220s and 1230s William of Auxerre and Philip the Chancellor began the task of facing and accommodating the newly acquired Greek and Arabic learning, as did Alexander of Hales and William of Auvergne, who became bishop of Paris just before the town-gown battle of 1228. In spite of official prohibitions, it is clear that Aristotle's libri naturales were being read, whether or not they were being taught, but it is not clear whether this was on the theological or Arts faculty. One must remember that masters were Artists before they were theologians, and they did not forget everything they had learned during the first seven years of their careers. Also, many came to study theology at Paris after having taken Arts degrees elsewhere, where the prohibitions against Aristotle were not in force. The result was the inexorable infiltration of the ideas contained in the Arabic (especially Averroes) and Greek (especially Aristotle) books, and an increasingly serious and successful effort to deal with them. This was a period of eclecticism in European philosophy when doctrines were taken from a variety of sources and roughly fitted together, sometimes with a modicum of critical thought but often without.

By the 1240s, we know that Aristotle's libri naturales were being read in the Arts curriculum. Roger Bacon was lecturing on them and says that they had arrived in his time, which would be consistent with the date of 1231. The Italian Bonaventure, later minister general of the Franciscan order and one of the great theologians of his day, reports his feeling of awe, wonderment, and disturbance when he first heard these strange and fascinating ideas being taught in a matter-of-fact way about 1245.

This period of acquisition and eclecticism came to an end in the works of a German Dominican, Albert von Lauingen, who studied and taught at Paris from 1240 to 1248. Albert the Great, as he is known to us, was the most prolific Christian author since Augustine. He was born about 1206 and died in 1280, so his life extended far into the period of mature scholasticism. Like Rabanus Maurus and Robert Grosseteste he outlived many of his pupils but retained to the end the intellectual orientation of his university days. He was the last and the most ambitious of the eclectic philosophers.

Albert had begun his university career at Bologna in 1222, but before the academic year was over he had moved to Padua, where he joined the Dominican order. After studying at the Dominicans'

Cologne studium for six years, he was sent to Paris from 1240 to 1248, where Thomas of Aquino was among his pupils. He returned to Cologne in 1248 to establish the Dominican studium generale there and at this time began the composition of a long series of philosophical works.

The basis of this corpus was the works of Aristotle. Albert used a considerable variety of other works to help him illuminate the often obscure text of Aristotle and to fill in the gaps in his treatment. Most important among these were Avicenna, pseudo-Dionysius, and Averroes, although Albert was enormously learned and there was not much available in Latin that he did not know. He considered himself an exegete rather than a philosopher, whose job it was to explain the meaning of the philosophers, to decide among conflicting interpretations, and to fill in the gaps with his own observations and experiments. Albert often adopted incompatible views of different philosophers, sometimes attempting a superficial accommodation and sometimes not. His doctrine of the soul is especially weak. He accepts both the Platonic-Augustinian-Avicennan view of the soul as a separate spiritual substance capable of an independent existence, and the Aristotelian view of the soul as the substantial form of the body and hence lacking any existence apart from the body. His opinion on the movers of the heavenly spheres was similarly confused, and like many of his contemporaries he did not seem to realize until quite late that both Avicenna and Averroes considered the active intellect to be one for all men and to be separate. Impressive as his work was, it was still a work of eclecticism, not of syntheseis or originality.

More important than the philosophical quality of his thought was Albert's success in winning for philosophy (in the broadest sense) an essential place in theological education, and in discriminating clearly between theology and philosophy, granting to each an autonomy of method and subject matter.[18] Like Grosseteste (whose works he knew well) he was convinced that one could not know theology adequately unless he was also expert in the knowledge of the world. And Albert's influence was perhaps even greater than Grosseteste's, at least in the late thirteenth century. His reputation for learning in his own day was justifiably enormous. His erudition awed his contemporaries as it awes us.

It was from among the young men who began their university careers during the decade of the 1240s that the first truly original and fully competent philosophical systems came. Needless to say, they disagreed violently with each other, but they represent the maturing of Latin Christian philosophy. The older, largely Avicennan approach, by now quite well accommodated to Christianity, was still shared by a majority of thinkers, who however disagreed with each other on specific doctrines. The works of Robert Grosseteste and Albert the Great were their most important aids in interpreting Aristotle, and they tended to share the following doctrines. First was the view of the soul as a separate substance from the body. It was sometimes viewed as composed of matter and form (for matter could be spiritual as well as corporeal), sometimes not. Also common to these thinkers was the doctrine of the plurality of forms in any given substance, and the accompanying doctrine of matter as possessing a kind of active and determinative potency (this would be a contradiction in terms to a strict Aristotelian), similar to the "seminal reasons" of Augustine's thought. Their epistemology leaned toward the doctrine of divine illumination, although there were many variations of this. They resisted the emanationist and necessitarian aspects of Greek and Arabic thought, usually holding that God creates without any intermediaries, and insisted on God's infinity and separateness from His creation; although, in what may at first glance appear to be an inconsistency, they also insisted on His intimate presence in creation, and its utter contingency and dependence upon Him. Men of this group were to be found in all the mendicant orders as well as among the secular masters. Among them were such renowned authors as Robert Kilwardby, John Pecham, and Giles of Rome. They unfortunately did not include any thinker of real genius, and they cast themselves as the upholders of tradition against the dangerous novelties of their opponents. This "tradition" was in many respects only a generation old, but in others it went back at least 300 years, and in some as far back as the age of the Fathers. It does violence to the facts, however, to label it as a Christian Augustinian tradition and to suppress its many elements of novelty.

A new group of brilliant, almost arrogantly confident young masters on the Arts faculty was determined to follow Aristotle, whose writings they equated with human reason, in all things. Their most highly regarded interpreter of Aristotle was Averroes, and they accepted from him the assertion that the philosopher's life as the highest calling of mankind, that theology is a watered-down version of philosophic truth for the consumption of weak minds, and that fables are a further dilution of truth for the masses, who are unable to understand anything else. Of this group, two men have been fairly well studied, Siger of Brabant and Boethius of Sweden (also known as Boethius of Dacia).

Siger[19] was born about 1240, in the late 1250s went to Paris to study Arts, and after receiving his degree began teaching on the Arts faculty. The content of that teaching has been preserved in a number of surviving treatises. He boldly asserted the independence and autonomy of philosophy, which he conceived as a purely rational enterprise with its own principles and methods. This of course continued a long tradition in Latin thought, going back to Anselm and Adelard of Bath, and whose most recent exponent had been Albert the Great. But this assertion acquired different nuances in the thought of one who had abandoned Anselm's viewpoint that philosophy is "faith seeking understanding" and the naive optimism of most twelfth-century and many thirteenth-century thinkers that the truth of God as revealed could not conflict with that arrived at by reason. Siger was fully aware of the fact that many of his philosophical positions were contrary to the teachings of the Christian faith. In such cases he always said that truth was to be found in faith, but that philosophy must be followed to its own conclusions and not contaminated by alien elements.

Siger's metaphysics, like that of most other thirteenth-century Latin philosophers, was a compound (not a mixture) of strict Aristotelianism and the Neoplatonic accretions found in the Arabic authors. The first principle of all things is First Being, which is eternal, simple, personal, and existing by virtue of itself (a se). Although its causality extends to every individual being in the universe, since it is simple and unique (unicus) it could only produce one effect immediately. This effect, the first of the separate intelligences, is, like its cause, eternal and necessary. It produces the second intelligence, and so on down to the area of generation and corruption below the moon. Thus God works by emanations through intermediaries, and the whole process is bound by necessity. Creatures have merely a capacity for existing, which is made actual by their participation in the perfection of God through the intermediaries of the intelligences. Since the cause of the universe is eternal, so too is the effect, i.e., the universe itself and all the species in it. Siger denies that existence is distinct from essence in creatures. Since the First Being exists a se and everything else exists from it, their existence is as necessary as that of their cause. So even in created (or caused) beings, existence belongs to their essence, and there is no need to posit an additional "act of being" to account for their existence.

The last of the separate intelligences constitutes the active (or agent) and passive (or possible) intellect of man. Man is composed of matter and form, the form being the sensitive (not the rational) soul. His intellectual functions are brought about by the activity of the agent intellect on the possible intellect, which is one for all mankind, although the effects differ in each individual because of differing capacities to receive them. Consequently there is no personal immortality. During the 1270s Siger modified, somewhat tentatively, his teaching on the unity of the intellect.

The human will Siger considered to be a passive power, subject to the images (or phantasms) evoked by the separate intellect, and hence man's actions are naturally determined. Since there is no personal immortality, there can be no rewards or punishments after death. Good and bad actions entail their own rewards and punishments in this life.

Siger's reputation was extremely high during his lifetime. He seems to have been an exciting young teacher who attracted a devoted following. His doctrine was clearly not strict Aristotelianism, as he claimed, or Averroism, as later writers have dubbed it. But it was a powerful and coherent synthesis, going far beyond the hesitant, partially rationalized systems of his predecessors.

Boethius of Sweden was the other most important leader of the philosophers of the Parisian Arts faculty. His works have not been studied so thoroughly as those of Siger, but considerable progress has been made in recent years and it is now possible to make some assessment of his views based on his own works rather than on the charges of his enemies.[20] He is probably the most extreme Latin exponent of the supreme value of a life of philosophical inquiry. This view is classical in origin and had been revived in Latin Europe in the twelfth century by such men as Adelard of Bath, Peter Abelard, John of Salisbury, and Daniel of Morley, but none of these men had perceived any conflict between philosophy and religion. Boethius, on the other hand, was not only aware of the conflict, but going beyond even Averroes, he insisted on it. He was willing to admit that the truth was to be found only in religion, but religion was based on revelation and belief and had nothing in common with philosophy. Philosophy was the investigation of natural causes by the use of human reason and was both the highest activity possible for man and the cause of his greatest happiness. There was no connection between it and theology. Faith does not shed light on human reason, and reason cannot help us understand what we believe by faith.

Like Siger, Boethius taught the doctrine of the eternity of the world, but like Thomas of Aquino he doubted that this could be proved or disproved by reason; it was merely a probable doctrine. From the list of propositions condemned by Stephen Tempier in 1277, we learn that he was also alleged to have taught that creation is impossible, that there was no first man and will be no last, and that the body, once corrupted, cannot return to life. The possibility of a future supernatural resurrection is not a proper subject for philosophical discussion since it is not capable of rational investigation.

Teaching on the theological faculty at about the same time that Siger and Boethius were lecturing in Arts was the brilliant and learned young Neapolitan, the Dominican Thomas of Aquino.[21] Although he disagreed with the Artists on several doctrines of crucial importance, he used the same sources and in many ways was a part of the same movement represented by them. But Thomas was above all a theologian. He had been born at Aquino in the kingdom of Naples in 1225 and had studied Arts at the recently founded university of Naples from 1239 to 1244. He joined the Dominican order, much to his noble family's horror, and was sent to study with Albert the Great, first at Paris, then at Cologne, from 1245 to 1252. He became a master of theology in 1256 and was appointed to one of the two Dominican chairs at Paris, where he taught from 1256 to 1259, during the heat of the conflict between the secular and mendicant masters. It was not until now, by which time he was in his mid-30s, that he began to write for publication. His writings are voluminous and cover a great range of subjects. One of his early works was the _Summa contra gentiles_, an aid to Christian missionaries trying to convert the Muslims. He also wrote commentaries on Aristotle's _libri naturales_, a commentary on the _Sentences_, and most important of all perhaps a _Summa theologiae_. In addition, he wrote a number of shorter works addressed to specific problems or discussing specific philosophical ideas.

Thomas made as extreme claims for theology as Siger and Boethius had for philosophy. Since all creatures, indeed all of creation, mirror God as their exemplar to some degree, and since human intellection must proceed upward from the data of sense experience, theology must include both philosophy and natural science. Thomas accordingly wrote detailed commentaries on the _libri naturales_ and included much material we would consider philosophical or scientific in his _Summa theologiae_ and other theological works. On the other hand, we cannot know nature adequately unless we know God, its creator and exemplar. Consequently Thomas' theology intimately influenced his philosophy, although he was scrupulous, in writing philosophical works, to use only philosophical principles and methods.

His metaphysics does not fall into any convenient category. In some respects it can be considered as a modification of Aristotle by some Neoplatonic and Muslim notions, but in fact, although it did take place within a definite tradition and a specific philosophical context, it was highly original. The cornerstone of his metaphysics was his doctrine of the composition of being and essence in creatures. This doctrine was an old one, but Thomas altered it in subtle but significant ways. After establishing that God is utterly simple, and that His being and essence are identical -- He is pure subsistent being -- Thomas contrasted this unique Being with all others. In every created being, he showed, its essence does not include its existence. God is free to create or not to create, and He could have created the world otherwise than He did; He could, in fact, have made it eternal. The fact that it had a beginning in time is not rationally demonstrable and is known only through revelation.

Therefore creatures are composed of essence and existence or being (Avicenna had emphasized the distinction of essence and being, while Thomas emphasized the composition). These are not two distinct things (_res_), one of which is added to the other. The nobler of them is being, since insofar as things are, they participate in the divine essence. But they are not pure being. Each one is a something. Until it is, it is nothing. All created beings, spiritual and corporeal, share this composition of essence and existence.

But Thomas eliminated from his thought the Augustinian notion of spiritual matter; only corporeal things were composed of matter and form. He also abandoned the seminal reasons and the plurality of forms. Reverting to a stricter Aristotelianism than many of his contemporaries would allow, Thomas taught the unity of substantial form. In man this form is the rational soul. Since the soul is a spiritual substance, it contains no matter per se, but only insofar as it informs the body. It nevertheless is not simple, but like the angels has composition only of essence and existence and can subsist as an independent entity apart from the body.

The originality of Thomas lay in his following out the implications for the Aristotelian system of the doctrines of divine being as pure act, and of divine infinity and freedom. But at the lower levels his thought is often quite a pure Aristotelianism, although placed in a new philosophical context. For example, he followed Arstotle's doctrine of cognition through intellectual abstraction from sense data, and he denied any intuitive knowledge of spiritual substances, or, on the natural level, of knowledge through divine illumination. He accepted the main outlines of Aristotle's universe, including the hierarchical structure, the reality of the intelligences and their necessity as movers of the heavens, and the composition of matter and form in corporeal beings. His thought could easily appear to be close to the naturalism of the Artists of his day, especially to sensitive and suspicious theologians who were alarmed about the introduction of dangerous novelties in university lectures.

During the late 1260s, the tensions between differing theologians, differing Artists, and between theologians and Artists grew more intense. One of the first to denounce the new trends publicly was the Franciscan theologian, Bonaventure, a man of deep spirituality, who was competent in philosophy but highly critical of excessive value's being conceded to it, and of the doctrines which were being openly taught. In 1267, in a series of lecture on the Ten Commandments, he issued a warning against many of the teachings of the philosophers; the next year, in a group of lectures on the gifts of the Holy Spirit, he attacked the doctrines that God cannot create out of nothing, that one separate intelligence can create another (emanationism), the eternity of the world, and the astrologically determined necessity of event on earth; and in 1273 in his lectures on the hexameron he repeated his strictures in much stronger language. In 1270 Thomas of Aquino published a treatise against the unity of the intellect, and the next year another work On the Eternity of the World, which claimed that the world's eternity could be neither proved nor disproved by reason, and we know it to be false solely by revelation, thus offending many theologians, especially Franciscans, who insisted that the non-eternity of the world could be rationally demonstrated. Some time during 1270 the Augustinian theologian, Giles of Rome, published a treatise against the errors of the philosophers.

By December of 1270 the situation had reached such proportions that the bishop of Paris, Stephen Tempier, formally condemned thirteen propositions, which admirably sum up the main points at issue: (1) the unity of the intellect in man; (2) it is false to say that man understands; (3) the human will does not have freedom of choice; (4) all mundane events are the necessary effects of the movements of the heavens; (5) the world is eternal; (6) there was no first man; (7) the soul passes away (is corrupted) when the body does; (8) after death the separated soul cannot suffer from corporeal fire; (9) freedom of choice is a passive, not an active power and is determined by the object desired; (10) God does not know particular things; (11) God known only Himself; (12) there is no divine providence ruling human actions; (13) God cannot give immortality to a mortal being.

The condemnation apparently had no effect, and the battle continued to rage. In 1271 John of Vercelli, the minister general of the Dominicans, wrote to several outstanding masters of the order, Robert Kilwardby, Albert the Great, and Thomas of Aquino, asking their opinions on several questionable doctrines, but the answers he received were so diverse that he could not have obtained much guidance from them. The debate continued, and in November, 1276 the inquisitor of France (at whose instigation we do not know) summoned Siger of Brabant and two other men of whom we know little, Goswin of la Chapelle and Bernier of Nivelles, to the inquisitorial court. Siger and his companions, accompanied by Boethius of Sweden fled from France and appealed their case to the papacy. They were apparently acquitted of heresy and remained at the papal court.

The pope at this time was John XXI, who as Peter of Spain had earlier been a famous master of Arts; his Summulae logicales was a widely used textbook in European universities. He was consequently not overly inclined to view academic controversies with alarm. But things had reached such a state by Janauary, 1277 that he could not ignore the Parisian situation (recall that the Parisian masters themselves had initiated their special relatonship with the papacy), and he accordingly sent a letter to bishop Tempier asking him to investigate the causes of the turmoil at Paris and report back to him. Instead, Tempier, on his own authority, appointed a commission of sixteen members, which in three weeks time assembled a jumbled and at times contradictory list of 219 propositions, which were declared heretical on March 7, 1277. All those who had taught or heard them were excommunicated unless they presented themselves for correction within seven days. In addition to the main points at issue, the list condemned Andreas Capellanus' Art of Love (by now apparently at least some people were taking it seriously) and books on geomancy and necromancy. It also cast its net widely enough to include about a dozen doctrines of Thomas of Aquino, the most important of which were that matter is the principle of individuation, that each angel constitutes a separate species, and that the will is subject to the judgment of the intellect.

Eleven days later, on March 18, the Dominican, Robert Kilwardby, archbishop of Canterbury, in a speech to the faculty and students of Oxford university, condemned a list of thirty errors in grammar, logic, and natural philosophy. Kilwardby was by now an old man. He had given up teaching in the mid-1250s and since then had confined his reading to the Bible and the Fathers. He was only dimly aware of the philosophical revolution which had recently transpired, but he did know that doctrines of questionable academic merit, and some even of doubtful orthodoxy, were being taught at Oxford. The doctrines he condemned, however, were not those at the heart of the Parisian controversy, and his condemnation was certainly not aimed on Thomas' teaching on the unity of substantial form,[22] a position which Kilwardby confesses has not been explained to him and which he does not understand. Kilwardby's condemnation had only a tenuous connection with Tempier's, but it must be considered as part of the same general disquietude among many philosophers and theologians over the growing acceptance of necessitarian and emanationist doctrines.

The effects of the 1277 condemnation are not yet fully understood, so any cause-effect relationship implied in what follows must be considered as tentative.[23] It must be understood that the condemnation at Paris was promulgated solely on the authority of the bishop of Paris and had only a local applicability (although there is evidence that some masters who worked at both Paris and Oxford felt bound by them even at Oxford), and that even there they were not strictly adhered to. The papacy's role in the affair did not extend to the condemnation, only to a request for an investigation of the turmoil. In fact there is no evidence that Tempier ever reported back to the pope as directed, although he may have. And the fact that the papacy probably acquitted and definitely protected Siger and his friends would indicate less than enthusiastic papal approval of the bishop of Paris' actions.

We know that the "philosophical" movement represented by Siger and Boethius continued to exist both at Paris and especially in Italy, where the university of Padua became a center of "Averroistic" studies. It is also clear that the older school, influenced more by the Neoplatonism of Augustine, pseudo-Dionysius, and Proclus, gained more vigor in the late thirteenth and the fourteenth centuries. The philosophy of Thomas became a political matter. Early in the fourteenth century, the Dominican order accepted it, after a period of hesitation, as its official philosophy and exerted pressure to have the condemnation of the Thomistic theses revoked. This pretty well obliged most Franciscans to oppose it, although it had a few adherents among that order. Its opponents wrote "Corrections" of it and its adherents wrote defenses of it. But, as often happens to men of originality and genius, Thomas was generally misunderstood by both parties and suffered as much from the efforts of his supporters as from his enemies. Within two generations after his death in 1274, his philosophy was labelled the via antiqua ("the old way"), so quickly does dangerous novelty become old-fashioned.

The history of philosophy in the fourteenth century is extremely complex and has not been so well studied as that of the thirteenth. It exhibits an increasing disengagement of philosophy and theology and a willingness on the part of philosophers to consider merely possible answers and then to suggest some bold hypotheses just to test their consequences. We shall consider only two additional thinkers of this vibrant and creative period, both Franciscans and both men of consummate ability, who gained adherents and founded "schools" of philosophy which would dominate the rest of the Middle Ages.

The first of these men is John Duns Scotus, born in 1266 and died in 1308. He studied at Oxford in the late 1280s and at Paris from 1293 to 1296, at a time when the philosophical divisions subsequent to the 1277 condemnations were just taking shape, and he took degrees in theology from both universities. John had joined the Franciscans in his youth and was familiar with the writings of Robert Grosseteste, which he probably read at the Oxford Franciscan convent, to which Grosseteste had bequeathed his library. In a sense he revived an older tradition which had been out of fashion for half a century, but like Thomas he was an acute and original thinker and not just the representative of a tradition. Following Grosseteste, he was fully aware of the limitations of human reason as well as its capacities, and he accepted Grosseteste's contention that the truths of Christianity aid human reason in its pursuits. It is therefore not surprising that he should have opposed Thomas' teaching on several crucial points.

John's works are extremely difficult. His arguments are complex and his distinctions are subtle and difficult to grasp. The following summary does not do him justice, but it should at least point out the leading characteristics of his thought. He disagrees with Thomas on the knowledge we have of God and on the relation of the Divine Ideas both to God and to creatures. Scotus argues that God and creatures share only one thing univocally (i.e., understood in a single sense in all cases), and that is being. But God is infinite being; in fact, infinity is the essential divine attribute. Divine goodness, wisdom, power, etc. are not identical with God's being and distinguished only by reason, but are themselves formally distinct (a formal distinction is not a real distinction, that is, a distinction of things). But since in God they exist in an infinite degree, they share this infinite existential mode and hence are ultimately not really distinct, but only formally so. The Divine Ideas are not the essences of created things, but exist only as the absolute objects of God's infinite knowledge. Of them, God freely chose to create some and thus make them real things, but not others. Creation is not determined by necessity; God could create infinitely many dissimilar universes if He chose.

Scotus also rejects Thomas' doctrine of the composition of being and essence in creatures, and that their essence is their idea in God's mind. To him, being and essence are really identical, with existence being a mode of essence. This leads him also to deny the Thomistic doctrine of the human soul. He says that reason can only show it to be the substantial form of man; everything else about it we know only from revelation.

He also rejects Thomas' teaching that matter is the principle of individuation and points out that it, like form, is common to all individuals of a species. Instead, he claims that we perceive not only individuals, but "common natures" in things, and that these common natures have a real existence outside the mind, although they do not exist apart from individuals. It is they that make it possible to say that some things are men, other horses, and still other stones. These common natures are the proper objects of our intellection, and when we abstract them from individuals they exist as universals in the mind (i.e., they can be predicated of many individuals), but in reality they exist only in individuals. If matter then is not the principle of individuation, what is? John's answer resulted in one of his less fortunate coinages: a "thisness" (haecceitas), that which makes an individual individual.

John's theory of knowledge may be characterized as an attempt to establish an area of certainty in the midst of growing philosophical skepticism. He divides human knowledge into two types: intuitive, by which we know something as definitely existing; and abstractive, by which we know things without regard to their existence or non-existence. He claimed that certainty is possible in three areas -- the famous Three Certitudes of Scotus. First are self-evident principles, such as "the whole is greater than the part," the law of non-contradiction, etc. Second are regularly repeated cause-effect relations in empirical fact, such as peppers' being hot to the taste and a solar eclipse's occurring when the moon passes between the sun and the earth. And third are our own actions and states of mind, such as grieving, rejoicing, thinking, feeling pain.

Scotus considered the human will to be the highest faculty in man and to determine all of his actions, even including intellection. It is the total cause of its own volition. A more radical disagreement with the Averroists, who claim that the will is subject to natural necessity, or even Thomas' claim that it is subject to the intellect, can hardly be imagined. With Scotus, the philosophical movement of the Middle Ages has come a long way, but his thought still contains some inconveniences, inconsistencies, and unnecessary complications. The culmination of medieval philosophy came with the work of the English Franciscan, William of Ockham.

Ockham was born shortly after 1280 and died a victim of the Black Death between 1347 and 1349. Until about two generations ago, he had been only slightly studied and greatly underappreciated. This was largely the result of the fact that he had made a personal enemy of the chancellor of Oxford, Luttrell, a confirmed Thomist, who refused to permit him to incept in theology and who, finding no sympathetic ear in England, journeyed to the papal court at Avignon to accuse William of heresy to pope John XXII. William obeyed the summons to Avignon, where he spent three years, probably at the Franciscan convent there, awaiting a verdict which never came. Also at Avignon at this time was Michael of Cesena, minister general of the Franciscan order and a champion of the original Franciscan teaching on apostolic poverty, which the pope violently opposed. William made common cause with him, and eventually the two angered the pope to the extent that they fled Avignon, met the pope's bitter enemy, the emperor Louis of Bavaria, at Pavia, and spent the remainder of their lives as advocates of the imperial cause. This accident of personal and political relations has cast a cloud over William's orthodoxy, which however has never seriously been questioned. He was disobedient to the pope, but aside from Luttrell, no one ever claimed to find any heresy in his philosophical works. His reputation has in recent years been restored. His doctrine, however, is enormously subtle and was not presented in systematic fashion. This, coupled with his highly technical vocabulary, makes interpretation of his teaching difficult, and many excellent scholars are still working on gaining a precise understanding of his views.[24] However, there are still widely varying opinions,[25] of which I take no account in the following summary.

Like all thinkers, Ockham had predecessors on whose views he built, and he did not create ex nihilo all the elements of his philosophy. But it was he who possessed the clarity of insight, the logical skills, and the scientific imagination to bring out the fullness of their meaning. Basic to William's thought are the following: (1) the principle of economy, or Ockham's razor; (2) the background of speculative grammar and of logic,[26] both of which had been developed to a high degree and in both of which William was expert; (3) an insistence that scientific demonstration is only possible by rigorous reasoning from necessary principles, and that demonstration be distinguished from mere "persuasions," or probable arguments.

Let us begin with a consideration of Ockham's razor, which he stated as: "That which can be done by fewer things is done vainly by more," or "Plurality should not be posited without necessity." This is a modification, on the level of methodology, of the Aristotelian pragmatic metaphysical principle that nature does nothing in vain, and it had been used in both ways by numerous thinkers before. But Ockham makes it central to his philosophical procedure. Unless one can give a sufficient reason for the existence of something, he is not justified in assuming it. By a rigorous application of this principle, he reduced Aristotle's categories from ten to two (substance and quality), got rid of "species" altogether, obliterated the "common natures" of Scotus and his successors, and eliminated the Divine Ideas, one of the oldest and most pernicious of the Neoplatonic accretions to Christianity. And he showed that reality is more, not less, intelligible by the elimination of these superfluous entities.

Now let us look at human cognition, which Ockham distinguished as intuitive and abstractive. Intuitive cognition is primary. Through our sense we immediately know the particular objects of knowledge. They are individual substances, and two partial causes cooperate in intuitive cognition, the knowing mind (or soul, in medieval terminology) and the thing known. No intermediate "species" is necessary to explain this act. What we have as a result of primary intuitive cognition is a concept, which is a natural sign signifying the object known. We also use words to signify the thing known. The concept remains in the soul virtually, so that our continuing knowledge of a thing does not depend on the thing's continuing existence. When the soul has accumulated a number of such concepts it can proceed to abstractive cognition, and by it can group concepts according to similarities. These similarities do not arise from some common nature; they are inherent in the individuals themselves. Hence, Ockham needs no principle of individuation, whether matter or haecceitas or anything else. Individuals are what we have immediate intuitive knowledge of. What is in need of explanation is universals. A universal is the very act of abstractive cognition. It corresponds to nothing existing outside the mind other than the individuals from which the abstraction was made. Then we use words to denote these universal concepts, but both the word and the universal concept are themselves singular, although they stand for a plurality of individuals.

Sciences are not of real things, but of propositions (composed of terms) about real things, ordered according to certain mental habits. They do of course treat of reality ultimately, but not directly, since the terms in logical propositions stand not for things, but for concepts.

Ockham had a very demanding standard for rational demonstration. Like Scotus, he was seeking for some basis of certitude, but his doctrine of divine omnipotence and freedom necessitated his setting his standards higher. Every creature is utterly contingent; it depends for its being and nature completely on God's free will. What exists is not necessary but could be otherwise, and so it is impossible to have strictly scientific knowledge of the actually existing world. This kind of knowledge can only be had of the possible order of creatures, and this includes any proposition that does not imply a contradiction. It can be obtained only by strict reasoning from propositions which are necessary, and outside logic and mathematics there are very few of these.

Why would Ockham have insisted on such a standard for scientific demonstration? It stems from his understanding of God as omnipotent, infinite, and utterly free. God, by His very omnipotence, knows all things, both actual and possible. There is no need to posit Divine Ideas to account for this. God knows all things just because he is God. His will is unconstrained. He was not bound to create this world or any world at all. He freely chose to create this one. Since He is infintely good, wise, and just, as well as omnipotent, His will is not arbitrary, and we may trust that this world will be regular. But Ockham insists that it could be otherwise, and since the only limitation on God's power is that He can do nothing that would involve a contradiction, we must investigate the possible order of creatures if we are seriously concerned with finding truth. Even the moral order is the result of God's will. There are no natural moral laws which determine what God must be like in order to be good. To do the good means to love God and obey His will.

God's creatures are consequently wholly contingent. On the level of causality, since God is the primary cuase of all things, he can do directly what in fact He does through secondary causes. That He chose to operate through secondary causes is a matter of His inscrutable will. Ockham does not, therefore, deny the reality of causality in the natural order, although he shows that we can have no demonstrative or intuitive knowledge of it. Our concept of causality is a mental habit derived from our observations of repeated sequences of events, but we cannot know a cause in itself.

Ockham's knowledge of God, and thus the consequences he drew from it, came from revelation, particularly the Bible and the Creed. He did not think that reason could give us much information about Him. Although we cannot prove that He is unique, we can prove that He exists; in fact, the only thing that can be predicated univocally both of God and creatures is being. Hence he denied the distinction between essence and existence, which he considers to be the same. But "being in general" does not exist. Single beings, including God, are, and so we can predicate being of them, but since we have no intuitive knowledge of infinite being we can have no concept of God that is both simple and adequate. The best we can do is combine concepts which we can have, such as being and first, and thus arrive at a concept of first being; but this is not simple. We can also deduce from His perfection that He is both intellect and will. But for the most part natural reason provides us with very little help in our quest to know God, and we must depend on what He has chosen to reveal to us about Himself.

With Ockham's philosophy the Middle Ages had achieved an admirable synthesis of the philosophical tradition of Antiquity with the revelation of the Christian faith. Faith teaches us of God's omnipotence (Ockham quotes the Creed: "I believe in God the Father Almighty"), and this implies the simplicity of God and the complete freedom of His will, which we could not know otherwise. From these things, the utter contingency of creation is a necessary consequence. All the rest of Ockham's thought follows from this. It is a wonderfully impressive intellectual achievement and a fitting climax to a 300 year philosophical tradition.

As the medieval period draws to a close, therefore, we do not have any unique synthesis encapsulating the essence of the age (nor did we earlier). Instead we have a variety of philosophical standpoints and systems. There are, at one extreme, the so-called Averroists, who consider philosophy to be man's highest calling and theology a diluted form of it for the consumption of weak minds, and who consider unaided human reason competent to discover truth. There are Thomists, who maintain the independence of philosophy and theology but who consider theology to embrace most of human learning, and who also place a very high value on human reason, which can explain anything natural but nothing miraculous. There is a much attenuated rationalism in Scotus, and the virtual elimination of philosophy from theology of the Ockhamists, in addition to many lesser trends which we have omitted from this discussion. It was a strong and varied tradition, which was an essential ingredient in the making of the modern world.

NOTES

1. The most satisfactory general histories of medieval philosophy are Armand A. Maurer, Medieval Philosophy (New York, 1962) for those who have no previous acquaintance with philosophy, and Etienne Gilson, History of Christian Philosophy in the Middle Ages (New York, 1955) for those who want a more technical treatment, as well as extensive bibliography. Extremely valuable, although limited in scope, is Fernand van Steenberghen, Aristotle in the West, tr. Leonard Johnston (2nd ed., Louvain, 1970).

2. William of Conches, De philosophia mundi, erroneously attributed to Honorius of Autun in PL 172: 39-40.

3. <u>Didascalion</u>, ed. C. H. Buttimer (Washington, D. C., 1939), 38-39.

4. On the development of the gloss, see Beryl Smalley, <u>The Study of the Bible in the Middle Ages</u> (Oxford, 1952), 46-66.

5. Among the best, though by now somewhat outdated, general treatments of the translations in English is C. H. Haskins, <u>The Renaissance of the Twelfth Century</u>, 278-302.

6. On the changing form of academic treatises during the thirteenth century, see Daniel A. Callus, "The Introduction of Aristotelian Learning to Oxford," <u>Proceedings of the British Academy</u> 29 (1943), 264-65.

7. See Daniel A. Callus, "The Treatise of John Blund <u>On the Soul</u>," <u>Autour d'Aristote</u>. <u>Recueil d'Etudes de Philosophie ancienne et médiévale affert à Monseigneur A. Mansion</u> (Louvain, 1955), 471-95. Blund's work has been edited by D. A. Callus and R. W. Hunt, <u>Johannes Blund</u>, <u>Tractatus de anima</u> (London, 1970).

8. The best summary treatment of Grosseteste's life and works is D. A. Callus, ed., <u>Robert Grosseteste</u>, <u>Scholar and Bishop</u> (Oxford, 1955).

9. R. C. Dales, "A Medieval View of Human Dignity," <u>Journal of the History of Ideas</u> 38 (1977), 557-72. The quotation is on pages 570-71.

10. ------, "Robert Grosseteste's Views on Astrology," <u>Mediaeval Studies</u> 29 (1967), 357-63.

11. See Richard C. Dales, "The De-Animation of the Heavens in the Middle Ages," <u>Journal of the History of Ideas</u> 41 (1980).

12. See S. H. Thomson, <u>The Writings of Robert Grosseteste</u> (Cambridge, 1940).

13. For a superb detailed study of this process, see D. A. Callus, "The Introduction of Aristotle to Oxford."

14. The <u>Quaternuli</u> (i.e., "notebooks") of David of Dinant has been ingeniously reconstructed by G. Théry, <u>Autour du décret de 1210: I. David de Dinant</u> (Kain, 1925).

15. The role of the theologians has been pointed out by Martin Grabmann, <u>I divieti ecclesiastici di Aristotele sotto Innocenzo III e Gregorio IX</u> (Rome, 1941).

16. On the date of the translations of Averroes, see R. de Vaux,

"La première entrée d'Averroës chez les Latins," <u>Revue de sciences philosophiques et théologiques</u> 22 (1933), 193-245.

17. See the summary above, chapter 11.

18. This is the judgment of Fernand van Steenberghen, <u>Aristotle in the West</u>, 176-77.

19. The best account of Siger in English is F. van Steenberghen, "Siger of Brabant," <u>The Modern Schoolman</u> 29 (1951), 11-27, reprinted, with slight changes, in the same author's <u>Aristotle in the West</u>, 209-229.

20. The most satisfactory treatment of Boethius in English is Armand Maurer, <u>Medieval Philosophy</u>, 199-204. Father Maurer is the discoverer and editor of several of Boethius' works.

21. The bibliography on Thomas is voluminous. The most recent scholarly treatment of him is James A. Weisheipl. <u>Friar Thomas d'Aquino, His Life, Thought, and Work</u> (Garden City, New York, 1974).

22. This is the conclusion of the perceptive and tightly reasoned essay by Leland E. Wilshire, "Were the Oxford Condemnations of 1277 Directed Against Aquinas?" <u>The New Scholasticism</u> 48 (1974), 125-32.

23. See especially Edward Grant, "The Condemnation of 1277, God's Absolute Power, and Physical Thought in the Late Middle Ages," <u>Viator</u> 10 (1979).

24. An excellent and accessible guide to Ockham's thought is <u>Philosophical Writings: Ockham</u>, tr. Philotheus Boehner (Bobbs-Merrill, LLA 193).

25. A superb review of recent Ockham scholarship is William J. Courtenay, "Nominalism and Late Medieval Thought: A Bibliograhpical Essay," <u>Theological Studies</u> 33 (1972), 715-34.

26. See A. Maurer, <u>Medieval Philosophy</u>, 245-54 for a non-technical summary of speculative grammar and the "new logic."

Chapter 13

Medieval Science

It is difficult to write about science, because the word (and the activity designated by it) has altered so drastically from time to time, and because the spectacular advances made by science in the modern world and the very high value now placed upon it often distort our perspective and make us look upon earlier science as merely quaint or at best a startling anticipation of the "truth" of modern science. But such an attitude does much violence to the realities of the development of human thought. That our science should have developed at all is highly unlikely, and the fact that it did owes much to the intellectual developments of western Europe from the twelfth through the fourteenth centuries.

The concept of a cosmos, or natural order, seems to have originated with the ancient Greeks, and in one form or another it was an important element in the thought of the Romans, the Christians (both Latin and Greek), the Jews, and the Muslims during succeeding centuries. But the classical Greek tradition of investigating this cosmos, both the general principles which govern its operation and the details of the ways in which it works, proved more fragile. By late Antiquity, among both Greeks and Latins, it was generally assumed that just about everything was known about nature. This "knowledge" was epitomized in a number of convenient handbooks and was the common property of the educated classes. It was a rare thinker, however, who undertook to question or extend this corpus in any rigorous manner.

There were some aspects of the thought of the Christian Fathers which would later lead men to prize nature highly and investigate it closely. Among these was the doctrine that the world, created by God according to number, weight and measure, was good and therefore worthy of man's attention. More important ultimately was the "creationist" view, which insists that God created the world out of nothing and without intermediaries, thus tending to minimize animism. The Fathers though were much more interested in other matters and so tended to ignore the physical world, except insofar as it exhibited God's goodness or mirrored the spiritual world.

Many of the repositories of ancient science had survived the demise of Antiquity and provided the sum total of Latin Europe's scientific knowledge before the mid-eleventh century. We have discussed them briefly in earlier chapters -- Pliny's Natural History, Seneca's Natural Questions, Macrobius' Saturnalia (especially Book VII) and Commentary on the Dream of Scipio, Plato's Timaeus, translated and provided with a commentary by Calcidius, Martianus Capella's Marriage of Mercury and Philology, Boethius' translations and textbooks, Isidore's Etymologies and De rerum *natura*, translations of fragments of the medical writings of Hippocrates and Galen, and a number of smaller works. This corpus of works embodying the remnants of ancient science remained nearly constant until the late tenth century and was not significantly expanded until the second quarter of the twelfth. Before the recovery of ancient science and the acquisition of Arabic science, a basic change occurred in the way at least some western European writers looked at and valued the world.

About the middle of the eleventh century, Latin thought began to become much more sophisticated than it had been since the Patristic era, and several attitudes important for the growth of science were developed over a period of about a century.

The first concerned the omnipotence of God. In a letter to Abbot Desiderius of Monte Cassino, known to us by the title De divina omnipotentia, Peter Damian made a frontal assault on all those (even including St. Jerome) who imputed any sort of impotence to God. The main assertion against which Peter argued was that God was powerless to cause a past event not to have happened. By reiterating the Patristic teaching that all things are present to God, and that past and future are consequences of the limited nature of our own being, Peter asserted that God could, if He chose, will a different world, in which what has happened would not happen, and in general dismissed any imputation of impotence to God as unacceptable. All the possibilities which were open to Him remain open to Him. Such a position could conceivably have been antithetical to science of any kind, since we could not reasonably expect any regularity in creation, but only the effects of God's whim. But this cannot be strictly inferred from Damian's treatise, and indeed it was not the way the doctrine of divine omnipotence was received into the European intellectual tradition. A generation after Damian, St. Anselm, while continuing to maintain God's complete freedom, developed the doctrine which would later be designated as God's ordered power (potentia ordinata), as distinguished from His absolute power (potentia absoluta). Anselm reasoned that since God had freely promised us certain things and had chosen to reveal to us something of His nature, the moral order, and His plan of redemption, He is bound by that freely given promise not to change His mind. So God has freely bound Himself to act in a certain way, and we may have complete confidence in this promise.

The second concerned the concept of the natural order.[1] During the early years of the twelfth century, the relationship between God and that part of creation which is called "natural" was worked out more completely. By far the most widely used and influential work of Greek science for the scientific thought of the twelfth century was Plato's Timaeus with Calcidius' commentary. It is interesting to see the interplay between the Platonic view of the world and the creationist position adopted by many of the Latin authors.

One of the first Europeans to express a new view of nature was Adelard of Bath, an Englishman who studied and taught in northern France and then travelled widely in search of Arabic wisdom. In one of his early works, the Natural Questions, he responded to his "nephew's" contention that all effects should be ascribed immediately to "the wonderful will of God," by saying: "I take nothing away from God, for whatever exists is from Him and because of Him. But the natural order does not exist confusedly and without rational arrangement, and human reason should be listened to concerning those things it treats of." Adelard insisted that the only standard of truth in philosophy is reason, since nature operates regularly and rationally. The content of his own science though is a grab-bag of fragments from the traditional sources. He praised both Aristotle and the Arabs highly in his writings, but at the time he wrote his Natural Questions he did not yet know either of them at first hand. He was grasping for an embodiment of his own ideal of nature and human reason and could not find it in any of his Latin sources. Consequently he assumed that it must exist in the writings of the Arabs, and in order to possess it he later learned Arabic and translated Euclid's Elements of Geometry and several important astronomical works into Latin.

Peter Abelard carried the matter further in his commentary on the creation story in Genesis (Hexameron). To Abelard, the creation of heaven and earth did not mean the creation of the spiritual and corporeal worlds, as it had to Augustine, but rather the creation of the four elements (fire, air, water, and earth). He explained that the six days of creation are not to be considered as six periods of twenty-four hours, or any other particular length of time, but rather as distinctions of God's works in bringing about the world. "Evening" means the creation of things in God's mind, and "morning" refers to the bringing to light of God's intention through His works. The first day contains all of creation potentially. Plato's intelligible world, he said, is "the very same Reason by which God made the world." But this Reason had to be completed in work. It was first hidden in the mind of God and "afterwards emerged through the produced works towards light." And so, despite the emanationist tendencies of his sources in this place, Abelard posits an absolute beginning, a creation by God in which he first planned rationally what He was going to do, and then without any intermediaries He did it. The fullest reality of the created world then is in its concrete existence, not, as with the Neoplatonic tradition, in the Divine Mind.

In his discussion of the knotty problem of how some of the waters got above the firmament, Abelard defined very clearly what he meant by "nature" and what should be considered the relationship of the natural world to God:

Although we now seek out or assign a power of nature, or natural causes, in certain effects of things, we should in no way do the same with regard to that prior work of God in forming the world, when God's will alone had the efficacy of nature in creating or arranging those things. We ought to assign natural causes only after those things were completed in six days by God's work. From then on, we are accustomed to give consideration to the force of nature; that is, when these natural things have already been thus made ready so that their nature or preparation might be sufficient to do anything at all without miracles. . . .Therefore, we call nature the power of things conferred upon them at the beginning which prepared them henceforth to give rise to anything; that is, sufficient to bring it about.

Thus when God created the natural world, He bestowed upon it everything it needed to operate by itself.

An even more extreme view of the self-sufficiency of nature was expressed by a contemporary of Abelard's, Thierry of Chartres. In his Hexameron, he states his intention "to explain the first part of Genesis literally and according to natural philosophy." He begins by adopting Aristotle's four causes as the framework for his discussion: the efficient cause is God; the formal cause is God's Wisdom (that is, the Son); the final cause is God's kindness (that is, the Holy Spirit); and the material cause is the four elements. "From these four causes," he says, "all corporeal substances have their subsistence." Primordial matter contained the four elements in a confused state in which each had some of the characteristics of the others; it did not precede the fully differentiated elements temporally, but only according to reason, as confusion naturally precedes articulation. He agreed with Abelard that by the term "heaven" the text meant fire and air, and by the term "earth" it meant earth and water.

Once this initial creation of "heaven and earth" (i.e., the four elements) had been accomplished by God, Thierry asserted that everything else occurred naturally. At this point fire, rather than God, became "as it were, the Artisan and efficient cause. ...For fire only acts, and earth is only acted upon; the two elements in the middle both act and are acted upon," and they "act as an administrator or vehicle of the power of fire toward the other elements." Thierry also taught that swiftness and slowness cannot exist apart from each other, because each depends upon the other. The rapid motion of light bodies surrounds and compresses slower bodies and makes them corpulent and solid. Reciprocally, fast-moving bodies must have something solid to "lean on," as when a man walks his foot must push against unyielding earth, or when a projectile is thrown, the finger must push against the hand, the hand against the arm, and so on.

And finally, Thierry seems to consider that even the apparently miraculous has a natural explanation: "We affirm that, in one of the aforesaid ways and from the originating causes which He bestowed on the elements in the space of six days, He produced whatever He created and still creates."

By the middle of the twelfth century, the main elements of this view of a self-subsistent and self-operating nature were simply assumed by some European scientists and used as a basis from which to push their investigations further. An anonymous scientist, who was probably a south Italian and a student of Thierry's, wrote an amazing work on the elements,[2] incorporating much of Thierry's teaching but going far beyond it. His other sources were Boethius, Calcidius, Macrobius, Lucan, and Virgil, and included what are probably the earliest quotations from Aristotle's Physics (grossly misunderstood) in Latin Europe. The author defines nature (physica) as "the natural motion of any element ex se. ... How and through what means these qualities of the elements work other effects in things is called physics. Now we shall tell how the qualities of the elements operate in the elements themselves or in other bodies by composition and resolution." He then begins the treatise proper by asserting that the elements clearly qualify as natural bodies. He next establishes the qualities of the elements, saying that they are eternally created by motion descending from God (he actually uses the Platonic term Craftsman -- artifex). First came the two extreme elements, fire and earth, fire resulting from swiftness, earth from slowness; then the two middle elements, water and air. The elements consist of tiny particles, or atoms, and swiftness or slowness of motion refer to the motions of the atoms, not to those of the elements as a whole. He borrows from Thierry the doctrine that fire acts as the Artisan, as well as Thierry's assertion that heaviness and lightness are mutually necessary, since the light (swift) elements make the heavy (slow) ones by compressing them, while the heavy ones provide a stable center against which the light ones lean. He then derives all the qualities of each of the elements from their proper motions and in the second section of his treatise rigorously applies his principles in explaining a number of meteorological phenomena and sense perception.

In spite of what seems to be a retreat from the creationist position in positing the eternity of the elements and considering God as the continuing source of the world's motion, the author maintains the self-sufficiency of the world of nature by following Thierry's lead concerning the role of fire in acting as the Artisan (i.e., efficient and formal causes). The rigor and the detail with which he deduces both the qualities of the elements and the interaction of the elements in observed phenomena from his first principle (i.e., that motion makes the elements) are clear advances over Thierry's treatment, and the resulting view of nature is more completely mechanistic.

At about the same time (that is, in the decade of the 1150s) another remarkable treatise on the elements was written by a man named Marius,[3] probably of Salernitan origin but writing somewhere in France. Although this work implies the same view of nature as we have been studying, it differs from the previously mentioned authors in certain important respects. Marius too posits a beginning, but in his teaching this is the creation by God of prime matter, totally devoid of qualities, which God then differentiated into the four elements, not only by moving different parts at different speeds, as was the case with the anonymous author, but also by adding two elemental qualities to each of his four divisions -- hot and dry for fire, hot and moist for air, moist and cold for water, cold and dry for earth. Then, because it pleased Him to do so, God set the elements in motion. Creation ceased at this point, and everything else occurred naturally through the mechanical interaction of the four elements. Unlike the other works we have been discussing, Marius' De elementis, while based on a firm theoretical foundation, is closely controlled by observation and experiment. Some of these experiments were standard and were derived from literary sources, but many others were clearly the result of Marius' own careful and wide-ranging observations. Marius is also totally materialistic, and he specifically rejects both animism and magic. He is preoccupied with process and is always at pains to explain how a given cause produces a given effect.

A third aspect of Latin European culture which influenced both the fact and the nature of the revival and growth of science was the mechanical and technological habit of mind, which has been well documented by historians from the late ninth century onward. It is difficult to explain why such an attitude came about (and many ingenious suggestions have been made), but of the fact there is no dispute. This can be illustrated by three quite dissimilar works. First is a book by a craftman-monk from northwestern Germany, written about 1122-23 under the pseudonym (for humility's sake) of Theophilus.[4] The bulk of it is a detailed description of the processes of the arts and crafts, especially metal work and glass making, an invaluable account of the actual technological practices of the early twelfth century. But in the prefaces to each of the three books of the work, Theophilus expresses his conviction that God delights in the arts and crafts and is pleased by those who work well in them. To him, a craftsman was engaged in a holy occupation.

Theophilus' attitude toward the crafts was quite in accord with that of his more famous monastic contemporary, Hugh of St. Victor. In his Didascalion, Hugh had included a classification of the sciences which, in stark contrast to similar works of late Antiquity, included the manual arts and crafts and saw them as having very great value.[5]

The same values are implicit in Marius' On the Elements, which we have already mentioned. This work abounds in descriptions of experiments and processes; indeed, no point, no matter how obvious, goes unillustrated by some reference to experience. Marius squeezes bellows, sucks skin into a glass tube, places a wineskin full of air under water and lets it go, heats an earthenware pot till it turns molten, changes the color of copper by applying the vapor of vinegar, churns and distills milk, places firebrands close together, and so on. Marius was an intellectual, as Theophilus was a craftsman, but he was well acquainted with the arts and crafts, as Theophilus was a participant in the written Latin culture of his day.

As we have noted earlier, Latin Europe never completely lost its contact with the Greek world, and there is no period in the Middle Ages, not even the dismal seventh and eighth centuries, when some translating was not being done. Contact with Arabic learning began by the late tenth century, although on a small scale. The translating movement (for such it became) began in the mid-eleventh century with the work of Alfanus and Constantine at Salerno and Monte Cassino. It received a major impetus from the enthusiasm and example of Adelard of Bath and reached its height (but by no means its end) in the work of Gerard of Cremona (d. 1175). It continued throughout the thirteenth century with Robert Grosseteste, Michael Scot, Bartholomew of Messina and William of Moerbeke and did not abate until around the second quarter of the fourteenth century.

The translators themselves came from every part of Europe -- Eugene the Admiral and Henry Aristippus from Sicily, James of Venice, Burgundio of Pisa, Plato of Tivoli, Moses of Bergamo and Gerard of Cremona from northern Italy, Robert of Chester, Adelard of Bath, Alfred Sareshel and Michael Scot from Britain, Herman of Carinthia, Rudolph of Bruges and Herman the German from the Empire, Cerbanus from Hungary, Hugh of Santalla, John of Seville and Dominic Gundissalinus from Spain. They were men of various circumstances. Some, such as the Sicilians Eugene and Aristippus, were members of a rich tri-lingual culture and were men of means and influence. Much the same is true of many of the Spaniards, for whom the books they sought and the facilities for learning Arabic were near at hand. The case was somewhat different for the north Italians, such as James of Venice, Moses of Bergamo, Plato of Tivoli and Burgundio of Pisa. They had learned Greek as a result of the diplomatic or commercial relations of their cities with the eastern Empire and had taken advantage of their acquisition of that tongue to translate some works which they were fortunate enough to come across in the East. And the most famous northern Italian translator, Gerard of Cremona, had made a long journey not to Constantinople but to Toledo and learned Arabic rather than Greek in a determined, fully conscious effort to recover the text of Ptolemy's Almagest, and he supported himself by teaching. Gerard was neither the first nor the most adventurous of our Arab-Latin translators, however, although he was certainly the most prolific. Adelard of Bath had travelled widely through southern Italy and the Near East as well as Spain (a Spanish sojourn seems highly likely, although there is no direct evidence of it) and in middle life had learned Arabic so that he might translate Euclid's Elements of Geometry and the astronomical tables of Al-Khwarismi. Like Gerard, he made his living as a teacher, although he also enjoyed the favor of several highly placed churchmen, as well as king Henry I of England. His countryman Robert of Chester (also known as Robert of Ketene), driven by curiosity about Arabic learning, wandered to Spain, learned Arabic, spent years in collaboration with his Dalmatian friend Herman of Carinthia, translated the Koran under the patronage of Peter the Venerable of Cluny, and eventually became bishop of Pamplona. These men then represented all sections of Europe and varied in status from impecunious scholars to great and wealthy politicians, but they all shared a common desire to acquire, by translation into Latin, the vast treasures of Greek and Arabic thought. Although luck undoubtedly played a significant part in determining which works were translated, there was also considerable conscious selection. These men were interested in works of science, philosophy and theology. They were not interested in purely literary works, although, in Constantinople at least, these were even more accessible than the works which were actually translated.

Among the translated works were some of crucial importance for the recovery and further development of science. Euclid's Elements of Geometry provided Latin Europe with its first knowledge of what Greek geometry actually was. This subject had been abominably treated in all the handbooks. Euclid's system of rigorous deduction from a limited number of definitions, axioms, and postulates provided a paradigm for mathematical-deductive science. Several translations were made of it, but that of Adelard was both first and most widely used. Other works by, or attributed to, Euclid were also translated -- the Catoptrica (on mirrors), Optics, and Data. Other works of geometry and geometrical optics were Apollonius' Conics, Archimedes' De mensura circuli, Hero of Alexandria's Catoptrica (attributed to Ptolemy), Alkind's De aspectibus, and, in the thirteenth century, Alhazen's Treasury of Optics.

The outstanding work of astronomy in the ancient world was Ptolemy's Almagest, which, after stating its principles, provided geometrical models for each of the planets, as well as elaborate tables to be used in computing planetary positions. Ptolemy had not been used by the Latin handbook authors (either because he was unknown to them or was too difficult for them), and his geometrical models were incompatible with the largely Platonic astronomy contained in the handbooks (as well as with the Aristotelian astronomy which was concurrently being recovered). However, the obvious excellence of Ptolemy's work soon won for it a place of honor as the authoritative astronomical treatise. But it was not the only work on astronomy which the Latins assimilated during the twelfth century. Many Arabic works by such authors as Al-Khwarismi, Messahale, Abu Ma'shar, Al-Battani, Ibn Thebit, and others, containing astronomical theory, planetary arguments, and appropriate tables, usually based on Ptolemy but often correcting him, were also translated.

With astronomy came also Hellenistic and Arabic astrology, probably the most highly regarded science by the twelfth-century avant garde. Ptolemy's Quadripartitum (Tetrabiblos), an astrological work, was more popular than his Almagest. There resulted a lively debate concerning both the validity and the orthodoxy of astrology, which continued throughout the Middle Ages. Many works of wisdom attributed to the "Thrice Great Hermes" were also rendered into Latin. "Hermes Tresmegistos" was a conflation of the Greek god Hermes with his Egyptian counterpart Toth. Between 200 B.C. and 200 A.D. a number of astrological, alchemical, and magical texts were composed and attributed to the god to give them greater authority. Among the earliest of such works to be translated were the Asclepius, which was used by Thierry of Chartres, and the Secrets of Nature, also attributed to Apollonius.

Probably the most important Arabic treatise to be translated during the first half of the twelfth century was Abu Ma'shar's Introduction to Astronomy (Ptolemy was translated at least four times, twice from Greek and twice from Arabic, but not until the third quarter of the century), through which much Aristotelian doctrine became known to the Latins.[6] During the last decades of the century, the most important author was Avicenna. Following Aristotle's example, he had written on all the same subjects, using the same titles, as the ancient Greek; and although Avicenna incorporated much Aristotelian teaching (and vocabulary) in his own essays, he interpreted it in the light of later Neoplatonic thought. Most significant of all his works was the Canon medicinae, based largely on Galen but including much original material.

Less numerous and influential (and also less well studied by modern historians) were treatises on alchemy, mineralogy, and geology. Works of medicine were among the earliest translations, and various treatises by "Hippocrates," Galen, Isaac Israeli, Ali ibn Abbas, Dioscorides, and others were prominent among the twelfth-century translations.

But by far the most important works to be acquired by the Latins were those of the great fourth century B.C. Greek philosopher, Aristotle, along with a number of works falsely ascribed to him. Previous to the mid-twelfth century, only Aristotle's elementary logical treatises were available in Latin -- Categories, Interpretation, and the Topics of Cicero or Boethius based on Aristotle's work of the same name. By the end of the twelfth century, nearly the entire corpus of his writings had been recovered: the advanced logical works, Prior Analytics, Posterior Analytics, and Sophistical Arguments; the treatises on physical science, Physics, The Heaven and the World (The World is falsely ascribed), Meteorology, On Coming to Be and Passing Away, culminating in the philosophical work Metaphysics; his treatment of the life sciences, Parts of Animals, History of Animals, Generation of Animals, the shorter works known collectively as the Parva naturalia, and On the Soul; the Nichomachean Ethics; as well as many works of false or questionable attribution: Secret of Secrets, Theology of Aristotle, On Plants, Mechanical Problems, the Properties of the Elements, and another work known simply as On the Elements. More scholarly effort has been expended on the history of the translation and reception of the works of Aristotle than of any other author, but there still remain large areas of ignorance. The earliest translations of the libri naturales, as the scientific works are called, are by James of Venice and may date from as early as 1120, and they were still being translated and retranslated as late as 1270. Knowledge of Aristotle's doctrine was often indirect in the twelfth century, coming from Cicero, Pliny, the church Fathers, or the newly translated Arabic works, especially those of Abu Ma'shar and Avicenna. Often the same work was translated several times, from Greek, from Arabic, or from both. There are many fragments of translations by unknown scholars and citations of Aristotle's works which do not match the wording of any known translation. As late as the end of the twelfth century, Aristotle was still not often used. But the organization of teaching in the universities of the early thirteenth century, as well as the recovery of commentaries on Aristotle's works by the great Greek commentators of late Antiquity, especially Simplicius, Themistius, and Alexander of Aphrodisias, and those of the Muslim Averroes, made it possible to subject his writings to systematic analysis, and by about 1255, Aristotle's works constituted over half of the required curriculum at the University of Paris, and probably of all other European universities as well.

The science of the twelfth century was much like that of fifth-century B.C. Greece -- what Thomas Kuhn has termed "pre-paradigm science."[7] It was imaginative, daring, and "free-wheeling." It had a strong indigenous motivation but was significantly influenced by the science of the more highly developed foreign cultures of the Greeks and Muslims (as the Greeks had been by those of Mesopotamia and Egypt). However, the strength and integrity of the medieval Latin world view resulted in the transformation of the exotic materials it absorbed. Still, no matter how brilliant and exciting such periods in the history of science are, there was too much freedom and diversity for progress to occur. At a certain point it is necessary for one of the competing views to win out and for the range of investigation to narrow.

The science of the thirteenth century is strikingly different from that of the twelfth. Intervening between the two were: the wealth of scientific knowledge contained in the translations; the development of more rigorous and highly specialized teaching techniques; and the working out of a new, more appropriate method of investigating nature. The works of Aristotle provided a highly articulated and hierarchically ordered cosmos, a technical vocabulary, and a vast amount of information about the physical world. These became accessible to Latin Europe through the carefully organized lectures in the universities. The development of the new scientific method was largely the work of one man, Robert Grosseteste, whose long life, from 1168 to 1253, bridged the two centuries.

Grosseteste was involved in most of the major intellectual developments of his time. He began lecturing at Oxford shortly before 1200 and studied theology, possibly at Paris, betwen 1209 and 1215. He was then appointed chancellor of Oxford -- very likely its first -- but continued to teach and write. In 1229 he became the first lecturer to the newly established Franciscan convent at Oxford and in 1235 was elected bishop of Lincoln, England's largest diocese and the one in which Oxford lay. When he was a young man, the twelfth-century translating activity was at its peak, and those works were just beginning to invade the curriculum. During his teaching days they were received into the mainstream of European thought, and Grosseteste himself was a leader in introducing them at Oxford. He translated many works from the Greek and provided commentaries to several of Aristotle's more difficult works, as well as short treatises on various aspects of the Philosopher's thought. He was also well versed in the Latin versions of Muslim and Jewish works, being an avid student of Muslim astronomy and astrology in his youth and one of the first Latins to use the works of Averroes after their arrival in 1231.

In a series of scientific works written between 1220 and 1235,[8] Grosseteste progressively developed his characteristic method of investigating nature, and during this same period he elaborated this method from a theoretical standpoint in his commentaries on Aristotle's Physics and Posterior Analytics and in two short works, On Lines, Angles and Figures and The Nature of Places.[9] According to this method, any complex phenomenon of nature must first be analyzed into its simplest components (he calls this analysis or resolutio). Then the investigator, relying on his scientific intuition, must frame a hypothesis which would show how these elements are combined so that they actually produce the phenomenon under investigation (this is the synthesis or compositio). In addition to this framework, Grosseteste employed experiments as an integral part of his investigation: as aids in accomplishing his analysis, as suggestions in framing his explanatory hypothesis, and as tests of the truth or falsity of a hypothesis. He also insisted that no accurate knowledge could be had of nature without mathematics, holding that since light is the cause of local motion, and light behaves according to geometric rules, therefore all local motion can be described mathematically. He also took over from Aristotle the principles of the uniformity and economy of nature, and he formulated, though he did not use, the principle that an experimental universal may be obtained from the observation that a given effect always results from a particular cause. When one controls his observations by eliminating any other possible cause of the effect, he may arrive at an experimental universal of provisional truth.

As an example of the new science, let us look at the work of Grosseteste's maturity, On the Heat of the Sun,[10] and notice both the salutary effects of investigating one strictly limited problem at a time and the power of Grosseteste's method. The question being investigated is "In what way does the sun generate heat?" The resolutio begins by asserting that there are three principles of the generation of heat: a hot body, motion, and a collection of rays. In all of these the proximate cause of heat is "scattering." How a hot body produces heat by scattering is evident, but how local motion and a collection of rays do so is difficult to see. In local motion, violent motion by conflicting with natural motion produces a scattering of parts, and thus heat. Scattering takes place through a concentration of rays because these rays are incorporated in a transparent medium; in a dense medium the incorporation is greater and in a subtle medium it is less. Hence the rays draw with them parts of the air in which they are incorporated, and when they are concentrated in one point a great scattering and consequently great heat result.

So if the sun generates heat, it will do so as a hot body, as a local motion, or as a collection of rays. It does not generate heat as a hot body does, for it is not in immediate contact with the heated thing. Neither does it generate heat by its motion, because its motion is circular and circular motion does not produce heat. Therefore, the sun must generate heat by a concentration of rays. The problem has now been reduced to a matter which can be investigated both mathematically and experimentally, and Grosseteste proceeds with the compositio.

The sun's rays, he says, are to some extent incorporated in the transparent medium of the air, a dense body. When these rays fall on the earth's surface, they are reflected at equal angles; so if they fall perpendicularly (as they will between the tropics of Cancer and Capricorn when the sun is at the zenith), the incident and reflected rays go along the same line in opposite directions, and there is a maximum of scattering and thus of heat. A similarly violent scattering and great heat can be produced by the concentration of rays refracted through a spherical body or reflected from a concave mirror.

North and south of the tropics, however, the sun's rays must always fall at less than right angles, so the paths of incidence and reflection will not be the same. It follows from this hypothesis that the farther a place is from the equator, the more obtuse will be the angle at which the sun's rays fall and are reflected, and so the scattering and heat will be proportionately less. This accords with observation.

There are, however, variations in temperature which cannot be accounted for solely by the hypothesis suggested and verified above. Consequently Grosseteste turns his attention from the rays themselves to the medium in which they are partially incorporated, i.e., the air. He proposes that the transparent medium and the corresponding degree of incorporation of the sun's rays are also directly proportional to the amount of heat generated. Then once again he deduces the consequences of this hypothesis and tests them either by reason or by experience. In the fifth element, he says, even if the sun's rays did intersect (and they do not), no heat would be generated because there is no dense nature; hence there is no incorporation and no scattering is possible. In the upper layers of air -- on mountain tops, for instance -- where the air is thinnest and the degree of incorporation slight, the least amount of heat is generated, as observation shows. But in a valley, where the air is more dense, there is a greater incorporation of rays and therefore more scattering and more heat.

During the second quarter of the thirteenth century, after a period of some resistance, the libri naturales of Aristotle had become required reading in most European universities. From this point on, impressive progress was made toward the solution of several scientific problems. Rather than attempt a complete account of all the types of scientific work being done in Europe during the thirteenth and fourteenth centuries, we shall focus our attention on the history of two problems, optics during the thirteenth century and local motion during the fourteenth. Most of the work we shall be discussing was done on the Arts faculties of the universities, but there were also wealthy patrons, such as the emperor Frederick II and several of the popes, and occasionally one of the religious orders. The only scientist I know of who refers to using his own fortune for scientific research was Roger Bacon.

During the thirteenth century probably more progress was made in the study of optics, particularly the problem of the rainbow, than in any other. Many highly advanced optical works of Antiquity had been translated during the twelfth century and the excellent Treasury of Optics of the Muslim Alhazen was translated from Arabic about 1250. But the principal motivation for the study of optics in the thirteenth century was the Metaphysics of Light developed by Robert Grosseteste. According to Grosseteste's understanding of the creation story in Genesis, in the beginning

God created the first corporeal form, light, which had the property of instantaneously multiplying itself infinitely in every direction; and simple matter, an unextended substance. The original point of light was joined to unextended matter (since matter and form never exist apart from each other) and in its expansion drew matter out into spatial dimensions. The resulting universe was a sphere, extremely rare at the outside but dense and opaque near the center. It was finite in size because of the limitations of matter and because a simple non-dimensional substance multiplied an infinite number of times would result in a finite quantity. The matter of the periphery was completely actualized and capable of no further change. When this first perfect body, containing only first matter and first form, had been created, it diffused its light back to the center, where it gathered together the mass existing below the first body, again rarefying the outermost parts and making the center more dense. The second sphere was thus formed, and by a similar process all thirteen spheres of our sensible world. On the outside of our universe, matter is completely actualized and capable of no further change, while at the center actualization is less, and matter remains susceptible of taking on a great variety of forms. Every subsequent form, either substantial or accidental, is generated from the first form, and every privation is generated by the privation of light. Grosseteste considered light to be the efficient cause of local motion as well as the principle of intelligibility in the created universe.

Optics was among the subjects studied at the universities, and by about 1263 a classic textbook of medieval optics, Perspectiva communis,[11] had been written by John Pecham. Within the science of optics, it was the problem of the rainbow which attracted the most attention and on which the greatest progress was made. The starting point of these studies was Aristotle's Meteorology, the turning point was Grosseteste's De iride, and the culmination was the work of Theoderic of Freiberg shortly after the beginning of the fourteenth century.

Aristotle taught that the rainbow was caused by the sun's rays being reflected from a cloud to the eye of the observer. The reason the bow was a band of colors and not simply an image of the sun was because the cloud was considered to be made up of tiny drops of water and air, each too small to reflect the sun itself, but capable only of reflecting its colors. These drops were considered, though, to constitute a single reflecting surface. To account for the shape of the bow, he resorted to an ingenious mathematical device, which could "save the appearances" but could hardly have been intended by him to be in accord with physical reality. He posited a hemisphere with its base on the plane of the horizon, with the observer situated at the center and the sun at some point on the circumference. Assuming the sun to be on the horizon (at which time the bow would have the maximum elevation), the rays would be reflected from a cloud also situated on the circumference of the hemisphere (and consequently the same distance from the observer as the sun!) to the eye of the observer. Assuming further that the lengths of the sides of the triangle thus formed are a constant, if one rotated the triangle around its base on the plane of the horizon, an arc of a circle would be described on the hemisphere. This accounts for the shape and position of the bow. In order to explain why only this bow-shaped band of colors appears, Aristotle asserted that only those rays which were reflected at the proper distance would produce the rainbow colors, and he gives precise directions for determining this distance.

During the twelfth century, Aristotle's Meteorology was translated into Latin by several authors, and the English scientist, Alfred Sareshel, provided it with a much-used commentary. In about 1235 Robert Grosseteste attempted a daring solution to the problem of the rainbow. He concluded that it was produced by the compound refraction of the sun's rays in the mist of a convex cloud. He then posited a cone of moisture descending from the cloud to the earth, rare at the top and more dense near the earth. There would consequently be four transparent media through which the sun's rays must pass -- the air containing the cloud, the cloud itself, the upper and rarer moisture, and the lower and denser moisture and the light would be refracted as it passed from one of these to another. Because of these refractions, the rays run together in the denser part of the moisture and are refracted there again and spread out into a figure like the curved surface of a cone expanded in the direction opposite the sun. When the upper portion of the hollow cone of rays falls on a second cloud, which is opposite the sun and acts as a screen, it produces a rainbow. This accounts for the bow's shape and position. The colors result from three factors: the density of the medium, the amount of light, and the brightness of the light. As the rays are progressively weakened by the series of refractions, the order of colors from red to violet appears. The role of refraction in this explanation is twofold: to cause the sun's rays to assume the shape of a cone; and, as a result of this, to weaken the light in such a way that the rainbow colors appear.

This explanation has a high degree of internal consistency, and its attempt to explain a complex phenomenon as the result of several simple ones is most impressive. But most important is the fact that Grosseteste had made a radical break from the Aristotelian tradition and had posed the problem in such a way that the correct (or nearly correct) solution could come from a series of criticisms of his shortcomings.

Albert the Great, a somewhat younger contemporary of Grosseteste, wrote a lengthy and diffuse work on the rainbow, which, while it did not present a carefully worked out theory, still aided in the solution of the problem. He adopted Grosseteste's theory with some modifications, emphasizing the part played by the individual drops in the formation of the rainbow, but he was not able to develop this suggestion. He was an indefatigable if unsystematic experimenter. He very carefully described what happens when one passes sunlight through prisms, spherical balls, and a glass hemisphere filled with black ink, and he reported seeing as many as four rainbows at once, although Aristotle said there could not be more than two.

The first really significant criticism of Grosseteste's theory was offered by Roger Bacon in his Opus maius. Grosseteste had considered his explanation finished when he traced the sun's rays to the cloud "opposite the sun" acting as a screen. He seemed to feel that it was objectively situated there. Bacon pointed out that, to the contrary, the rainbow moves as the observer moves, and each observer sees a different rainbow; at all times (as Aristotle had noted) the sun, the observer, and the center of the bow are all situated on the same straight line. This, Bacon claimed, is inconsistent with the laws of refraction, and as evidence of its inconsistency he called attention to cases of images caused by refracted light -- clouds, crystalline stones, a stick placed in water -- which are stationary and do not move with the observer. Bacon also noted that a rainbow can occur in an irregular spray, such as that caused by splashing oars, where Grosseteste's four media and three refractions could not possibly exist. He pointed out that the refractions posited by Grosseteste would produce a solid cone of bright rays, and not just the surface of a cone. Following Aristotle, Seneca, and St. Albert, he emphasized the importance of the individual drops in causing the rainbow, but he was not able to go beyond Aristotle in describing that role. He did however realize that the bow was seen in a different set of drops by each observer. In explaining why the colors appeared in the particular drops they did and not in others, he followed Aristotle in asserting that this would only occur when there was the proper amount of light and the necessary darkness of the background. He added to this the observation that the colors appeared when light was reflected to the eye at the correct angle, but he could not explain why a given angle was "correct." Still, his insistence on this aspect of the phenomenon was of crucial importance to the solution of the problem. Bacon also provided the first bit of accurate measurement of any aspect of the rainbow: he gave the radius of the bow as forty-two degrees, a value very close to the modern one. In his criticism of the weaknesses of Grosseteste's explanation, his refocusing of attention on the individual drops of moisture, his body of experimental work, his realization that each observer saw a different bow, and his measurement of the bow's radius, Bacon significantly advanced the study of the rainbow.

The next steps of basic importance were taken by the Polish scholar, Witelo, who was born about 1230 and wrote his Optics between 1270 and 1278. He had the great advantage of knowing the Treasury of Optics of the great Muslim scholar, Alhazen, which had been translated into Latin around 1250. He resumed Grosseteste's emphasis on refraction, but instead of Grosseteste's cumbersome mechanism, he concentrated on the behavior of light in individual drops. He investigated experimentally the paths of light through glass spheres filled with water (which he treated much like a microcosmic analogue to Grosseteste's cloud and mist), and he studied the production of colors by light rays refracted through hexagonal crystals.

Striving to construct a satisfactory theory, he seems to have borrowed suggestions from both Grosseteste and Bacon and then to have gone beyond either of them. He asserted that the rainbow is caused by both reflected and refracted light. Since clouds, he said, are composed of both moist and dry vapors, and light does not penetrate dry vapors but does pass through moist ones, some light would be reflected from the outer surface of the cloud (from drops of dry vapor) and some would penetrate to the interior of the cloud where they would be condensed by refraction and then reflected from other drops to the eye of the observer. The weakening of the sun's light, caused by both reflection and refraction, produced the colors of the bow, and this would happen only when the rays were reflected at the "correct" angle (forty-two degrees more or less, depending on the density of the cloud).

The high point of medieval rainbow studies came shortly after the turn of the fourteenth century in the work of the German Dominican, Theoderic of Freiberg. It is a beautiful example of the employment of the mathematical experimental method which had been worked out at Oxford during the preceding century. Theoderic's work went beyond that of his predecessors on two counts. First, it was based on a much fuller and more precise experimental foundation. And second, Theoderic had that flash of insight into the problem which no amount of experimentation could compensate for -- he realized that the colors of the rainbow were formed by the refraction, internal reflection, and second refraction of rays of light in individual raindrops, and that large numbers of drops close together, each reflecting one color to the eye (depending on the angle made by the sun's rays and the line of sight) constitute the rainbow.

This was the most important single discovery in the whole long history of the study of the rainbow, but it did not constitute the entire solution. Theoderic realized correctly that all the drops reflecting the sun's rays at the same angle to the eye would appear to have the same color and would have the shape of a bow, but he incorrectly followed Aristotle in thinking this depended on the "effective ratio" between the lines from the sun to the drops and from the eye to the drops. He also erred in concentrating his attention on the size of the arc between the incident and emergent rays. There are two more ways in which Theoderic's work was faulty. First, his theory of color was still based (with slight modifications) on the Aristotelian notion that color is produced by the weakening of white light. And second, he inexplicably used the value twenty-two degrees rather than forty-two degrees for the radius of the rainbow. But in spite of these admitted shortcomings, Theoderic's solution of the rainbow problem remains one of the monuments of medieval science.

Fashions are constantly changing in science as in everything else. Shortly after Theoderic published his work on the rainbow, European scientists quickly lost interest in geometric optics. Gaining in popularity for several decades was a different branch of physics, the study of local motion.

Once Aristotle's Physics and On the Heaven had been studied carefully, it became evident that there were serious difficulties in several aspects of his treatment of local motion, and it was in elaborating and criticizing his remarks that medieval scientists did some of their most impressive and fruitful work. The commentators of late Antiquity had attempted some clarification, and both the Muslims and the thirteenth-century Latins had dealt with the problem, but it was not until the early fourteenth century that significant progress was made. This progress resulted for the most part from the rigorous application of mathematics to the study of motion; the experimental side of the question was largely ignored. The scholars involved made many references to everyday experience, but they did not devise specific experiments the way that Roger Bacon, Witelo, and Theoderic of Freiberg had done.

In Aristotle's analysis, local motion was one of four possible species of motion, the others being change of substance, quality, or quantity. Change of place, or local motion, could be either natural or violent. Natural motion occurred when a body, having been removed from its "natural place," returned to it. There were two qualities of bodies which determined this motion: heaviness in the case of earth and to a lesser extent water, and lightness in the case of fire and to a lesser extent air. Violent motion occurred when some exterior force caused the body to move in some direction other than its natural inclination moved it. Such a force, in his view, could act only by maintaining permanent contact with the object it moved, and when this contact ceased, the violent motion should also cease.

Aristotle also held that natural motions accelerated, but his description of this acceleration and his attempts to account for it were extremely inadequate. His Muslim commentator, Averroes, attributing human qualities to these bodies, interpreted Aristotle as meaning that as bodies neared their natural place, they became more desirous of reaching home as quickly as possible and so hastened their speed. But Aristotle also stated that velocity increased with the distance a body moved in natural motion.

In any case, he tended to ignore the factor of acceleration in his further analysis of natural motion and to treat it as being of constant velocity. The weight (or lightness) of a body and the resistance of the medium through which motion occurred were considered to be the crucial factors determining velocity, since the motion would be caused by the weight or lightness of the body and impeded by the resistance of the medium. He considered resistance an essential factor, claiming that without it motion would be instantaneous, which is impossible.

In violent motion, Aristotle held that velocity was determined by the ratio between the force moving the body and the resistance of the medium. He was not consistent in his treatment of this question either, and although he said that there would be no motion unless the force were greater than the resistance, a rigorous application of the principles he enunciated would necessitate some motion for any values of these two factors.

During the last quarter of the thirteenth century, Europeans gave more attention to the problem of local motion than they had before. Their works often took issue with Aristotle but remained largely within the Aristotelian frame of reference. They made some progress and foreshadowed many of the fourteenth-century developments, which indeed depended to some extent on them. In kinematics (i.e., the formal relationships of time, distance, and velocity) it was noticed that in the case of freely falling bodies, continuingly greater units of space are traversed in successive equal period of time, and that velocity of fall increased with distance from the beginning of the fall rather than with proximity to natural place. In dynamics (the study of the actual forces involved in motion) there were several attempts to account for the continued motion of a projectile after it had lost contact with the mover and to explain the acceleration of a body in free fall. But these insights, important as they were, were not worked out, nor were either their consequences or the exact definitions of their terms made explicit.

It was during the fourteenth century that the medieval study of motion reached its height, especially at the universities of Oxford and Paris. It took place within the Aristotelian tradition, usually in the form of lectures on Aristotle's Physics or On the Heaven and the World, but its net result was the destruction of the Aristotelian world view during the sixteenth and seventeenth centuries.

The first important studies of this sort were carried on at Merton College, Oxford by a group of natural scientists who were greatly interested in the application of mathematics to physics. The major figure among the Merton scholars was Thomas Bradwardine. In the year 1328 he composed a treatise On the Proportions of the Speed of Motions[12] for the purpose of giving a clear mathematical account of the laws of motion and the relationship between force, resistance, and velocity. His procedure was rigorously mathematical, beginning with a theoretical analysis of proportionality and then proceeding to deduce eight theorems from eight axioms. On the basis thus established, Bradwardine first disproved four widely held theories and then went on to construct his own views.

He concluded that the proper relationship could be expressed as $n^V = F/R$ (in modern terminology), V being velocity, F force, and R resistance, and that consequently any given velocity may be doubled by squaring or halved by extracting the square root of the proportion associated with that velocity. In answering possible objections which might be brought against him, Bradwardine developed the concept of velocity as an instantaneous quality of motion, as distinct from a simple function of time and distance. This use of infinitesimals to express an instantaneous velocity considered as a quality of motion, and the unanswered question thus raised concerning the relationship between this quality of motion and the quantity of motion possessing this quality, were enormously fruitful in subsequent studies of motion from the fourteenth to the seventeenth centuries.

Bradwardine's Proportions was not only a work of the first importance, considered in itself, but it was also extremely influential. Within a very short time it penetrated to Paris, eastern Europe, and northern Italy. At Merton College itself Bradwardine was succeeded by a group of mathematical physicists known as the Calculatores. Chief among them are Richard Swineshead, William Heytesbury, and John Dumbleton. Among their major achievements were: the Merton "mean speed" theorem, by which it was proved that in any uniformly accelerated motion, the velocity reached at the mid-point is equal to the average velocity of the entire movement; the equivalent of the correct formula (i.e., $S = 1/2\ at^2$) in relating elapsed time to distance traversed in a uniformly accelerated motion; and the use of line segments as primitive graphs, visually representing arithmetic and logical procedures in relating such terms as velocity and distance. Bradwardine's work and that of the other Mertonians spread across Europe within a few years' time and directly influenced almost all subsequent discussions of dynamics.

Mathematics, however, can only describe how things happen. Why motion occurred was another question which occupied the attention of many fourteenth-century writers, as Aristotle's contention that contact between mover and moved must constantly be maintained began to break down under close scrutiny. Probably the most fruitful concept to come out of the discussions of this problem was that of "impetus," first fully developed in Latin Europe by

John Buridan of Paris, although similar theories had been developed by several Arabic authors during the preceding three centuries. There had been several approaches to the impetus theory among the ancients, the Muslims, and the Latins, but Buridan's statement of it, while still containing a few ambiguities, is more comprehensive and precise than any which preceded him.

Buridan, born sometime before 1300 and dying in 1358, spent most of his adult life as a lecturer on the Arts faculty at Paris, expounding the books of Aristotle's natural philosophy. In the study of motion, his most important contribution was his doctrine of impetus. His problem was to explain why a body continues in motion after it loses contact with its original mover. After examining in detail and finding unsatisfactory the answers given by Aristotle and others, he proposed his own solution: that in addition to imparting motion to a body, the original moving force, whether gravity in the case of natural motion, or a human hand, a machine or a bowstring in the case of violent motion, also imparts an impetus -- "a kind of force," he says, "but not what we usually mean by force." The nature of this impetus is somewhat ambiguous. Since its primary function is to keep a body in motion, it must be some sort of force or cause of motion. But since it arises from motion itself it must also be, to some extent, a result of motion or a quality of motion. If Buridan had meant it only in the latter sense, it would be identical with the "momentum" of Newtonian physics, and in any case it is defined by the same factors: the more matter in a body and the greater its velocity, the greater the impetus. But he more often considered it as a force continuing to act on a body.

An interesting aspect of Buridan's impetus is its permanence. It would apparently keep a body in motion forever if it were not corrupted by contrary forces, such as internal resistance, gravity, or resistance of the medium. In fact Buridan twice applies it in this way, once in the example of the revolving mill wheel which would turn forever if the mill did not wear out and there were no resistance, and once in his suggestion that God may have given each of the heavenly bodies the impetus He desired at the time He created them, and they have been running on their own impetus ever since, because there is no resistance or other corrupting force in the heavens.

The most important of Buridan's successors was his pupil, Nicole Oresme, an extremely able scientist and mathematician. Oresme modified his teacher's doctrine on impetus in two important ways. First he held that it arose from acceleration, and not simply velocity, although this left unanswered the question of where the initial acceleration in free fall comes from. And secondly, he denied that it was permanent in nature.

The study of local motion was, along with astronomy, at the very center of the scientific revolution of the seventeenth century, and the work of these medieval scientists was crucial in determining what problems should be investigated, which aspects of the problems were most significant, and what methods a physical scientist should employ in his investigations.

NOTES

1. See Richard C. Dales, "A Twelfth Century Concept of the Natural Order," Viator 9 (1978), 179-92.

2. See Richard C. Dales, "Anonymi De elementis: From a Twelfth-Century Collection of Scientific Works in British Museum MS Cotton Gala E. IV," Isis 56 (1965), 174-189.

3. English translation in R. C. Dales, ed. and tr., Marius On the Elements (Berkeley, 1976).

4. English translations, with very helpful introductions, in C. R. Dowell, ed. and tr., Theophilus, De diversis artibus (London, 1961) and John H. Hawthorne and Cyril Stanley Smith, On Divers Arts: The Treatise of Theophilus (Chicago, 1963). See also the review essay of Lynn T. White, Jr., "Theophilus Redivivus," Technology and Culture 5 (1964), 224-233.

5. C. H. Buttimer, ed., Hugh of St. Victor, Didascalion (Washington, 1939), 38-39.

6. See Richard Lemay, Abu Ma'shar and Latin Aristotelianism in the Twelfth Century (Beirut, 1962).

7. Thomas S. Kuhn, The Structure of Scientific Revolutions (2nd ed., Chicago, 1970).

8. See Richard C. Dales, "Robert Grosseteste's Scientific Works," Isis 52 (1961), 381-402.

9. On Grosseteste's method, see A. C. Crombie, Robert Grosseteste and the Origin of Experimental Science, 1100-1700 (Oxford, 1952), 44-134.

10. English translation in R. C. Dales, The Scientific Achievement of the Middle Ages (Philadelphia, 1973), 68-72.

11. David C. Lindberg, ed. and tr., John Pecham and the Science of Optics: "Perspective Communis," (Madison, Wisconsin, 1970).

12. H. Lamar Crosby, Jr., ed. and tr., Thomas of Bradwardine His Tractatus de Proportionibus (Madison, Wisconsin, 1955).

Chapter 14

Sub-University Culture

During the thirteenth and fourteenth centuries, the number of laymen interested in learning grew constantly.[1] Part of this growth was no doubt due to the drop-outs from the universities, but there were many who never attended a university and never aspired to who were nevertheless interested in intellectual matters. There were many grammar schools maintained by religious orders (both the Dominicans and Franciscans were active in this regard), by municipalities, by guilds, or by private masters. Many people were literate in their own language but not in Latin, thus creating a demand for translations. Others studied the ars dictaminis rather than the lengthy and demanding university curriculum, since the course was short, relatively easy, and led rather quickly to reasonably lucrative employment. The increasingly technical nature of university education had cut off the semilearned (who in an earlier age could have kept abreast of current learning) from access to what was going on in the educated world. So for a variety of reasons there was a new and different public for intellectual productions from the early thirteenth century on. We shall in this chapter investigate briefly some of the literary works which catered to this demand.

The encyclopedic tradition, as we have seen in earlier chapters, was very old. Encyclopedias first served to communicate the basic facts of knowledge in all fields, in a non-technical way, to an educated but non-specialist public. In late Antiquity this changed to an attempt to salvage the essentials of human learning during a period of rapid decline. During the Carolingian age, it was to collect as much knowledge as possible in one place. During the twelfth century the encyclopedic framework was used for several original works of very high quality, which were not so much interested in collecting more snippets from more sources as with applying more hard thought to what was already at hand. Two outstanding examples of this type are William of Conches' Philosophia and Daniel of Morley's The Natures of Things Above and Below. Both were addressed to the learned public, the first with an eye to imposing greater clarity on man's concepts, the second largely to propagandizing the new Arabic learning, and both have a clear overall strucutre which is, in the long run, more important than the constituent parts.

Near the end of the twelfth century a transitional type of encyclopedic work, the De naturis rerum,[2] was composed by the English savant Alexander Neckam. Although Alexander was a secular for most of his life, this book has many hallmarks of a monastic work, particularly in its constant and often quite strained attempts to moralize every bit of information it gives about natural science. The range of Alexander's reading is quite impressive, and his presentation of the material is popular and non-technical. He was clearly not writing for his peers (Alexander had studied Arts, law, medicine, and theology at Paris and was well versed in all these subjects), but his audience did have to know Latin. One of the most charming aspects of the book is Alexander's liberal use of anecdotes, popular stories, folk practices, and remarks on contemporary culture. In short it has many characteristics of a popular work -- its readers or hearers certainly would not have been university people -- but its language was Latin. There could not as yet have been a large number of English laymen who knew Latin. The intended audience must have been the semi-educated clergy, regular and secular, or grammar school students (Alexander had spent some years as teacher at the grammar school at Dunstable). As the number of literate laymen grew, so did interest in De naturis rerum.

Of quite a different type, and clearly written for an intelligent lay audience, is Bartholomew the Englishman's De proprietatibus rerum.[3] Its structure is quite similar to that of William of Conches' Philosophia, but it is several times longer and is not intended for the intelligentsia. Its material is taken indiscriminately from a great variety of sources of different types and quality -- Gregory the Great, Augustine, Isidore, Solinus, and Pliny, the major classical authors, the medical writers, especially those translated by Constantine (Bartholomew is extremely well read in medical literature), several of the Greek Fathers, including pseudo-Dionysius, a number of twelfth-century writers, and pope Innocent III and Michael Scot, his near contemporaries.

Bartholomew justifies his preoccupation with the corporeal universe by quoting pseudo-Dionysius to the effect that we can only rise to the contemplation of the incorporeal universe by first mastering the corporeal.[4] He moves rather quickly through the Trinity and angels to man, a subject which interests him greatly. He discusses man's dignity, the human soul in its various aspects, and its powers. Here he compounds elements from Augustine, Aristotle, and the medical writers so skillfully that one hardly notices that these three notions of the soul are mutually incompatible. The powers of the soul lead him into a discussion of human physiology, the five senses, the four elements, the primary qualities (hot and cold: active, moist and dry: passive), the humors, the parts of the body (these include both external factors, such as head, eyes, nose, breasts, knees, etc., and the internal organs, bones, and nerves). Then in Book VI he begins discussing man with respect to the differences of age, sex, and nature, including a number of diseases and their causes. Book VIII turns to a discussion of the world, which begins with astronomy and continues through the whole range of human physical sciences.

Bartholomew never taxes his reader's brain with difficult or involved reasoning. His presentation is clear and fluid and is couched in a simple unpretentious Latin. It is both easy and fun to read. He had read very widely, but he shows no sense of discrimination among his authorities; he will cite Isidore or Gregory the Great alongside Galen or Avicenna on medical topics. His citations of Aristotle are brief paraphrases, and he thus spares his readers the struggle of wading through Aristotle's own words. His work was deservedly popular, as were the slightly later encyclopedias of Vincent of Beauvais and Thomas of Cantimpré.

These works were primarily concerned with the human and physical sciences, but they should not be considered as representative of thirteenth-century science. They were competent and successful attempts to popularize learning, but they drew more heavily on the outmoded science of late Antiquity and the early Middle Ages than on the current science of their own day. They are valuable as guides to what popular learning consisted of, but not what was going on in the universities.

The principal form of communication in the Middle Ages -- legal, governmental, diplomatic, propagandistic, and personal -- was the letter. The importance of letters then was much greater than it is in the modern world, which offers many alternative forms of communication. Therefore, the study of letter writing, or the ars dictaminis, was very important. We have already noted several proto-dictaminal works of the tenth century, and we have seen how the study of rhetoric was modified, at least on one level, to the study of prose epistolary composition. Rules were established, few and simple at first, more numerous and complicated later, concerning the parts of the letter, order of names in the salutation (Heloise's second letter to Abelard begins by her taking him to task for improperly placing her name ahead of his in the salutation), forms of the captatio benevolentiae (how to get the good will of the recipient), and so on. These matters seem to have been taught orally for some time. No manual of rules earlier than about 1100 survives, but long before this the form assumed by letters written all over Europe clearly implies some sort of general agreement and formal teaching on the rules of composition.[5]

By about 1100, the earliest formal treatises on the ars dictaminis were composed, probably by teachers of the art, and they proliferated during the next half-century. The earliest names are Alberic of Monte Cassino, Albert of Samaritani, Henry Francigena, Hugh and Bernard of Bologna, and Albert de San Martino. Although the authors of these treatises often vilify each other and warn students to avoid the worthless and fraudulent teaching of their rivals, in fact the manuals are quite similar. Included in letter writing was the drafting of legal documents, another highly formalized procedure. At least a modicum of Latin grammar was taught in the dictaminal courses, but only enough to enable the student to get his job done. Since his own knowledge of literature was often slight, the student was taught how to adorn his composition through the use of florilegia, although excessive ornamentation was usually frowned on. This was a strictly business course, just the sort of thing that serious scholars all over Europe were deploring in the twelfth century. Henry Francigena bragged that his treatise was so self-sufficient that even people with slight intelligence could become accomplished letter writers by following its rules. But it was apparently lucrative, and employment opportunities for dictatores were excellent. They ranged from the lower echelons of chancery or civic bureaucracies to ambassadorial appointments or university teaching.

The art developed significantly during the twelfth century, and about 1200 Buoncompagno da Segna, one of the most famous of the dictatores, had created out of it a literary technique using an exchange of fictitious letters as a means of telling a story. Although most practitioners of the ars dictaminis continued to function on the purely practical level, it has been suggested that the professional humanists of the Italian Renaissance had their origins in the dictaminal tradition of the preceding two centuries.[6] Certainly the dictatores constituted a large and important class in European society, semi-educated but often susceptible to the delights of literature, science, and philosophy. They were an important segment of the sub-university literate laity of the late Middle Ages.

There are other types of literature, both Latin and vernacular, peripheral to the subject of this chapter, which we shall only mention and not discuss in detail. Most important are the sermons. Both Dominicans and Franciscans were devoted to preaching, and the sermon became a literary type of great popularity during the thirteenth and fourteenth centuries. Some of our most valuable information on Franciscan preaching comes from the Chronicle of the Italian Franciscan, Salimbene of Parma,[7] a masterpiece in its own right. It is written in Latin but is a gossipy, anecdotal, intensely personal, popular book. This was also the great age of histories and chronicles, genres which seem to have had considerable appeal. Then there are some works such as the Philosophia pauperum or Stanington's summaries of the libri naturales whose purpose is not clear. They were probably intended for poor students at the universities or substitute Arts courses for friars and not for lay or "sub-university" consumption. There is also a series of astrological treatises by Michael Scot. By no means intended for the learned, they were both a bit of pleading for astrology and an elementary course in how to be an astrologer. Scot himself claims that they are strictly elementary and suitable even for those of weak minds (the same group that Henry Francigena had courted).

It was during the twelfth and thirteenth centuries that the vernacular literatures of the European peoples came into their own. They have varying histories, and we shall not try to give an account of any of them as a whole, but during the thirteenth and fourteenth centuries many of them reached a point, both in quality and in popularity, that they might be considered a part of the sub-university intellectual culture.

German vernacular literature[8] developed rapidly during the twelfth century and reached impressive heights in Wolfram von Eschenbach, Walter von der Vogelweide, Hartmann von Aue, and Gottfried von Strassburg. But its decline during the thirteenth was precipitous and by the fourteenth, except for the vernacular sermon, it was moribund. English literature has an atypical history because of the importation of the French language among the ruling classes of church and state consequent upon the Norman conquest, which arrested the development of a very promising Old English literature. For about the first two centuries of Middle English there is little of note in the vernacular. But late in the thirteenth century English writers again began producing excellent literature of a variety of types, and by the end of the fourteenth England had her first writer of classic status in Geoffrey Chaucer. The Italian vernacular was late developing as a literary vehicle, perhaps because it was so close to Latin, but once it began it quickly produced a group of classically excellent works in the writings of the Florentine trio, Dante, Petrarch, and Boccaccio. It was the French vernacular which achieved maturity first and which dominated European vernacular literature from the twelfth through the fourteenth centuries.

Until the end of the twelfth century, most vernacular literature was designed for the military and the courts or for the clergy. Near the end of the twelfth century, a new genre, much broader in its appeal, was established in France and spread throughout Europe. This was the _fabliau_, which in spite of its trivial subject matter and low style has exerted an enormous and enduring influence on subsequent European literature.

The _fabliau_ is a short humorous story in verse (eight syllable rhymed couplets). Its language is, with few exceptions, simple and often crude and obscene, its style is broad and often tends toward parody. It depends largely on the old reliable sources of humor, sex, scatology, and slapstick. Its characters range through all the social classes. We have knights and their ladies, merchants, priests and monks, tavern keepers, butchers, peasants, "poor clerks," and in one _fabliau_ even the great philosopher Aristotle. Characterization, however, is not their strong point. They are rather of the nature of cartoons or burlesque sketches, and the characters are stock comic types: the crafty and avaricious merchant, the greedy and lecherous priest or monk, the stupid peasant, etc. Settings are not dwelt on but are swiftly and deftly established -- the tavern, the merchant's house, the hayloft, the bedroom. These are not, however, artless tales composed by unskilled semi-literates but are carefully constructed stories with a characteristic style. The names of many of the authors are known. A few were university trained and held responsible positions; others were university drop-outs, who probably conformed more nearly to the Goliardic stereotype than did the authors of the Goliardic poetry; many were jongleurs, professional entertainers, and a few were minstrels attached to courts. The fabliaux seem to have been popular among all classes of the population from the nobility to the peasantry, and the old notion that they were essentially middle-class urban literature is no longer held (although the middle class clearly constituted a large part of their audience), and some stories exist in several versions, each tailored to the tastes and prejudices of a different audience.

Their moral tone, or lack of it, makes them unique in medieval literature. Unlike the fables (fablaux) they have no moral lesson to preach, or if they do it is not to be taken seriously. The only quality which is given any moral value at all is cleverness -- having one's own way, gaining revenge on one's enemies, and coming up smelling like a rose. The characters who possess this quality are most often women, and although the fabliaux are usually considered anti-feminist in the extreme, since their female characters are forever cuckolding their husbands, lying, cheating, and bringing general misfortune upon the dull-witted men they married, they are nearly always the victors in a game of wits[9] (The Snow Child and The Woman Who Was Castrated are notable exceptions). Men often deceive other men too, but they are usually assisted by dumb luck or by a woman. The only males who are treated kindly by the authors are poor clerks and students, the very class of people who composed many of the tales.

A summary of the plots of several fabliaux[10] will provide some feeling for their general character. Brunain, the Priest's Cow, written by Jean Bodel of Arras, is one of the earlier and shorter of the fabliaux. A peasant and his wife went to church and heard the priest say in his sermon that if one gave freely to the church, God would return to him twice as much as he gave. So the peasant, stupid enough to take this literally, gave the priest his cow (which didn't give much milk anyway). The priest's servant tied it to the priest's own cow, Brunain (which he claimed not to possess), and the peasant's cow returned home, still tied to Brunain. And so the Lord's promise was fulfilled.

Another fabliau about a stupid peasant, who nevertheless shows a streak of low cunning when pushed to extremities, is The Peasant Doctor. In this story a rich but crude peasant is married to the daughter of an impoverished nobleman. The peasant realizes that his wife does not love him and worries about the priest or someone else seducing her while he is away every day ploughing the fields.

He reasons that if he beats her every morning before he leaves, she will be red-eyed and unattractive all day to would-be seducers, and at night he will beg forgiveness and thus spend a pleasant evening and night with her. After two days of this treatment, the wife finds a way to get even when two messengers from the king stop at her house seeking a skilled physician to dislodge a fishbone from the throat of the king's daughter. The wife tells them that her husband is a wonderfully skillful doctor, but because of a personality quirk he expects to be beaten before he will say or do anything for anyone. The messengers find the peasant in the field and ask him to come with them to cure the king's daughter. He of course answers that he knows nothing of such matters, so they beat him until he agrees to come along. He succeeds in dislodging the bone by stripping himself naked, lying over a fire, and scratching and currying himself. The girl is so surprised by this unexpected outrageous behavior that she bursts out laughing, and the bone comes free. The king is delighted and insists that the peasant stay on at court as the royal physician. Again, the peasant protests, is beaten, and agrees. Then the king commands him to cure eighty of the sickest people in the realm. Again protestations, beating, and agreement. The peasant sends all but the sick away, then says he will cure them by roasting the sickest of them over a fire, making a powder of his remains, and administering it to the others. They all instantly insist that they are cured. The king is so pleased that he gives the peasant great wealth and permission to return to his wife, whom he never beats again.

The man seldom comes off so well though. In The Wife of Orleans a wealthy merchant, suspecting his wife (correctly) of infidelity, announces that he is taking an extended business trip but goes only a short way and comes back at nightfall pretending to be the young clerk who he knows, through a household spy, is planning to share his wife's bed that night. But the wife recognizes her husband and, thinking fast, pretends she thinks he is the lover and locks him in a hayloft, promising to send for him when it is safe. Then she goes into the house and tells the family and servants that a young clerk has been pestering her for sexual favors and she has told him that she would grant his wishes to-night; but she has managed to lock him in the loft. She orders them all to take clubs and beat him soundly so that he will never bother her again. They obey with great gusto, and the poor husband is soundly beaten. Meanwhile, the wife has been enjoying the services of her lover, the clerk. When the husband recovers from his beating and finds that it was meant for the clerk, he is delighted with his wife's virtue and faithfulness and abandons his suspicions. So the husband is cuckolded but happy, the wife is faithless but trusted and is free to continue her affair without interference from her husband.

Many of the fabliaux have to do with contented or helpless cuck-

-291-

olds. Sometimes the lovers are clerks, sometimes priests or monks, sometimes even knights. One of the funniest is <u>Beranger Longbottom</u>. Again we have an interclass marriage. The son of a wealthy peasant is knighted and married to the daughter of an impecunious nobleman. The peasant-knight is a coward and a glutton, and his wife comes to loathe him. In order to gain status in her eyes the knight rides out into the forest, hangs his shield on a tree, and hacks it to bits with his sword. Then he breaks his lance into pieces and rides back telling of his valorous military exploits. He does this day after day, becoming more arrogant and insufferable with each new "victory." At last his wife becomes suspicious, and after he leaves on one of his expeditions she dons armor and follows him. Catching him in the act of beating his shield with his sword, she (pretending to be a knight) offers him a choice between fighting (and dying if he should lose) or kissing her ass. The knight, claiming that he has taken an oath not to fight, chooses the latter alternative and is amazed by the length of her rectal crease, never thinking to attribute it to the difference between male and female anatomy. He asks the name of his conqueror and is told that it is Beranger Longbottom, the scourge of all cowards. Then the wife hurries home, takes off her armor, and summons a young man she has coveted from before her marriage. They go shamelessly to bed, and when the husband returns home, discovers and threatens them, she tells him that if he causes any trouble she will tell Beranger Longbottom. The moral of this tale is: "When the shepherd is weak, the wolf shits wool."

This type of coarse language is carried to an extreme in the tale of Aubigier. The story itself is incidental and is merely an excuse for piling up references to excrement, urine, latrines, dungheaps, and coprophiliac sexual acts, much like several of the comic strips in the <u>National Lampoon</u>. This <u>fabliau</u> was extremely popular and was considered to be funny, although much of the humor is lost on a modern audience.

But another of the more obscene <u>fabliaux</u> is also one of the funniest, namely <u>The Knight Who Made Cunts and Assholes Speak</u>.[11] Unlike most <u>fabliaux</u> it does have a touch of the magical in it, but this was obviously not taken seriously. A valorous, idealistic, unemployed knight and his cynical and world-wise squire Hugh are riding out in search of tourneys so the knight may recoup his fortunes. Hugh, riding ahead, sees three beautiful young girls bathing naked in a stream. He steals their clothes, hoping to sell them for a hundred pounds, but the knight, riding up to Hugh, will have nothing to do with such ungallant behavior and orders his squire to return the garments. The girls (were they fairies of not?), out of gratitude, each bestow a gift on the knight. The first says that henceforth all men will make him welcome and give him whatever he needs. The second makes him blush by saying that he shall have the power to make cunts speak, and the third adds that if the cunt should be stopped up and unable to speak he would

-292-

be able to make assholes speak. The knight at first thinks that they are making a fool of him, but when they meet a rich priest and he offers them his hospitality, he begins to wonder. So to test his powers, he orders the cunt of the priest's mare to speak. When it obeys, the priest runs off, leaving them his mare and all his money. When they arrive at the count's castle for the tourney, they are extravagantly welcomed. That night the countess ordered one of her most attractive servants to share the knight's bed, but when the knight tried out his new powers on her cunt she leapt out of bed in fright and told her mistress everything. The next night the countess related this to all present and bet the knight forty pounds against his horse and armor that he could not make her cunt talk. To insure her victory, she excused herself for a moment and stuffed it with cotton. So, when the knight ordered it to speak there was only silence. But Hugh reminded the knight of the third girl's gift, and the countess' asshole revealed the lady's strategem. The count ordered her to remove the cotton and the knight won his bet.

There are in all about 160 fabliaux extant, and many have been lost. As a distinct genre they came to an end in 1346 with the death of Jean de Condé, but they have provided material for storytellers from Boccaccio and Chaucer in the fourteenth century to Balzac in the nineteenth.

While some may question the inclusion of so low a type of literature as the fabliaux in a discussion of intellectual culture, whether sub-university or otherwise, there can be no doubt as to the intellectual content of Jean de Meun's continuation of the Romance of the Rose. Jean Clopinel was born a Meun-sur-Loire, not far from William of Lorris' birthplace, in the late 1230s. He was mostly likely a master of Arts at Paris, but it is not known whether he was a regent master. In any case he kept in close touch with university affairs and lived in the Faubourg St. Jacques, close to the left-bank schools. He seems to have considered himself a popularizer of intellectual culture. He translated Vegetius' De re militari into French for the benefit of military engineers, and Boethius' Consolation of Philosophy and the letters of Abelard and Heloise for the benefit of intelligent non-Latin speaking laymen. Two other translations intended for the latter audience have not survived, namely Aelred of Rievaulx's Spiritual Friendship[12] and Gerald of Wales' Topographia hibernica. From the late thirteenth century onward, there was a steady stream of translations of classical and scholastic works into the vernacular tongues, especially French.

It was for this same class of readers that Jean intended his continuation of the Romance of the Rose. In it he uses many of the types that were common in the fabliaux (the jealous and brutal husband, the bitter and garrulous old hag, the clever and faithless wife), but its purpose is to consider love from every point

of view and in the process to pass along to the reader in a simplified form a large portion of the Latin intellectual heritage,
from the classical and patristic ages to the productions of his
own day. It is much like an adult education extension course
presented in one of the more popular literary forms of the time.

But the work is not essentially an extension Arts course; it is
essentially a poem, to which Jean himself gave the title Mirror
for Lovers. Since Jean is bound to present all points of view
about love, it is pointless to try to discover what his own views
were. He includes the obligatory anti-feminist polemic, but he
also includes some quite liberal views which he might easily have
left out. The only opinions expressed in the poem which we can be
sure are those of the author are the vicious attacks on the mendicants. Otherwise he is faithfully reflecting the variety of views
on the subject of love in all its manifold meanings.

Consequently, Jean's concept of what he was doing was quite different from William of Lorris' poem, the autobiography of a lover
presented as an allegorical courtly romance. This is enough to
explain the differences in tone, structure, style, and technique.
Jean has undertaken to finish William's story, and he eventually
gets around to it, but the narrative element is almost an intru-
sion in the structure of the poem. The continuation is about five
times the length of the original, and very little of it is given
over to the small amount of narration that remained. Jean drops
the tightly-knit allegory and in its place uses the similar devices of personification (Reason, Nature) or types (Jealous Husband, Duenna) as vehicles for the discussion of love.

As Jean de Meun's part of the poem begins, the Lover is trying to
keep from losing hope and remembers the earlier words of the God
of Love that he would gain his end unless he behaved in an un-
courtly manner, but that this would take time. Then Reason
appears to try to dissuade the Lover from his irrational quest.
She points out that the God of Love deceives his followers and
leaves them miserable; that Nature's purpose in sex is the continuation of the race and that it is made pleasurable only to induce
men to have children; and that carnal pleasure only impersonates
true love. She then argues that friendship is the highest form of
love (based on Cicero's De amicitia), and that it remains firm
despite the vagaries of Fortune, which is then discussed at some
length (based on Boethius' Consolation). She attempts to define
true happiness, again depending largely on Boethius, and the
fleetingness of worldly goods and honors. She then gets back to
the theme of the highest love, which is greater even than Justice.
Reason then uses a bit of matter-of-fact coarse language in recounting that Jupiter had "cut off his father's balls." The Lover
is offended, and there follows a discussion of plain speaking,
euphemism, and dirty language. Reason then commits an astounding
act by offering herself to the Lover as a rival to the Rose and

urges him to accept her friendship and abandon Fortune, who is then discussed again, along with her wheel, at great length, with examples from Greek and Roman mythology and history and from contemporary events, including the deposition of Manfred, king of Sicily, by Charles of Anjou (this is one of the criteria for dating the poem -- Charles died in 1285).

After a resumption of the argument over crude words, the Lover declines Reason's offer, and Friend steps in to offer some corrupt and cynical advice, which the Lover virtuously scorns. Friend then backs off a bit but continues to argue that trickery and deceit are acceptable and necessary if the Lover is to succeed. This makes possible a discussion of poverty and a contrast of the present day to the Golden Age. It is also in Friend's speech that the caricature of the Jealous Husband is presented. He is a totally despicable man, the kind who drives a woman to "typically feminine" behavior. As part of his abuse of his wife, the Jealous Husband contrasts her with Heloise, the perfect woman. This is the first reference to the correspondence of Abelard and Heloise in literature, over 150 years after it was alleged to have been written.

After a good deal more ranting about the evils of women, the husband beats his wife and is gone. Friend observes that it would be impossible for any woman to love such a man, since whatever she does, he will arbitrarily change the rules and she will be wrong. For love to flourish there must be equality between the two lovers. In spite of the venom of the husband's speeches, the wife certainly comes off looking better than her abusive mate. Since Friend is a neutral character, it is quite possible that he is voicing Jean's own views here.

After Friend has delivered himself of a long string of platitudes -- conventional wisdom on how to get along with women -- the story resumes briefly. But the battle preparations are interrupted for a brief history of the composition of the Romance of the Rose, begun by William of Lorris and continued after a lapse of more than forty years by Jean Clopinel. Then the God of Love summons his barons and somewhat incongruously includes False Seeming and Forced Abstinence (two vicious caricatures of the mendicants) among his troops. They are necessary now but will be dismissed as unsuitable wretches when their services are no longer required. This diatribe goes on for many pages, as Jean concentrates his accumulated hatred of the mendicants into a devastating portrayal of their hypocrisy and venality.

In the course of their wicked activities, False Seeming and Forced Abstinence commit an allegorically impossible murder by killing Evil Tongue and force their way into the castle where the Rose and Fair Welcome are being held. They come upon the Duenna, whose job it is to guard the Rose, and bribe her to act as go-between for the Lover and Fair Welcome. This gives Jean an opportunity to paint a scathing picture of a once-fair old woman who has been (deservedly) ill-treated by men and wants above all things to get even.

After a short interruption to offer a justification of his portrayal of women and friars (compare Boccaccio's Decameron), Jean begins to describe the assault of the forces of the God of Love against the castle. It proceeds as a series of individual combats in the manner of Prudentius' Psychomachia or Alan of Lille's Anticlaudianus. The outcome is in doubt, but Venus comes to the rescue. This results in a 4,000 line interruption of the story, while Nature (borrowed from Bernard Silvestris and Alan of Lille) makes a somewhat gratuitous appearance (the excuse is that a battle means deaths, and Nature's reproduction closely follows death). The description of Nature's function is followed by a short course in alchemy. Nature then goes for confession to her priest, Genius, who somewhat ungallantly interrupts it with a rehearsal of the faults of the female character, illustrated by a comic character sketch of a greedy and demanding wife. Finally Nature begins her confession, saying that she regrets only one thing she has done. But before we find out what that is, we must hear of all the things she has done that she does not regret, which amounts to a textbook on the natural sciences.

At last, though, we find out that man has been her mistake, because he alone refuses to follow her precepts and work hard at reproducing his kind. She then sends Genius to carry her message to the God of Love and urge him on. Genius obeys and urges the barons to plow their fields well and carry on Nature's never-ending battle with death. For in so doing, they are not only obeying Nature but the Author of all things. By pleasing Him they will attain the eternal meadow, where the sheep munch forever on grass that immediately renews itself, and where there is no death or corruption. Compared to this garden, round in shape, the square garden of Sir Mirth pales into insignificance.

Thus inspired, the forces of the God of Love, led by Venus, attacked the Tower of Shame (interrupted by the story of Pygmalion), which fell easily. The Lover then made his way to the Ivory Tower and, in one of the more erotic passages in European literature, he followed Nature's commandments and impregnated the Rose.

Jean has managed to include a considerable portion of the literary, scientific, and religious traditions of the West in his poem, and near the end he even managed an accommodation between the commands of the God of Love and the will of God as represented by the laws of Nature. But despite one short salley into heaven, his is an earthbound poem. It is intensely interested in man, whom it portrays as summing up the entire created universe, sharing being with the stones, life with plants, feeling with the beasts, and intellection with the angels -- a small world in himself. Its main fault is that it has no central character -- we hardly know the Lover -- and consequently no clear controlling vision to impose order on the constituent parts. It was nevertheless the most popular poem of the Middle Ages (over 200 manuscripts are still extant) and remained for two centuries a topic of learned conversation and a source of disagreement for those who reacted differently towards its portrayal of women, sexuality, religion, or morality. It was read by royalty, by burghers, by knights, and by women. It was the medieval poem par excellence.

As the fourteenth century began, France was the leading nation of Europe. Her capital, Paris, had perhaps 100,000 inhabitants, making it one of the largest cities in Christendom. Its university was unparalleled in reputation. Its art, architecture, and literature set the standard for all of Europe. The French king was the most powerful monarch in Europe; the pope was in Avignon, dependent upon his protection. The countryside was densely populated and prosperous. But France was about to undergo the most disastrous century in her history, as the Hundred Years War, peasant uprising, civic strife, bourgeois rebellion, and the Black Death all put unbearable strains on her institutions, and her dominance slowly subsided.

Italy had been a dependent territory throughout the Middle Ages, subject to the incursions and rule of the Lombards, Franks, Byzantines, Muslims, Normans, Germans, and French. The wars of the Normans in the eleventh century, of Frederick Barbarossa in the twelfth, and of Frederick II and his successors in the thirteenth had wrought much physical destruction. Italy had never known any political unity, but her urban life had always been vigorous and grew more so with the expansion first of trade and then of manufacturing, especially textiles, during the thirteenth and fourteenth centuries. While French culture was beginning to lose its vigor and integrity, Italian culture attained a high degree of coherence, and the preoccupation of the rest of Europe with the Hundred Years War left the Italians free to fight each other with little outside interference and to develop in their own way. The resulting movement, known as "humanism" or the "Italian Renaissance" had complex origins,[13] but its most obvious and most remarked characteristic was the revival of the cult of classical literature. The relationship of the Italian Renaissance to twelfth-century humanism has not been sufficiently studied. There was obviously some, but we are hard put to offer more than a few details. The fourteenth-century Italians, especially Petrarch, felt that something enormously precious had been lost and was being recovered in their own day. Petrarch and his friends were enthusiastic, even fanatical, cultivators of the ancient literary ideal, which they considered a guide to life, morality, religion, and culture. They were contemptuous of the scientific culture, essentially French and centered in the universities, which still dominated intellectual life. While French medieval culture was suffering the shock of the Hundred Years War, the Black Death, and their attendant horrors, the Italian enthusiasts restored classical studies to dominance and inaugurated a new age in European intellectual history.

But much more was involved in the outburst of creative activity of fourteenth-century Italy than the revival of classicism. The relationship of "scholasticism" and Italian "humanism" has not been suffficiently explored, nor has that of the Italian movement to the parallel movement in France been the subject of much study. These are difficult and extremely complex problems, and much hard basic work remains to be done. Much that was supposedly "Renaissance" was in fact scholastic,[14] and the humanists' characterization of scholasticism as a futile, logic-chopping, mind-numbing waste of time is clearly vastly exaggerated. We should not accept an enemy's evaluation as objective, although it may point up areas of major value conflict.

But one thing is clear. The Italians took intellectual culture out of the universities and provided an attractive alternative for those lovers of literature and elegance who felt alienated by the stylized procedure and scientific outlook of the universities. It was the Italians who first created an extra-university intellectual culture that rivalled or even excelled that of the universities.

NOTES

1. A general preliminary study of lay literacy is James Westfall Thompson, The Literacy of the Laity in the Middle Ages (Berkeley, California, 1939; reprint New York, 1960).

2. There is available only an amateurish edition with a fatuous introduction by Thomas Wright, Alexandri Neckam De naturis rerum (London, 1863; reprint 1967). Rolls Series, 34.

3. Bartholomaeus Angelicus (sic!) De rerum proprietatibus (Frankfurt, 1601; reprint 1964).

4. Praefatio, ed. cit., 2.

5. This is the thesis of William D. Patt, "The Early 'Ars Dictaminis' as the Response to a Changing Society," Viator 9 (1978), 133-155.

6. Paul Oskar Kristeller, Renaissance Thought: The Classic, Scholastic, and Humanist Strains (2 vols., New York, 1961; Harper Torchbook TB48), I, 12-13.

7. It is largely accessible in English in the translated sections in G. G. Coulton, From St. Francis to Dante (London, 1906; reprint University of Pennsylvania Paperback, 1972).

8. For a competent elementary summary in English of medieval German literature, see Paul Salman, Literature in Medieval Germany (New York, 1967).

9. See Norma Jean Thompson, The Old French Fabliau: A Classification and Definition, unpublished Ph.D. thesis, University of Southern California, 1972.

10. English translation of a good sampling of the fabliaux are available in Fabliaux: Ribald tales from the Old French, ed. and tr. Robert Hellman and Richard O'Gorman (New York: Apollo Editions A-134, 1965) and Bawdy Tales from the Courts of Medieval France, tr. and ed. Paul Brians (Harper Torchbook 1725, 1972).

11. There is a brilliant verse translation of this in Hellman and O'Gorman, Fabliaux, 105-122.

12. See Southern, Medieval Humanism, 35 for a brief evaluation of Aelred's Spiritual Friendship.

13. Wallace K. Ferguson, The Renaissance in Historical Thought (Boston, 1948); Paul Oskar Kristeller, Renaissance Thought: The Classic Scholastic, and Humanist Strains; Walter Ullman, Medieval Foundations of Renaissance Humanism (Ithaca, New York, 1977); Hans Baron, The Crisis of the Early Italian Renaissance: Civic Humanism and Republican Liberty in an Age of Classicism and Tyranny. (Rev. ed. Princeton, 1966): Colin Morris, The Discover of the Individual, 1050-1200 (Harper Torchbook 1718, 1972) will give some idea of the complexity of the problem and the haziness of its conceptualization.

14. This is strikingly true in science. Compare J. H. Randall, "The Development of Scientific Method in the School of Padua," Journal of the History of Ideas 1 (1940), 177-206 with A. C. Crombie, Robert Grosseteste and the Origins of Experimental Science, 1100-1700.

EPILOGUE

One of the most renowned American historians of the Middle Ages, Henry Osborn Taylor, ended his survey of medieval thought with a brilliantly written and erudite chapter entitled "The Medieval Synthesis," and his view of the thought of the High Middle Ages has dominated our conception of them ever since. But I have never been able, try as I might, to perceive the medieval synthesis in the manifold reality of medieval texts. What I see is rather a rich diversity of incompatible elements, often highly rationalized, which were not and cannot be synthesized.

What we call the Middle Ages are the first several stages of the development of Western European civilization. Europeans made use of many diverse elements in contriving a new culture, never uniform, out of disparate elements from the ancient Near East and the eclectic civilization of Rome, blended more or less successfully with the folk cultures of Europe's many peoples. The most comprehensive legacy from Antiquity was the Christian church, itself heir to a variety of traditions. From a nearly illiterate group of societies, all to some extent Christian, Europe slowly developed an advanced and widely diffused intellectual culture and gave birth to several characteristic institutions and values which set it off from other cultures; but it did this without ever becoming homogenized. The high value placed upon physical nature, the conviction of the dignity of labor, the empirical and mechanical habit of mind are all characteristically Latin European, but none of these was universally held. One might as easily choose the European concept of romantic love (whether we wish to call it "courtly" or not), but scholars are still seriously questioning whether such a thing ever existed, and it is likely that the fabliaux and the older romances give us a better approximation of actual attitudes towards love and sex than do the troubador lyrics, the courtly romances, or even the vast amount of Latin love literature in the Ovidian tradition. The classical literary tradition was firmly established as the basis of medieval education, and although "grammar" was down-graded to a preparatory subject during the thirteenth century, the classical thread was never broken, and the literary ideal was reaffirmed by the fourteenth and fifteenth-century Italians as a learned alternative to the scientific and vocational emphasis of the universities. A selection of classical authors continued to be read, even in the universities, and the works of the great twelfth-century poets remained popular. Latin poetry continued to be written during the thirteenth century, and while it was generally not very good, it included the great Dies irae, probably by Thomas of Celano, which is superb. But there had always been those who feared and deplored the reading of any pagan works, whether literature, drama, or philosophy, and these remained even beyond the Middle Ages.

The High Middle Ages are on the surface intensely materialistic, but the spiritual ideal of the mendicants was the most popular and influential force of the time. In philosophy there was the unresolved tension between the necessitarian view inherited from Antiquity and embodied in the works of nearly all the great philosophers, which in effect denied freedom to God and insisted that what is must be because God is what He is; and the opposing view, developed during the eleventh and twelfth centuries, that God is utterly free and could create any kind of world He chose. There were fundamental disagreements over the whole range of philosophical questions from epistemology to physics, and the whole range of theological questions. (Some of these had indeed been settled and were no longer subjects for argument, but they were far fewer than is commonly realized.) While there may have been many attempts at synthesis, none was universally accepted, and all were mutually incompatible -- certainly Dante was no Thomist -- and none of them can be held to speak for an entire age. Most thinkers in fact did not feel compelled to seek a synthesis, but from the third quarter of the thirteenth century preferred to concentrate on small, clearly defined questions and not worry too much about the "big picture."

The work which best reflects the nature of medieval thought is Jean de Meun's continuation of the Romance of the Rose. As pure literature it might be inferior to the best of Dante or Chaucer, but as an expression of the quintessence of an age it is unsurpassed. It is a work neither of analysis nor of synthesis. It was rather, in the author's own words, a mirror, and a mirror reflects what is.

What is most enchanting about medieval thought is its diversity and its vigor. We do great violence to the Middle Ages if we insist on seeing them as a time of universal acceptance of some hierarchical system of thought in which all questions were answered. Their essence lay in the fact that no (or very few) questions were definitely answered, and all were in need of further investigation.

local motion 276, 275, 280-3
logic 45, 105, 134, 148, 158, 198, 200, 203, 212, 218, 224, 236, 243, 254, 257, 272; "New Logic" 158, 201, 224, 237; "Old Logic" 201, 224, 237
Logos 12, 99
Louis VII, king of France 175, 198
Louis of Bavaria 91, 110
Louis the Pious 82, 84, 87, 92, 98
Lucan 12, 63, 111, 128, 133, 199, 202, 222, 267
Lucilius 12
Lucretius 2, 16
Lupitus of Barcelona 136
Luttrell 257
Luxeuil 37, 62, 68, 75
Macer 222
Macrobius 8, 26-7, 134, 162, 195, 203, 263, 267
magic 154, 158, 269, 271
Mailduib 63
Man 99, 194-8, 286
Manichaeans 13, 30, 31
Marbod of Rennes 154-5
Marcellus See: Moengal
Marcellus Empiricus 118
Marie, countess of champagne 175, 176, 177
Marius of Salerno 268
Marius Victorinus 11, 12, 13, 43, 112
Martial 128, 156, 199, 222
Martianus Capella 27-8, 52, 97, 111, 112, 121, 128, 134, 146, 162, 187, 194, 203, 263
Martin of Braga 38, 57, 69
Martin of Tours, St. 53, 55, 56
mass 102, 115, 116
mathematics 5, 38, 43, 46, 77, 105, 131, 134, 160, 161, 224, 237, 241, 143, 258, 274, 279, 281, 282
Matthaeus Platearius 210
Maurdramnus, abt. of Corbie 75
Mauricius the Spaniard 244
Maurus of Salerno 149, 210, 222
Maximus the Confessor, St. 99
medicine, medical 58, 113, 131,

136, 149, 158, 161, 162, 209-11, 213, 221, 222, 225, 233, 238, 263, 271, 286
mendicants 216, 226, 243, 251
Menippean satire 28, 194
Merton College, Oxford 227, 281, 282
Messahale 271
Metamorphosis Goliae episcopi 187
metaphysics 218, 224, 240, 248, 252, 258, 275
meteorology 58, 241, 267
Michael of Cesena 257
Michael Scot 224, 245, 269, 286, 288
Middle Academy 3
Middle English 288
Middle Platonism 3
mineralogy 58, 271
Minucius Felix 9, 10, 12-13
Modoin 89
Moengal (Marcellus) 106, 110, 111-12
Mont Ste. Geneviève 160, 163, 201
Montanists 10
Monte Cassino 49, 69, 74, 75, 80, 81, 110, 146, 148, 209, 264, 269
Montpellier 146, 153, 225
Moses of Bergamo 269
Muses 28
music 5, 43, 113, 116, 121, 134, 137, 148, 222
Muslims 69, 87, 105, 110, 126, 129, 136, 148, 158, 224, 240, 251, 263, 272, 275, 279, 280, 283, 297
mystery cults 3
Naples, Neapolitan 69, 250
nature 98-99, 107, 119, 149, 162, 198, 239, 251, 259, 267, 273
Nature, goddess 196, 197
Neckam, Alexander See: Alexander Neckam
Nemesius of Emesa 149, 203, 209
Neoplatonism 3-6, 26-7, 30, 31, 45, 98, 233, 240, 248, 251, 255, 258

Scotland 62, 227
script 37, 74-75
scriptorium 75, 78
Secundus, Chronicle 81
Sedulius 14, 38, 40, 63, 111, 122
Sedulius Scotus 96-97, 101, 106
Seneca 44, 106, 133, 222, 263
Sens 187, 222, 236, 244
Sequence 106, 113, 116-17, 119, 138
sermons 288, 289
Servatus Lupus, abt. of Ferrières 70, 95-96 102, 106, 133, 137
Sicily 50, 269, 295
Sidonius Apollinaris 38, 222
Siger of Brabant 248-50, 253
Simon of Bredon 225
Simon of Poissy 198
Simplicius 272
Snow Child, The 119, 138, 290
Socrates, historian 48
Socrates, philosopher 233
Solinus 154, 222, 285
Sozomen 48
Spain, Spanish, Spaniard 49, 57, 69, 125, 129, 131, 136, 152, 158, 224, 236, 270, 274
Statius 108, 111, 133, 222
Stephen of Provins 245
Stephen Tempier 250, 253
Stoic 3, 13, 22, 34
studium generale 207, 212, 217, 246
Suetonius 79, 88, 133
Sulpicius Severus 39, 88
Supreme Mind See: Idea of Good, the One, God
surgery 211, 212
Sybilline books 12
Symmachus, father-in-law of Boethius 45
Symmachus, senator 18-19, 25, 44, 222
Tacitus 28, 29, 40, 88, 128
Taylor, Henry Osborn 56, 203
Tempier, Stephen See: Stephen Tempier
Terence 12, 105, 111, 122, 125, 126, 128, 133, 137, 147

Tertullian 1, 9-10, 23, 196
Tertullianists 9
Thais 123, 124
Themistius 272
Theobald, abp. of Canterbury 198
Theodore of Tarsus 62-63
Theodoret 48
Theoderic 42, 43, 45, 92
Theodosius, emperor 18
Theodulf of Orleans 61, 74, 78, 82-84, 87, 88, 96, 101, 103
Theophanou 127, 128
Theophilus German monk 268-269
Theophilus Protospatharius 162, 210, 211, 222
Thierry of Chartres 158, 161-62, 194, 198, 236, 266-67, 271
Thomas of Aquino, St. 226, 240, 250-53
Thomas Becket, St. 198
Thomas Bradwardine 225, 282
Thomas of Cantimpré 287
tides 65
Toledo 69, 269
Toth, Egyptian god 271
Toulouse 70, 245
Tours 52, 55, 76, 79, 89, 146, 152, 155, 158, 160, 185
tragedy 222
translations, translators, 2, 11, 24, 25, 29, 39, 43, 44, 45, 48, 52, 98, 112, 117, 132, 133, 136, 148-50, 153, 160-62, 201, 209-10, 224-25, 234, 239, 243, 245, 264, 265, 269-73, 286, 293
transubstantiation 102-3, 156, 236
Trogus Pompeius 222
trivium 198, 200
Trope 196, 115, 116, 117, 137, 138
troubador 168, 175
Tuotilo of St. Gall 114, 115
Ulrich, St. 110
uncial 37, 74-75, 78
universals 46, 47
University College, Oxford 228, 240
Urso of Calabria 149, 210
Vandals 35, 38, 41, 42